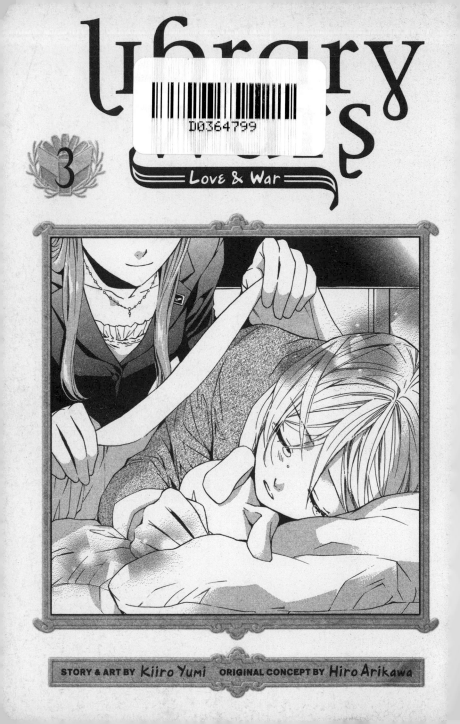

library wars

3

Love & War

D0364799

STORY & ART BY *Kiiro Yumi*   ORIGINAL CONCEPT BY *Hiro Arikawa*

Library Wars

Love & War

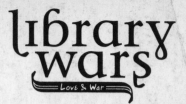

Contents

The Library Freedom Act

Libraries have the freedom to acquire their collections.

Libraries have the freedom to circulate
materials in their collections.

Libraries guarantee the privacy of their patrons.

Libraries oppose any type of censorship.

When libraries are imperiled,
librarians will join together
to secure their freedom.

library wars
Love & War

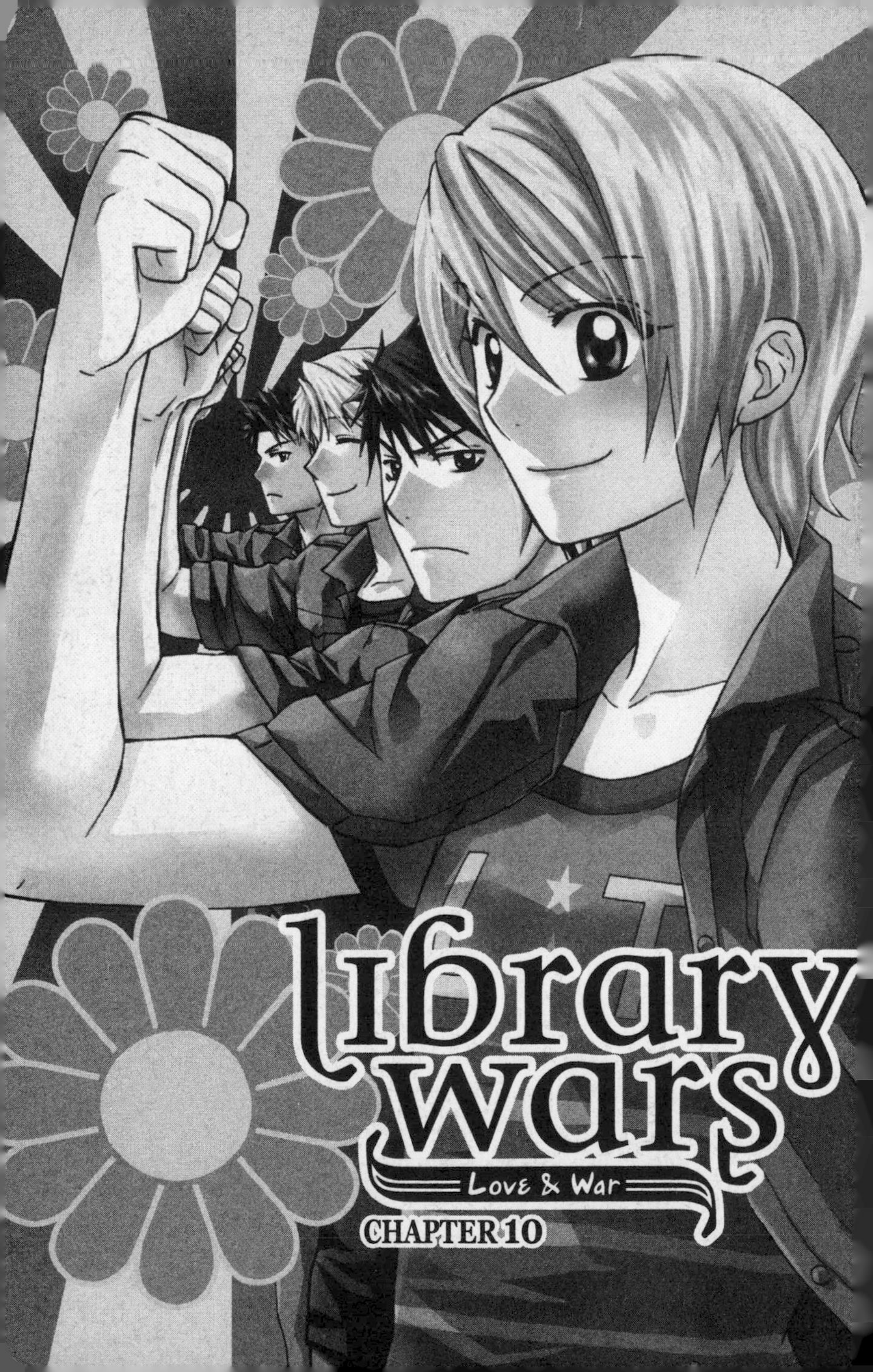
library wars
Love & War
CHAPTER 10

Library Wars LOVE & WAR 3

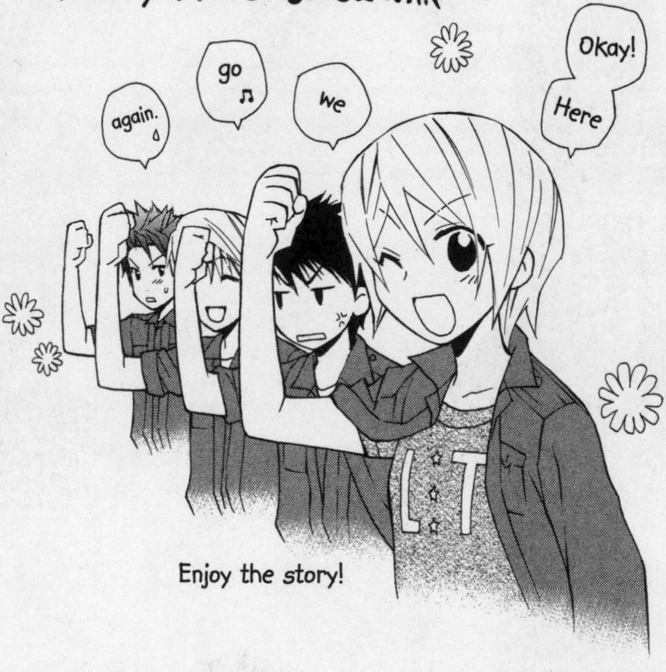
Okay!
Here
we
go ♫
again.
Enjoy the story!

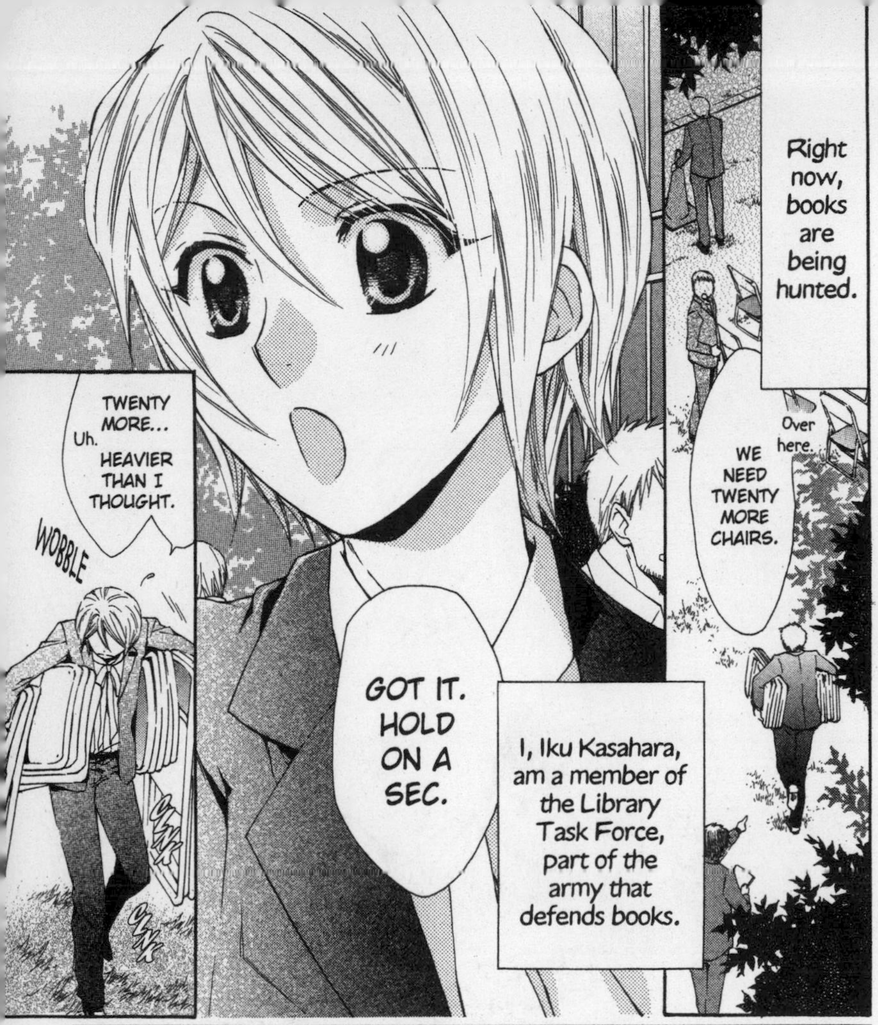
Right now, books are being hunted.
Over here.
WE NEED TWENTY MORE CHAIRS.
GOT IT. HOLD ON A SEC.
I, Iku Kasahara, am a member of the Library Task Force, part of the army that defends books.
TWENTY MORE... Uh. HEAVIER THAN I THOUGHT.
WOBBLE
CLINK
CLINK

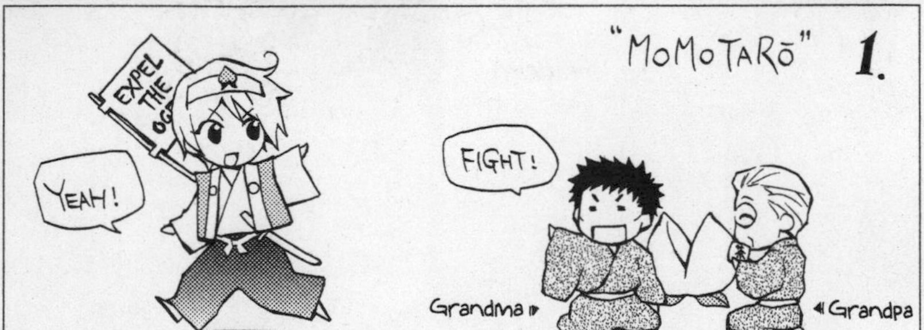
"MOMOTARŌ" 1.
Grandpa
Grandma
FIGHT!
YEAH!
EXPEL THE

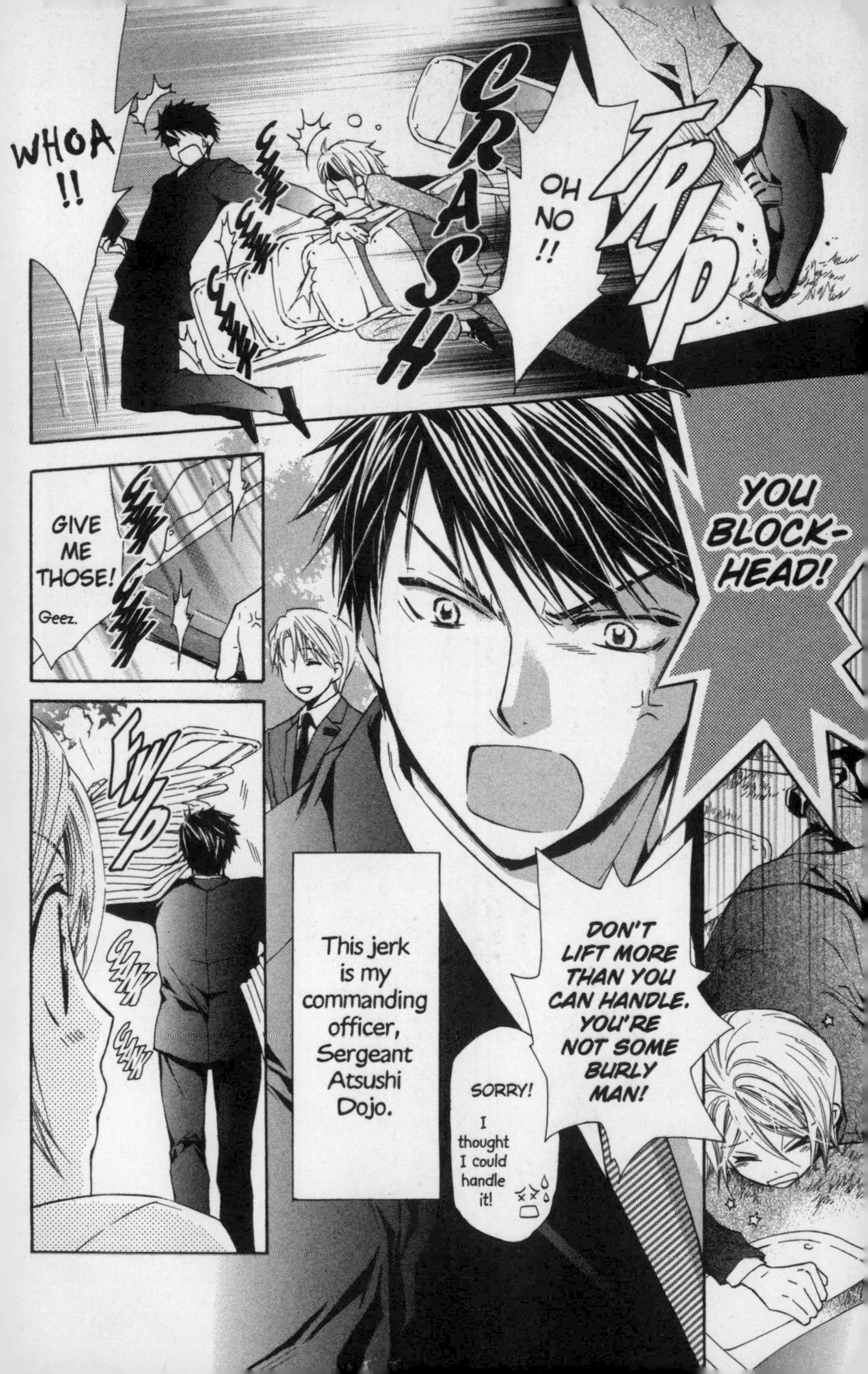
TRIP
OH NO!!
CRASH
CLANK CLANK CLANK CLANK
WHOA!!
YOU BLOCK-HEAD!
DON'T LIFT MORE THAN YOU CAN HANDLE. YOU'RE NOT SOME BURLY MAN!
SORRY!
I thought I could handle it!
This jerk is my commanding officer, Sergeant Atsushi Dojo.
CLANK CLANK
GIVE ME THOSE!
Geez.
WHIP
CLANK
CLANK

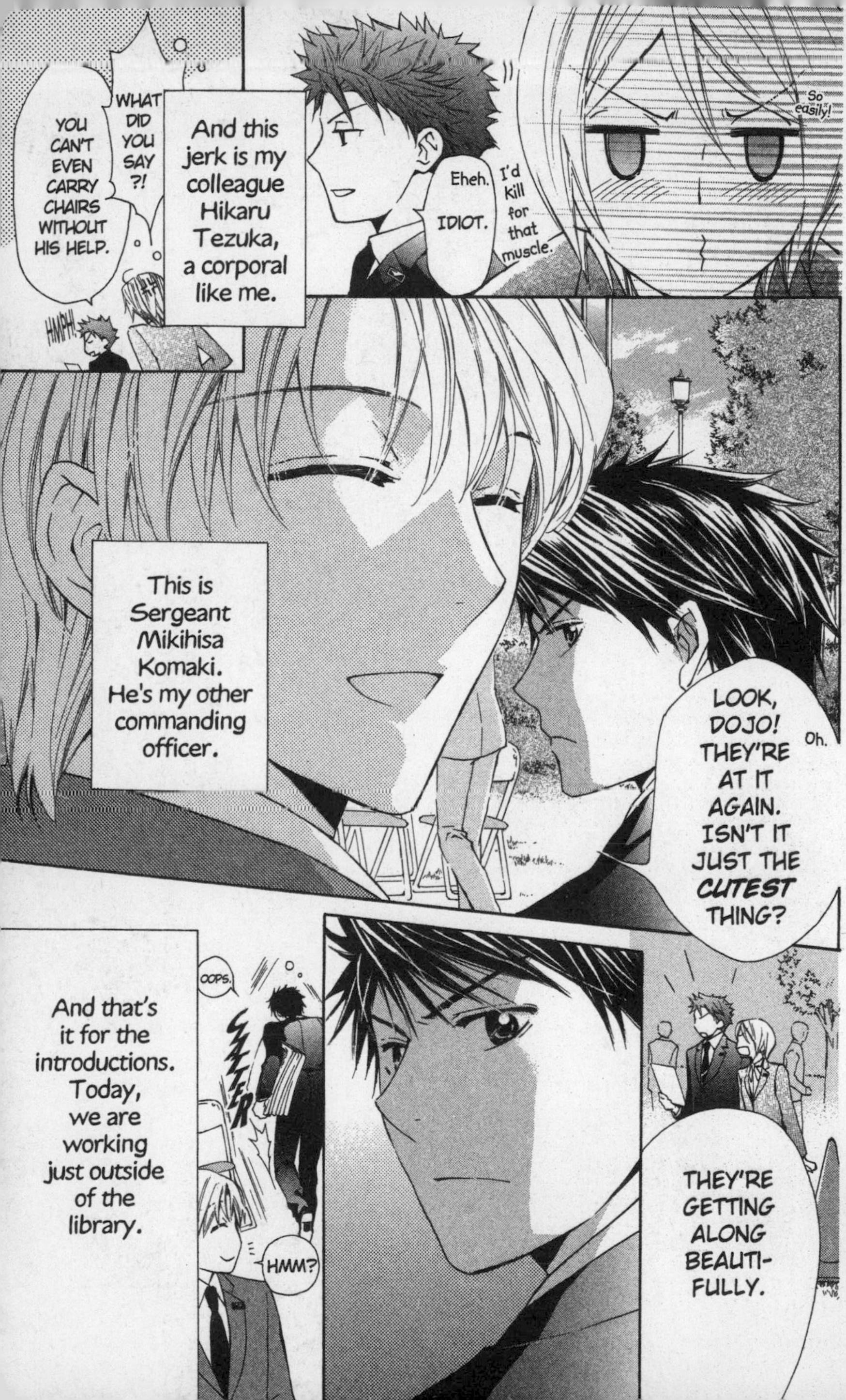
So easily!
I'd kill for that muscle.
Eheh. IDIOT.
And this jerk is my colleague Hikaru Tezuka, a corporal like me.
WHAT DID YOU SAY?!
YOU CAN'T EVEN CARRY CHAIRS WITHOUT HIS HELP.
HMPH!
LOOK, DOJO! THEY'RE AT IT AGAIN. ISN'T IT JUST THE CUTEST THING?
Oh.
This is Sergeant Mikihisa Komaki. He's my other commanding officer.
THEY'RE GETTING ALONG BEAUTIFULLY.
OOPS.
HMM?
And that's it for the introductions. Today, we are working just outside of the library.

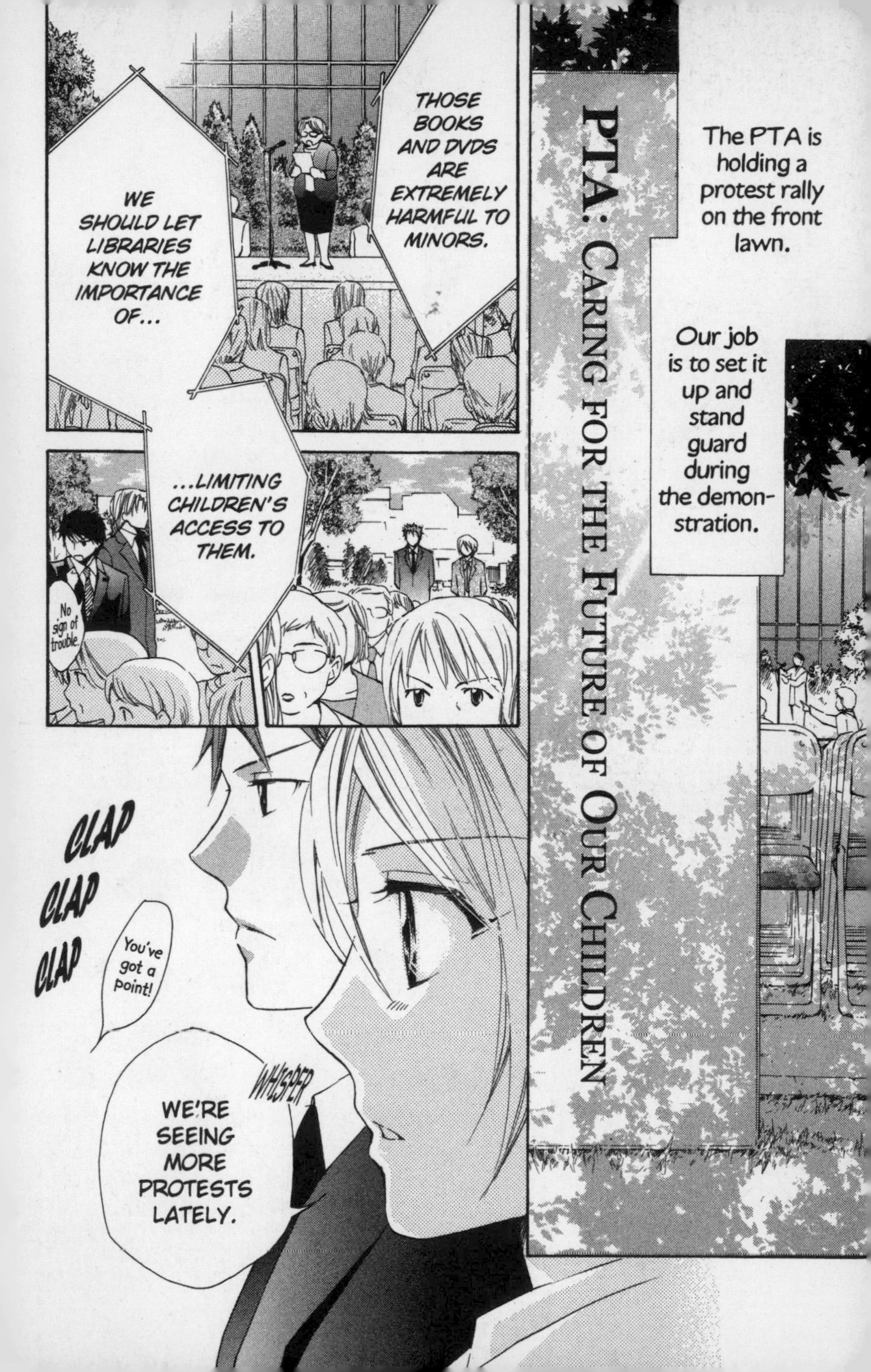
The PTA is holding a protest rally on the front lawn.
Our job is to set it up and stand guard during the demonstration.
PTA: CARING FOR THE FUTURE OF OUR CHILDREN
THOSE BOOKS AND DVDS ARE EXTREMELY HARMFUL TO MINORS.
WE SHOULD LET LIBRARIES KNOW THE IMPORTANCE OF...
...LIMITING CHILDREN'S ACCESS TO THEM.
No sign of trouble.
CLAP
CLAP
CLAP
You've got a point!
WHISPER
WE'RE SEEING MORE PROTESTS LATELY.

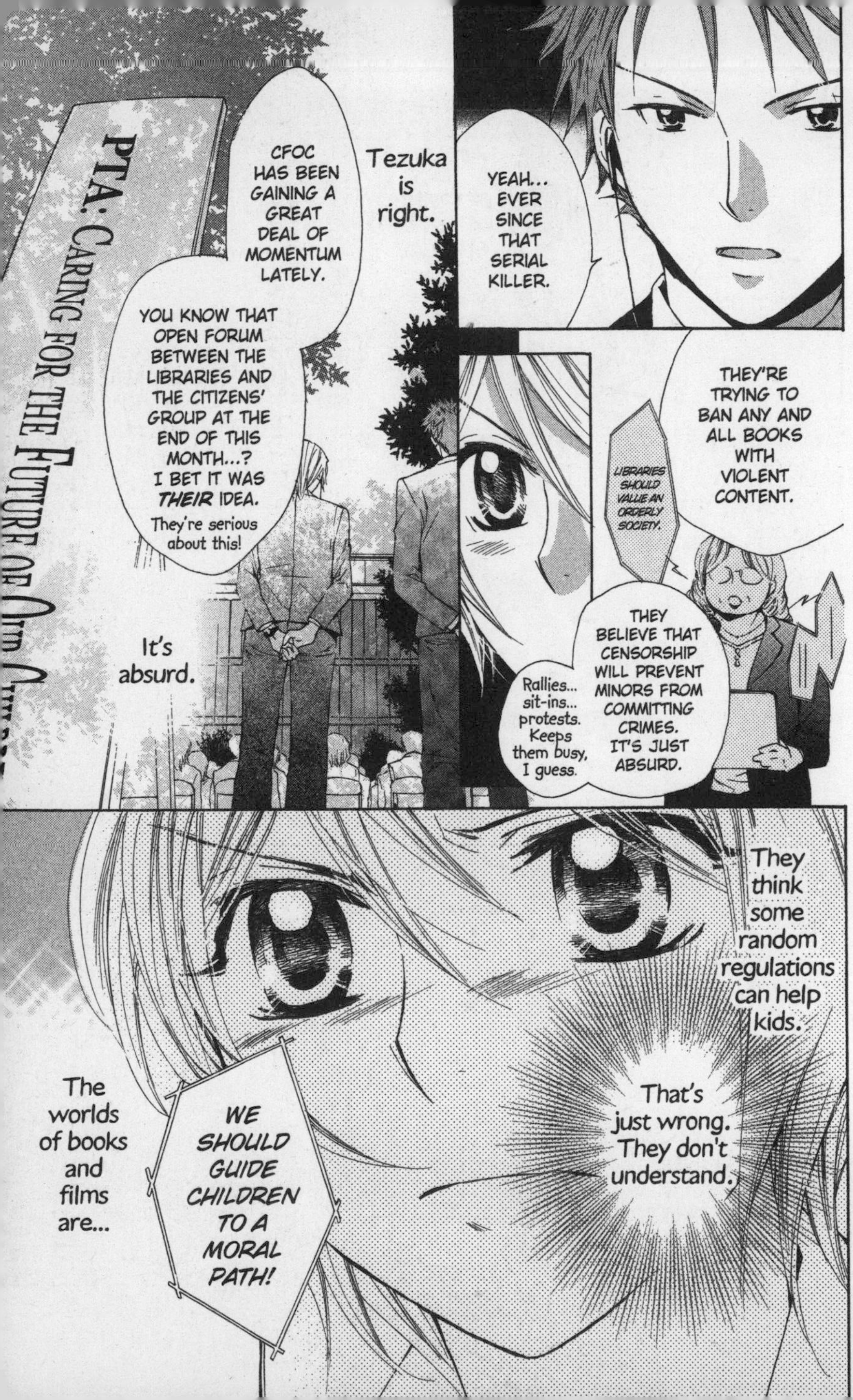
YEAH... EVER SINCE THAT SERIAL KILLER.
THEY'RE TRYING TO BAN ANY AND ALL BOOKS WITH VIOLENT CONTENT.
LIBRARIES SHOULD VALUE AN ORDERLY SOCIETY.
THEY BELIEVE THAT CENSORSHIP WILL PREVENT MINORS FROM COMMITTING CRIMES. IT'S JUST ABSURD.
Rallies... sit-ins... protests. Keeps them busy, I guess.
CFOC HAS BEEN GAINING A GREAT DEAL OF MOMENTUM LATELY.
Tezuka is right.
PTA: CARING FOR THE FUTURE OF
YOU KNOW THAT OPEN FORUM BETWEEN THE LIBRARIES AND THE CITIZENS' GROUP AT THE END OF THIS MONTH...? I BET IT WAS THEIR IDEA.
They're serious about this!
It's absurd.
They think some random regulations can help kids.
That's just wrong. They don't understand.
WE SHOULD GUIDE CHILDREN TO A MORAL PATH!
The worlds of books and films are...

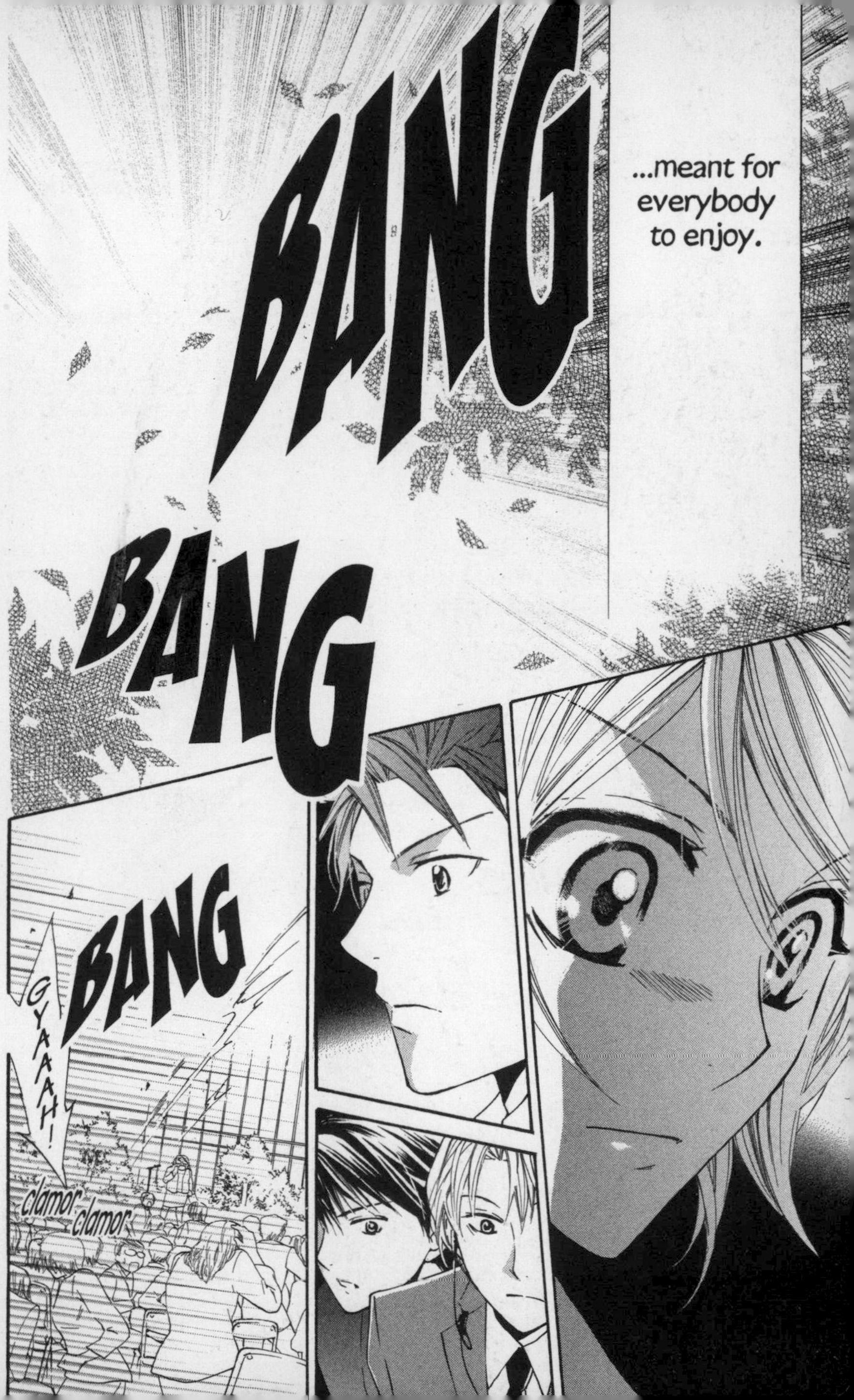
...meant for everybody to enjoy.
BANG
BANG
BANG
GYAAAH!
clamor clamor

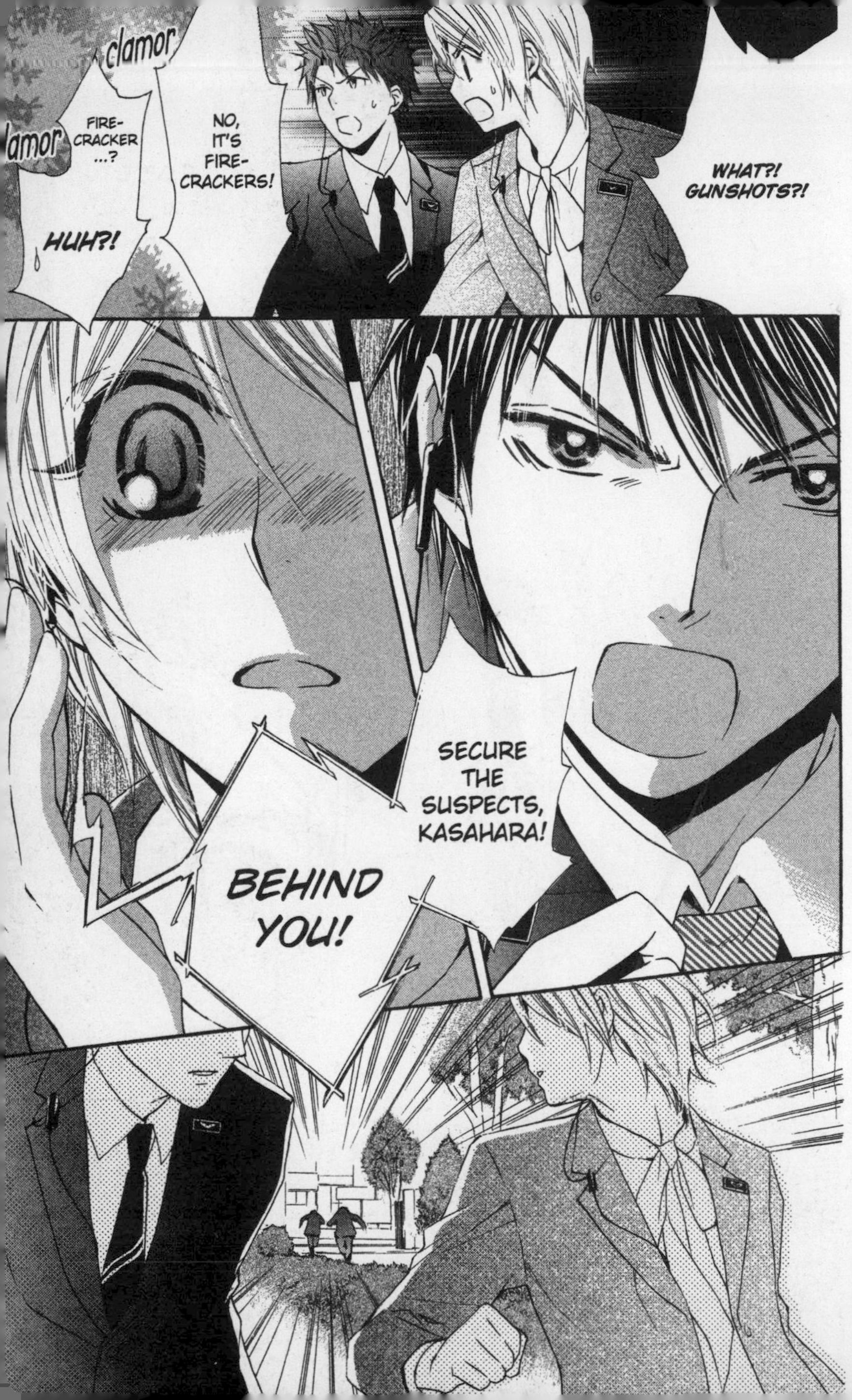
WHAT?! GUNSHOTS?!
clamor
NO, IT'S FIRE-CRACKERS!
FIRE-CRACKER ...?
HUH?!
SECURE THE SUSPECTS, KASAHARA!
BEHIND YOU!

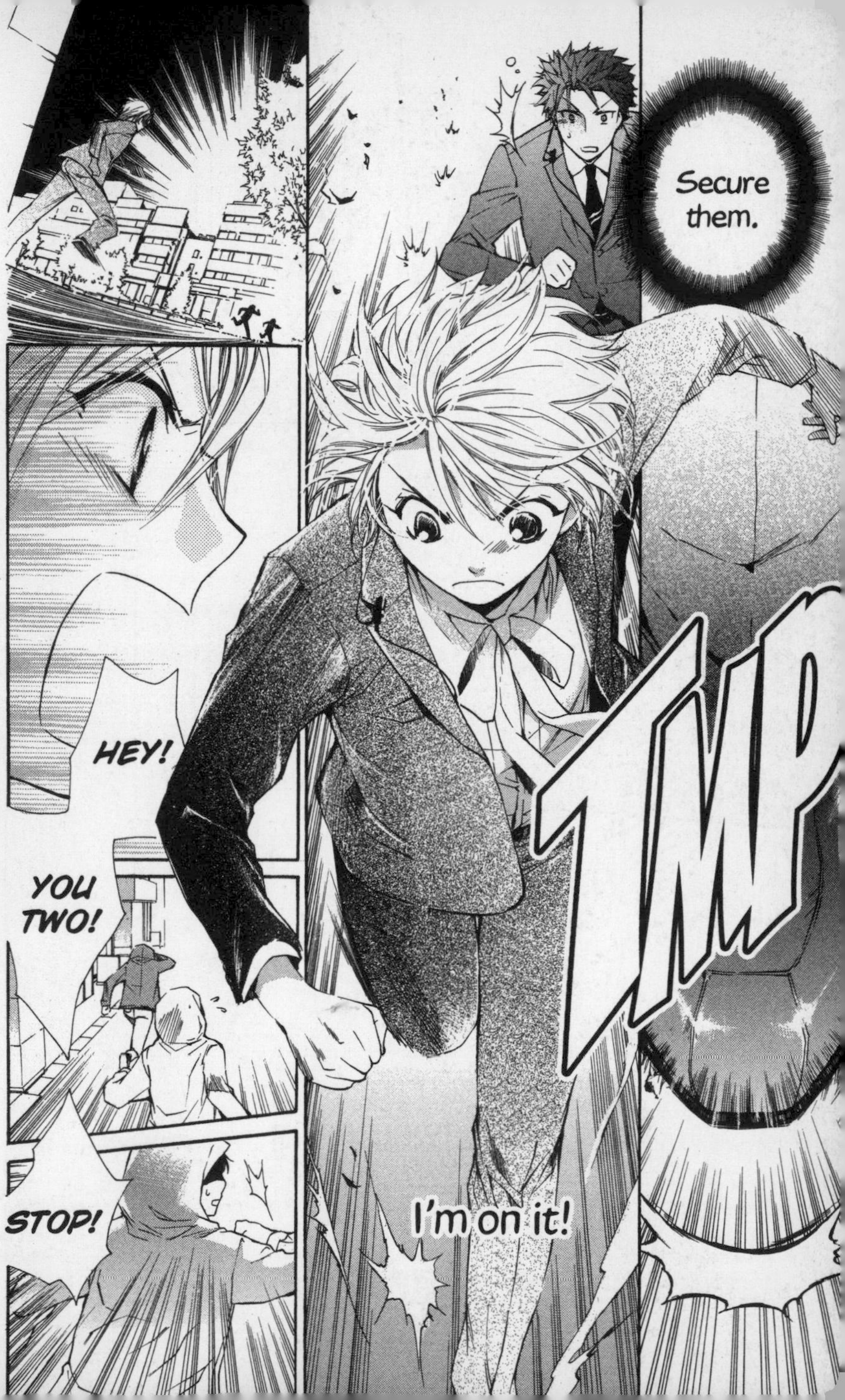
Secure them.
TMP
I'm on it!
HEY!
YOU TWO!
STOP!

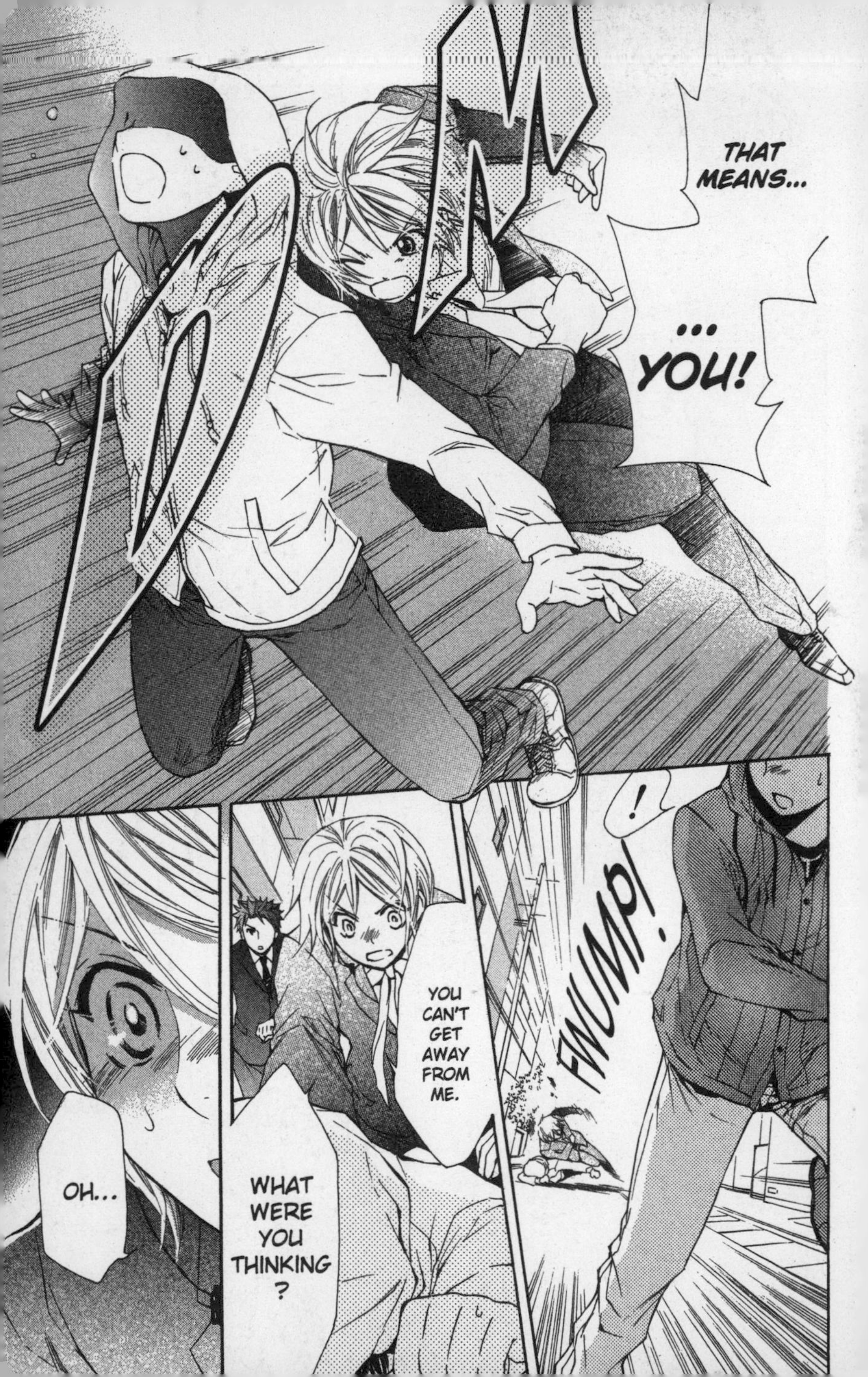
THAT MEANS...
...YOU!
!
FWUMP!
YOU CAN'T GET AWAY FROM ME.
WHAT WERE YOU THINKING?
OH...

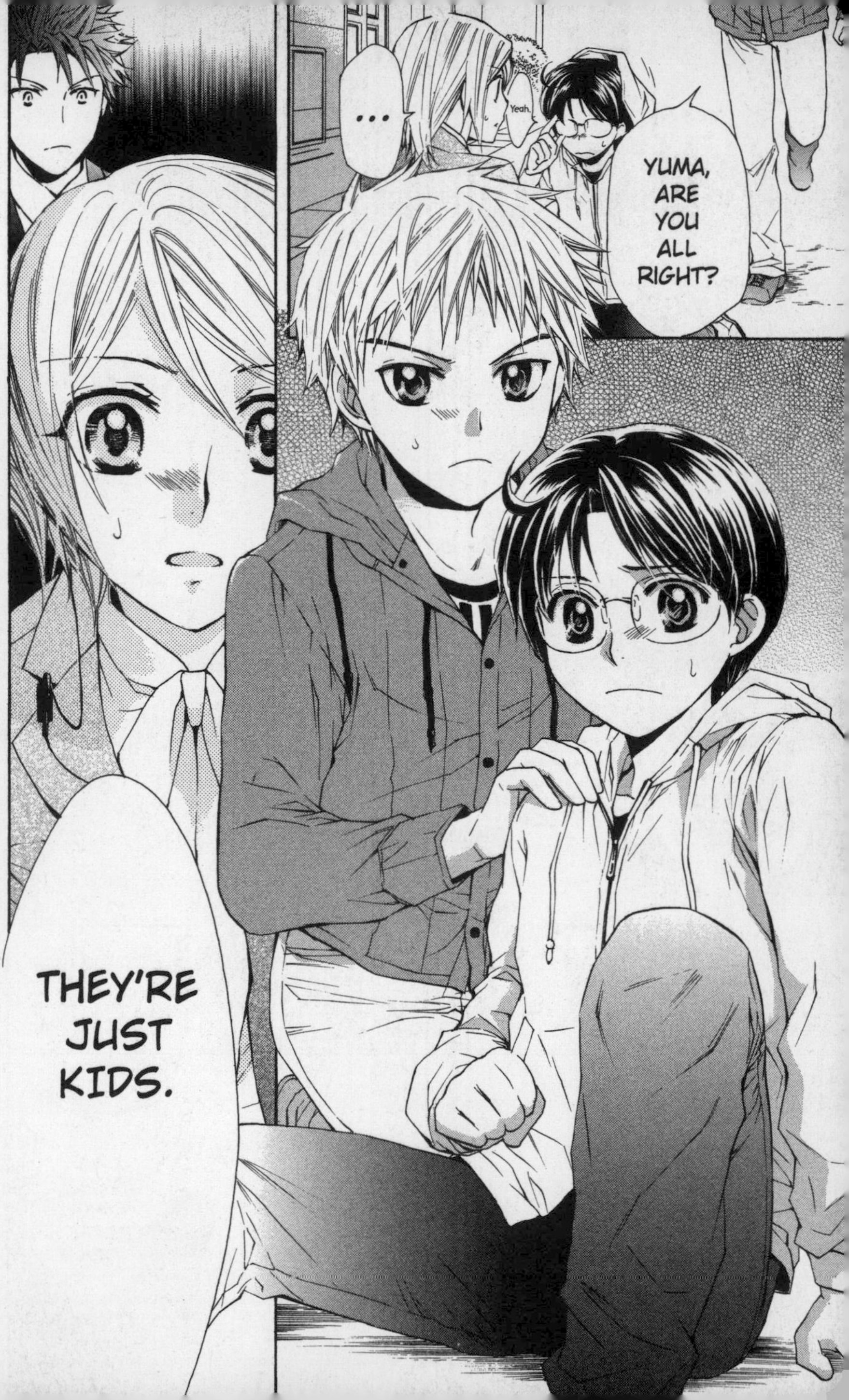
YUMA, ARE YOU ALL RIGHT?
Yeah.
...
THEY'RE JUST KIDS.

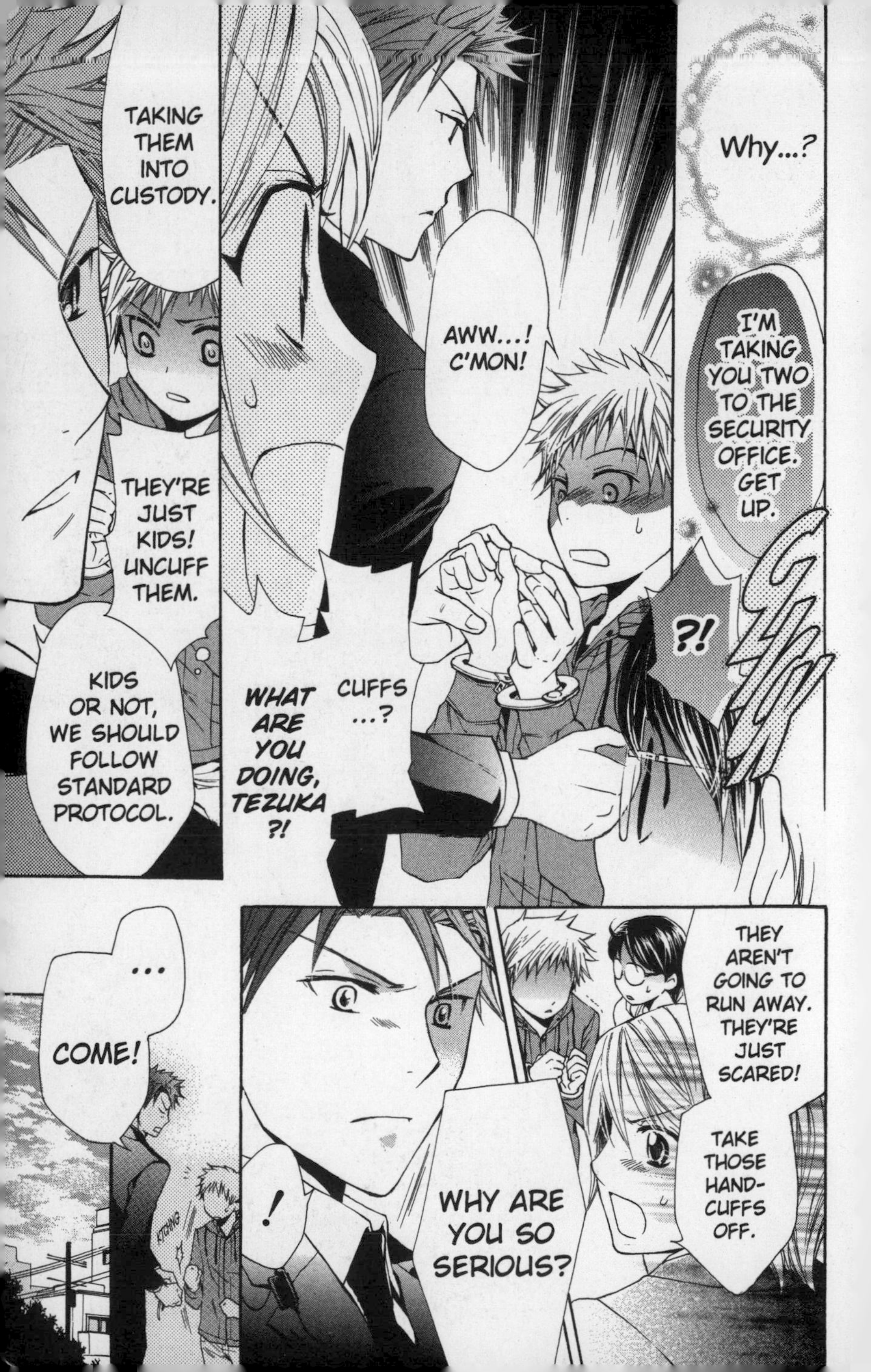
Why...?
I'M TAKING YOU TWO TO THE SECURITY OFFICE. GET UP.
?!
AWW...! C'MON!
CUFFS ...?
WHAT ARE YOU DOING, TEZUKA?!
TAKING THEM INTO CUSTODY.
THEY'RE JUST KIDS! UNCUFF THEM.
KIDS OR NOT, WE SHOULD FOLLOW STANDARD PROTOCOL.
THEY AREN'T GOING TO RUN AWAY. THEY'RE JUST SCARED!
TAKE THOSE HAND-CUFFS OFF.
WHY ARE YOU SO SERIOUS?
!
...
COME!

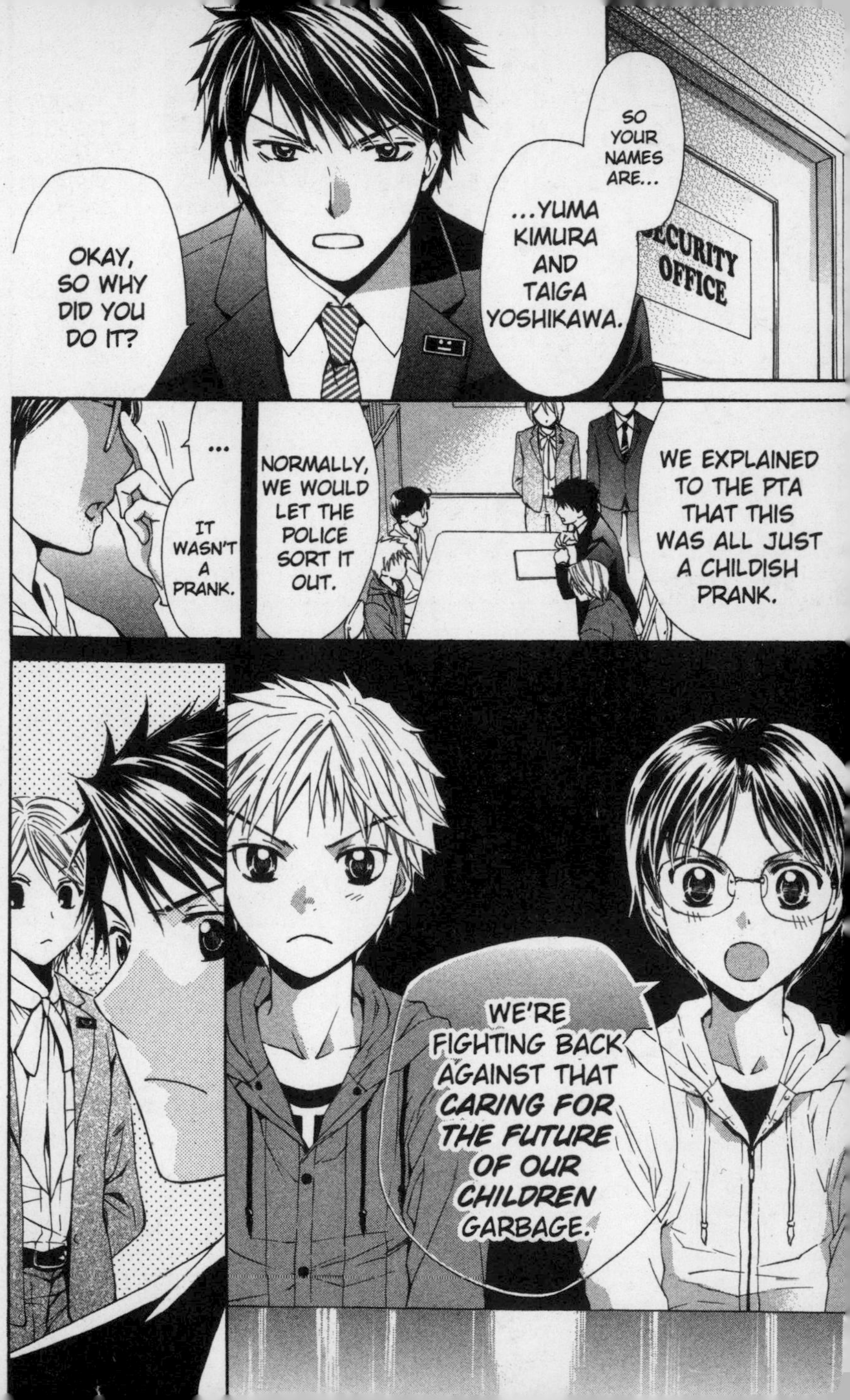
SO YOUR NAMES ARE...
...YUMA KIMURA AND TAIGA YOSHIKAWA.
SECURITY OFFICE
OKAY, SO WHY DID YOU DO IT?
WE EXPLAINED TO THE PTA THAT THIS WAS ALL JUST A CHILDISH PRANK.
NORMALLY, WE WOULD LET THE POLICE SORT IT OUT.
...
IT WASN'T A PRANK.
WE'RE FIGHTING BACK AGAINST THAT *CARING FOR THE FUTURE OF OUR CHILDREN* GARBAGE.

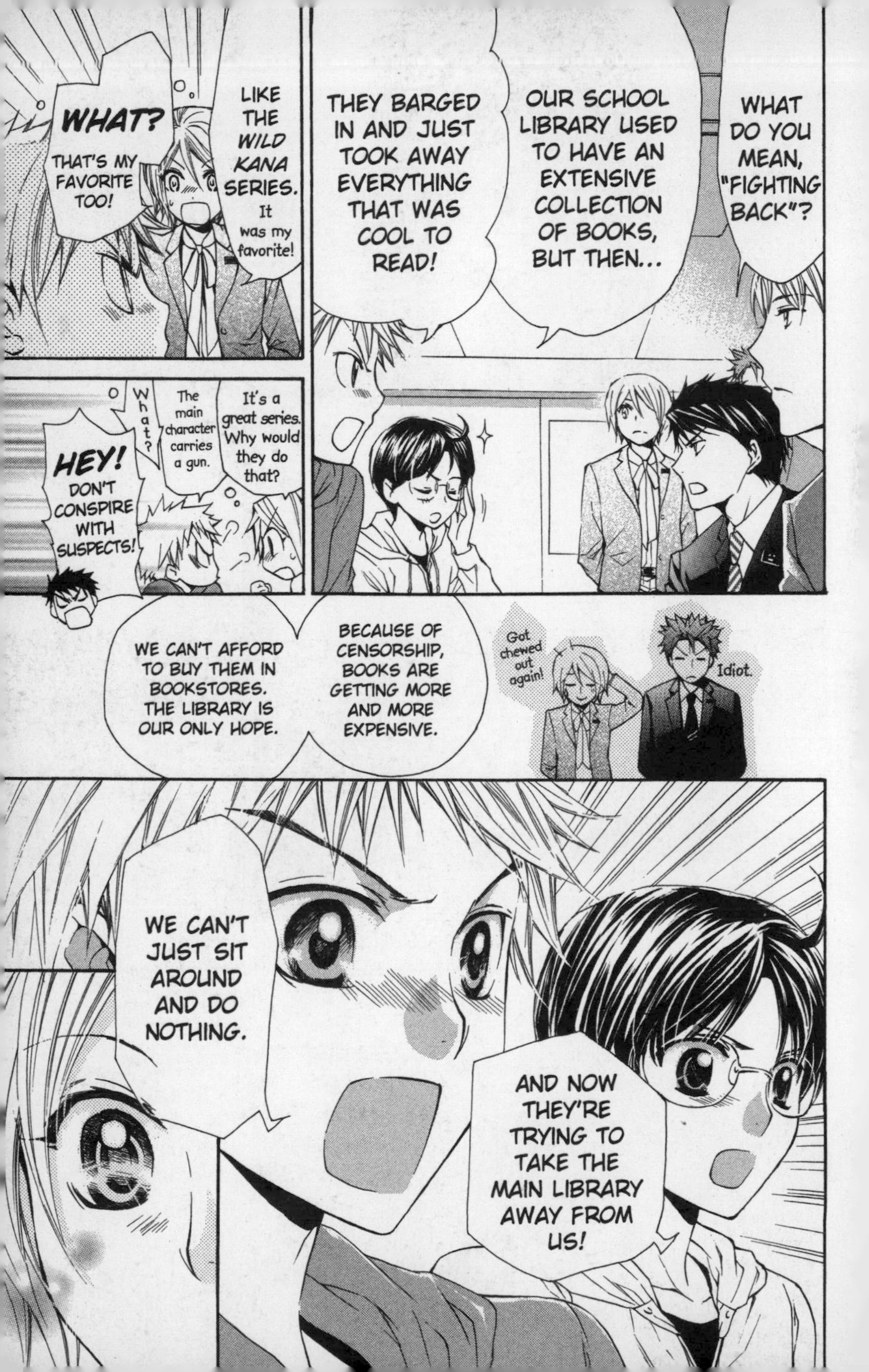
WHAT DO YOU MEAN, "FIGHTING BACK"?
OUR SCHOOL LIBRARY USED TO HAVE AN EXTENSIVE COLLECTION OF BOOKS, BUT THEN...
THEY BARGED IN AND JUST TOOK AWAY EVERYTHING THAT WAS COOL TO READ!
LIKE THE WILD KANA SERIES.
It was my favorite!
WHAT?
THAT'S MY FAVORITE TOO!
It's a great series. Why would they do that?
The main character carries a gun.
What?
HEY!
DON'T CONSPIRE WITH SUSPECTS!
Idiot.
Got chewed out again!
BECAUSE OF CENSORSHIP, BOOKS ARE GETTING MORE AND MORE EXPENSIVE.
WE CAN'T AFFORD TO BUY THEM IN BOOKSTORES. THE LIBRARY IS OUR ONLY HOPE.
AND NOW THEY'RE TRYING TO TAKE THE MAIN LIBRARY AWAY FROM US!
WE CAN'T JUST SIT AROUND AND DO NOTHING.

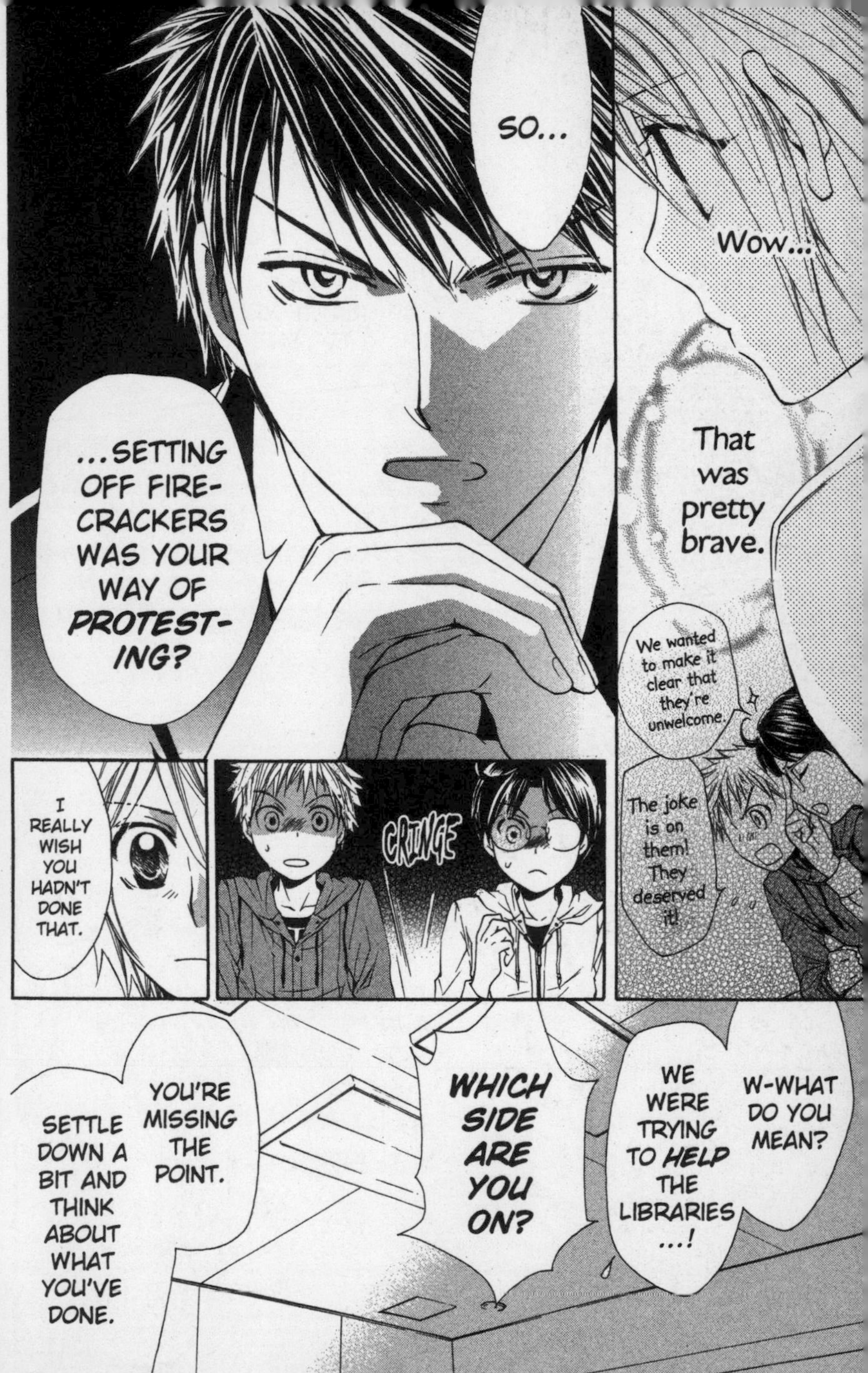
SO...
...SETTING OFF FIRE-CRACKERS WAS YOUR WAY OF *PROTESTING?*
Wow...
That was pretty brave.
We wanted to make it clear that they're unwelcome.
The joke is on them! They deserved it!
I REALLY WISH YOU HADN'T DONE THAT.
CRINGE
W-WHAT DO YOU MEAN?
WE WERE TRYING TO *HELP* THE LIBRARIES ...!
WHICH SIDE ARE YOU ON?
YOU'RE MISSING THE POINT.
SETTLE DOWN A BIT AND THINK ABOUT WHAT YOU'VE DONE.

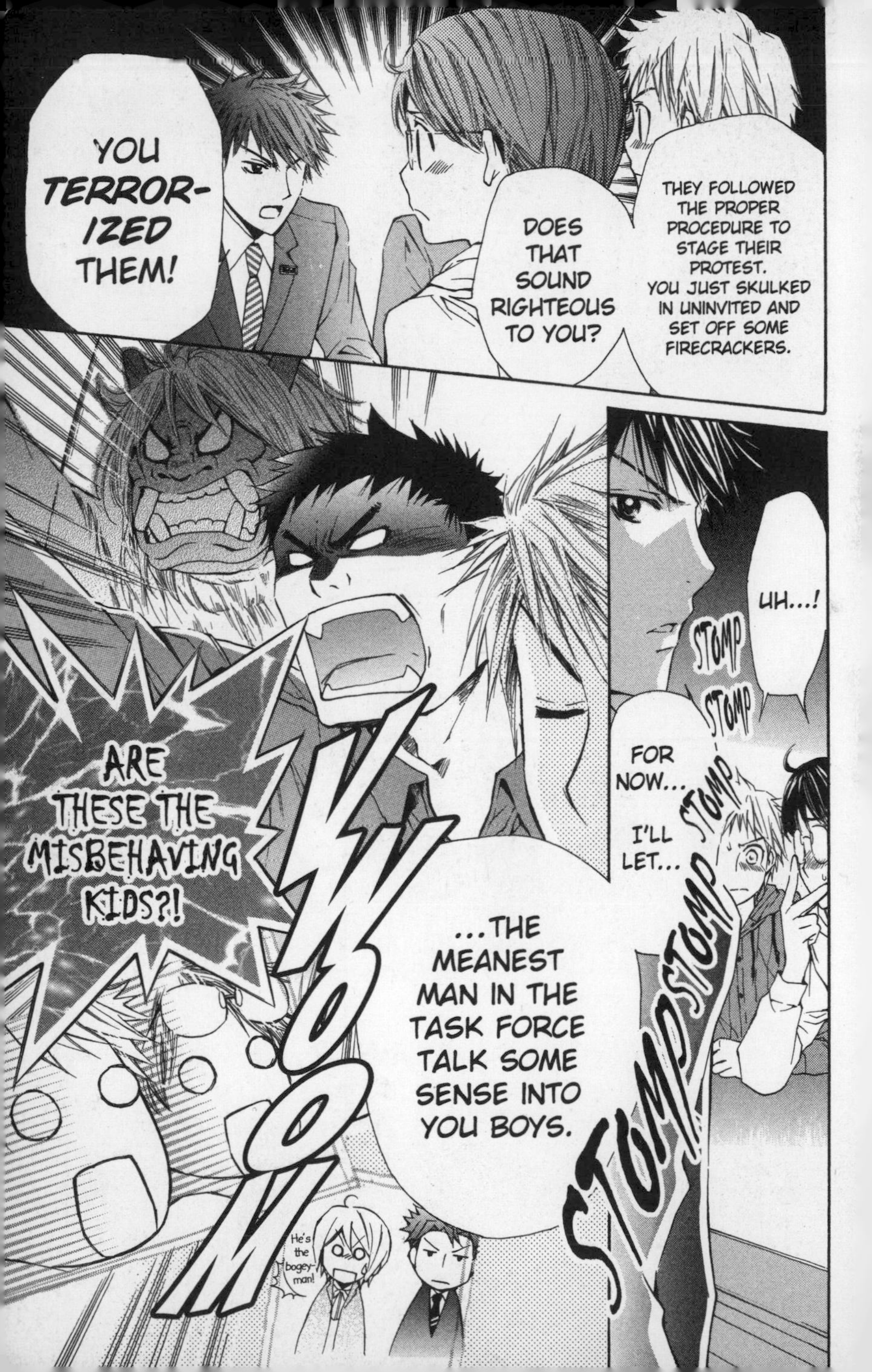
THEY FOLLOWED THE PROPER PROCEDURE TO STAGE THEIR PROTEST. YOU JUST SKULKED IN UNINVITED AND SET OFF SOME FIRECRACKERS.
DOES THAT SOUND RIGHTEOUS TO YOU?
YOU TERROR-IZED THEM!
UH...!
STOMP
STOMP
FOR NOW...
I'LL LET...
STOMP
STOMPSTOMPSTOMP
ARE THESE THE MISBEHAVING KIDS?!
WHOOOM
...THE MEANEST MAN IN THE TASK FORCE TALK SOME SENSE INTO YOU BOYS.
He's the bogey-man!

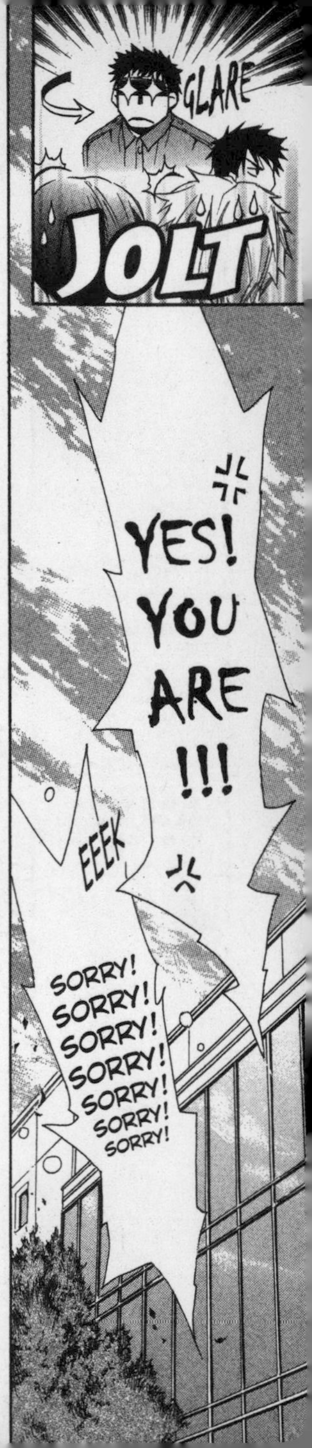
GLARE
JOLT
YES! YOU ARE!!!
EEEK
SORRY! SORRY! SORRY! SORRY! SORRY! SORRY! SORRY!

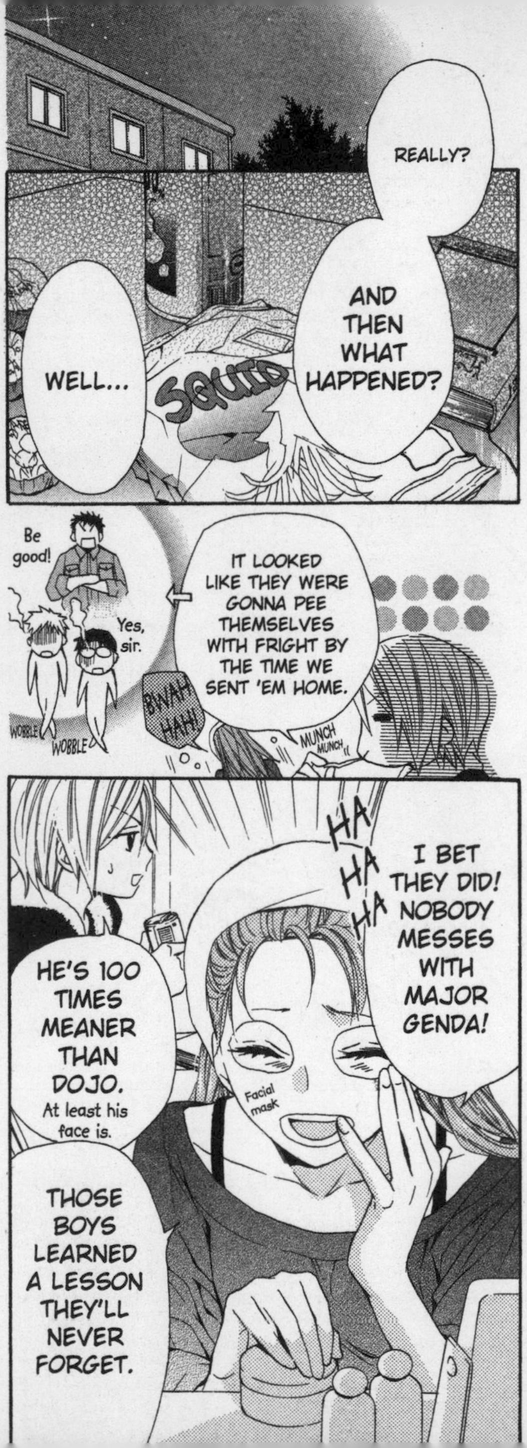
REALLY?
AND THEN WHAT HAPPENED?
SQUID
WELL...
IT LOOKED LIKE THEY WERE GONNA PEE THEMSELVES WITH FRIGHT BY THE TIME WE SENT 'EM HOME.
Be good!
Yes, sir.
WOBBLE
WOBBLE
BWAH HAH
MUNCH MUNCH
HA HA HA
I BET THEY DID! NOBODY MESSES WITH MAJOR GENDA!
HE'S 100 TIMES MEANER THAN DOJO.
At least his face is.
Facial mask
THOSE BOYS LEARNED A LESSON THEY'LL NEVER FORGET.

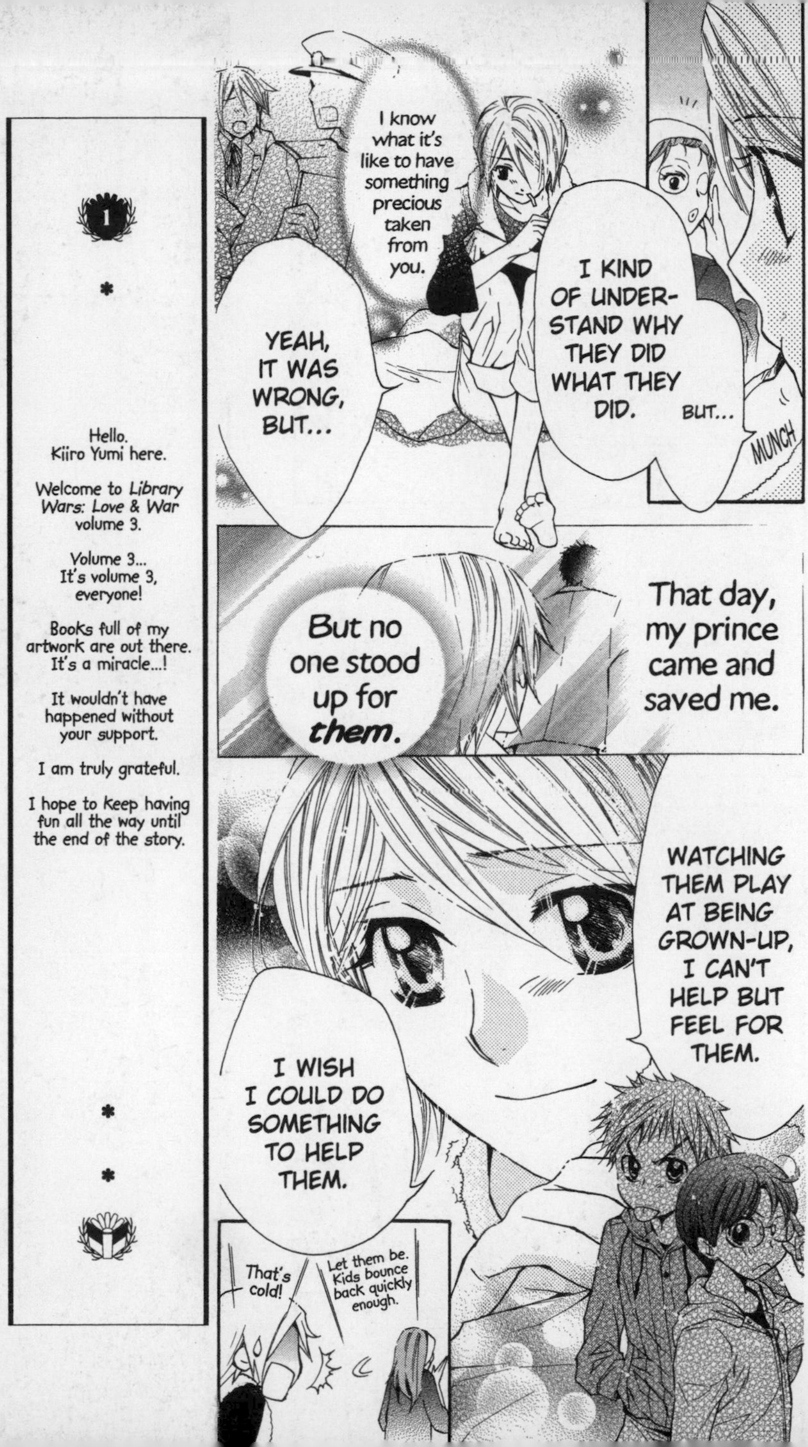
I know what it's like to have something precious taken from you.
MUNCH
I KIND OF UNDER-STAND WHY THEY DID WHAT THEY DID.
BUT...
YEAH, IT WAS WRONG, BUT...
That day, my prince came and saved me.
But no one stood up for *them*.
WATCHING THEM PLAY AT BEING GROWN-UP, I CAN'T HELP BUT FEEL FOR THEM.
I WISH I COULD DO SOMETHING TO HELP THEM.
Let them be. Kids bounce back quickly enough.
That's cold!

1

*

Hello.
Kiiro Yumi here.

Welcome to *Library Wars: Love & War* volume 3.

Volume 3...
It's volume 3, everyone!

Books full of my artwork are out there. It's a miracle...!

It wouldn't have happened without your support.

I am truly grateful.

I hope to keep having fun all the way until the end of the story.

*

*

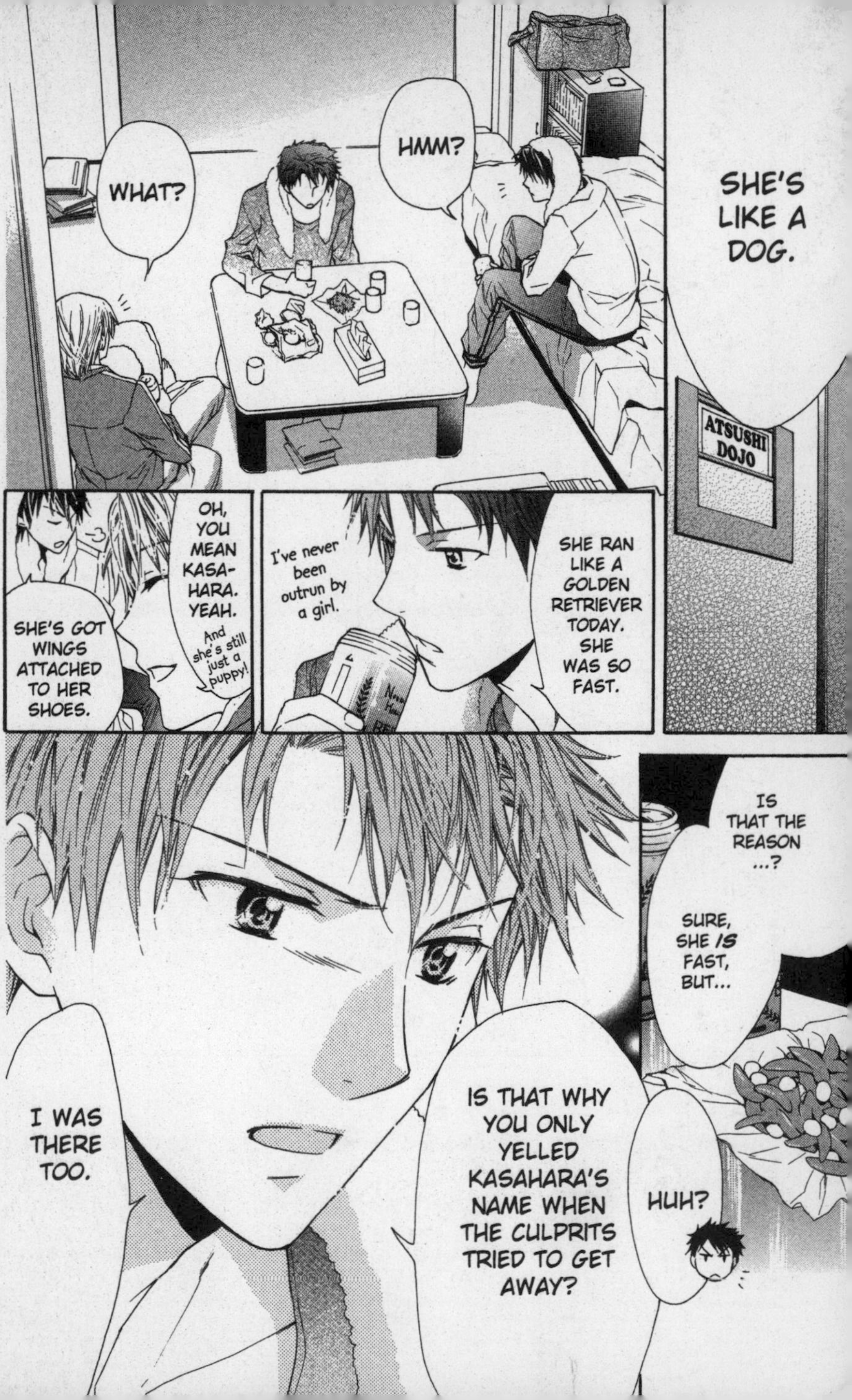
SHE'S LIKE A DOG.
ATSUSHI DOJO
HMM?
WHAT?
SHE RAN LIKE A GOLDEN RETRIEVER TODAY. SHE WAS SO FAST.
I've never been outrun by a girl.
OH, YOU MEAN KASA-HARA. YEAH.
And she's still just a puppy!
SHE'S GOT WINGS ATTACHED TO HER SHOES.
IS THAT THE REASON ...?
SURE, SHE *IS* FAST, BUT...
IS THAT WHY YOU ONLY YELLED KASAHARA'S NAME WHEN THE CULPRITS TRIED TO GET AWAY?
HUH?
I WAS THERE TOO.

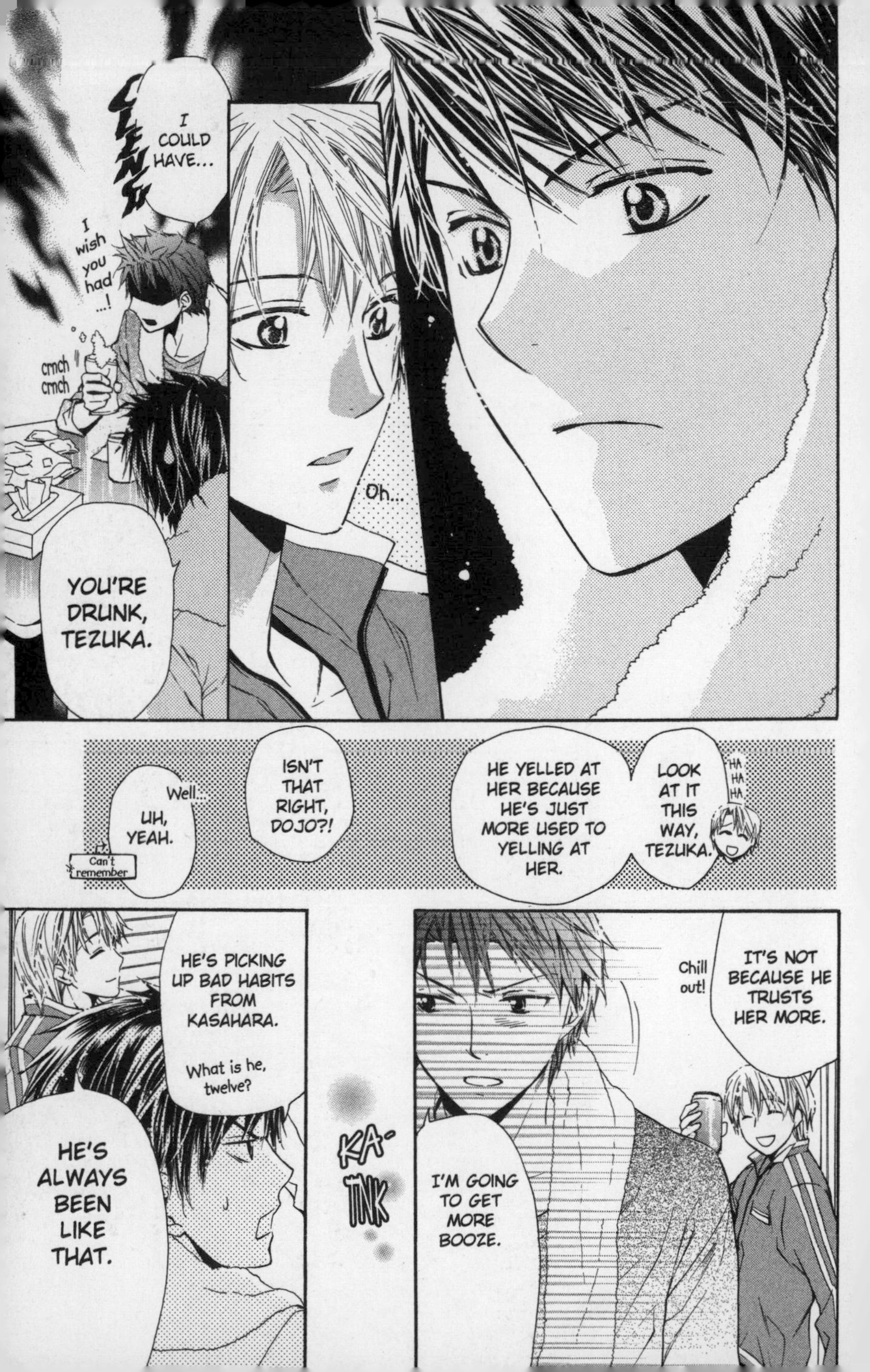
I COULD HAVE...
CLENCH
I wish you had...!
crnch crnch
YOU'RE DRUNK, TEZUKA.
Oh...
HA HA HA
LOOK AT IT THIS WAY, TEZUKA.
HE YELLED AT HER BECAUSE HE'S JUST MORE USED TO YELLING AT HER.
ISN'T THAT RIGHT, DOJO?!
Well...
UH, YEAH.
Can't remember
IT'S NOT BECAUSE HE TRUSTS HER MORE.
Chill out!
I'M GOING TO GET MORE BOOZE.
KA-TNK
HE'S PICKING UP BAD HABITS FROM KASAHARA.
What is he, twelve?
HE'S ALWAYS BEEN LIKE THAT.

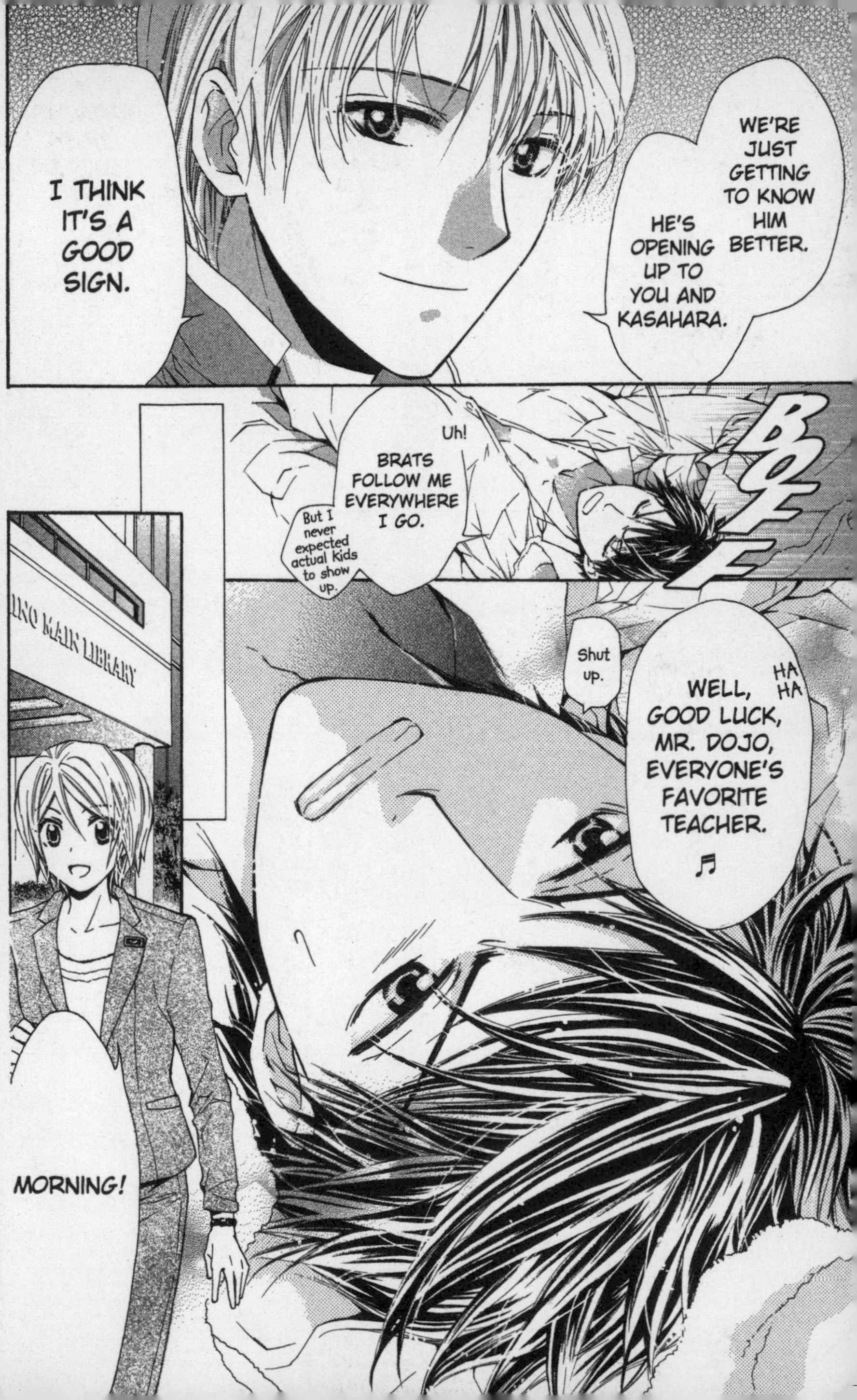
WE'RE JUST GETTING TO KNOW HIM BETTER.
HE'S OPENING UP TO YOU AND KASAHARA.
I THINK IT'S A GOOD SIGN.
BOFF
Uh!
BRATS FOLLOW ME EVERYWHERE I GO.
But I never expected actual kids to show up.
HA HA
WELL, GOOD LUCK, MR. DOJO, EVERYONE'S FAVORITE TEACHER. ♫
Shut up.
MAIN LIBRARY
MORNING!

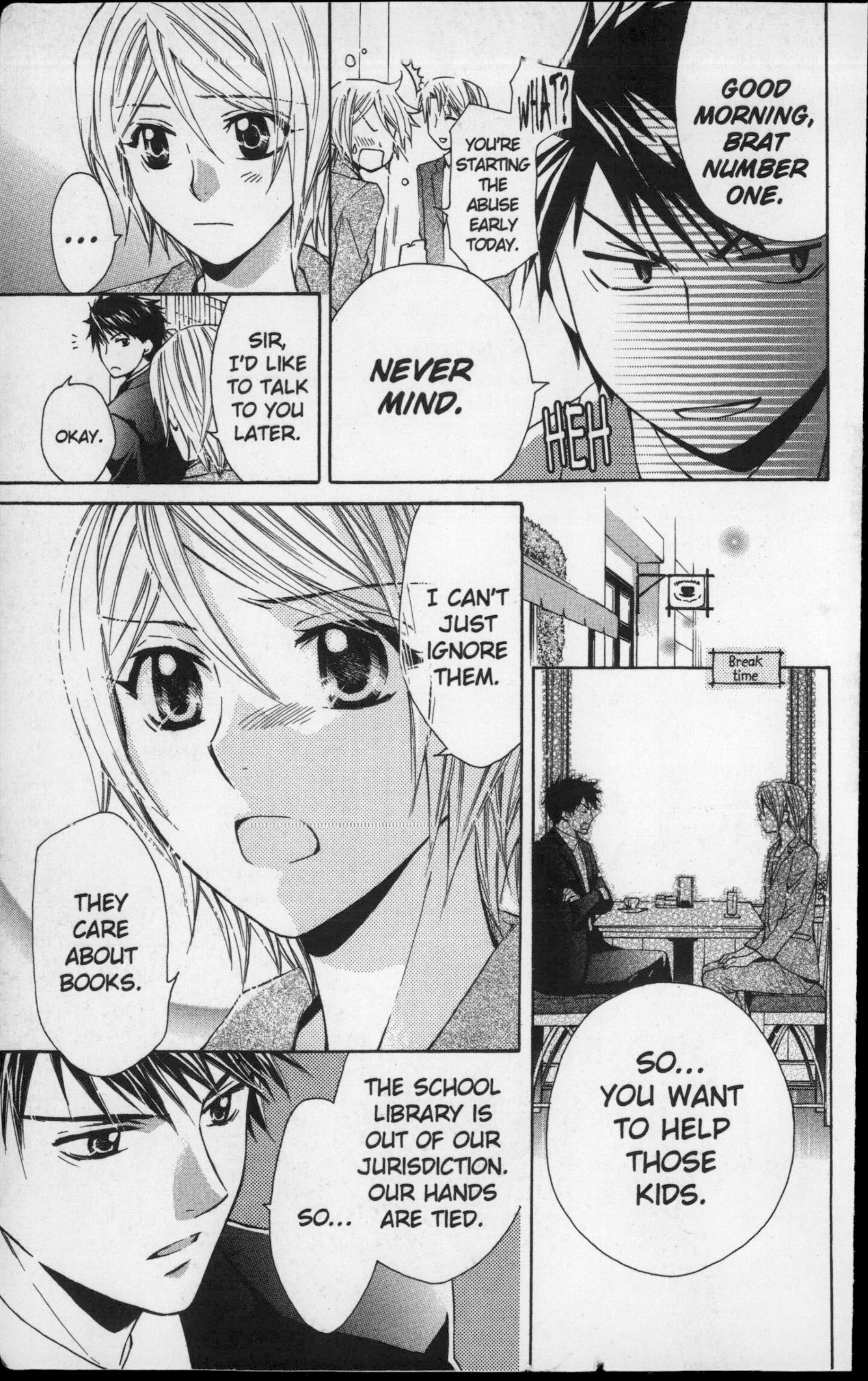
GOOD MORNING, BRAT NUMBER ONE.
WHAT?
YOU'RE STARTING THE ABUSE EARLY TODAY.
HEH
NEVER MIND.
...
SIR, I'D LIKE TO TALK TO YOU LATER.
OKAY.
Break time
SO... YOU WANT TO HELP THOSE KIDS.
I CAN'T JUST IGNORE THEM.
THEY CARE ABOUT BOOKS.
THE SCHOOL LIBRARY IS OUT OF OUR JURISDICTION. OUR HANDS ARE TIED.
SO...

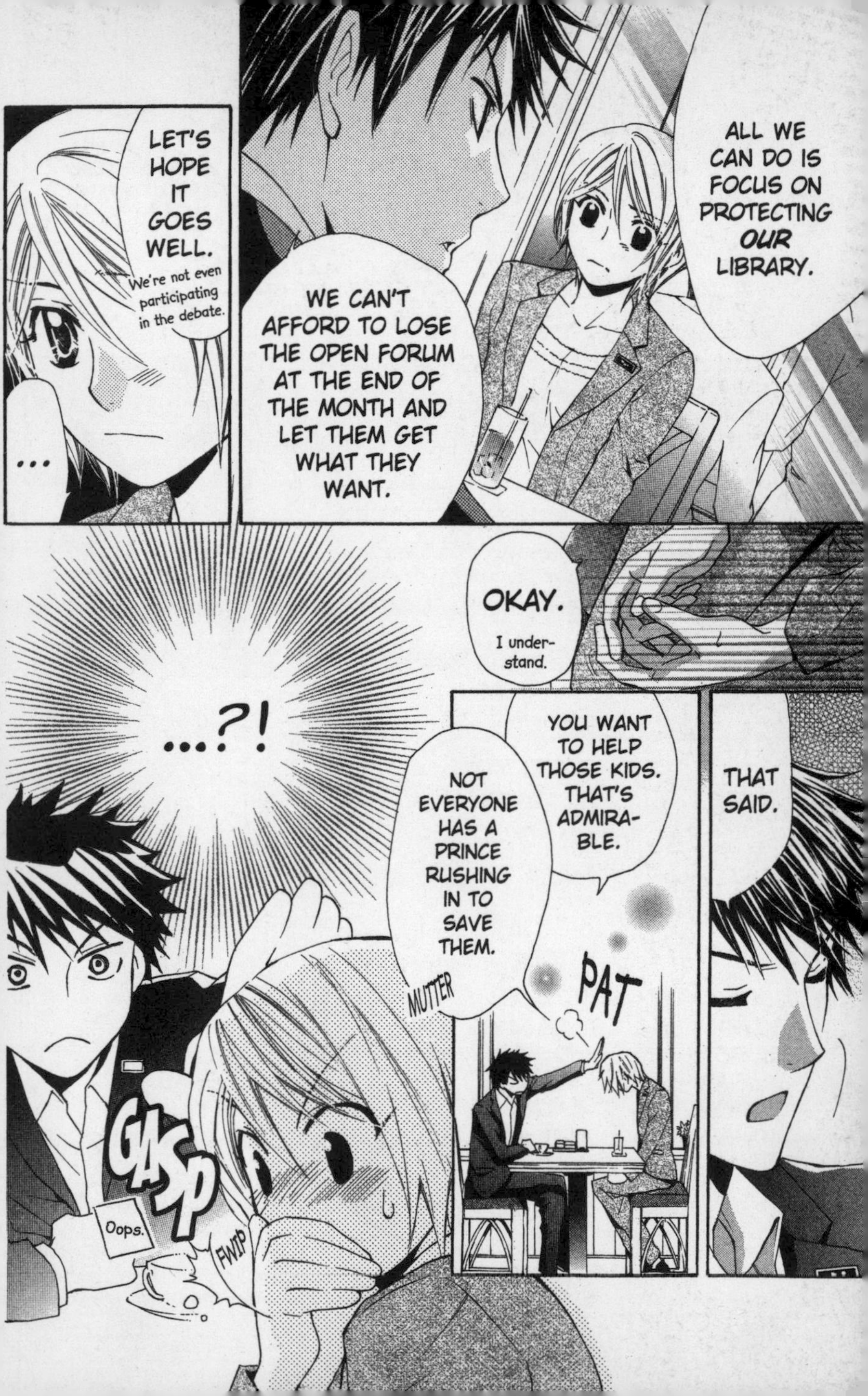
ALL WE CAN DO IS FOCUS ON PROTECTING OUR LIBRARY.
WE CAN'T AFFORD TO LOSE THE OPEN FORUM AT THE END OF THE MONTH AND LET THEM GET WHAT THEY WANT.
LET'S HOPE IT GOES WELL.
We're not even participating in the debate.
...
OKAY.
I understand.
THAT SAID.
YOU WANT TO HELP THOSE KIDS. THAT'S ADMIRABLE.
NOT EVERYONE HAS A PRINCE RUSHING IN TO SAVE THEM.
MUTTER
PAT
...?!
GASP
Oops.
FWIP

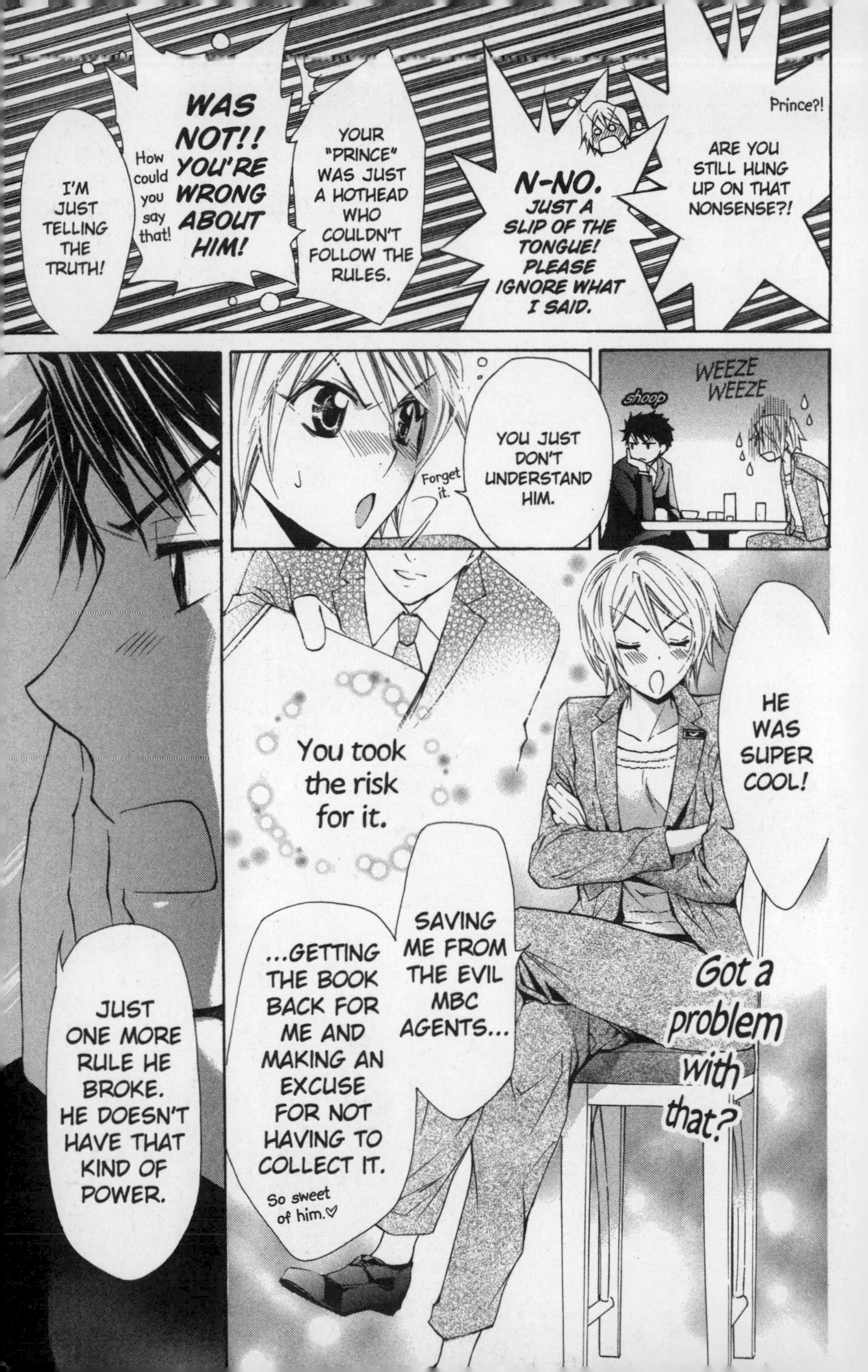

Prince?!
ARE YOU STILL HUNG UP ON THAT NONSENSE?!
N-NO. JUST A SLIP OF THE TONGUE! PLEASE IGNORE WHAT I SAID.
YOUR "PRINCE" WAS JUST A HOTHEAD WHO COULDN'T FOLLOW THE RULES.
WAS NOT!! YOU'RE WRONG ABOUT HIM!
How could you say that!
I'M JUST TELLING THE TRUTH!
WEEZE WEEZE
shoop
YOU JUST DON'T UNDERSTAND HIM.
Forget it.
HE WAS SUPER COOL!
Got a problem with that?
SAVING ME FROM THE EVIL MBC AGENTS...
...GETTING THE BOOK BACK FOR ME AND MAKING AN EXCUSE FOR NOT HAVING TO COLLECT IT.
So sweet of him.♡
You took the risk for it.
JUST ONE MORE RULE HE BROKE. HE DOESN'T HAVE THAT KIND OF POWER.

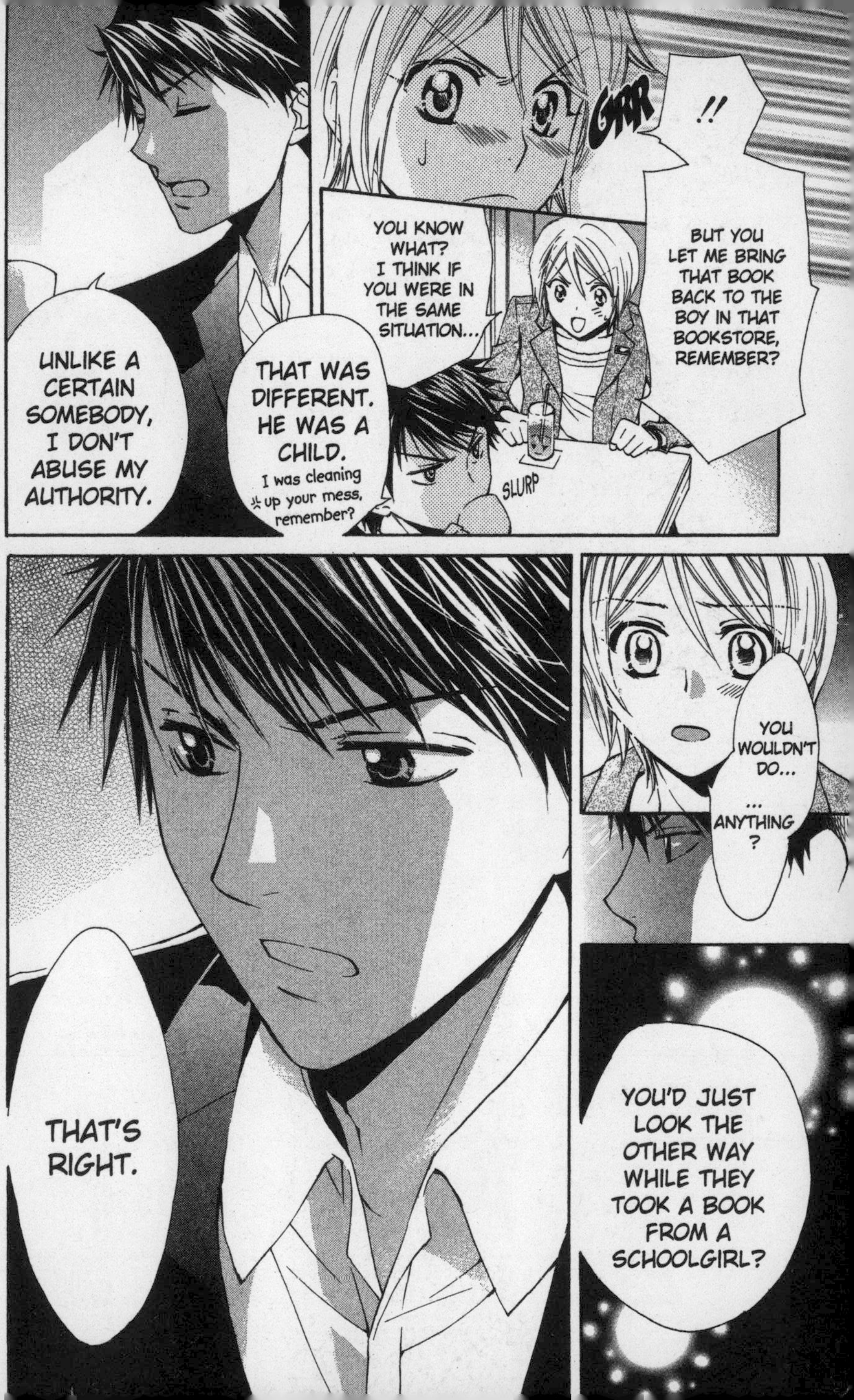
GRR
!!
BUT YOU LET ME BRING THAT BOOK BACK TO THE BOY IN THAT BOOKSTORE, REMEMBER?
YOU KNOW WHAT? I THINK IF YOU WERE IN THE SAME SITUATION...
THAT WAS DIFFERENT. HE WAS A CHILD.
I was cleaning up your mess, remember?
SLURP
UNLIKE A CERTAIN SOMEBODY, I DON'T ABUSE MY AUTHORITY.
YOU WOULDN'T DO...
...ANYTHING?
YOU'D JUST LOOK THE OTHER WAY WHILE THEY TOOK A BOOK FROM A SCHOOLGIRL?
THAT'S RIGHT.

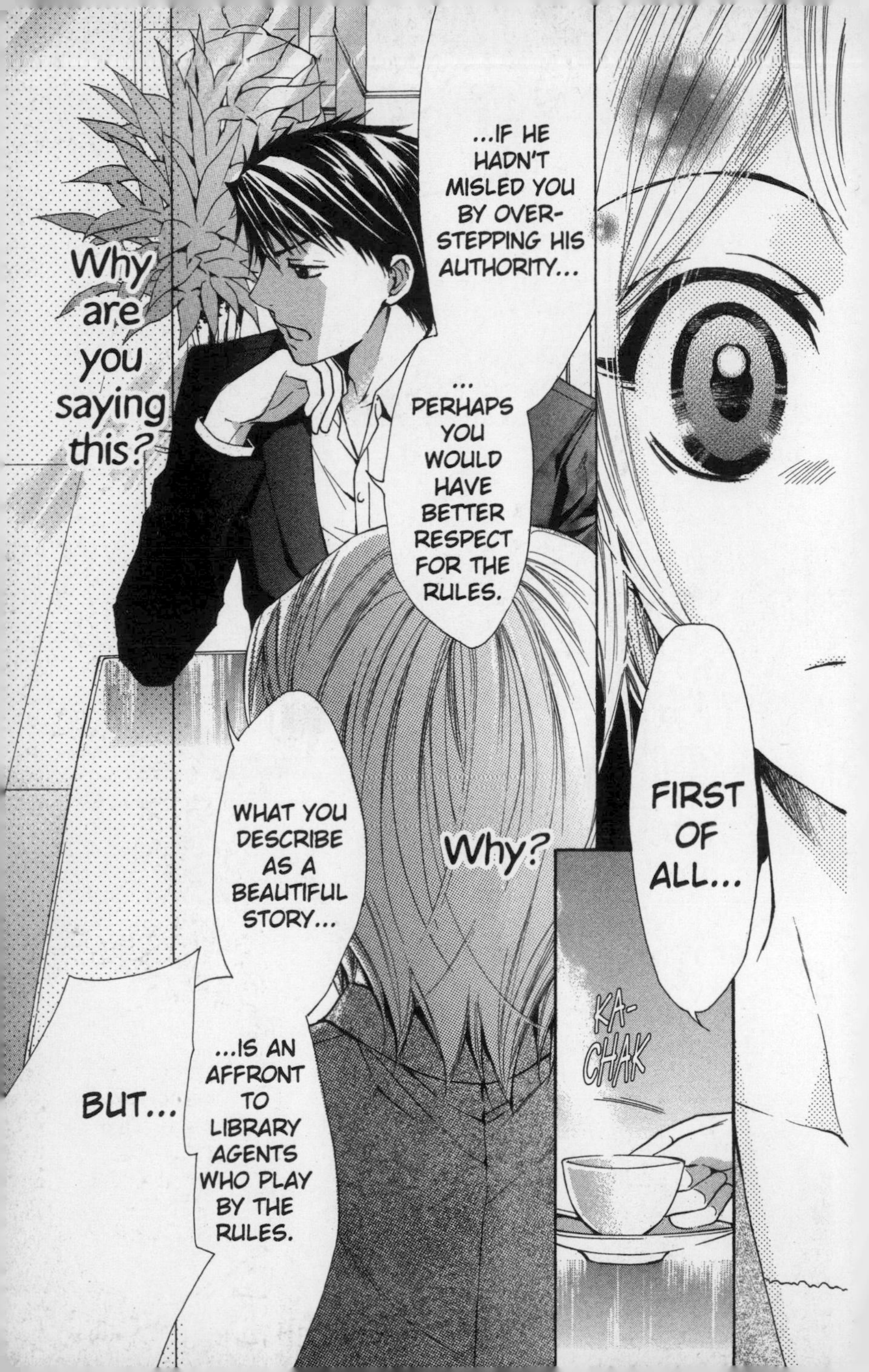
FIRST OF ALL...
KA-CHAK
WHAT YOU DESCRIBE AS A BEAUTIFUL STORY...
...IS AN AFFRONT TO LIBRARY AGENTS WHO PLAY BY THE RULES.
BUT...
...IF HE HADN'T MISLED YOU BY OVER-STEPPING HIS AUTHORITY...
... PERHAPS YOU WOULD HAVE BETTER RESPECT FOR THE RULES.
Why?
Why are you saying this?

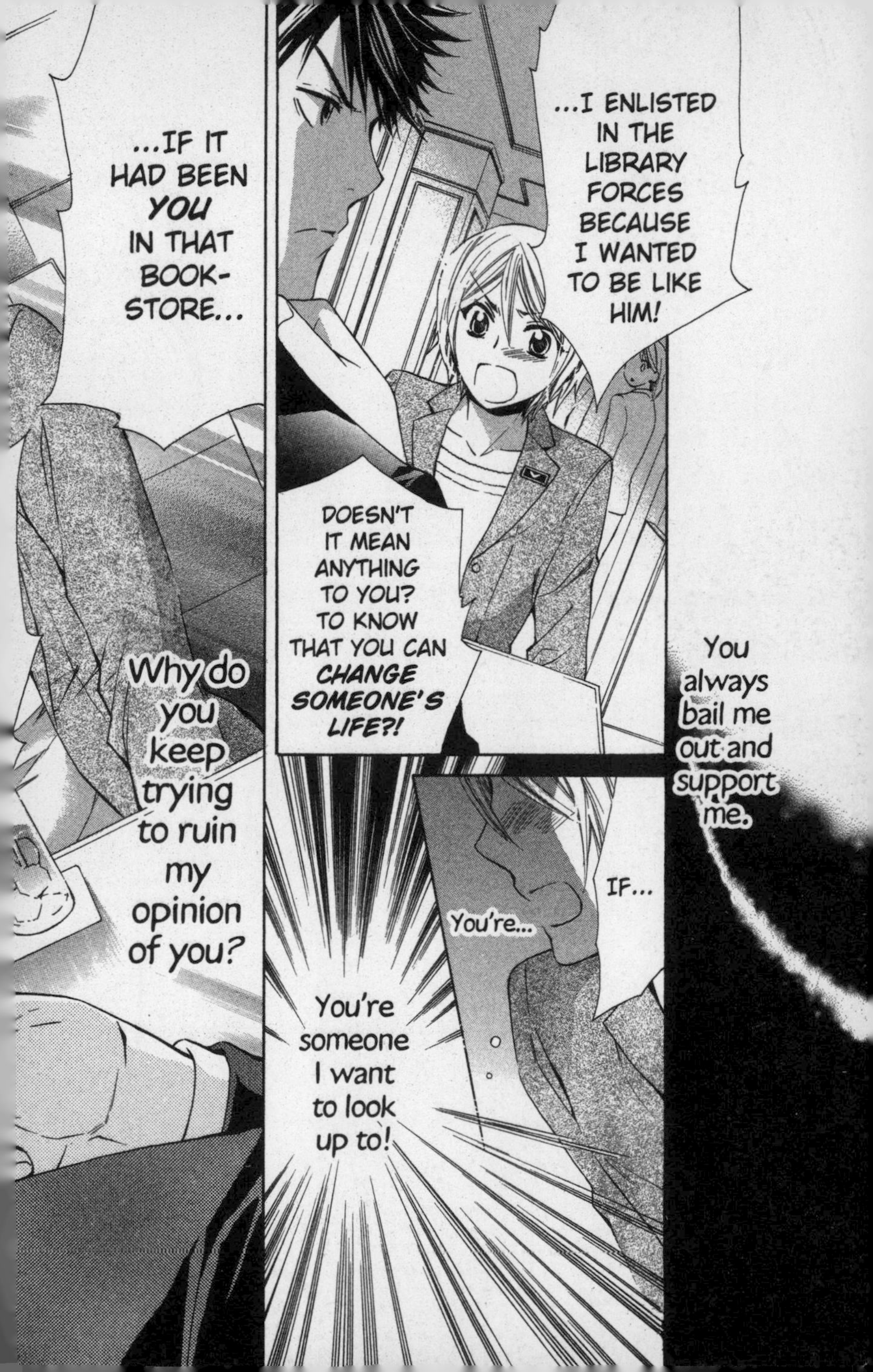
...I ENLISTED IN THE LIBRARY FORCES BECAUSE I WANTED TO BE LIKE HIM!
DOESN'T IT MEAN ANYTHING TO YOU? TO KNOW THAT YOU CAN *CHANGE SOMEONE'S LIFE?!*
You always bail me out and support me.
IF...
You're...
You're someone I want to look up to!
...IF IT HAD BEEN *YOU* IN THAT BOOK-STORE...
Why do you keep trying to ruin my opinion of you?

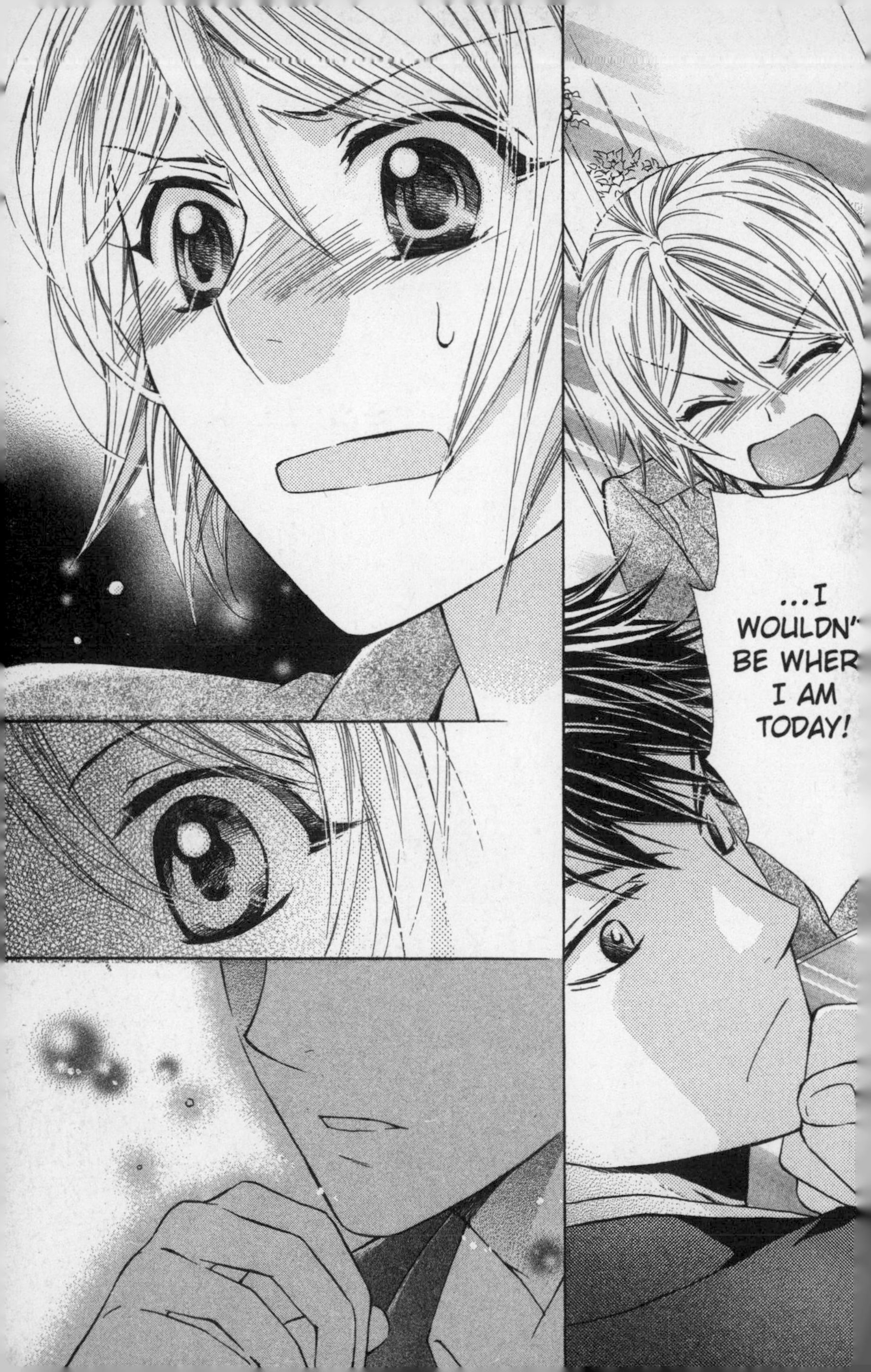
...I WOULDN' BE WHER I AM TODAY!

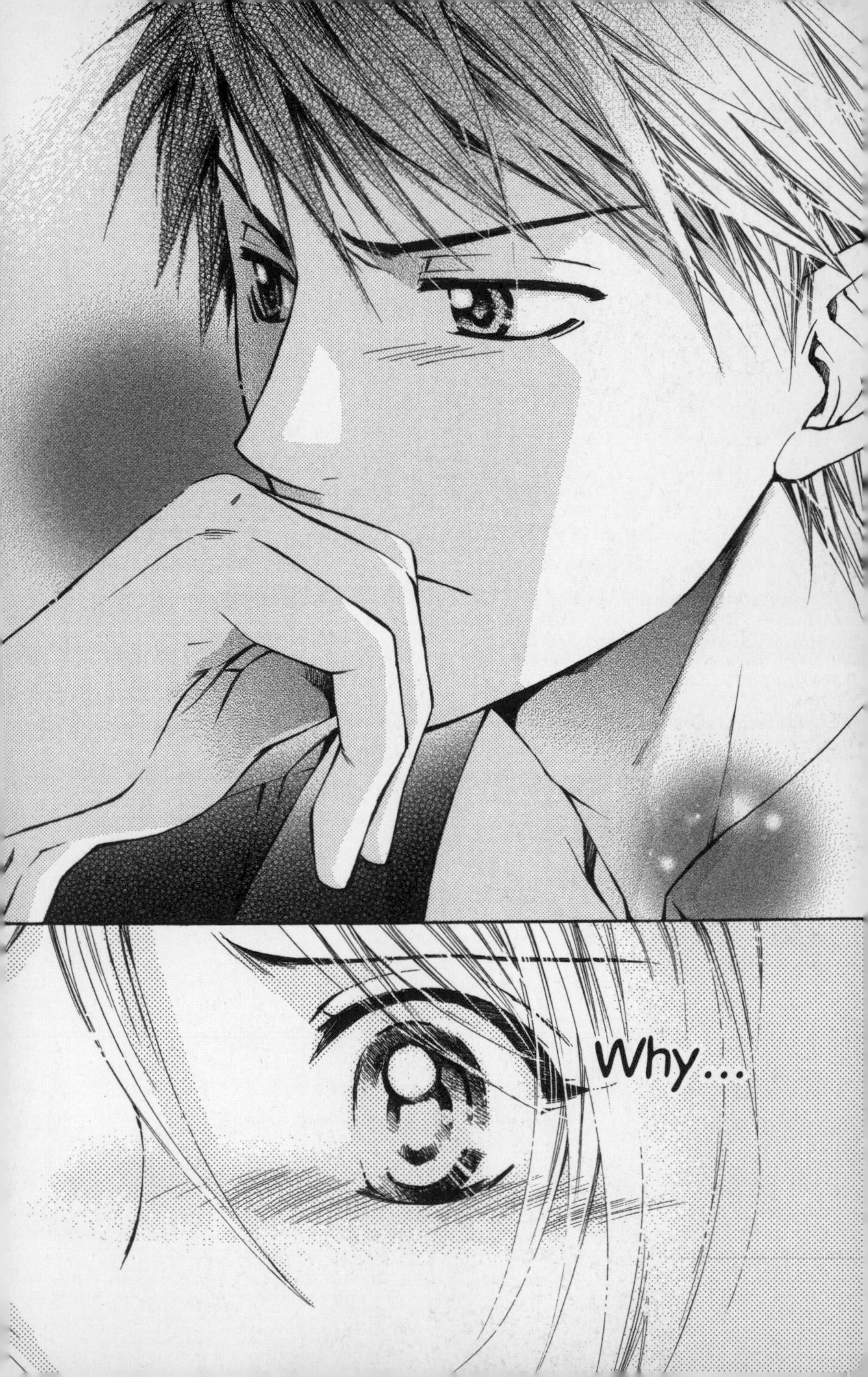
Why....

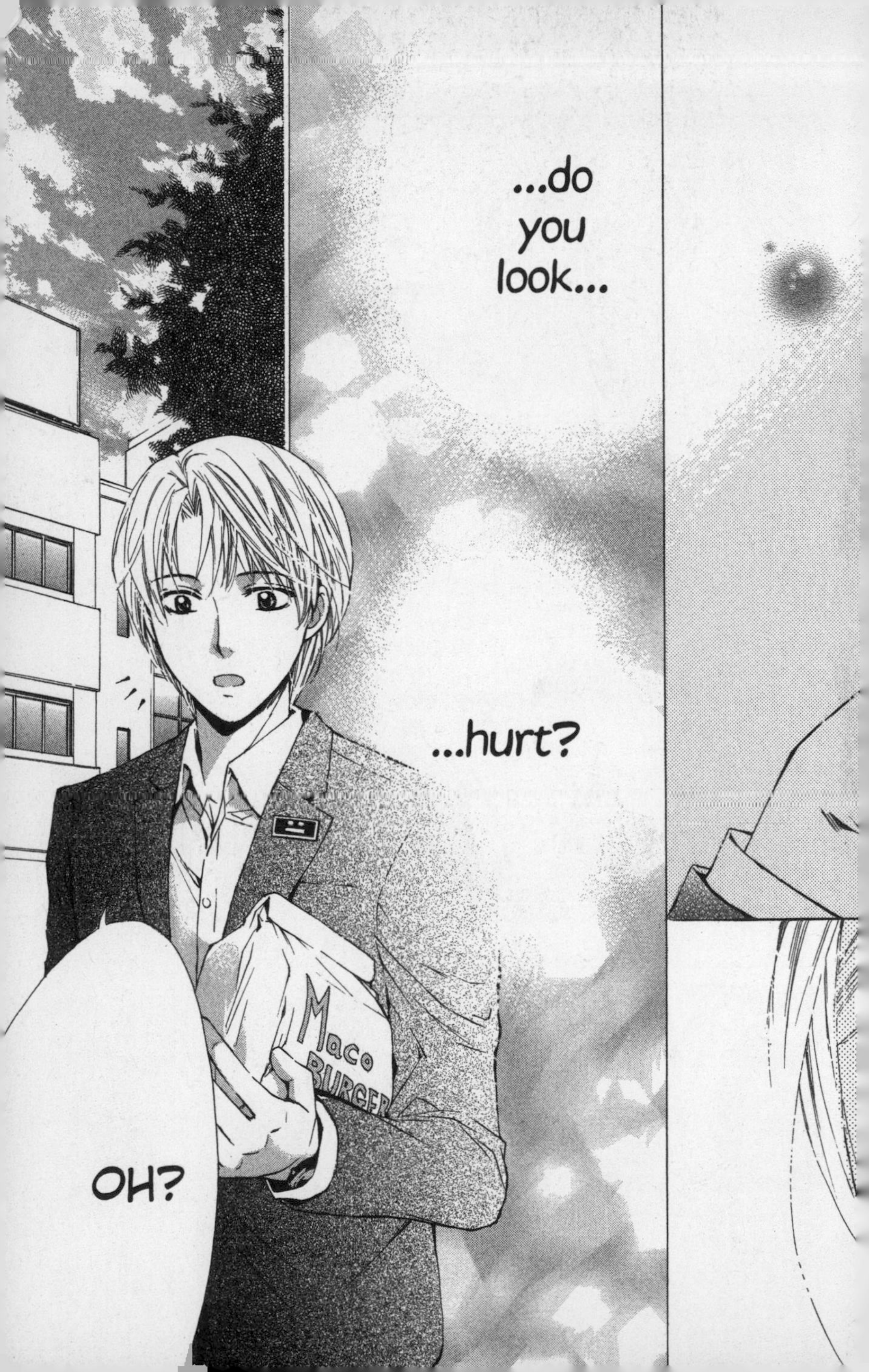
...do you look...
...hurt?
OH?

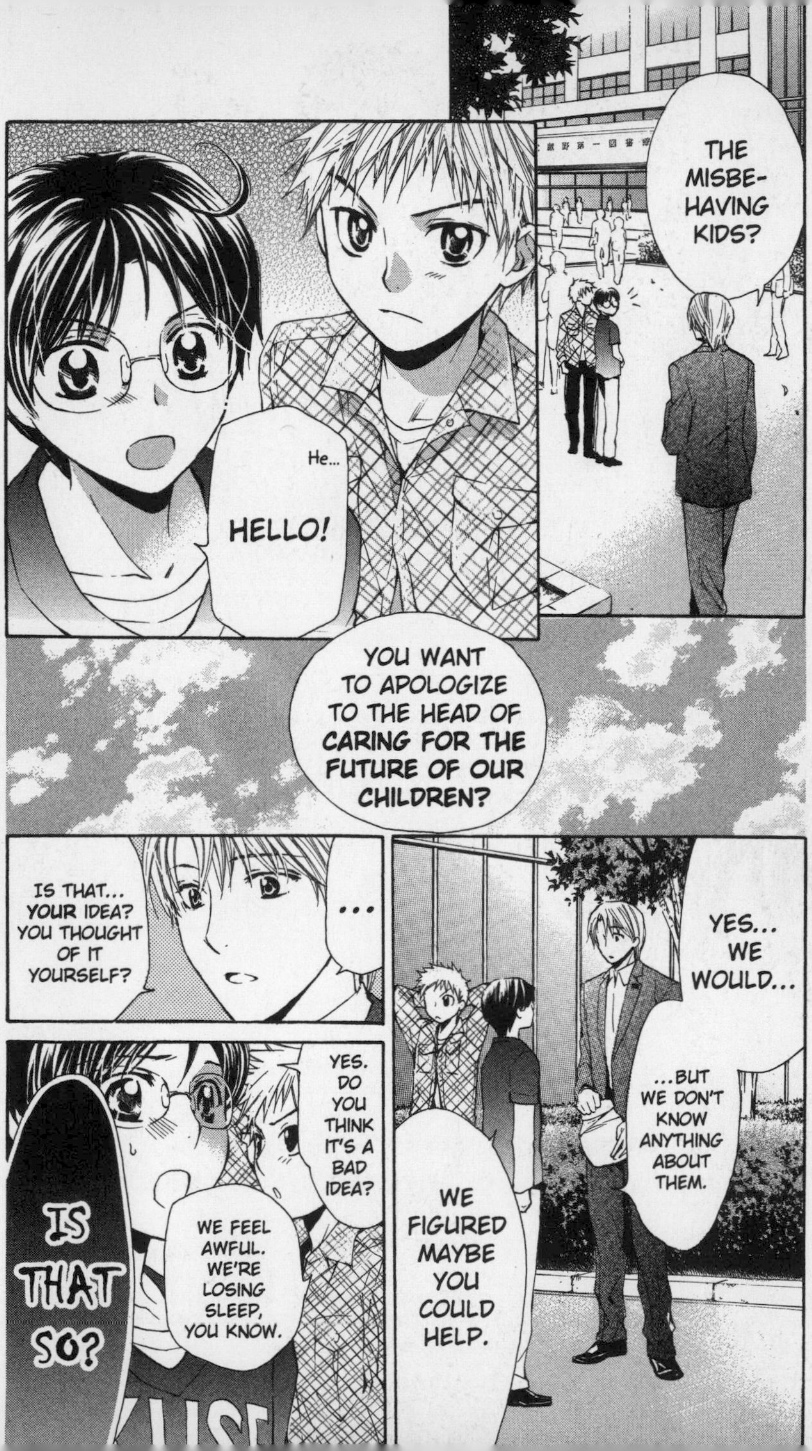
THE MISBE-HAVING KIDS?
He...
HELLO!
YOU WANT TO APOLOGIZE TO THE HEAD OF CARING FOR THE FUTURE OF OUR CHILDREN?
YES... WE WOULD...
...BUT WE DON'T KNOW ANYTHING ABOUT THEM.
WE FIGURED MAYBE YOU COULD HELP.
...
IS THAT... YOUR IDEA? YOU THOUGHT OF IT YOURSELF?
YES. DO YOU THINK IT'S A BAD IDEA?
WE FEEL AWFUL. WE'RE LOSING SLEEP, YOU KNOW.
IS THAT SO?

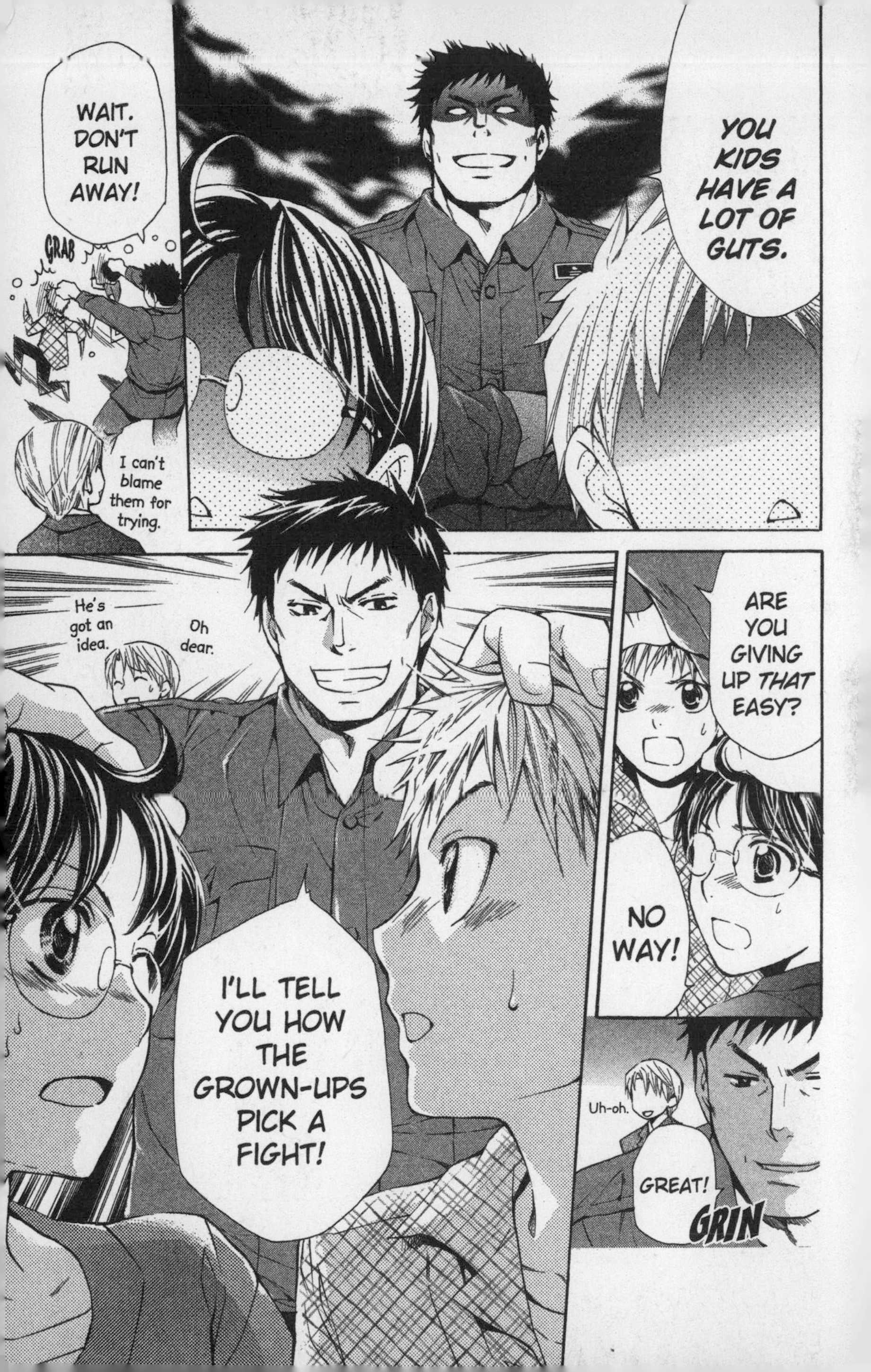
YOU KIDS HAVE A LOT OF GUTS.
WAIT. DON'T RUN AWAY!
GRAB
I can't blame them for trying.
ARE YOU GIVING UP THAT EASY?
NO WAY!
Uh-oh.
GREAT!
GRIN
He's got an idea.
Oh dear.
I'LL TELL YOU HOW THE GROWN-UPS PICK A FIGHT!

Shibazaki's Imagination

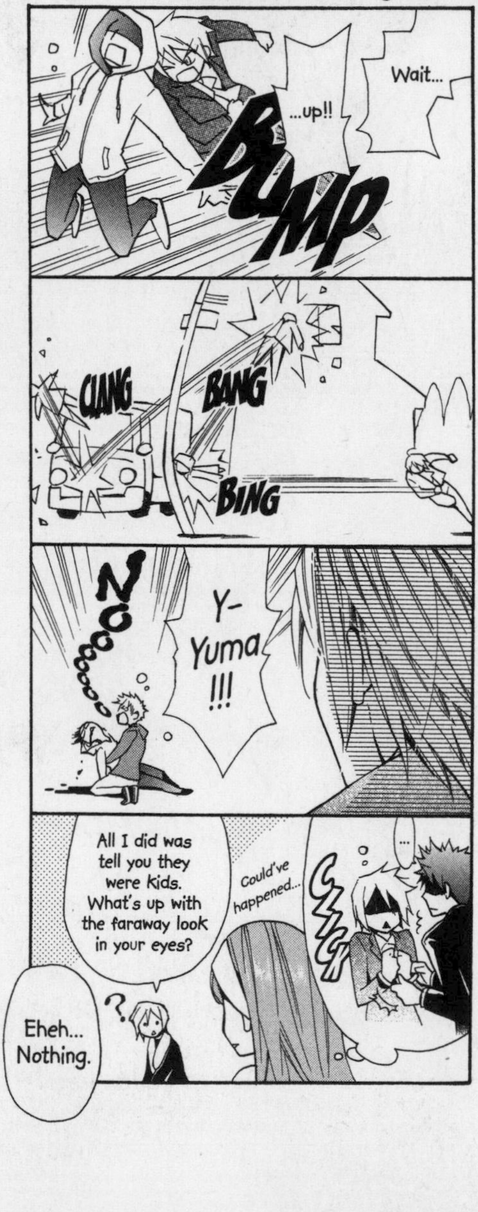
Wait...
...up!!
BUMP
BANG
CLANG
BING
Y-Yuma!!!
NOooooooo
...
CLICK
Could've happened...
All I did was tell you they were kids. What's up with the faraway look in your eyes?
Eheh... Nothing.

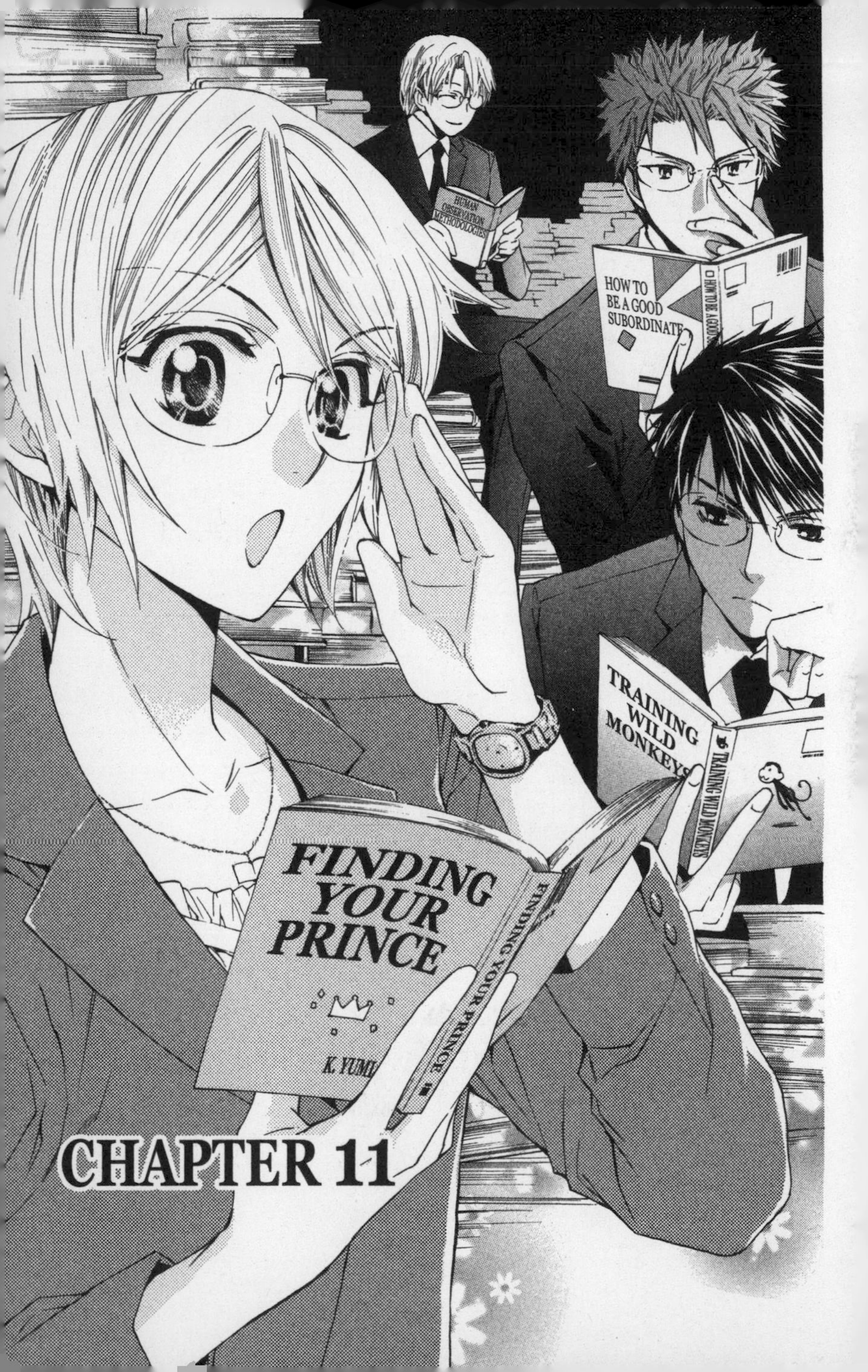
HUMAN OBSERVATION METHODOLOGIES
HOW TO BE A GOOD SUBORDINATE
TRAINING WILD MONKEYS
TRAINING WILD MONKEYS
FINDING YOUR PRINCE
K. YUMI
FINDING YOUR PRINCE
CHAPTER 11

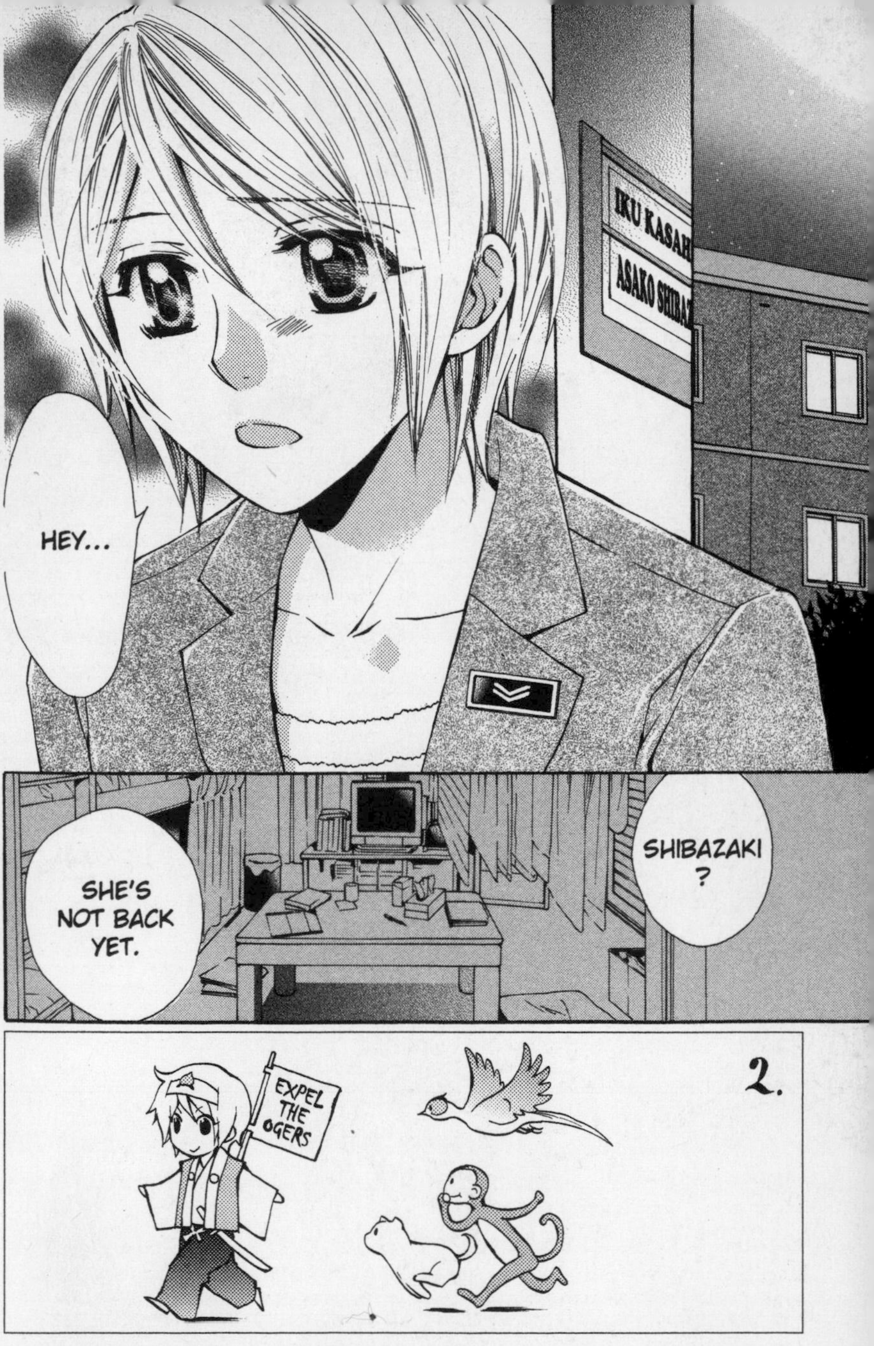
HEY...
SHIBAZAKI ?
SHE'S NOT BACK YET.
2.
EXPEL THE OGERS

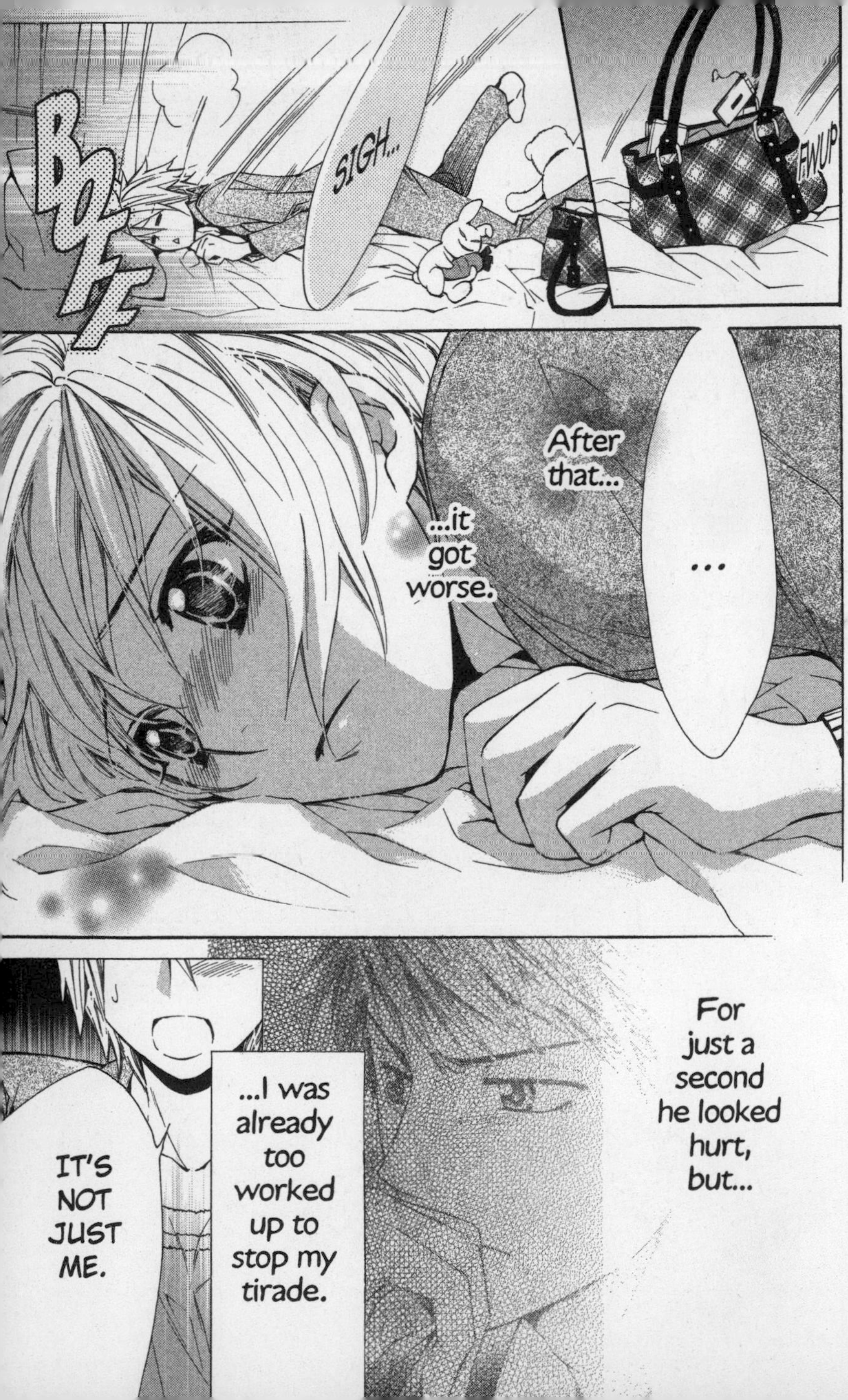
FWUP
SIGH...
BOFF
...
After that...
...it got worse.
For just a second he looked hurt, but...
...I was already too worked up to stop my tirade.
IT'S NOT JUST ME.

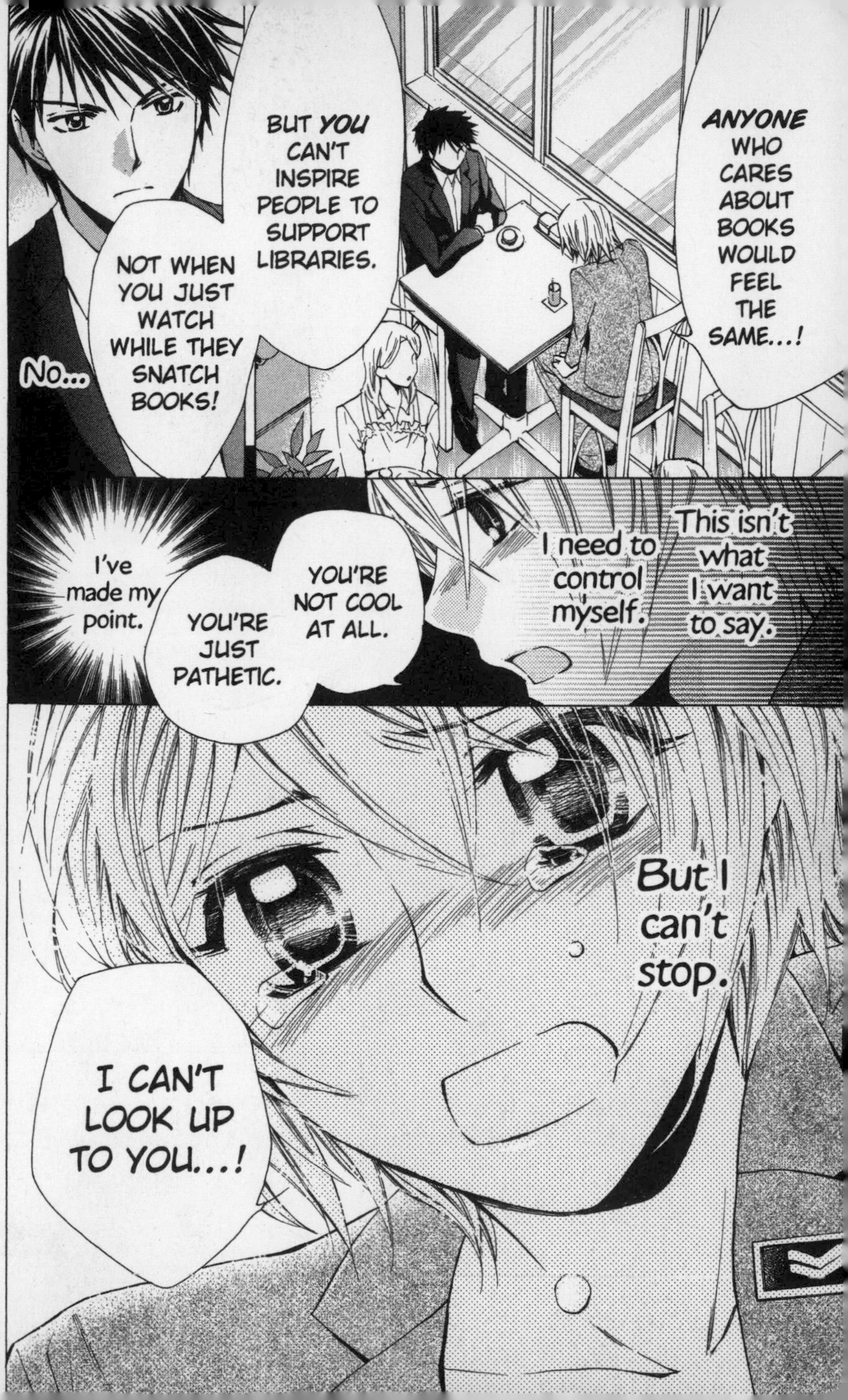
ANYONE WHO CARES ABOUT BOOKS WOULD FEEL THE SAME...!
BUT YOU CAN'T INSPIRE PEOPLE TO SUPPORT LIBRARIES.
NOT WHEN YOU JUST WATCH WHILE THEY SNATCH BOOKS!
No...
This isn't what I want to say.
I need to control myself.
YOU'RE NOT COOL AT ALL.
YOU'RE JUST PATHETIC.
I've made my point.
But I can't stop.
I CAN'T LOOK UP TO YOU...!

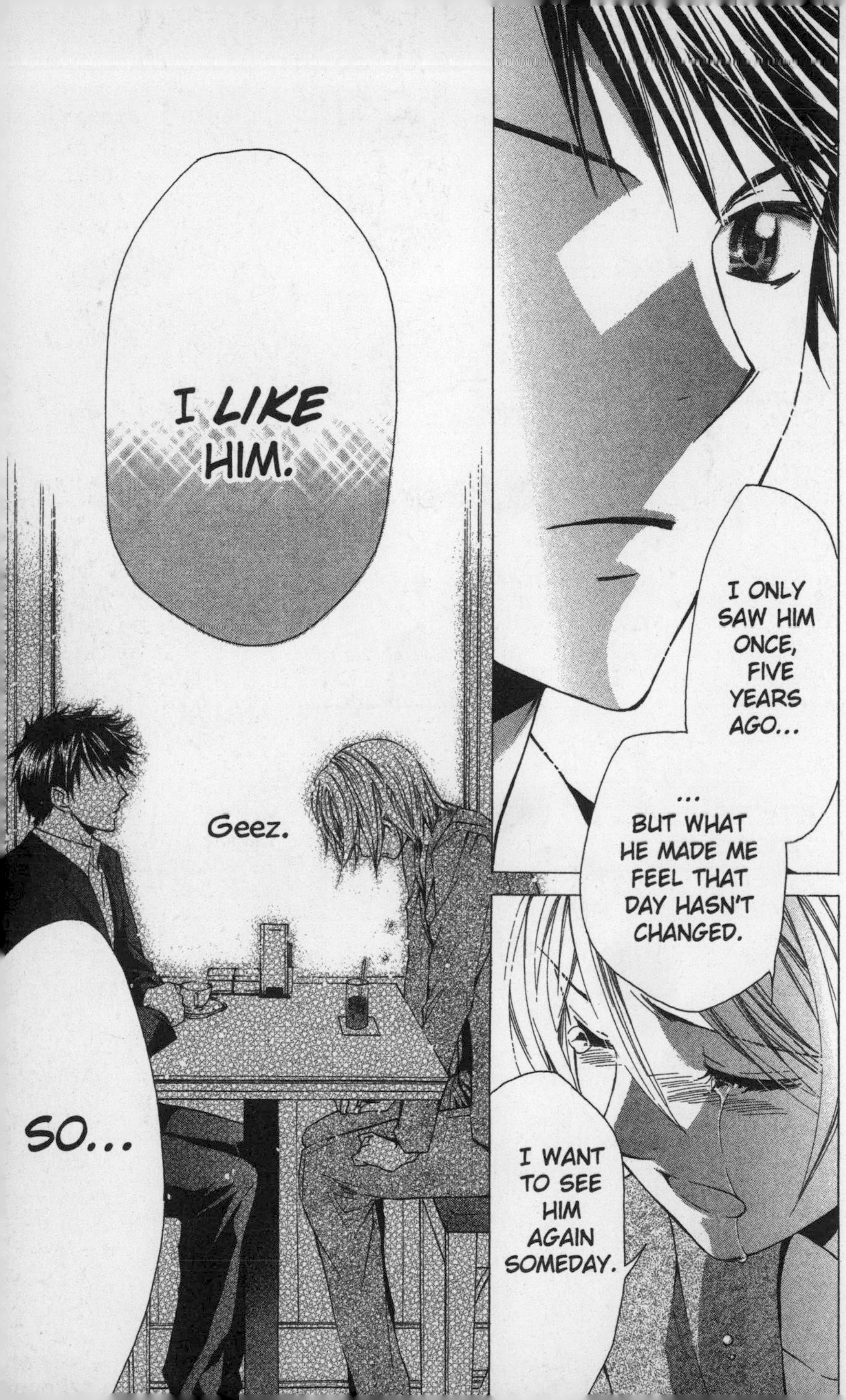
I ONLY SAW HIM ONCE, FIVE YEARS AGO...
... BUT WHAT HE MADE ME FEEL THAT DAY HASN'T CHANGED.
I WANT TO SEE HIM AGAIN SOMEDAY.
I LIKE HIM.
Geez.
SO...

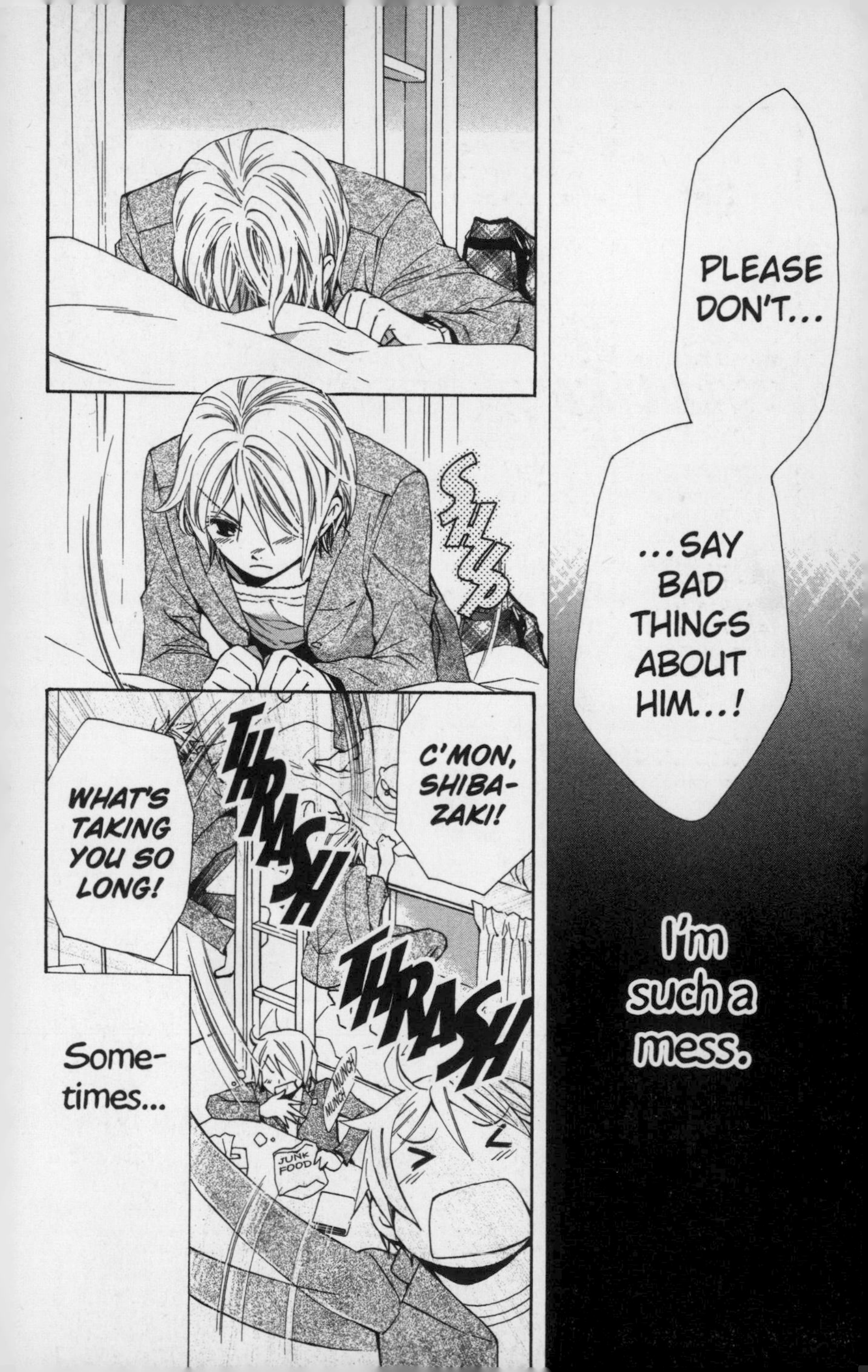
PLEASE DON'T...
...SAY BAD THINGS ABOUT HIM...!
I'm such a mess.
SHHP
C'MON, SHIBA-ZAKI!
THRASH
WHAT'S TAKING YOU SO LONG!
THRASH
MUNCH MUNCH
JUNK FOOD
Some-times...

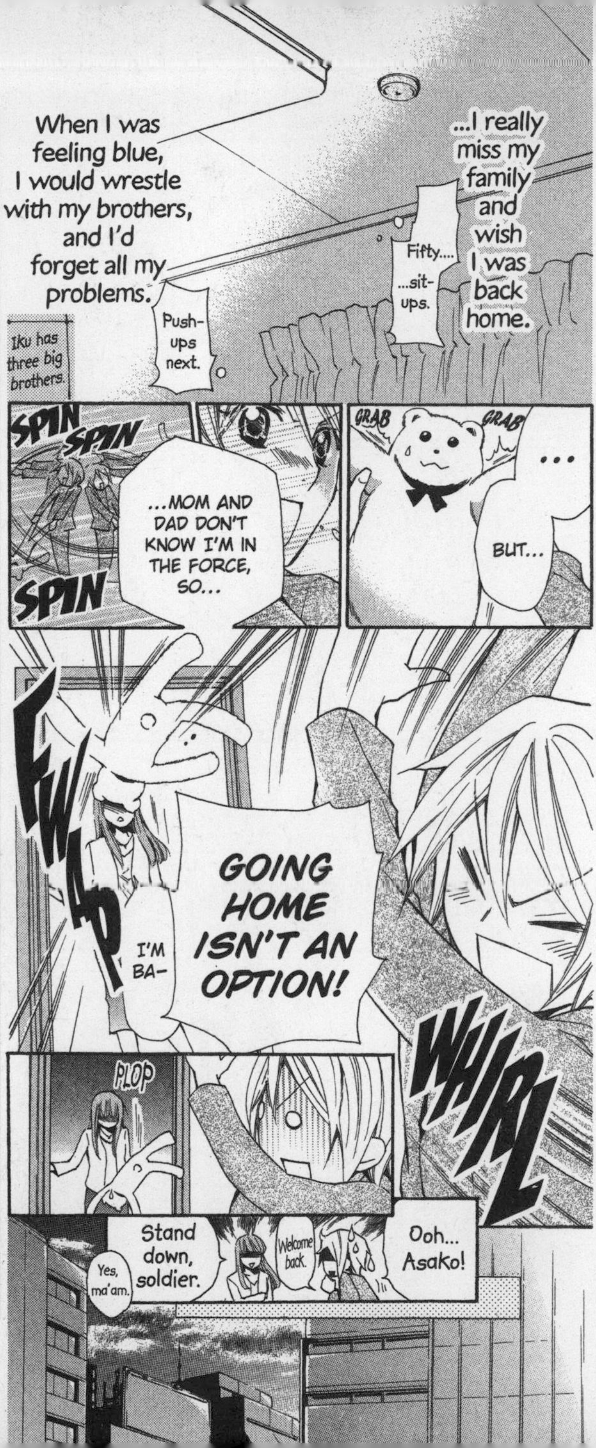
...I really miss my family and wish I was back home.
Fifty.... ...sit-ups.
When I was feeling blue, I would wrestle with my brothers, and I'd forget all my problems.
Push-ups next.
Iku has three big brothers.
GRAB GRAB
...
BUT...
...MOM AND DAD DON'T KNOW I'M IN THE FORCE, SO...
SPIN SPIN
SPIN
WHIRL
GOING HOME ISN'T AN OPTION!
I'M BA-
FWAP
PLOP
Ooh... Asako!
Welcome back.
Stand down, soldier.
Yes, ma'am.

2

*

I know.
Iku and Dojo look unnaturally friendly in the back cover illustration.

I drew it for Lala's cover in October 2008.

That was my first time seeing my work on a magazine cover... It was just amazing, but not good for my heart...

I went to a bookstore to see it for myself but couldn't bear to look.
So I ran away like I did when volume 1 came out.
Why do I get so embarrassed about it...?!
The project itself was a lot of fun.
I can handle unnatural. *

*

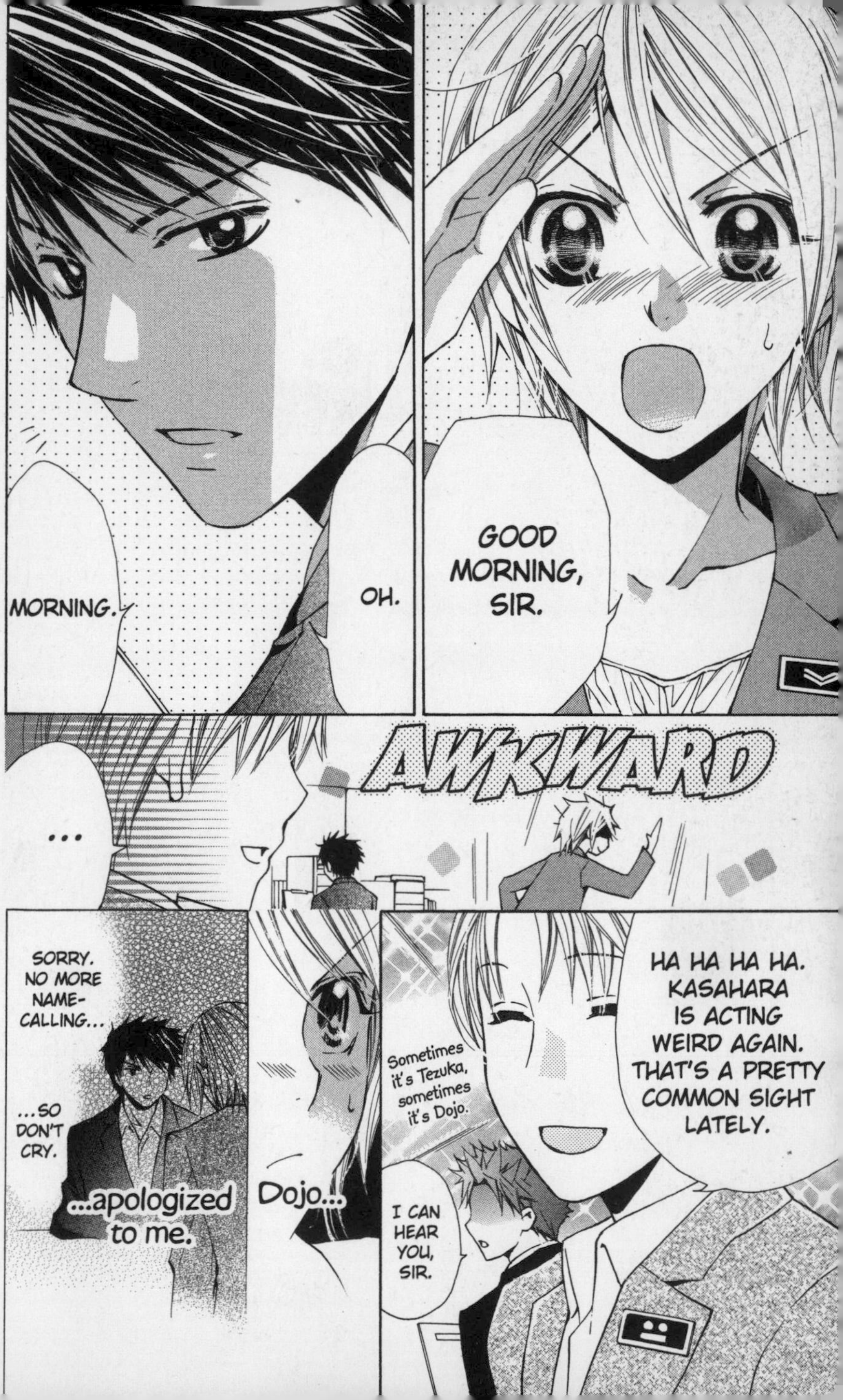
GOOD MORNING, SIR.
OH.
MORNING.
AWKWARD
...
HA HA HA HA. KASAHARA IS ACTING WEIRD AGAIN. THAT'S A PRETTY COMMON SIGHT LATELY.
Sometimes it's Tezuka, sometimes it's Dojo.
I CAN HEAR YOU, SIR.
Dojo...
SORRY. NO MORE NAME-CALLING...
...SO DON'T CRY.
...apologized to me.

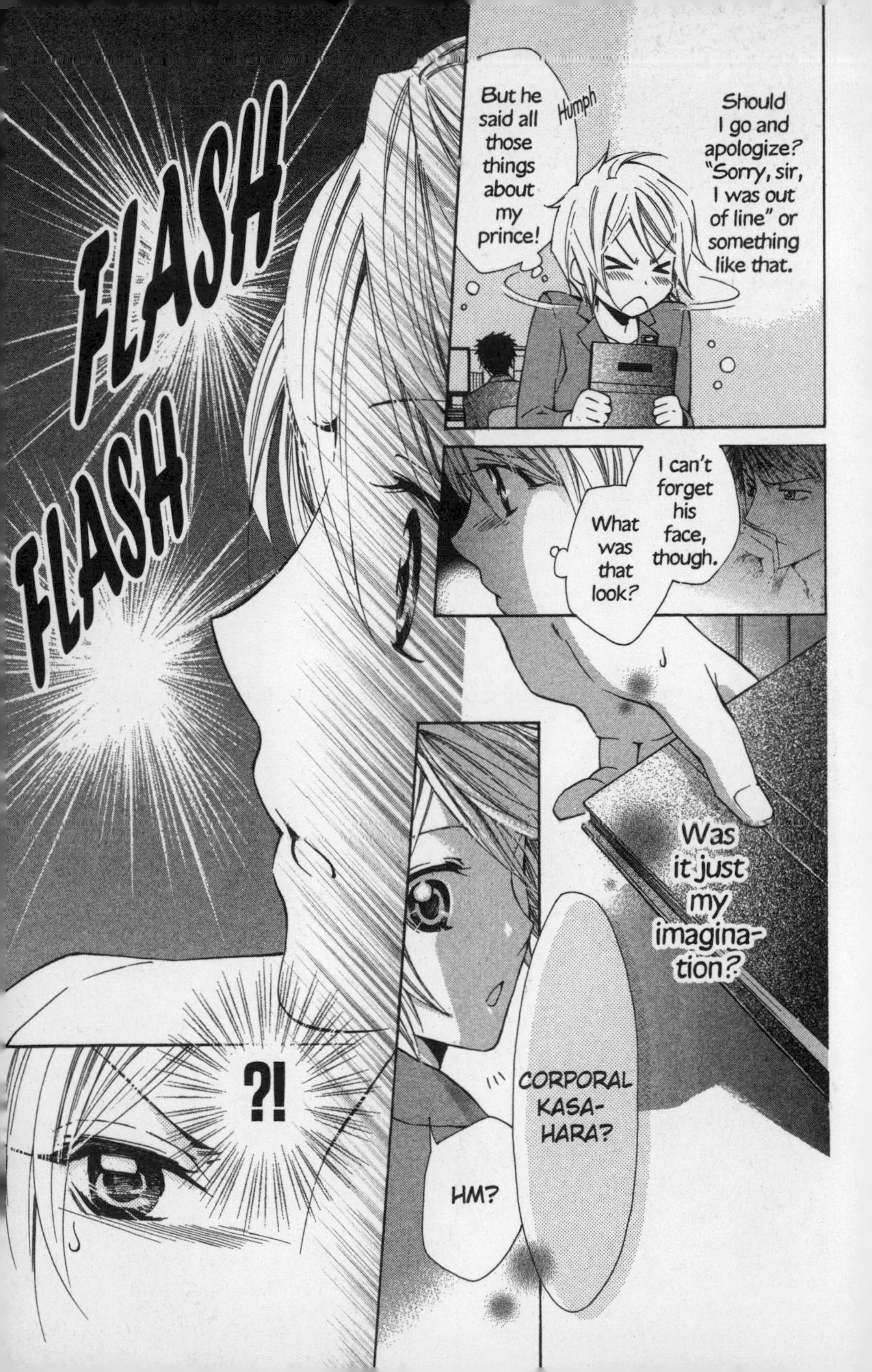
Should I go and apologize? "Sorry, sir, I was out of line" or something like that.
Humph
But he said all those things about my prince!
I can't forget his face, though.
What was that look?
Was it just my imagination?
CORPORAL KASA-HARA?
HM?
FLASH
FLASH
?!

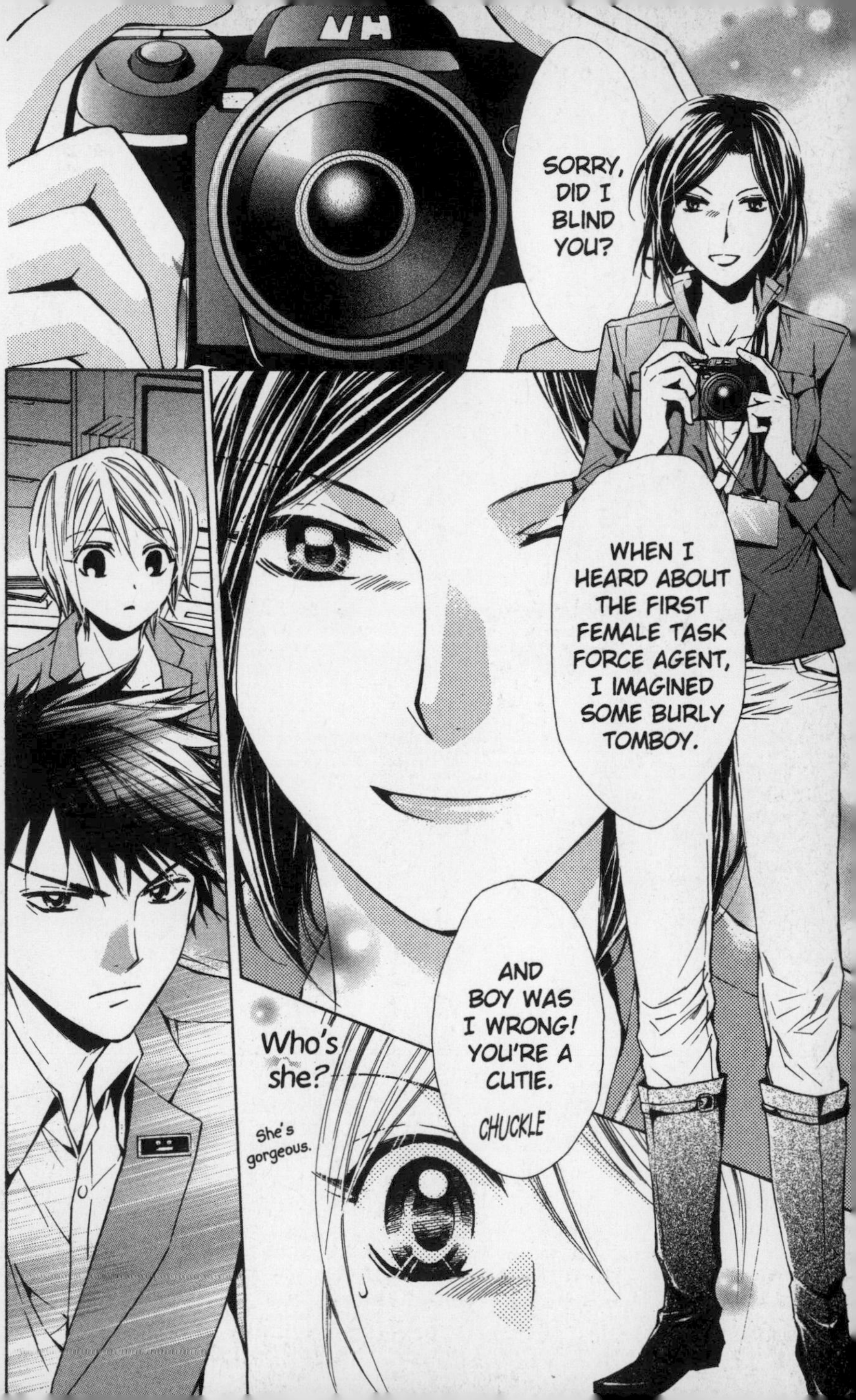
SORRY, DID I BLIND YOU?
WHEN I HEARD ABOUT THE FIRST FEMALE TASK FORCE AGENT, I IMAGINED SOME BURLY TOMBOY.
AND BOY WAS I WRONG! YOU'RE A CUTIE.
CHUCKLE
Who's she?
She's gorgeous.

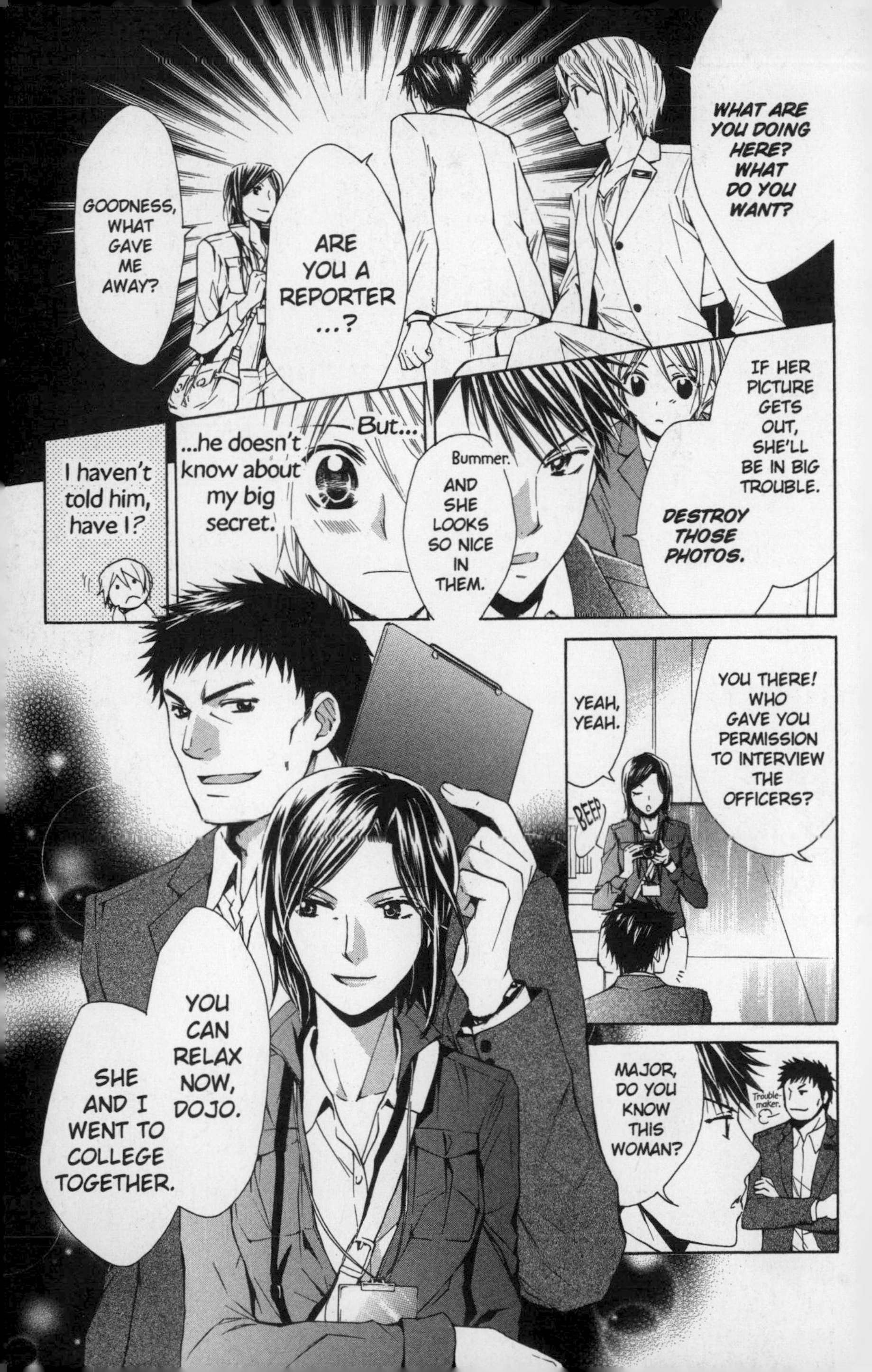
WHAT ARE YOU DOING HERE? WHAT DO YOU WANT?
ARE YOU A REPORTER ...?
GOODNESS, WHAT GAVE ME AWAY?
IF HER PICTURE GETS OUT, SHE'LL BE IN BIG TROUBLE.
DESTROY THOSE PHOTOS.
AND SHE LOOKS SO NICE IN THEM.
Bummer.
But...
...he doesn't know about my big secret.
I haven't told him, have I?
YOU THERE! WHO GAVE YOU PERMISSION TO INTERVIEW THE OFFICERS?
YEAH, YEAH.
BEEP
MAJOR, DO YOU KNOW THIS WOMAN?
Trouble-maker.
YOU CAN RELAX NOW, DOJO.
SHE AND I WENT TO COLLEGE TOGETHER.

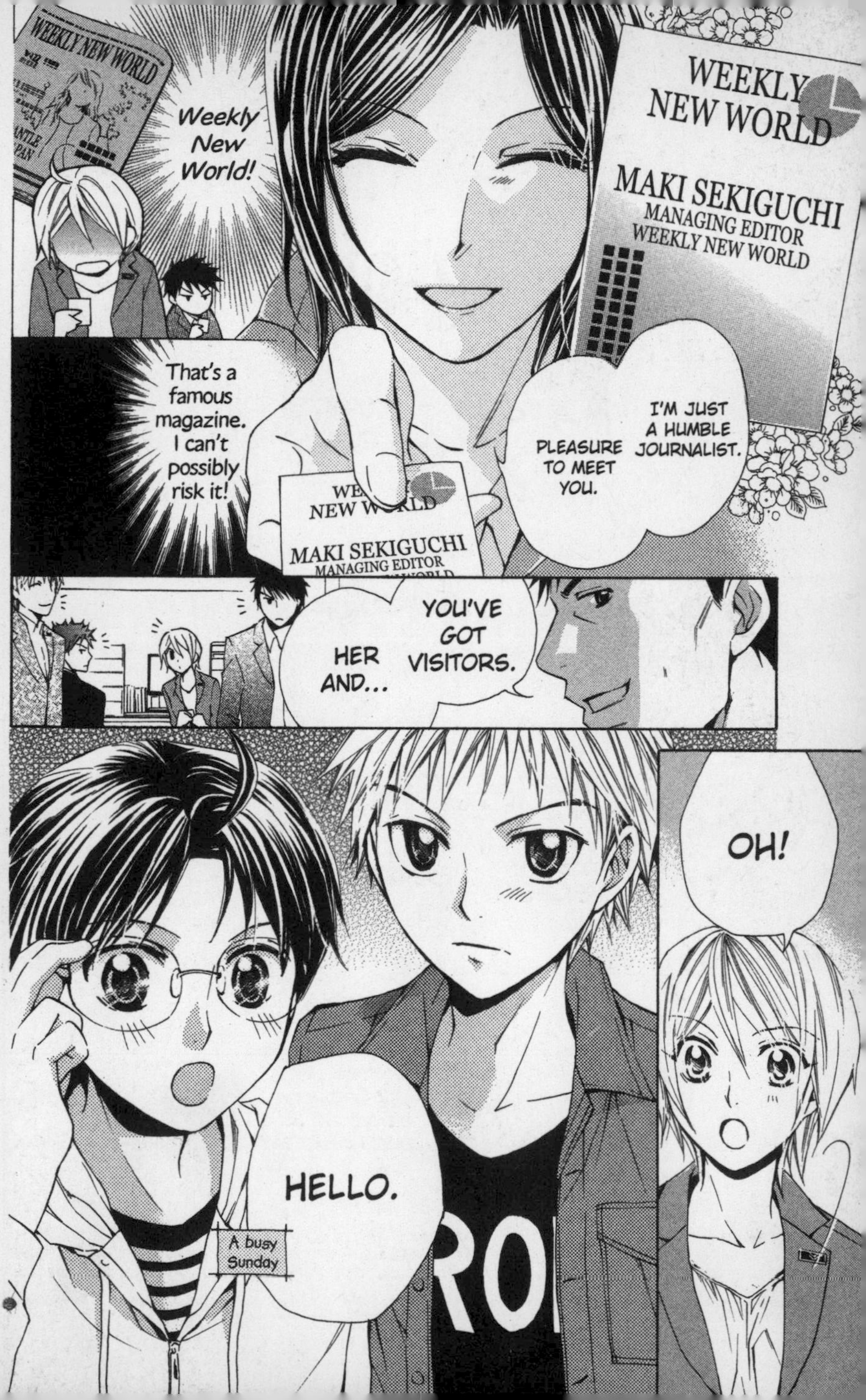
WEEKLY NEW WORLD
MAKI SEKIGUCHI
MANAGING EDITOR
WEEKLY NEW WORLD
I'M JUST A HUMBLE JOURNALIST.
PLEASURE TO MEET YOU.
MAKI SEKIGUCHI
MANAGING EDITOR
WEEKLY NEW WORLD
Weekly New World!
That's a famous magazine. I can't possibly risk it!
YOU'VE GOT VISITORS.
HER AND...
OH!
HELLO.
A busy Sunday

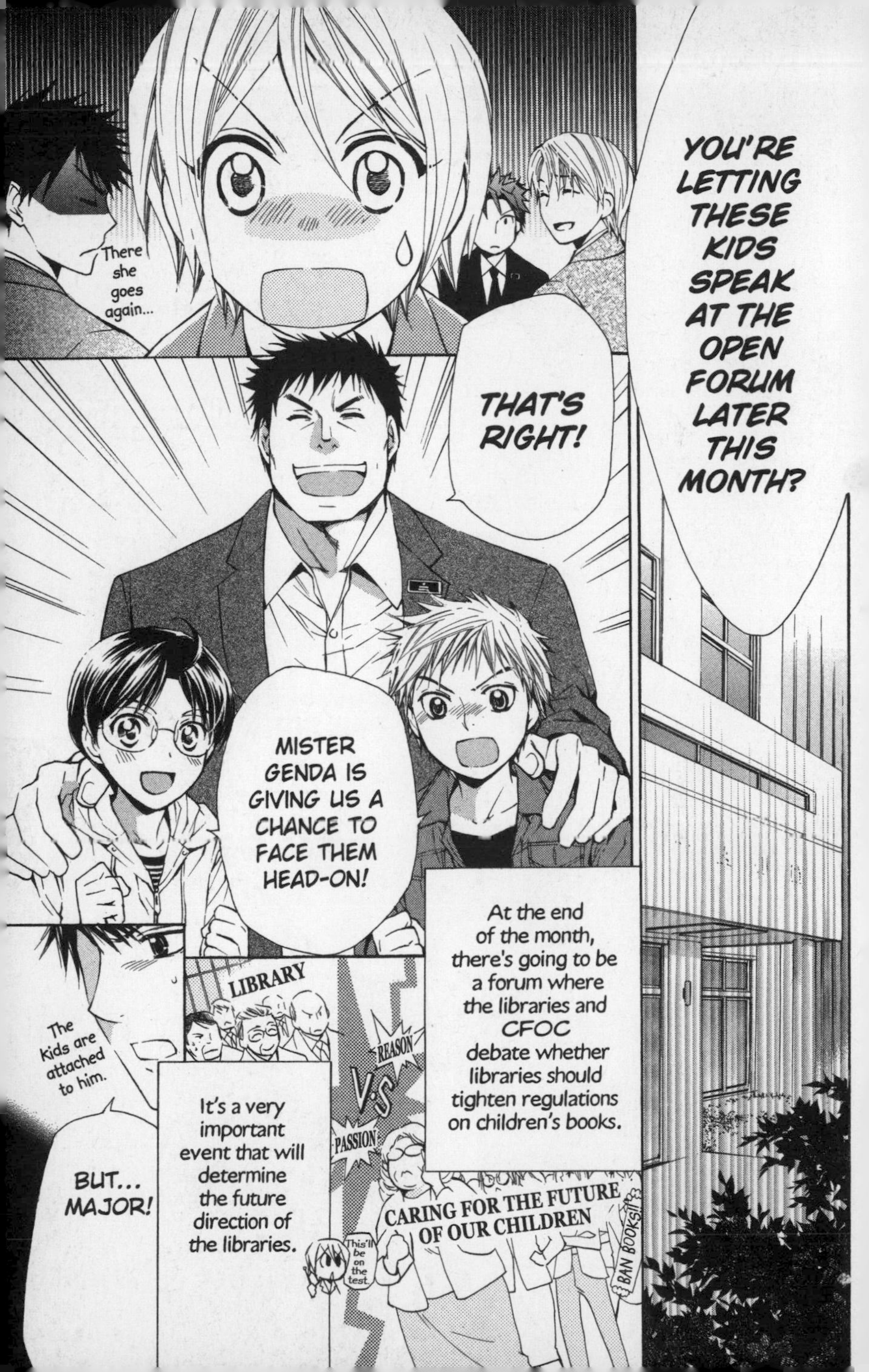
YOU'RE LETTING THESE KIDS SPEAK AT THE OPEN FORUM LATER THIS MONTH?
There she goes again...
THAT'S RIGHT!
MISTER GENDA IS GIVING US A CHANCE TO FACE THEM HEAD-ON!
At the end of the month, there's going to be a forum where the libraries and CFOC debate whether libraries should tighten regulations on children's books.
LIBRARY
REASON
VS
PASSION
CARING FOR THE FUTURE OF OUR CHILDREN
BAN BOOKS!!
It's a very important event that will determine the future direction of the libraries.
This'll be on the test.
The kids are attached to him.
BUT... MAJOR!

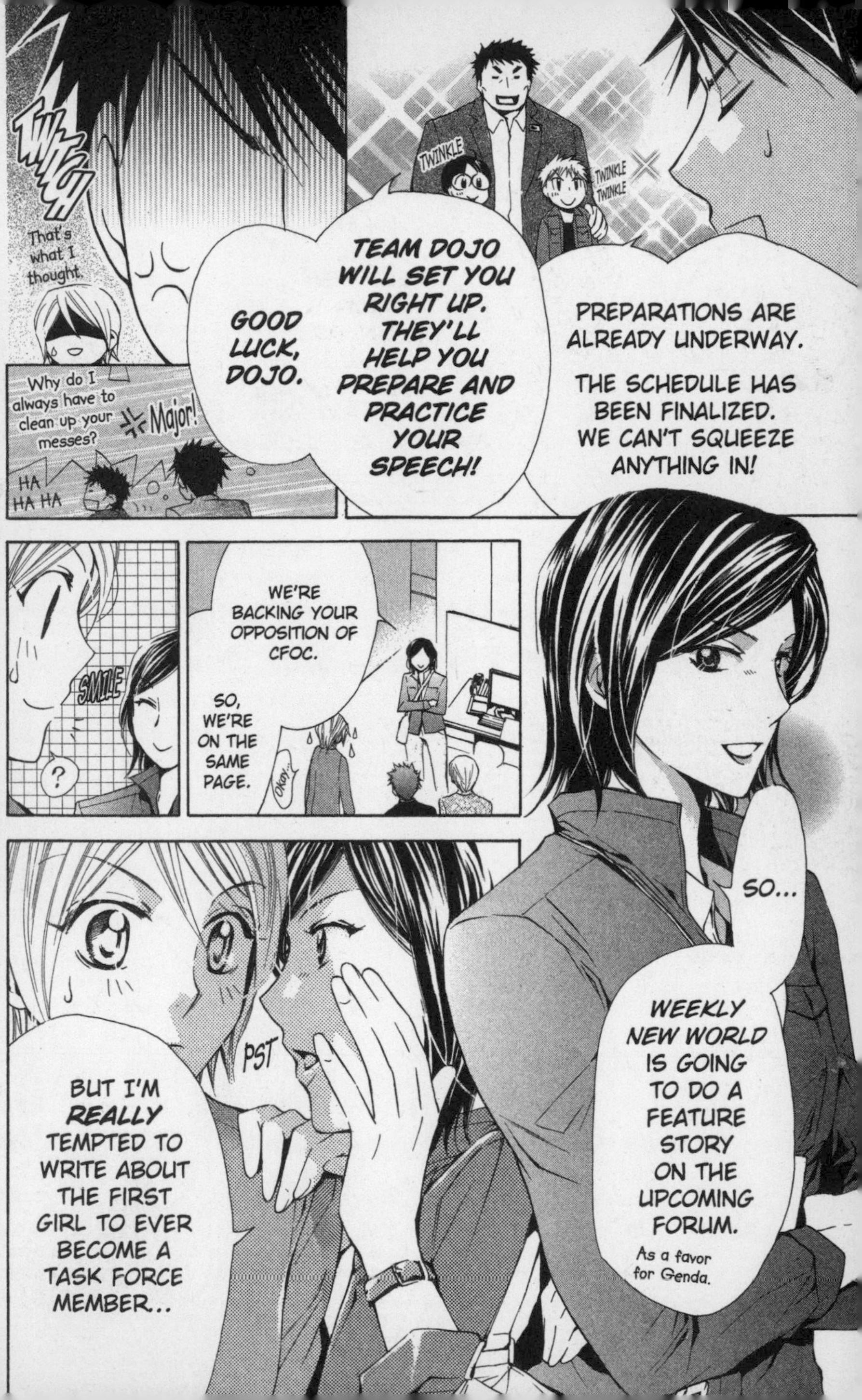
PREPARATIONS ARE ALREADY UNDERWAY.
THE SCHEDULE HAS BEEN FINALIZED. WE CAN'T SQUEEZE ANYTHING IN!
TEAM DOJO WILL SET YOU RIGHT UP. THEY'LL HELP YOU PREPARE AND PRACTICE YOUR SPEECH!
GOOD LUCK, DOJO.
TWINKLE
TWINKLE TWINKLE
TWITCH
That's what I thought.
Why do I always have to clean up your messes?
Major!
HA HA HA
SO...
WEEKLY NEW WORLD IS GOING TO DO A FEATURE STORY ON THE UPCOMING FORUM.
As a favor for Genda.
WE'RE BACKING YOUR OPPOSITION OF CFOC.
SO, WE'RE ON THE SAME PAGE.
Okay...
SMILE
?
PST
BUT I'M *REALLY* TEMPTED TO WRITE ABOUT THE FIRST GIRL TO EVER BECOME A TASK FORCE MEMBER...

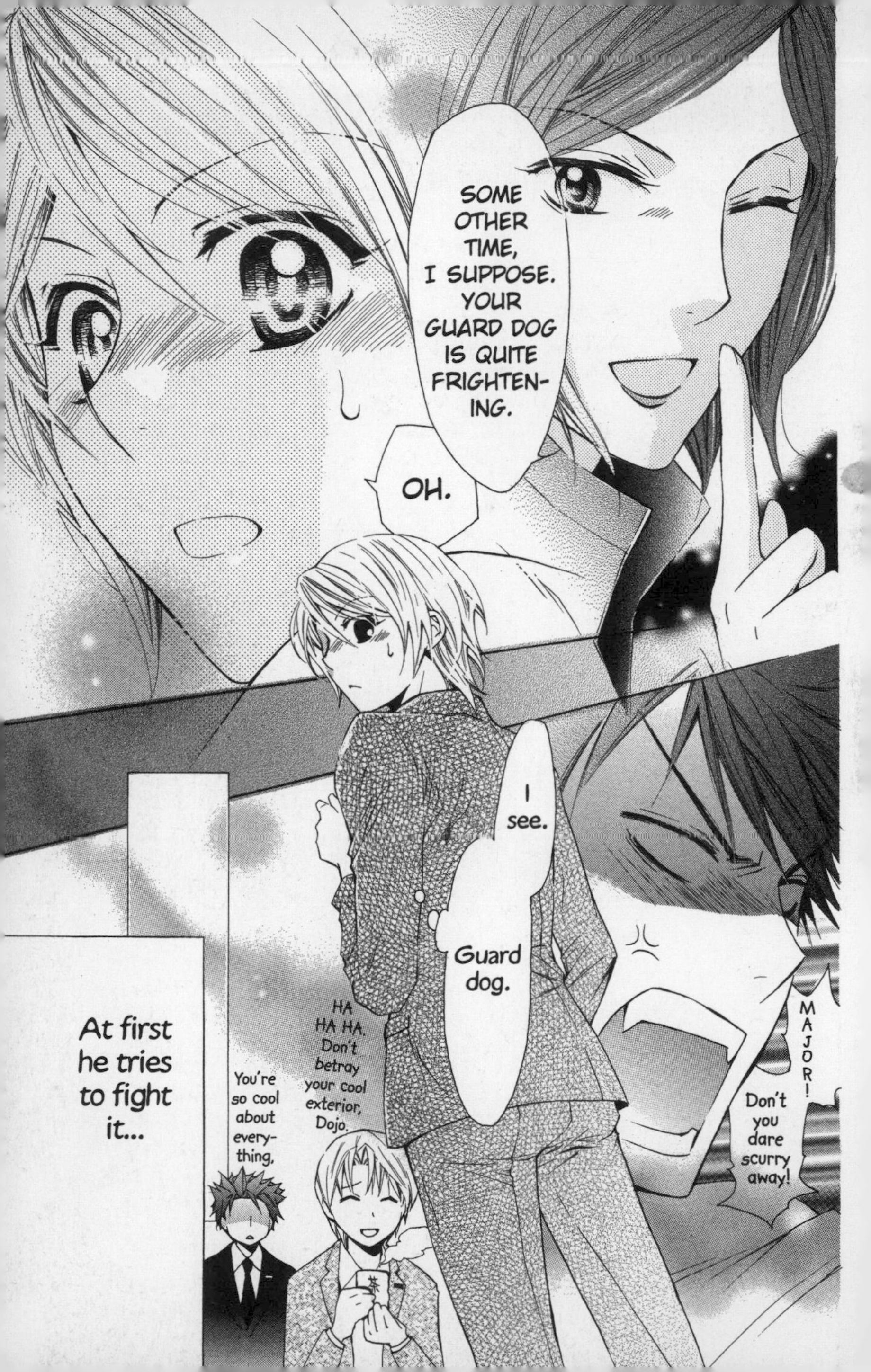
SOME OTHER TIME, I SUPPOSE. YOUR GUARD DOG IS QUITE FRIGHTEN-ING.
OH.
MAJOR!
Don't you dare scurry away!
I see.
Guard dog.
HA HA HA. Don't betray your cool exterior, Dojo.
You're so cool about every-thing,
At first he tries to fight it...

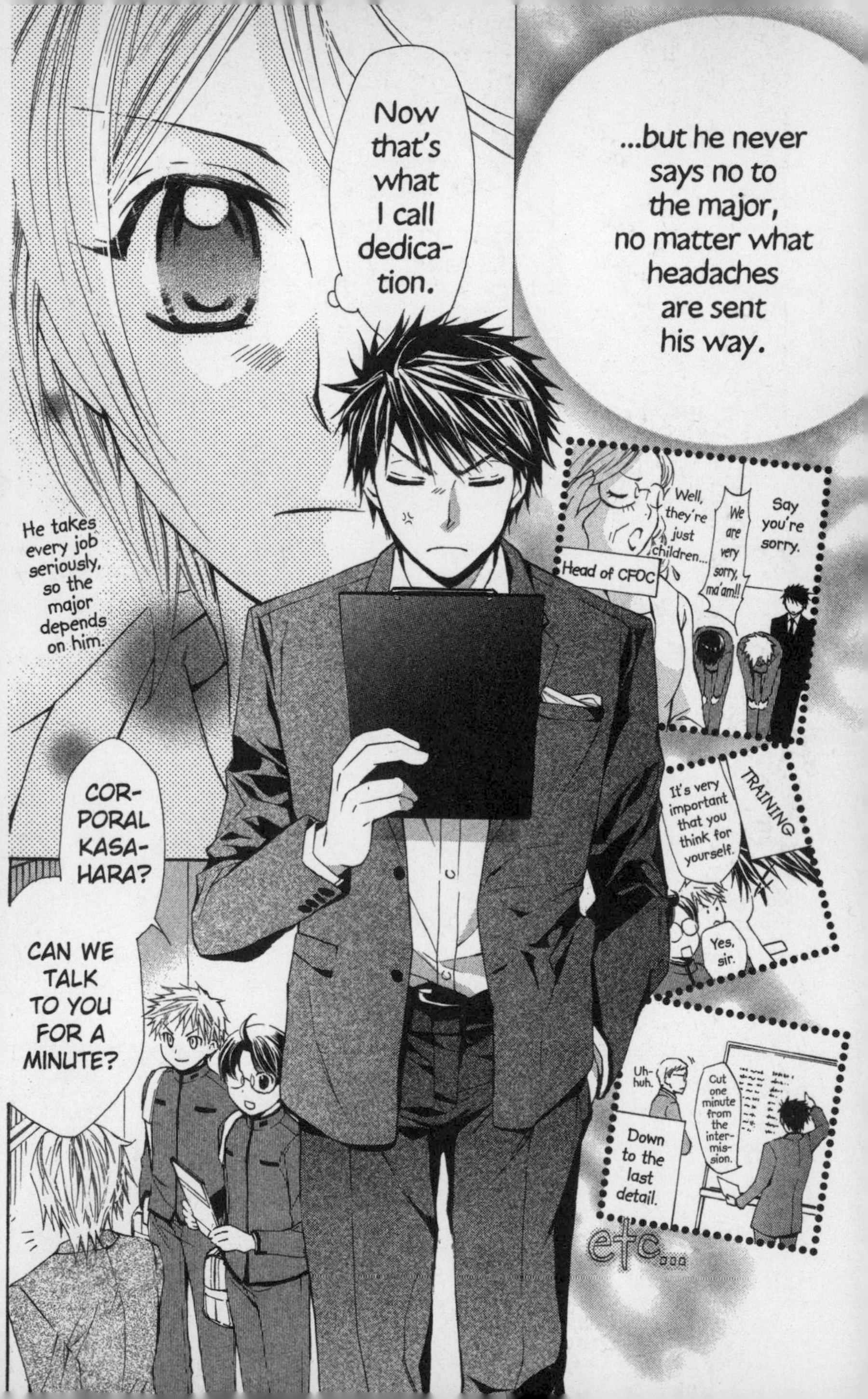
...but he never says no to the major, no matter what headaches are sent his way.
Say you're sorry.
We are very sorry, ma'am!!
Well, they're just children...
Head of CFOC
TRAINING
It's very important that you think for yourself.
Yes, sir.
Cut one minute from the intermission.
Uh-huh.
Down to the last detail.
etc...
Now that's what I call dedication.
He takes every job seriously, so the major depends on him.
CORPORAL KASAHARA?
CAN WE TALK TO YOU FOR A MINUTE?

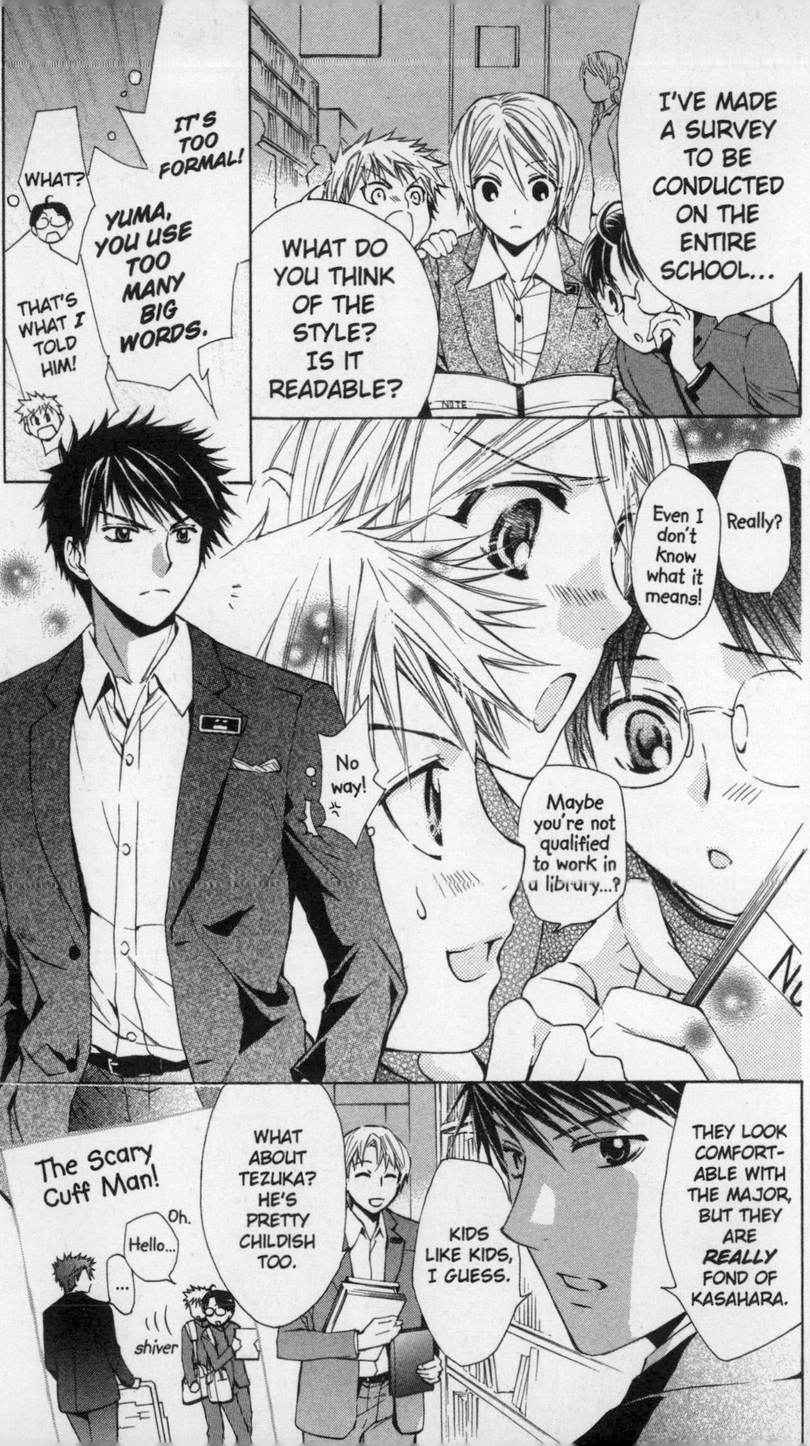
I'VE MADE A SURVEY TO BE CONDUCTED ON THE ENTIRE SCHOOL...
WHAT DO YOU THINK OF THE STYLE? IS IT READABLE?
IT'S TOO FORMAL!
YUMA, YOU USE TOO MANY BIG WORDS.
WHAT?
THAT'S WHAT I TOLD HIM!
Really?
Even I don't know what it means!
Maybe you're not qualified to work in a library...?
No way!
THEY LOOK COMFORT-ABLE WITH THE MAJOR, BUT THEY ARE REALLY FOND OF KASAHARA.
KIDS LIKE KIDS, I GUESS.
WHAT ABOUT TEZUKA? HE'S PRETTY CHILDISH TOO.
The Scary Cuff Man!
Oh.
Hello...
...
shiver

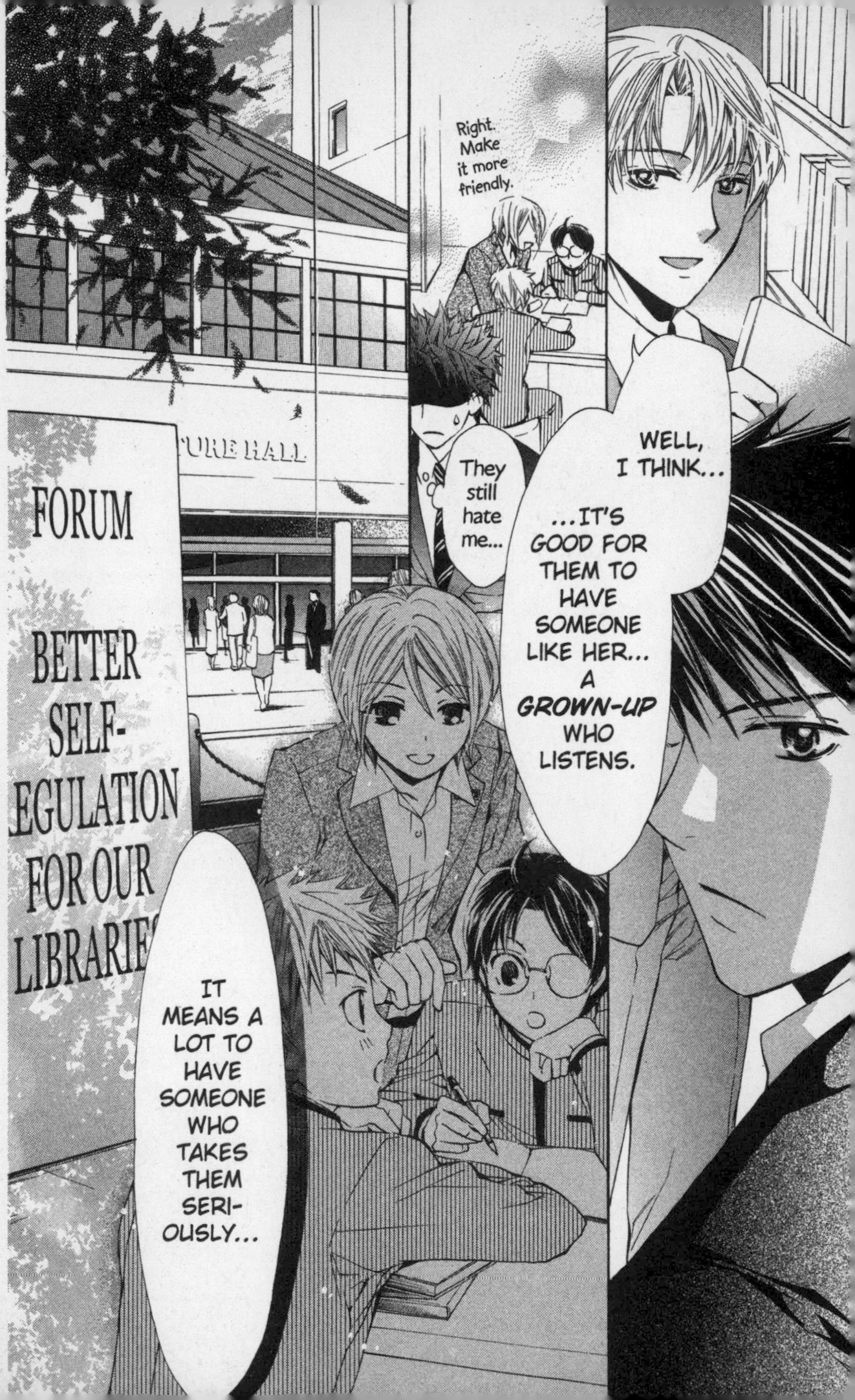
WELL, I THINK...
...IT'S GOOD FOR THEM TO HAVE SOMEONE LIKE HER... A *GROWN-UP* WHO LISTENS.
Right. Make it more friendly.
They still hate me...
URE HALL
FORUM
BETTER SELF-
EGULATION FOR OUR LIBRARIE
IT MEANS A LOT TO HAVE SOMEONE WHO TAKES THEM SERI-OUSLY...

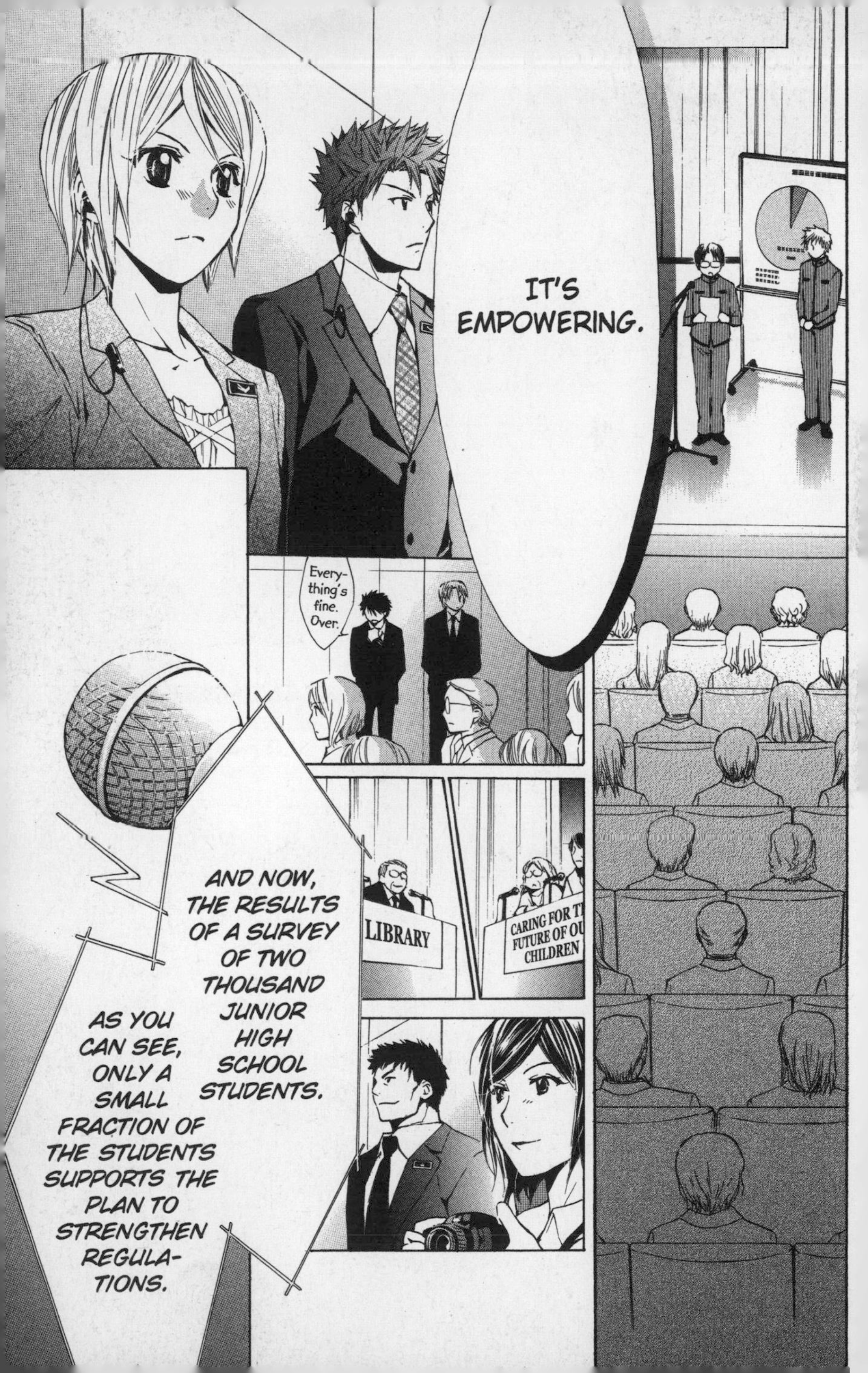
IT'S EMPOWERING.
Everything's fine. Over.
CARING FOR TH
FUTURE OF OU
CHILDREN
LIBRARY
AND NOW, THE RESULTS OF A SURVEY OF TWO THOUSAND JUNIOR HIGH SCHOOL STUDENTS.
AS YOU CAN SEE, ONLY A SMALL FRACTION OF THE STUDENTS SUPPORTS THE PLAN TO STRENGTHEN REGULA-TIONS.

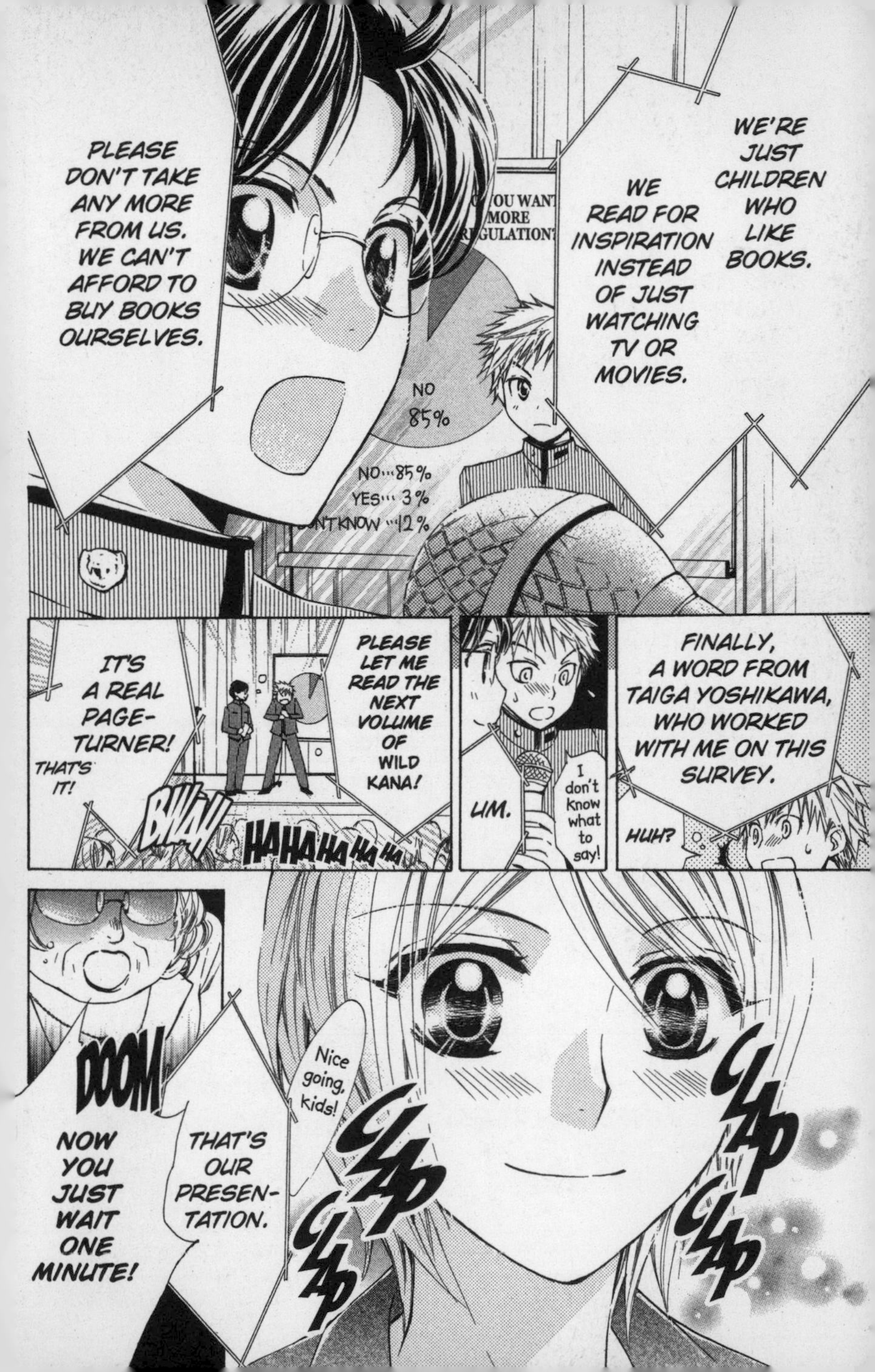

WE'RE JUST CHILDREN WHO LIKE BOOKS.
WE READ FOR INSPIRATION INSTEAD OF JUST WATCHING TV OR MOVIES.
PLEASE DON'T TAKE ANY MORE FROM US. WE CAN'T AFFORD TO BUY BOOKS OURSELVES.
MORE
NO 85%
NO…85%
YES… 3%
FINALLY, A WORD FROM TAIGA YOSHIKAWA, WHO WORKED WITH ME ON THIS SURVEY.
HUH?
UM.
I don't know what to say!
PLEASE LET ME READ THE NEXT VOLUME OF WILD KANA!
IT'S A REAL PAGE-TURNER!
THAT'S IT!
BWAH
HAHAHAHAHAHA
THAT'S OUR PRESENTATION.
Nice going, kids!
CLAP CLAP
CLAP CLAP
DOOM
NOW YOU JUST WAIT ONE MINUTE!

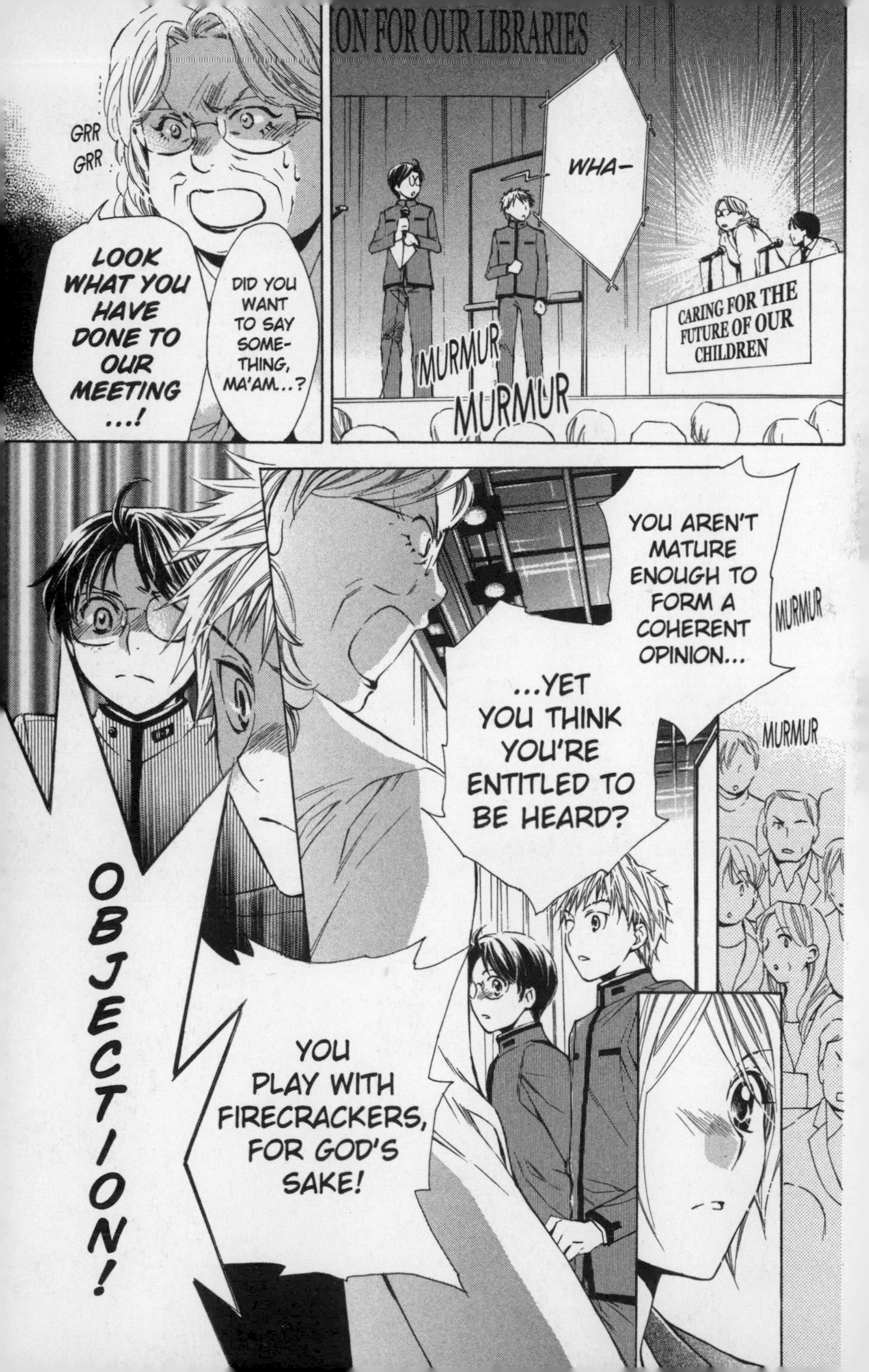
ON FOR OUR LIBRARIES
WHA-
CARING FOR THE FUTURE OF OUR CHILDREN
MURMUR
MURMUR
GRR
GRR
DID YOU WANT TO SAY SOME-THING, MA'AM...?
LOOK WHAT YOU HAVE DONE TO OUR MEETING ...!
YOU AREN'T MATURE ENOUGH TO FORM A COHERENT OPINION...
MURMUR
...YET YOU THINK YOU'RE ENTITLED TO BE HEARD?
MURMUR
YOU PLAY WITH FIRECRACKERS, FOR GOD'S SAKE!
OBJECTION!

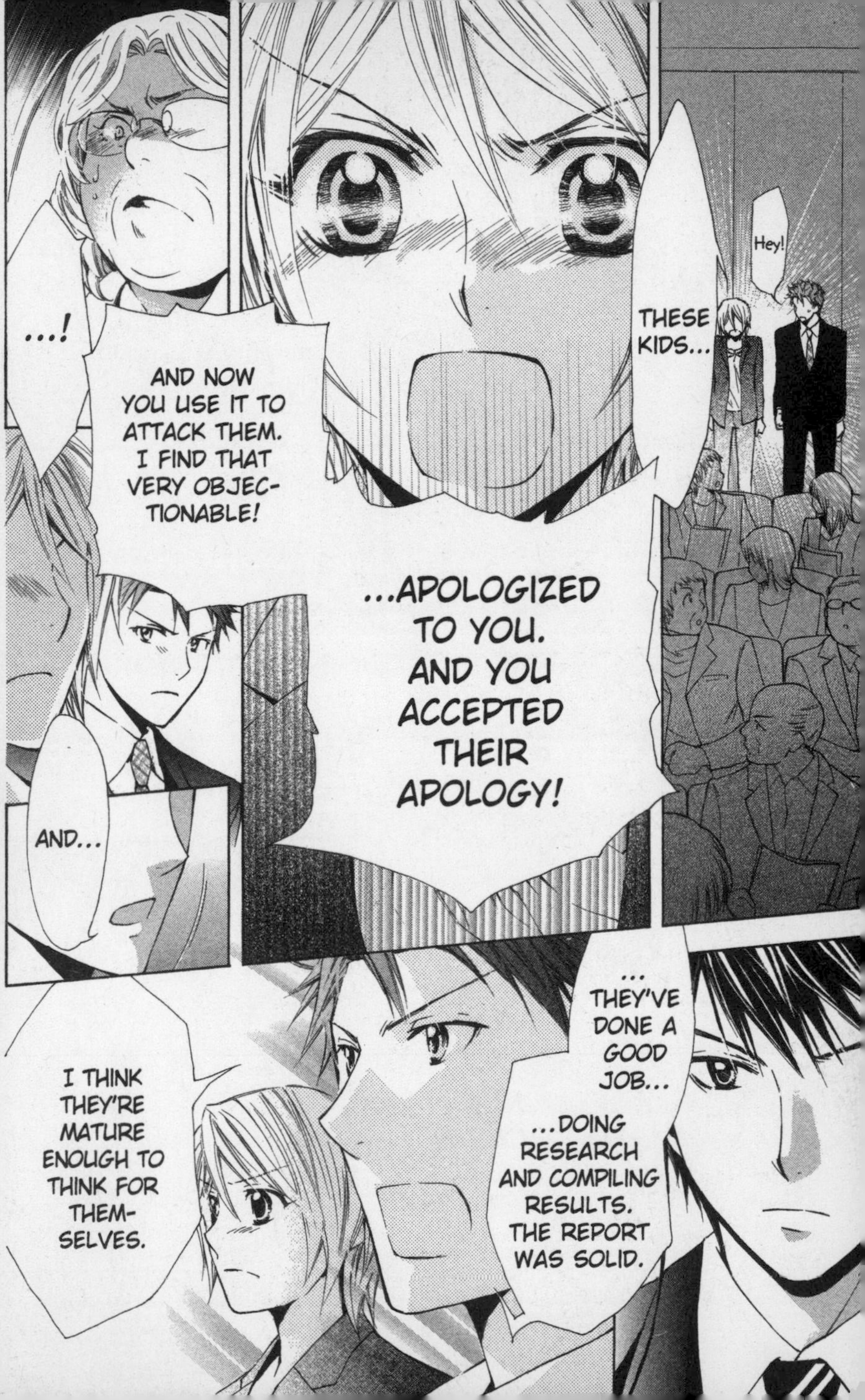
Hey!
THESE KIDS...
...APOLOGIZED TO YOU. AND YOU ACCEPTED THEIR APOLOGY!
...!
AND NOW YOU USE IT TO ATTACK THEM. I FIND THAT VERY OBJECTIONABLE!
AND...
... THEY'VE DONE A GOOD JOB...
...DOING RESEARCH AND COMPILING RESULTS. THE REPORT WAS SOLID.
I THINK THEY'RE MATURE ENOUGH TO THINK FOR THEMSELVES.

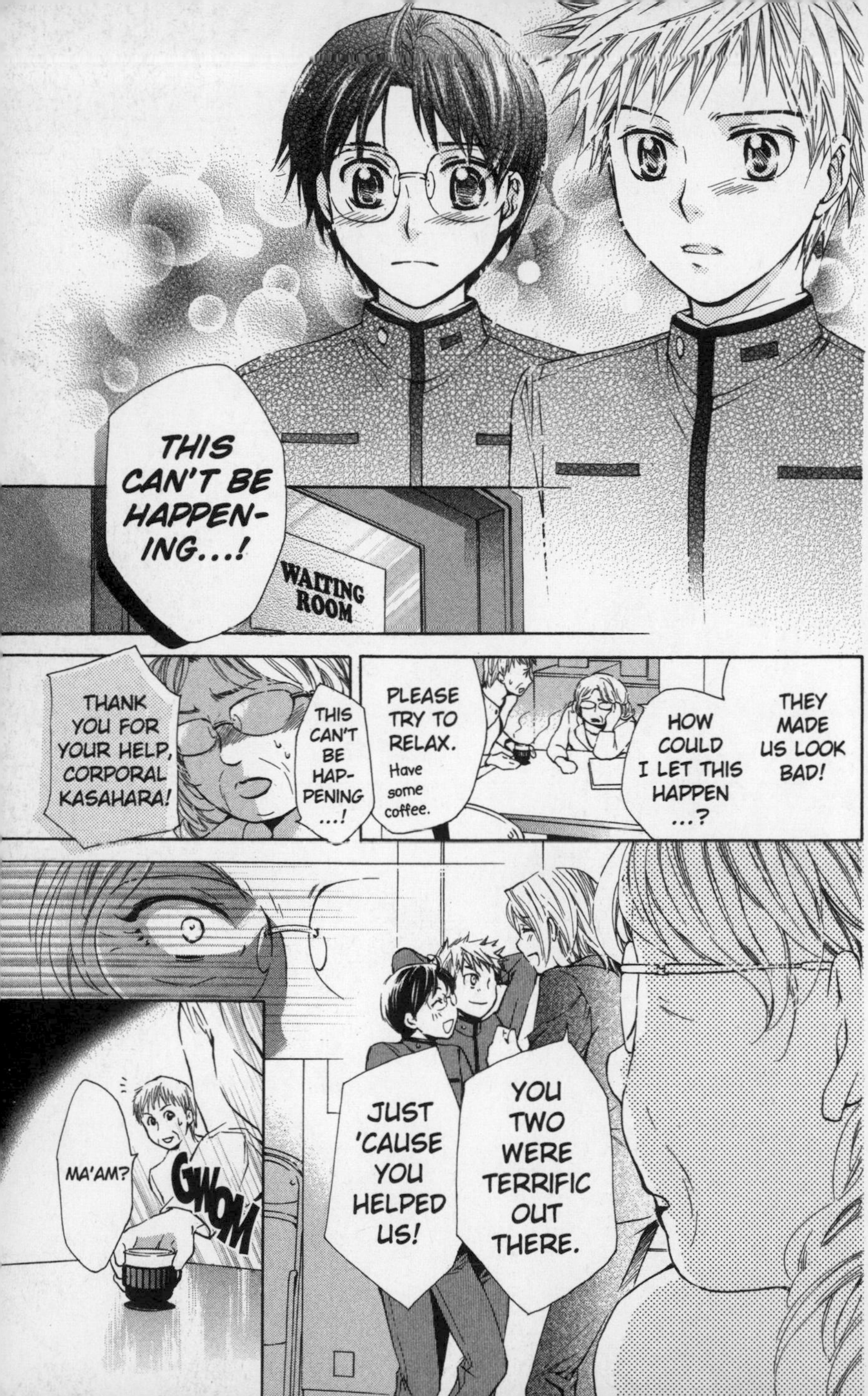
THIS CAN'T BE HAPPEN-ING...!
WAITING ROOM
THEY MADE US LOOK BAD!
HOW COULD I LET THIS HAPPEN ...?
PLEASE TRY TO RELAX. Have some coffee.
THIS CAN'T BE HAP-PENING ...!
THANK YOU FOR YOUR HELP, CORPORAL KASAHARA!
YOU TWO WERE TERRIFIC OUT THERE.
JUST 'CAUSE YOU HELPED US!
GWOM
MA'AM?

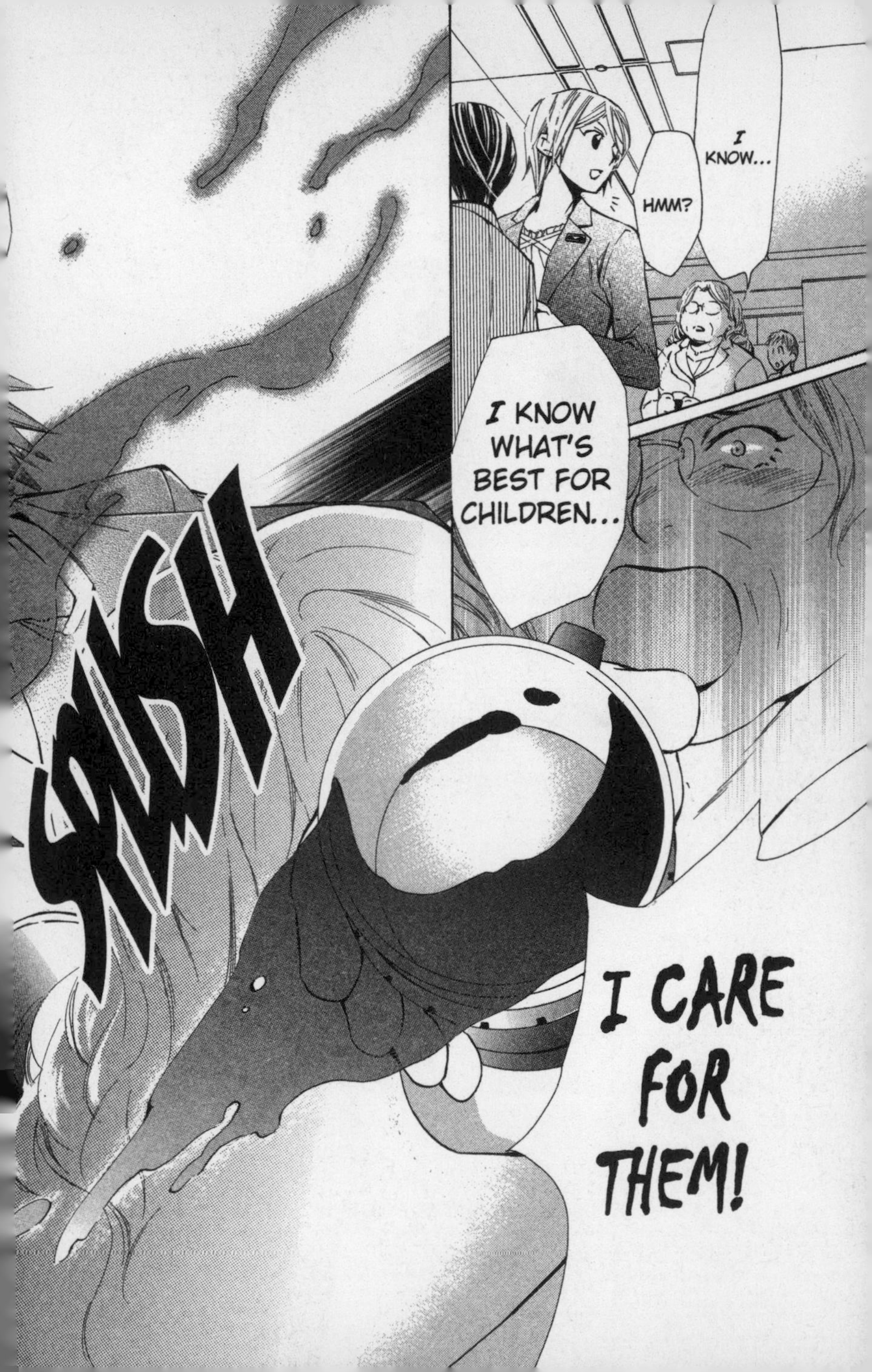
I KNOW...
HMM?
I KNOW WHAT'S BEST FOR CHILDREN...
I CARE FOR THEM!
SPLISH

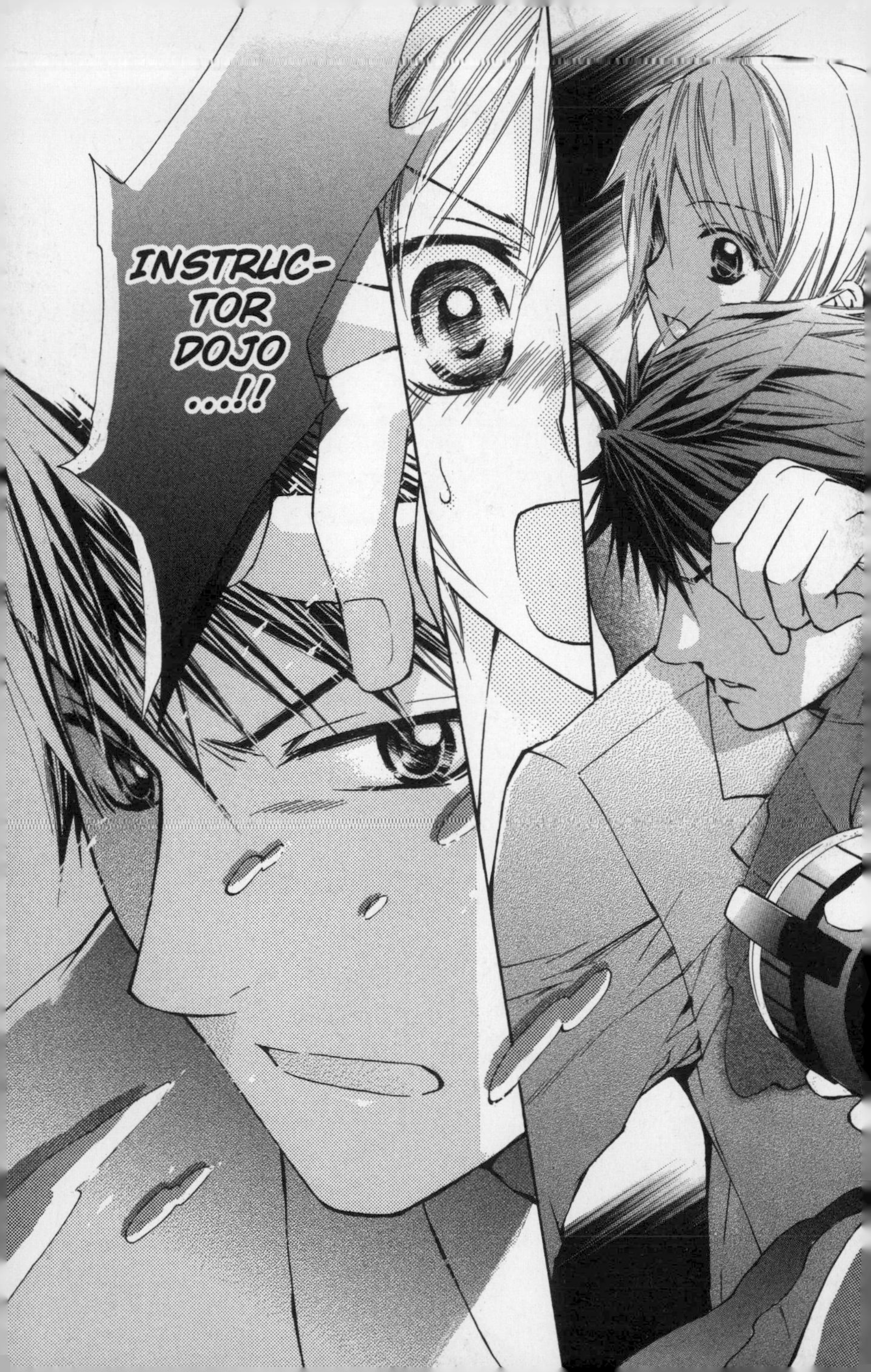
INSTRUC-
TOR
DOJO
...!!

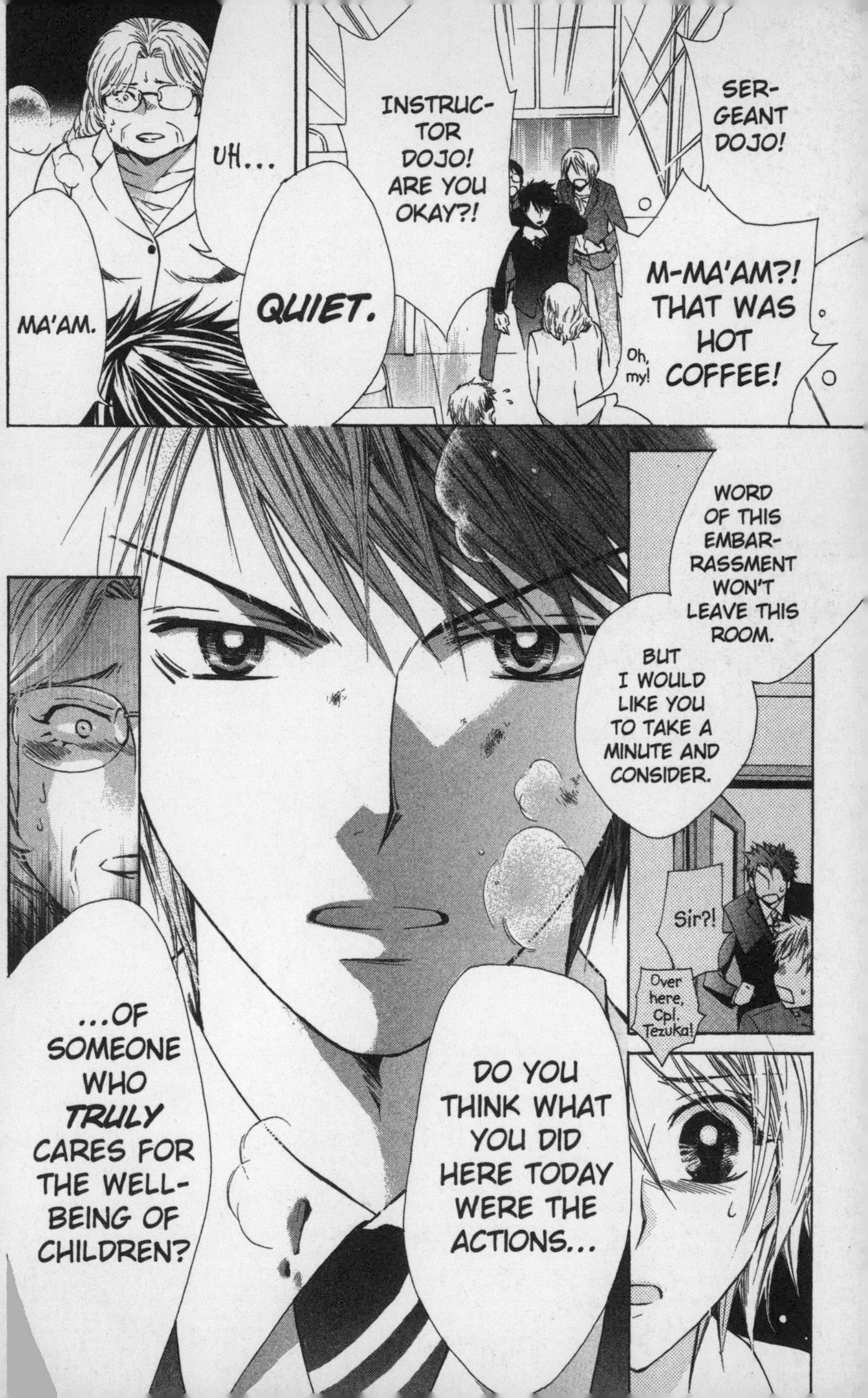
SER-GEANT DOJO!
M-MA'AM?! THAT WAS HOT COFFEE!
Oh, my!
INSTRUC-TOR DOJO! ARE YOU OKAY?!
QUIET.
UH...
MA'AM.
WORD OF THIS EMBAR-RASSMENT WON'T LEAVE THIS ROOM.
BUT I WOULD LIKE YOU TO TAKE A MINUTE AND CONSIDER.
Sir?!
Over here, Cpl. Tezuka!
DO YOU THINK WHAT YOU DID HERE TODAY WERE THE ACTIONS...
...OF SOMEONE WHO *TRULY* CARES FOR THE WELL-BEING OF CHILDREN?

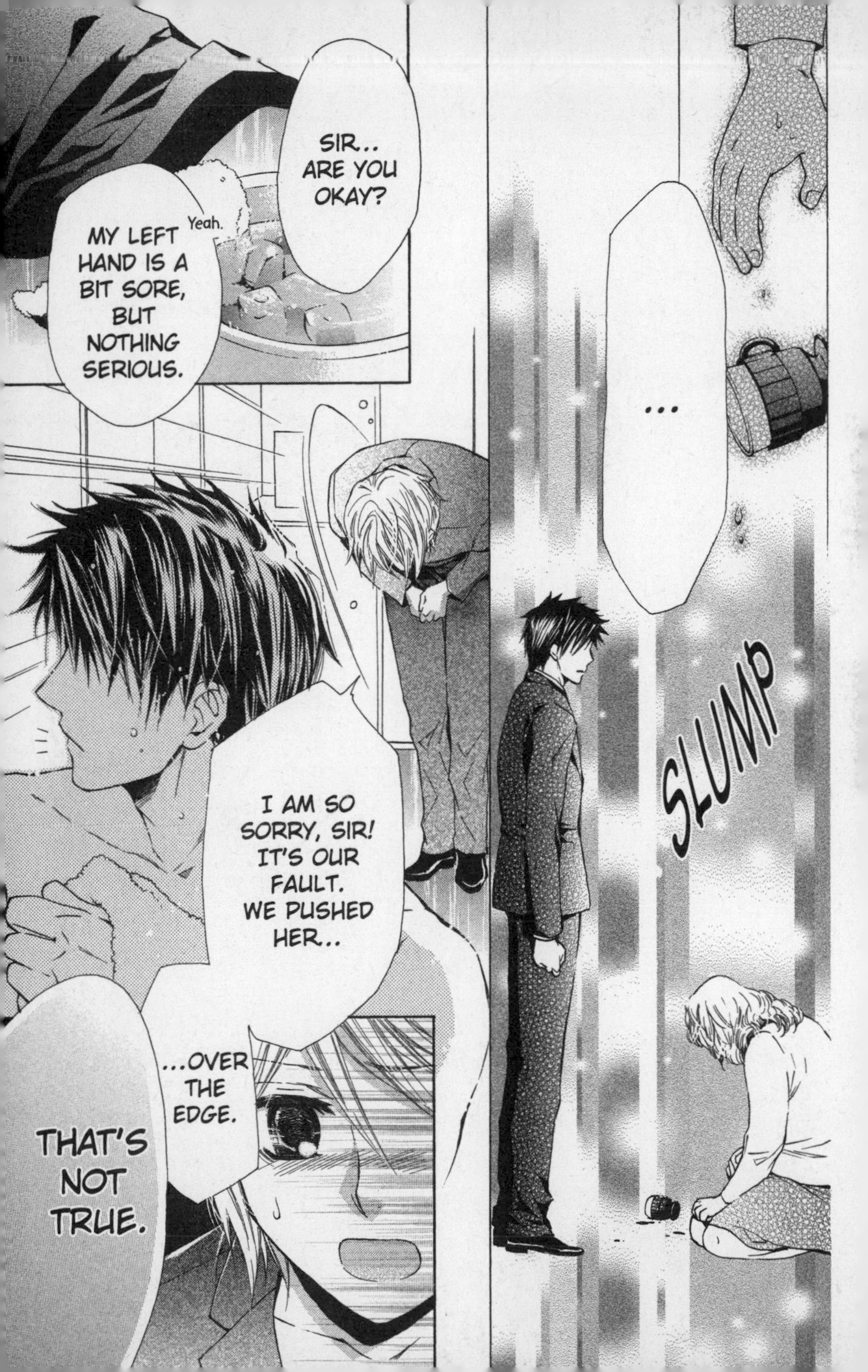
...
SLUMP
SIR... ARE YOU OKAY?
Yeah.
MY LEFT HAND IS A BIT SORE, BUT NOTHING SERIOUS.
I AM SO SORRY, SIR! IT'S OUR FAULT. WE PUSHED HER...
...OVER THE EDGE.
THAT'S NOT TRUE.

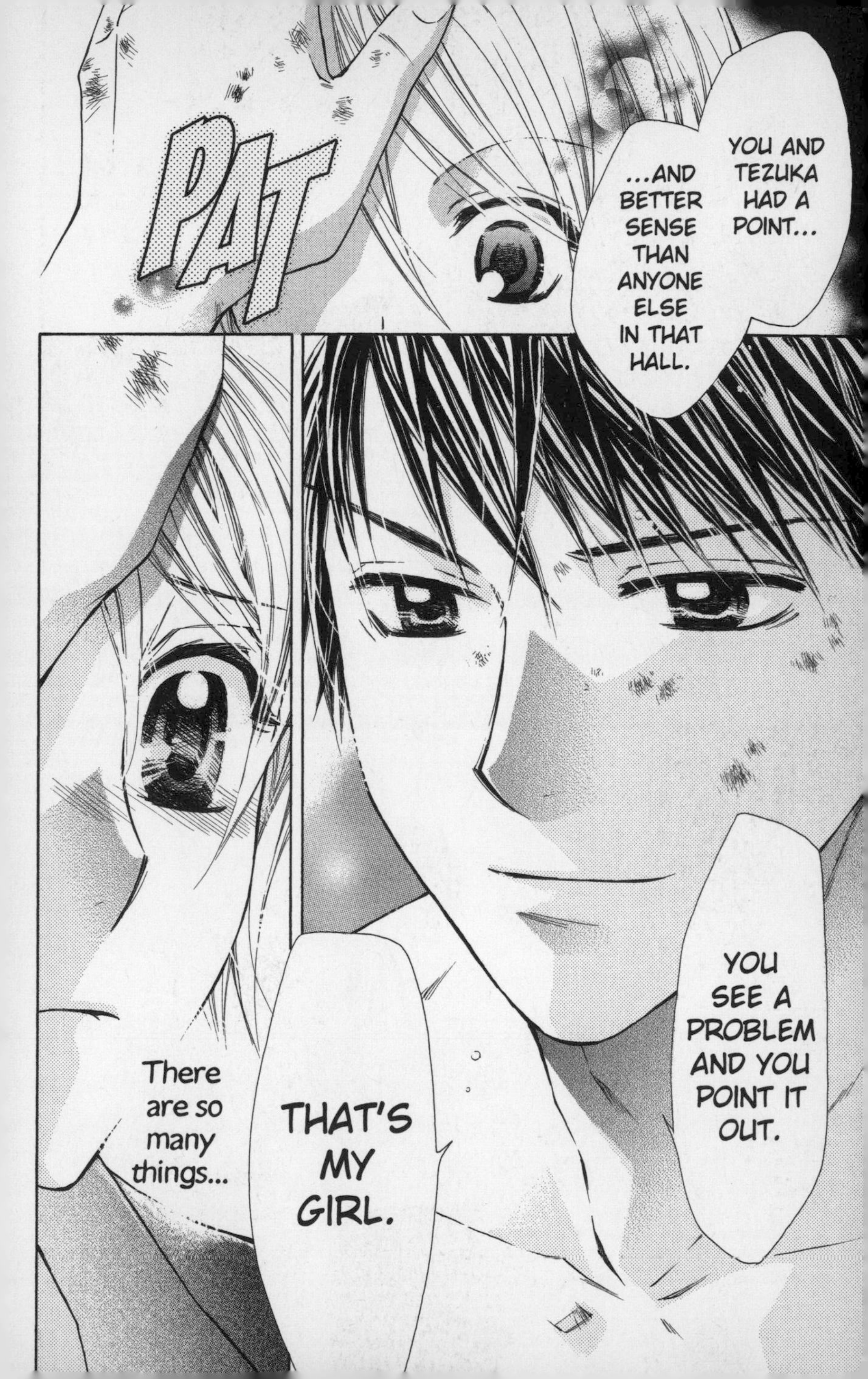
YOU AND TEZUKA HAD A POINT...
...AND BETTER SENSE THAN ANYONE ELSE IN THAT HALL.
PAT
YOU SEE A PROBLEM AND YOU POINT IT OUT.
THAT'S MY GIRL.
There are so many things...

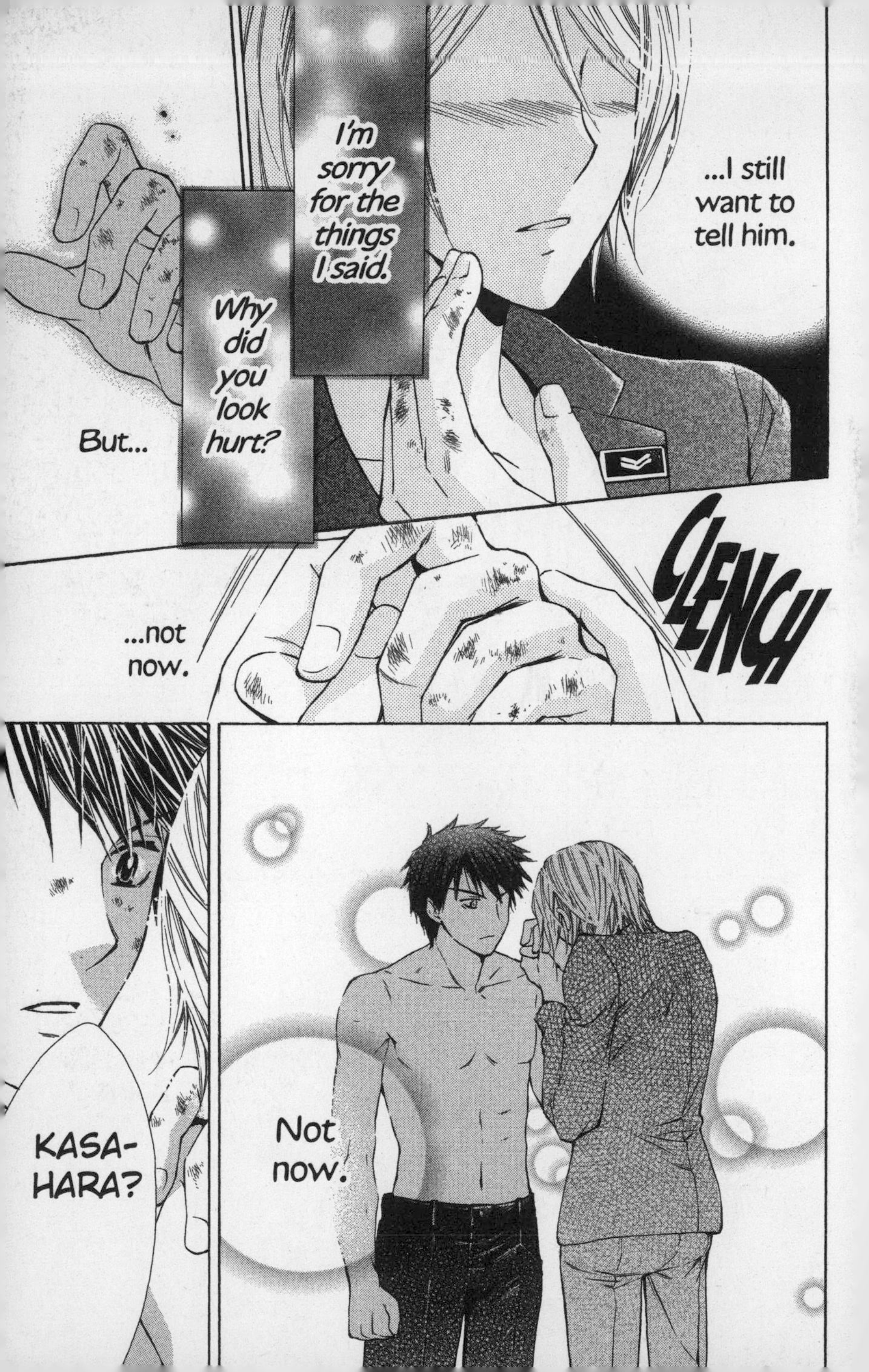
...I still want to tell him.
I'm sorry for the things I said.
Why did you look hurt?
But...
CLENCH
...not now.
Not now.
KASA-HARA?

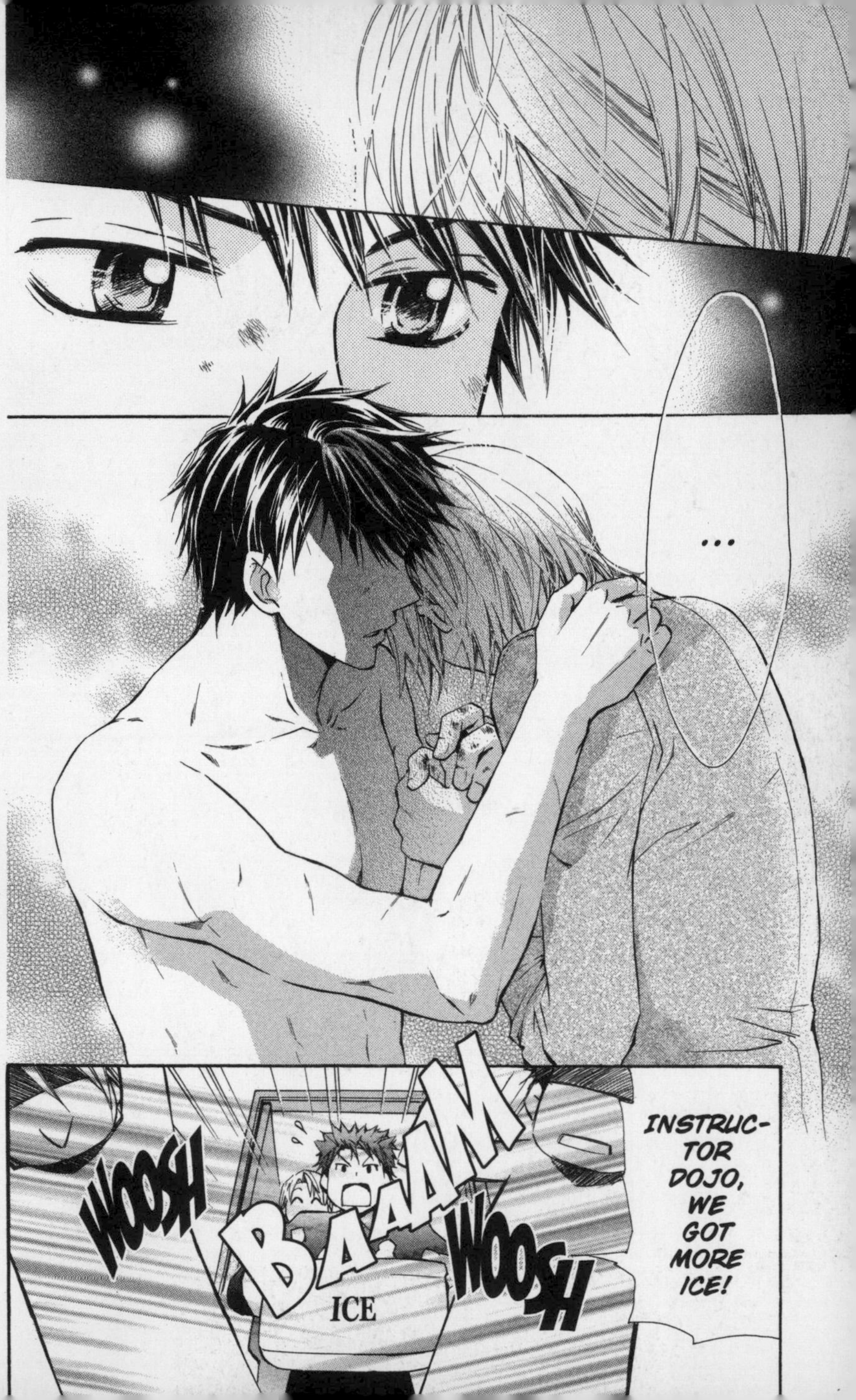
...
INSTRUCTOR-TOR DOJO, WE GOT MORE ICE!
WOOSH
BAAAM
WOOSH
ICE

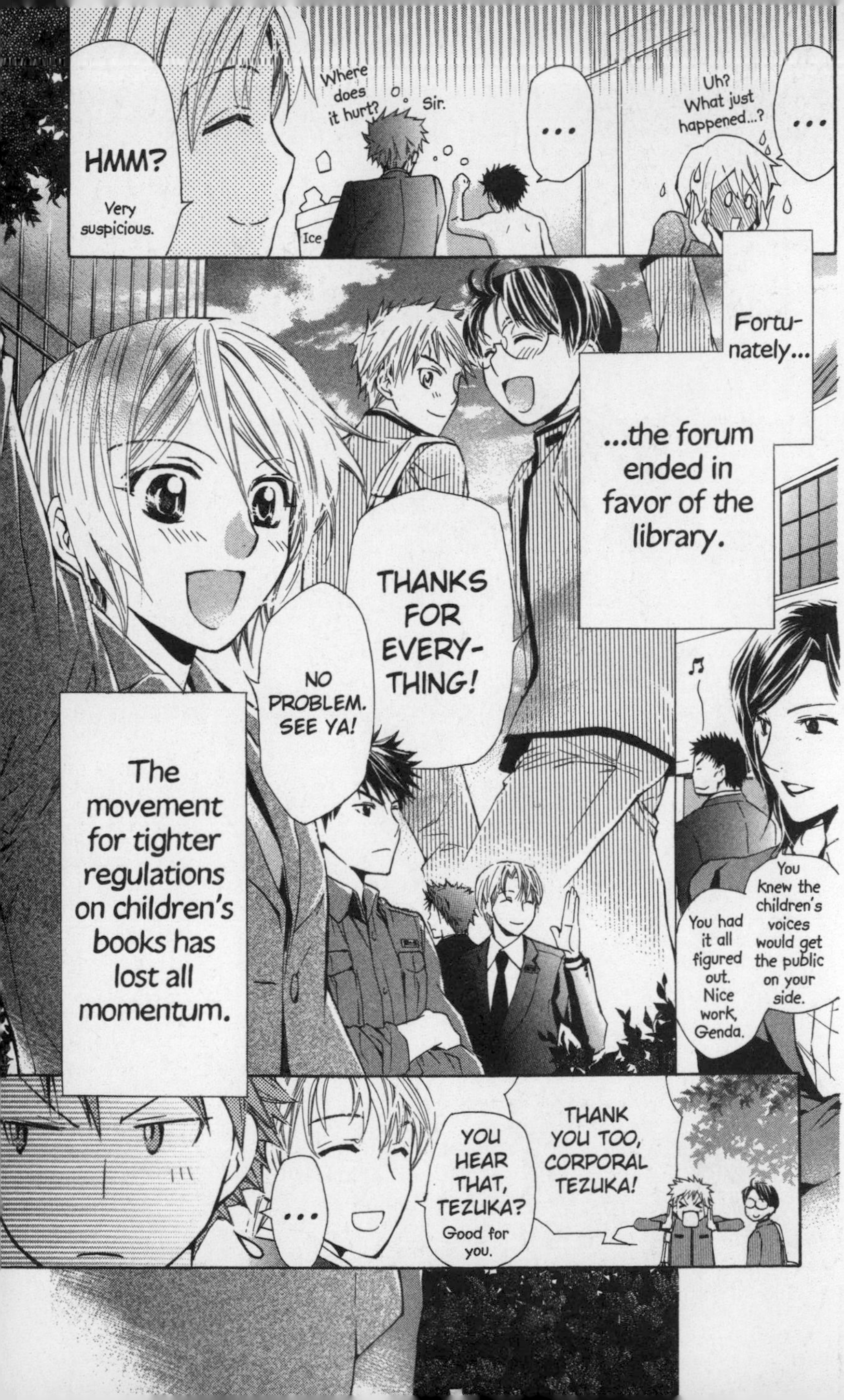
...
Uh? What just happened...?
...
Sir.
Where does it hurt?
Ice
HMM?
Very suspicious.
Fortunately...
...the forum ended in favor of the library.
THANKS FOR EVERYTHING!
NO PROBLEM. SEE YA!
The movement for tighter regulations on children's books has lost all momentum.
You knew the children's voices would get the public on your side.
You had it all figured out. Nice work, Genda.
THANK YOU TOO, CORPORAL TEZUKA!
YOU HEAR THAT, TEZUKA? Good for you.
...

Exemplary Adult

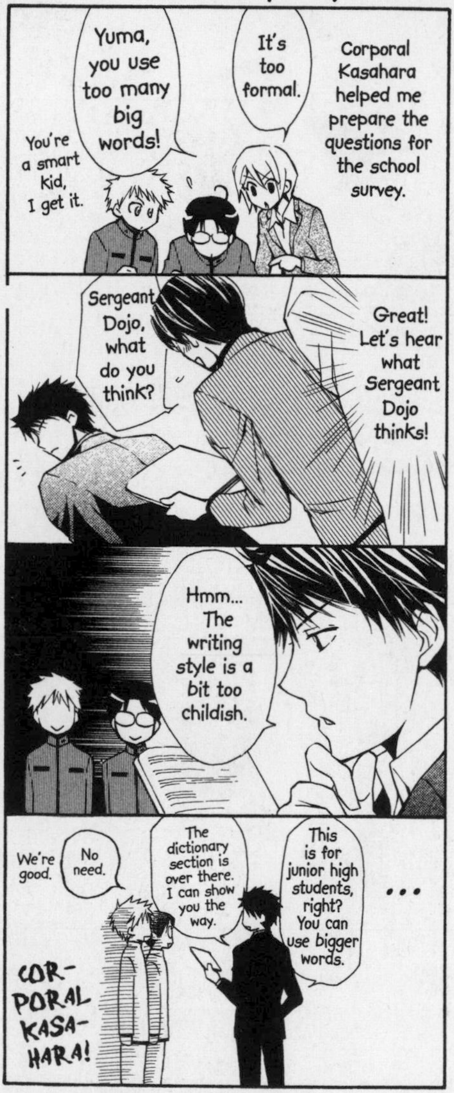
Corporal Kasahara helped me prepare the questions for the school survey.
It's too formal.
Yuma, you use too many big words!
You're a smart kid, I get it.
Great! Let's hear what Sergeant Dojo thinks!
Sergeant Dojo, what do you think?
Hmm... The writing style is a bit too childish.
...
This is for junior high students, right? You can use bigger words.
The dictionary section is over there. I can show you the way.
No need.
We're good.
CORPORAL KASAHARA!

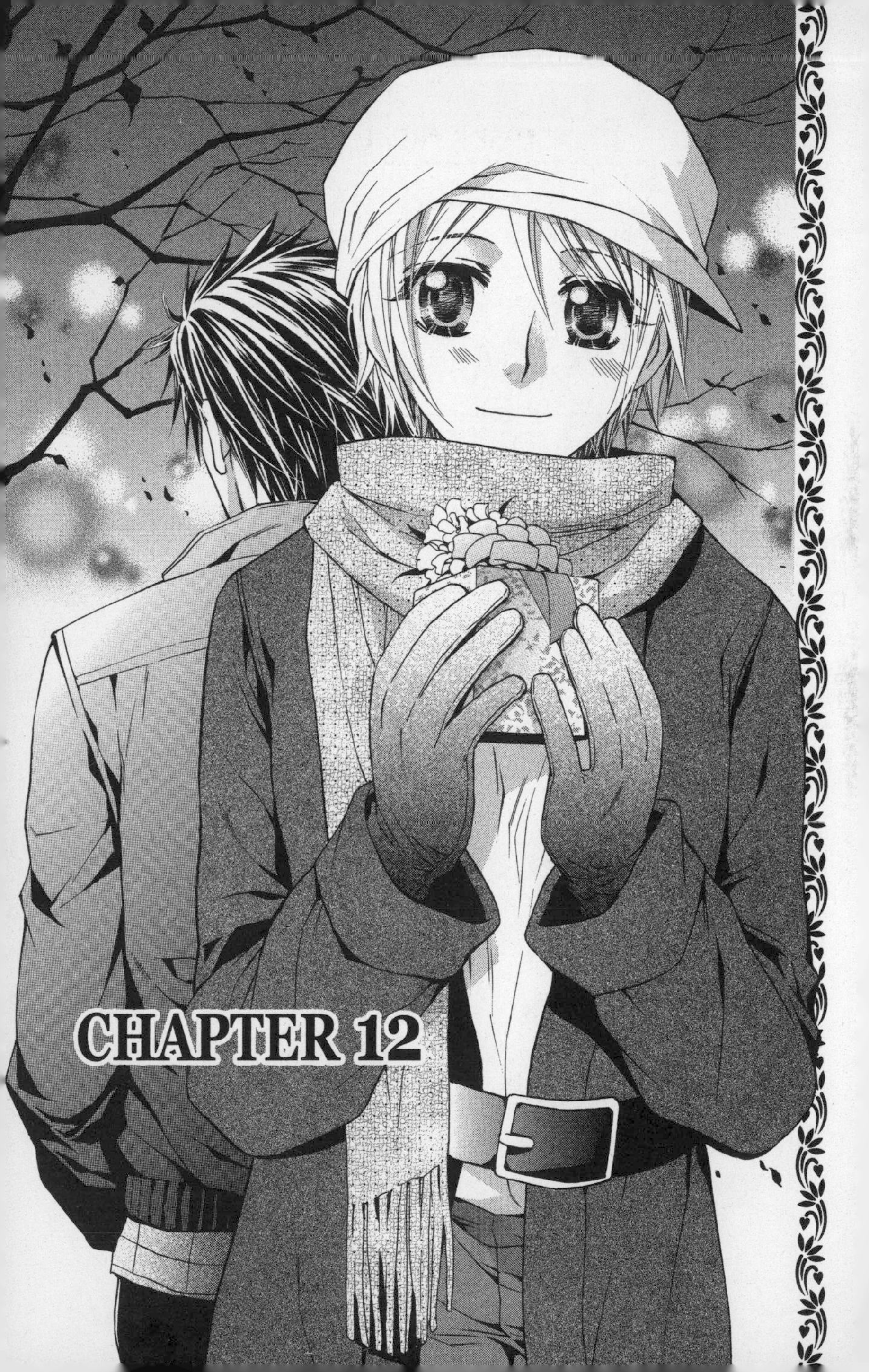
CHAPTER 12

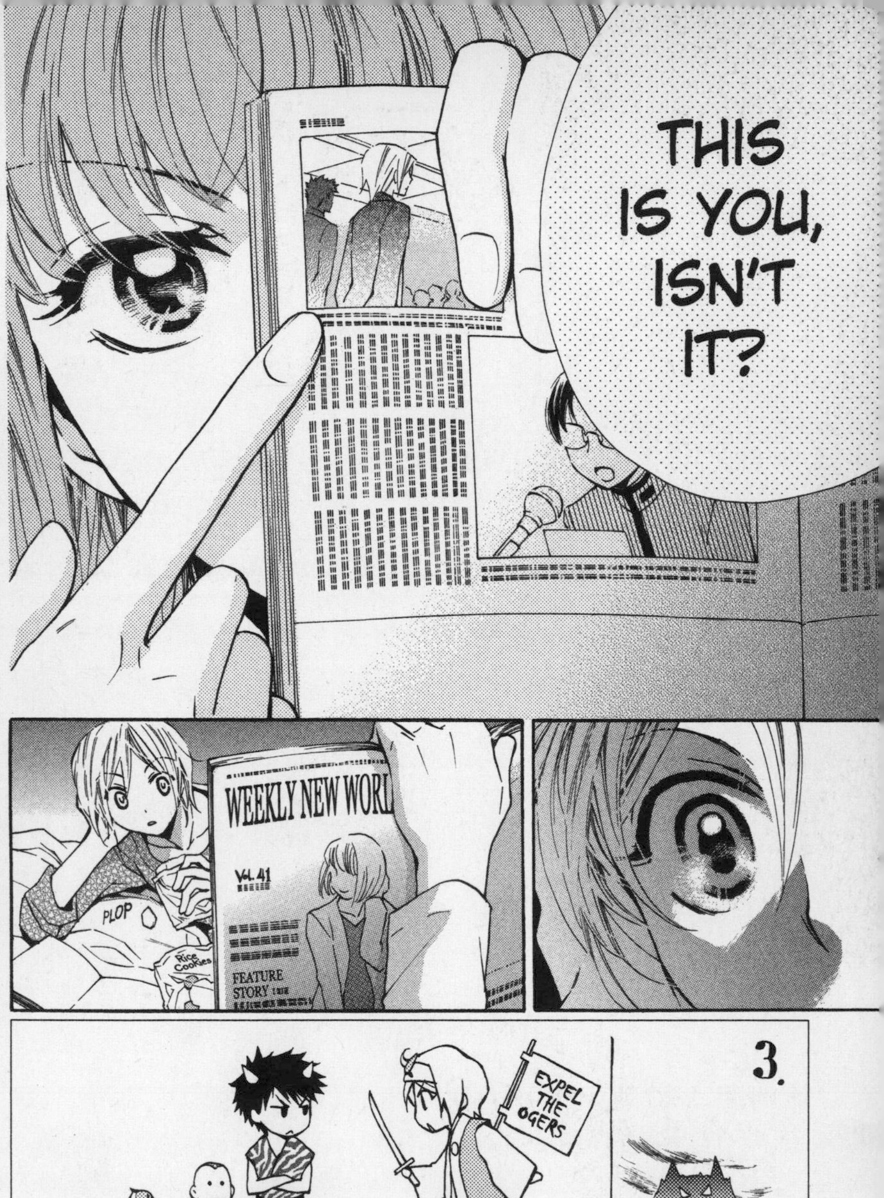
THIS IS YOU, ISN'T IT?
WEEKLY NEW WORLD
Vol. 41
FEATURE STORY
PLOP
Rice Cookies
3.
Ogre Island
EXPEL THE OGERS

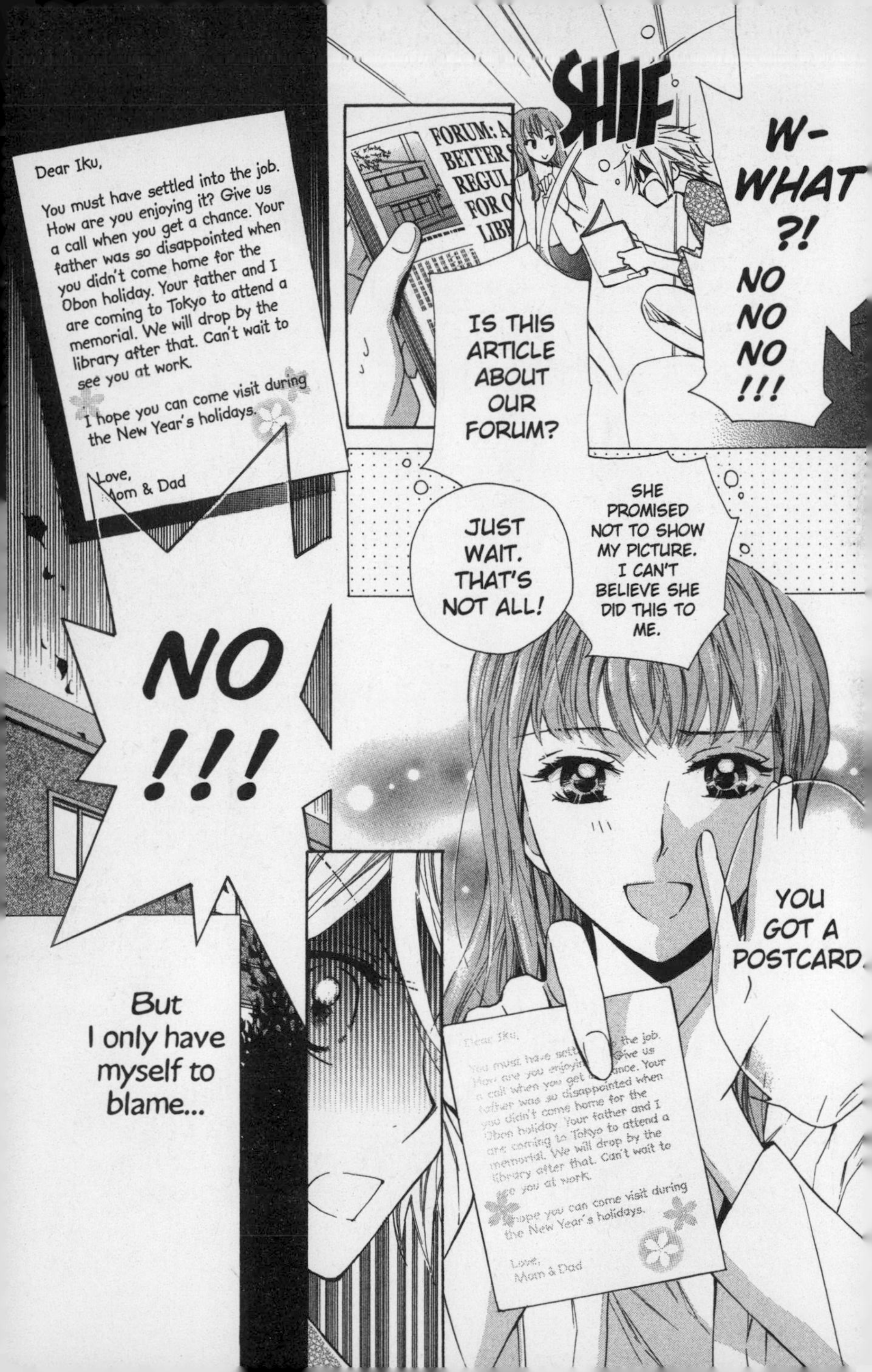
SHIF
W-WHAT?!
NO NO NO!!!
FORUM: A
BETTER
REGUL
FOR
LIBR
IS THIS ARTICLE ABOUT OUR FORUM?
SHE PROMISED NOT TO SHOW MY PICTURE. I CAN'T BELIEVE SHE DID THIS TO ME.
JUST WAIT. THAT'S NOT ALL!
YOU GOT A POSTCARD.
Dear Iku,
You must have settled into the job. How are you enjoying it? Give us a call when you get a chance. Your father was so disappointed when you didn't come home for the Obon holiday. Your father and I are coming to Tokyo to attend a memorial. We will drop by the library after that. Can't wait to see you at work.
I hope you can come visit during the New Year's holidays.
Love,
Mom & Dad
NO!!!
But I only have myself to blame...

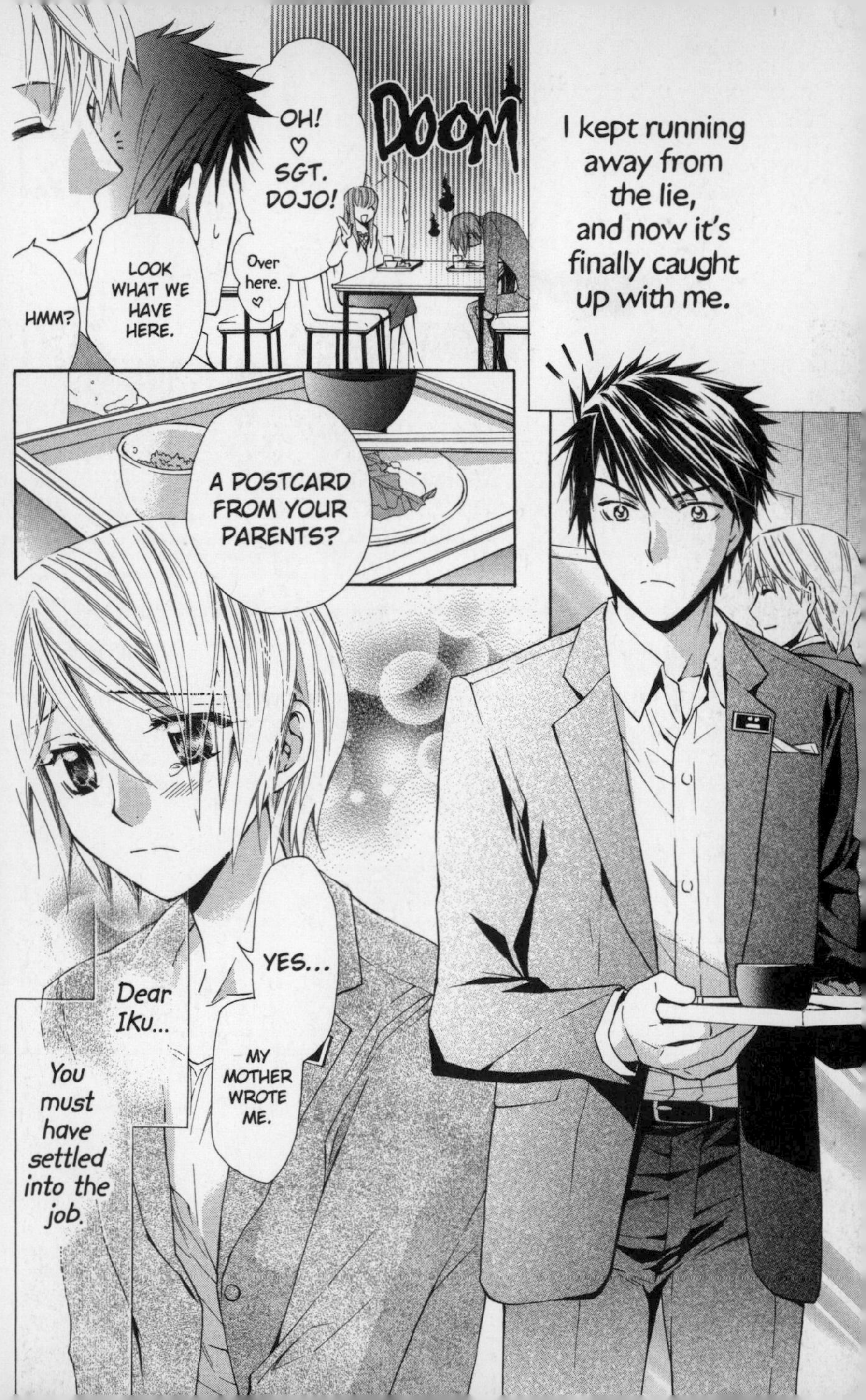
I kept running away from the lie, and now it's finally caught up with me.
DOOM
OH! ♡ SGT. DOJO!
Over here. ♡
LOOK WHAT WE HAVE HERE.
HMM?
A POSTCARD FROM YOUR PARENTS?
YES...
MY MOTHER WROTE ME.
Dear Iku...
You must have settled into the job.

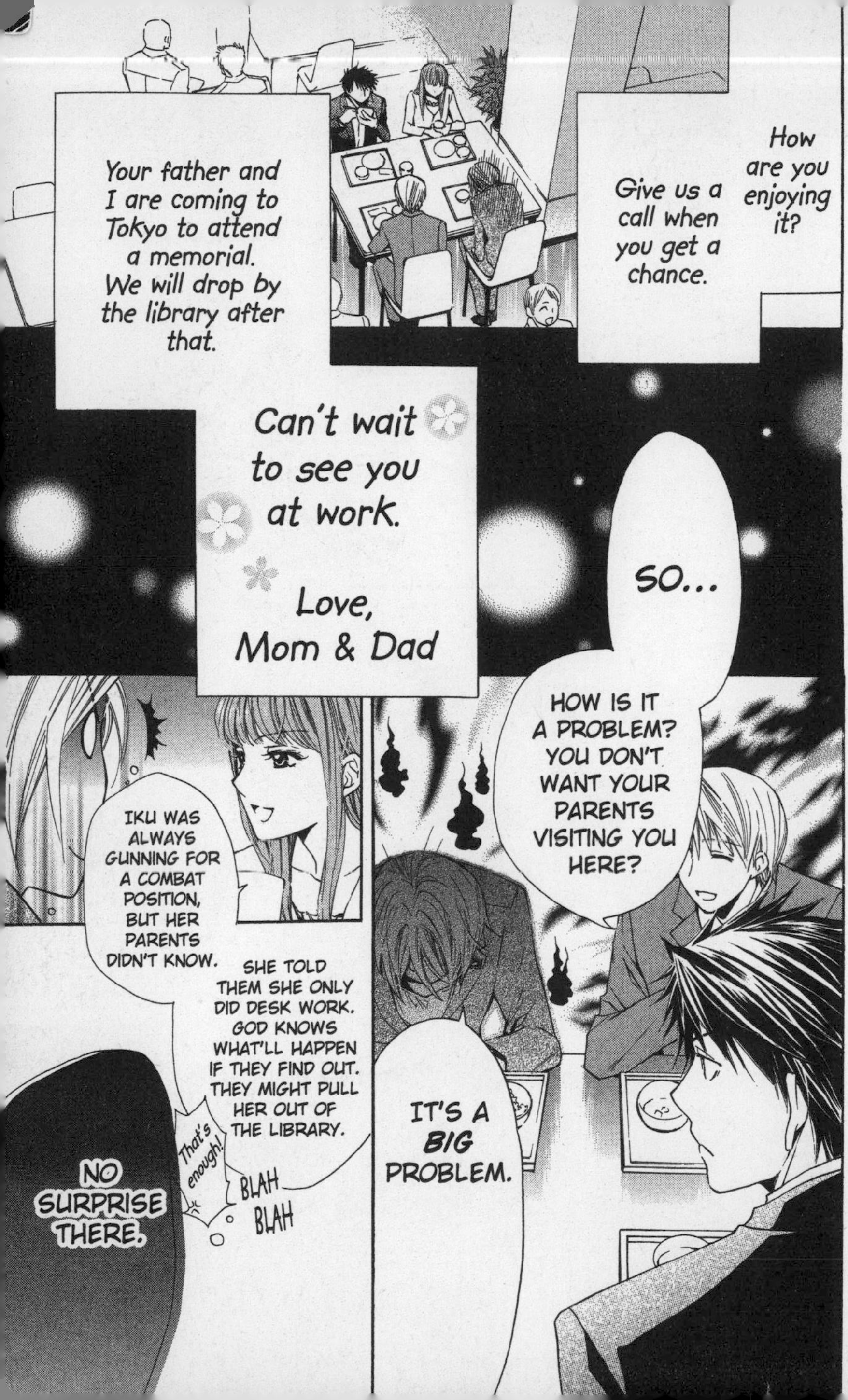
How are you enjoying it?
Give us a call when you get a chance.
Your father and I are coming to Tokyo to attend a memorial. We will drop by the library after that.
Can't wait to see you at work.
Love, Mom & Dad
SO...
HOW IS IT A PROBLEM? YOU DON'T WANT YOUR PARENTS VISITING YOU HERE?
IT'S A BIG PROBLEM.
IKU WAS ALWAYS GUNNING FOR A COMBAT POSITION, BUT HER PARENTS DIDN'T KNOW.
SHE TOLD THEM SHE ONLY DID DESK WORK. GOD KNOWS WHAT'LL HAPPEN IF THEY FIND OUT. THEY MIGHT PULL HER OUT OF THE LIBRARY.
That's enough!
BLAH BLAH
NO SURPRISE THERE.

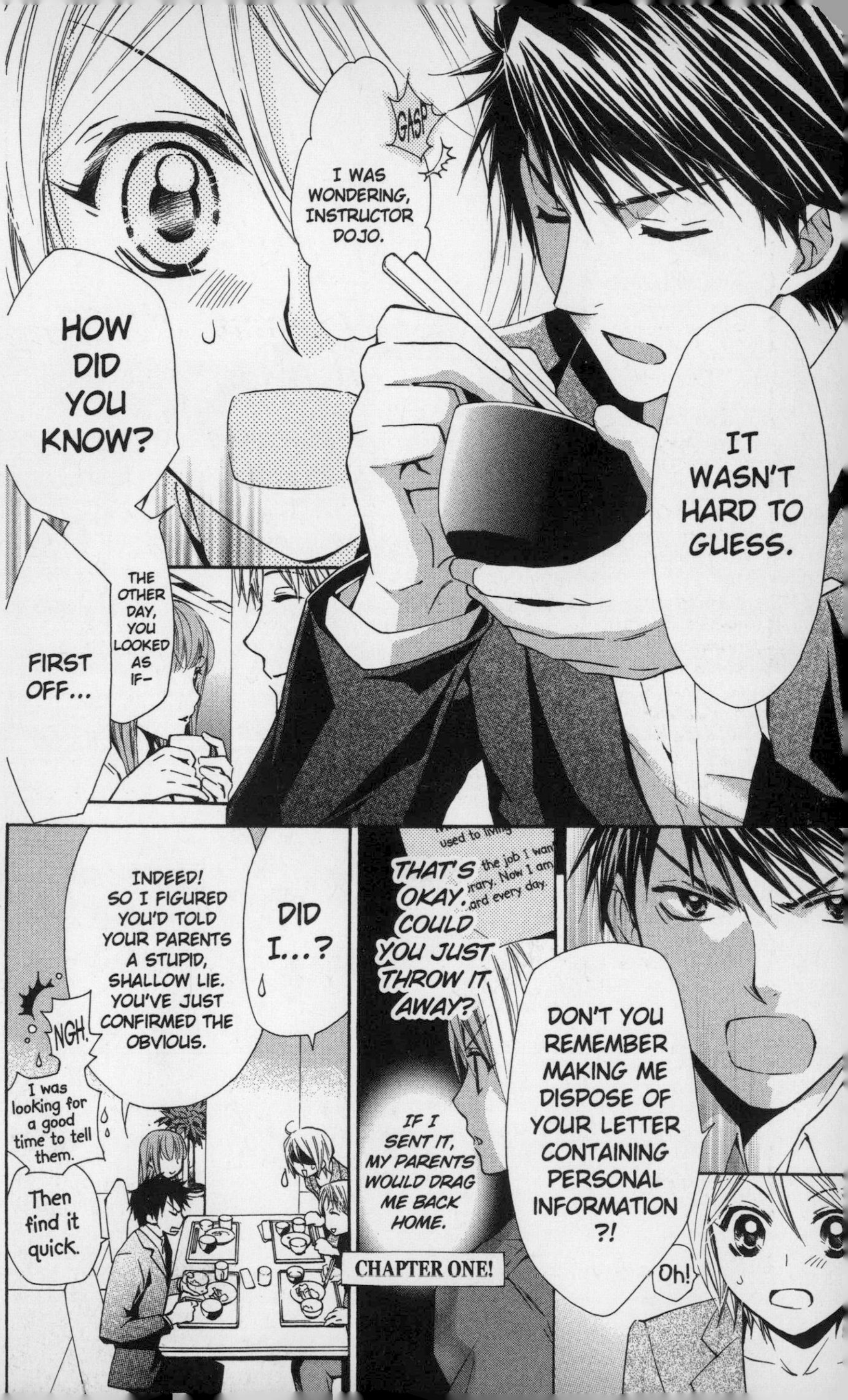
GASP
I WAS WONDERING, INSTRUCTOR DOJO.
HOW DID YOU KNOW?
IT WASN'T HARD TO GUESS.
FIRST OFF...
THE OTHER DAY, YOU LOOKED AS IF-
DON'T YOU REMEMBER MAKING ME DISPOSE OF YOUR LETTER CONTAINING PERSONAL INFORMATION ?!
Oh!
THAT'S OKAY. COULD YOU JUST THROW IT AWAY?
IF I SENT IT, MY PARENTS WOULD DRAG ME BACK HOME.
CHAPTER ONE!
DID I...?
INDEED! SO I FIGURED YOU'D TOLD YOUR PARENTS A STUPID, SHALLOW LIE. YOU'VE JUST CONFIRMED THE OBVIOUS.
NGH!
I was looking for a good time to tell them.
Then find it quick.

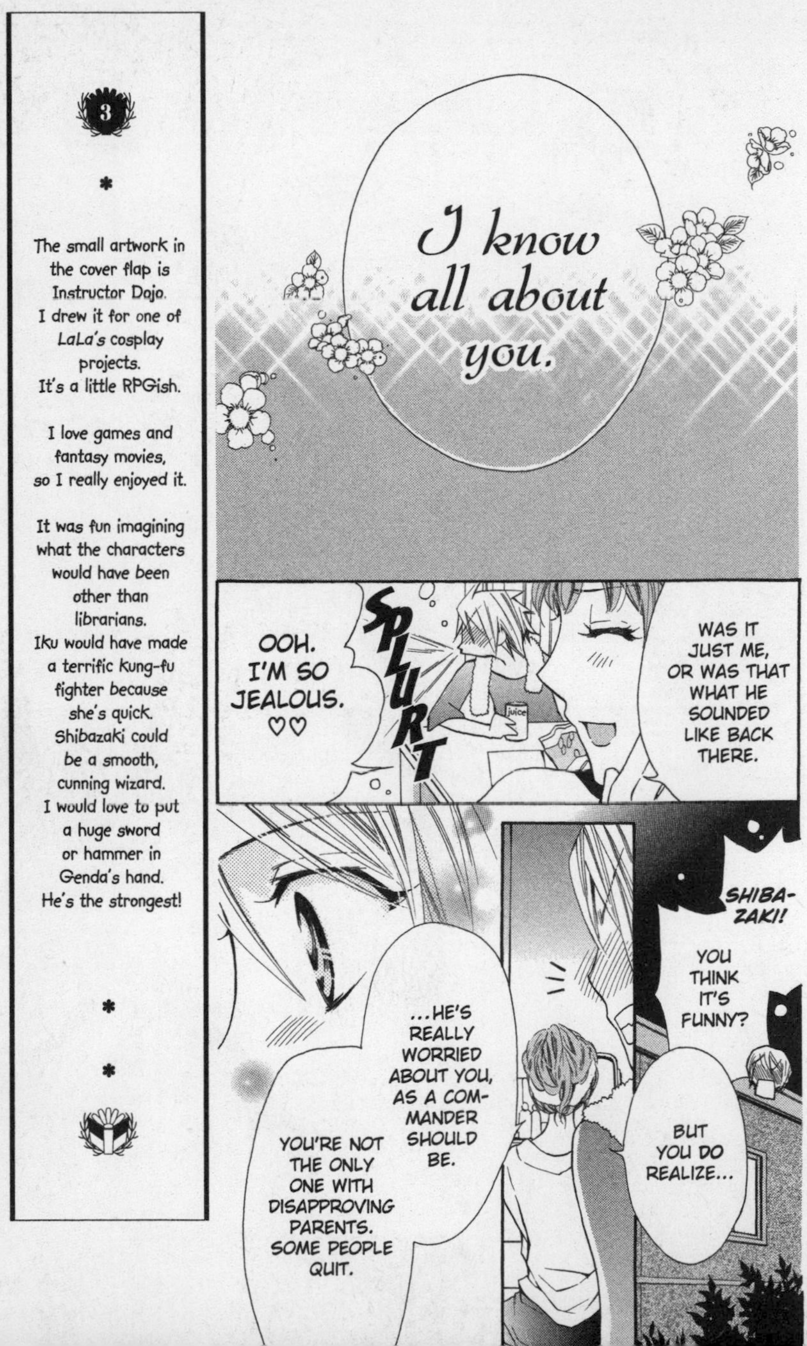
I know all about you.
WAS IT JUST ME, OR WAS THAT WHAT HE SOUNDED LIKE BACK THERE.
SPLURT
juice
OOH. I'M SO JEALOUS. ♡♡
SHIBA-ZAKI!
YOU THINK IT'S FUNNY?
BUT YOU DO REALIZE...
...HE'S REALLY WORRIED ABOUT YOU, AS A COMMANDER SHOULD BE.
YOU'RE NOT THE ONLY ONE WITH DISAPPROVING PARENTS. SOME PEOPLE QUIT.

3

*

The small artwork in the cover flap is Instructor Dojo. I drew it for one of *LaLa's* cosplay projects. It's a little RPGish.

I love games and fantasy movies, so I really enjoyed it.

It was fun imagining what the characters would have been other than librarians. Iku would have made a terrific kung-fu fighter because she's quick. Shibazaki could be a smooth, cunning wizard. I would love to put a huge sword or hammer in Genda's hand. He's the strongest!

*

*

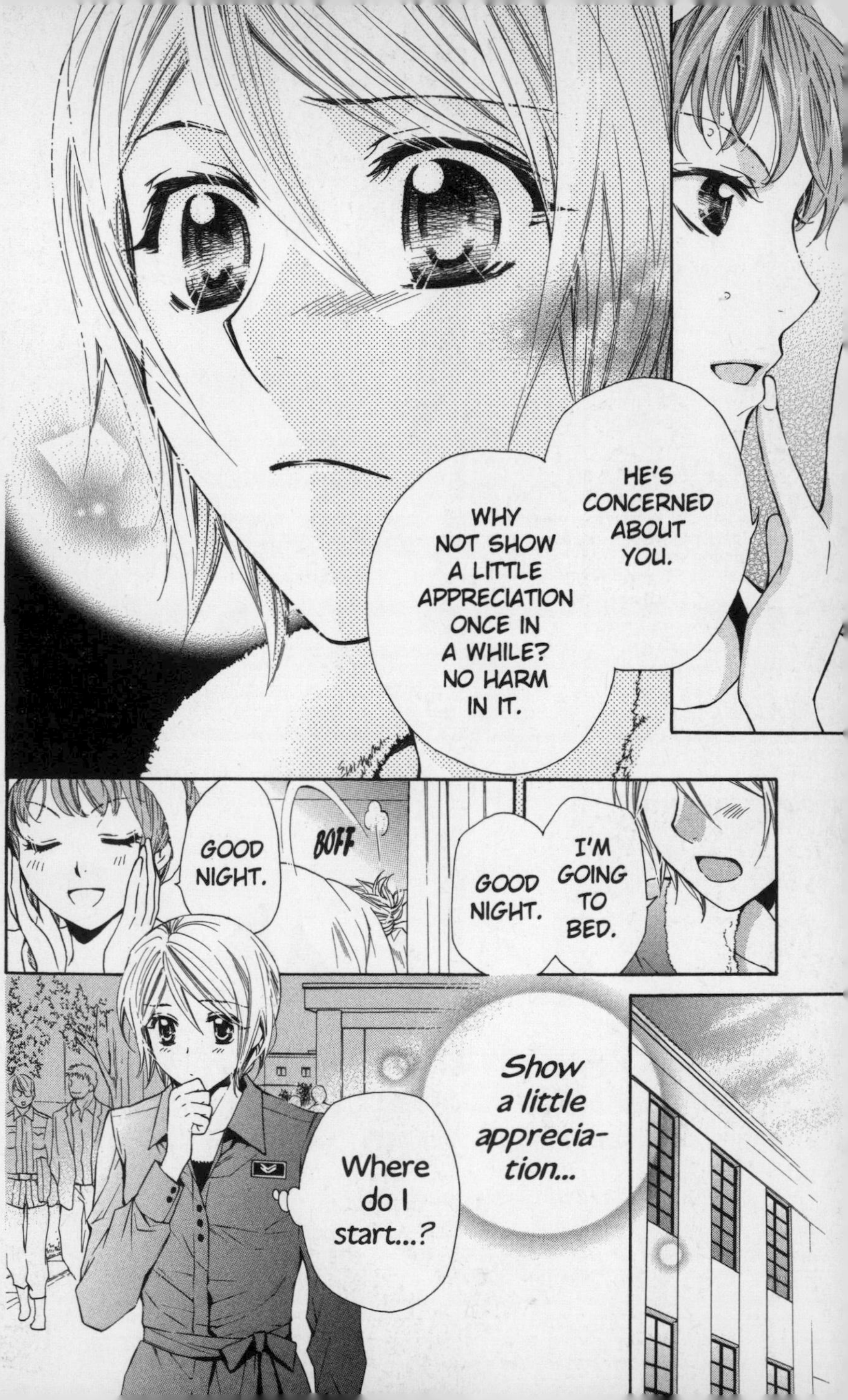
HE'S CONCERNED ABOUT YOU.
WHY NOT SHOW A LITTLE APPRECIATION ONCE IN A WHILE? NO HARM IN IT.
I'M GOING TO BED.
GOOD NIGHT.
BOFF
GOOD NIGHT.
Show a little apprecia-tion...
Where do I start...?

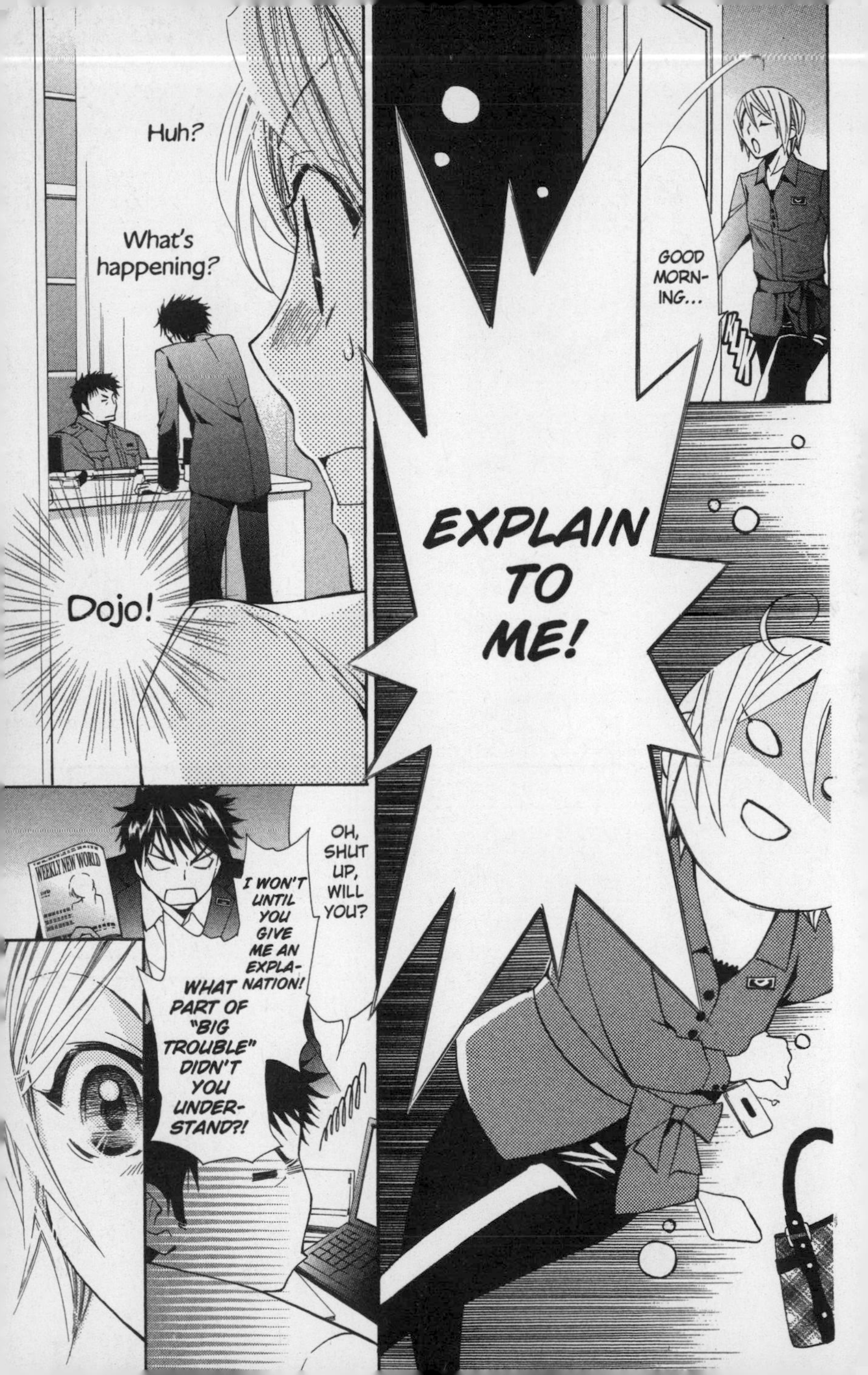
GOOD MORNING...
KLIK
EXPLAIN TO ME!
Huh?
What's happening?
Dojo!
OH, SHUT UP, WILL YOU?
I WON'T UNTIL YOU GIVE ME AN EXPLANATION!
WHAT PART OF "BIG TROUBLE" DIDN'T YOU UNDERSTAND?!
WEEKLY NEW WORLD

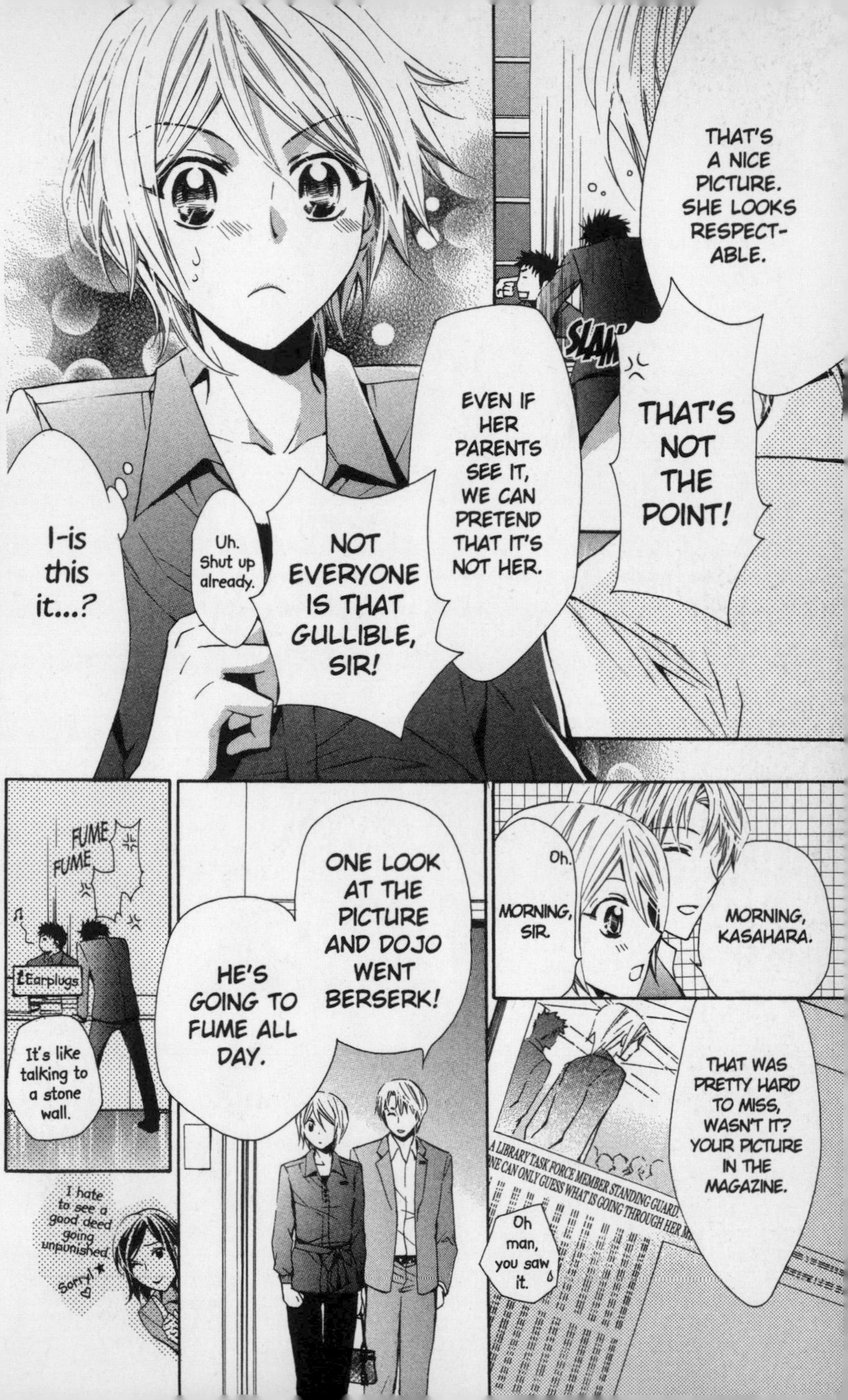
THAT'S A NICE PICTURE. SHE LOOKS RESPECT-ABLE.
SLAM
THAT'S NOT THE POINT!
EVEN IF HER PARENTS SEE IT, WE CAN PRETEND THAT IT'S NOT HER.
NOT EVERYONE IS THAT GULLIBLE, SIR!
Uh. Shut up already.
I-is this it...?
MORNING, KASAHARA.
Oh.
MORNING, SIR.
THAT WAS PRETTY HARD TO MISS, WASN'T IT? YOUR PICTURE IN THE MAGAZINE.
A LIBRARY TASK FORCE MEMBER STANDING GUARD.
Oh man, you saw it.
ONE LOOK AT THE PICTURE AND DOJO WENT BERSERK!
HE'S GOING TO FUME ALL DAY.
FUME
FUME
Earplugs
It's like talking to a stone wall.
I hate to see a good deed going unpunished.
Sorry!★♡

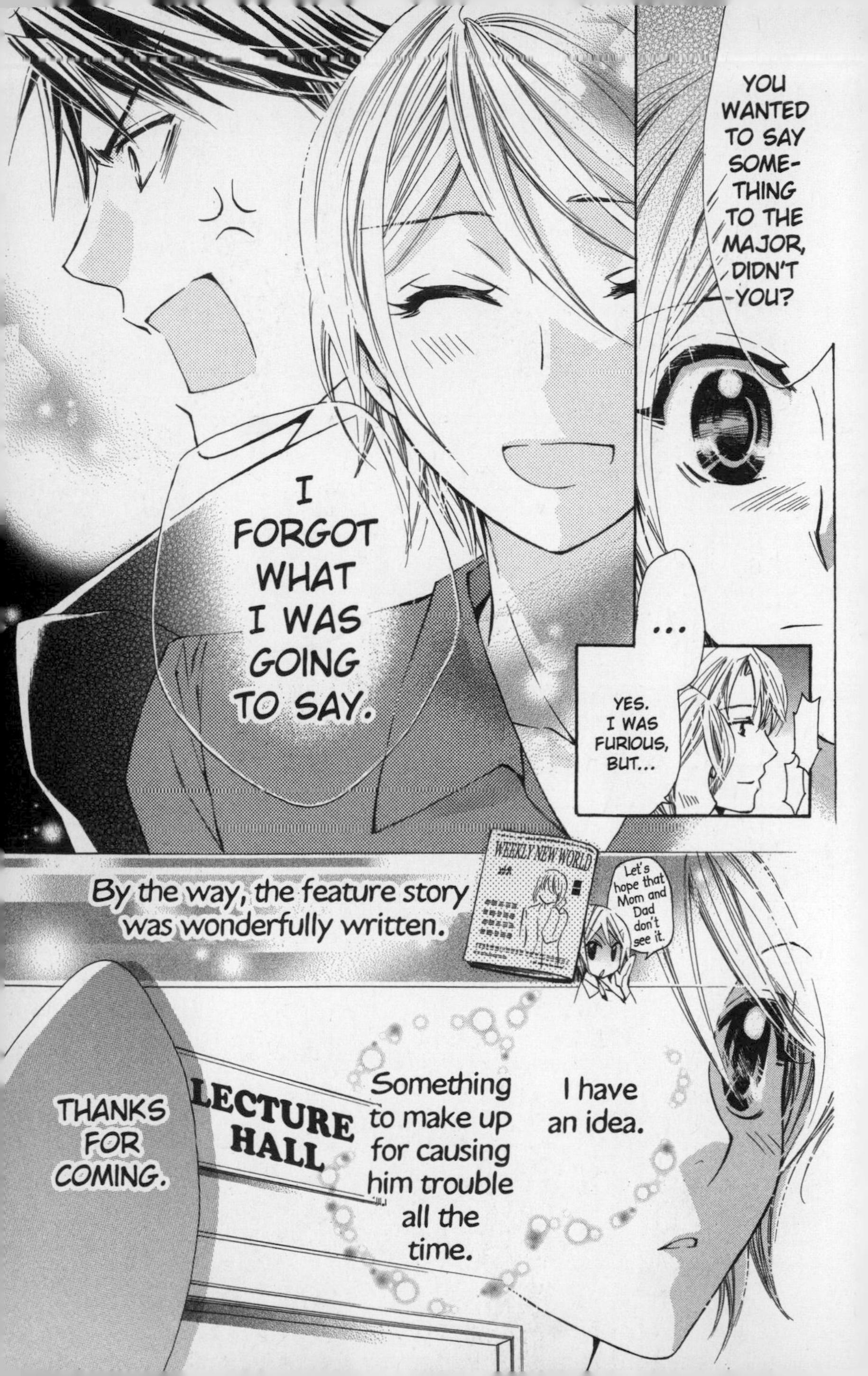
YOU WANTED TO SAY SOMETHING TO THE MAJOR, DIDN'T YOU?
...
YES. I WAS FURIOUS, BUT...
I FORGOT WHAT I WAS GOING TO SAY.
WEEKLY NEW WORLD
Let's hope that Mom and Dad don't see it.
By the way, the feature story was wonderfully written.
I have an idea.
Something to make up for causing him trouble all the time.
LECTURE HALL
THANKS FOR COMING.

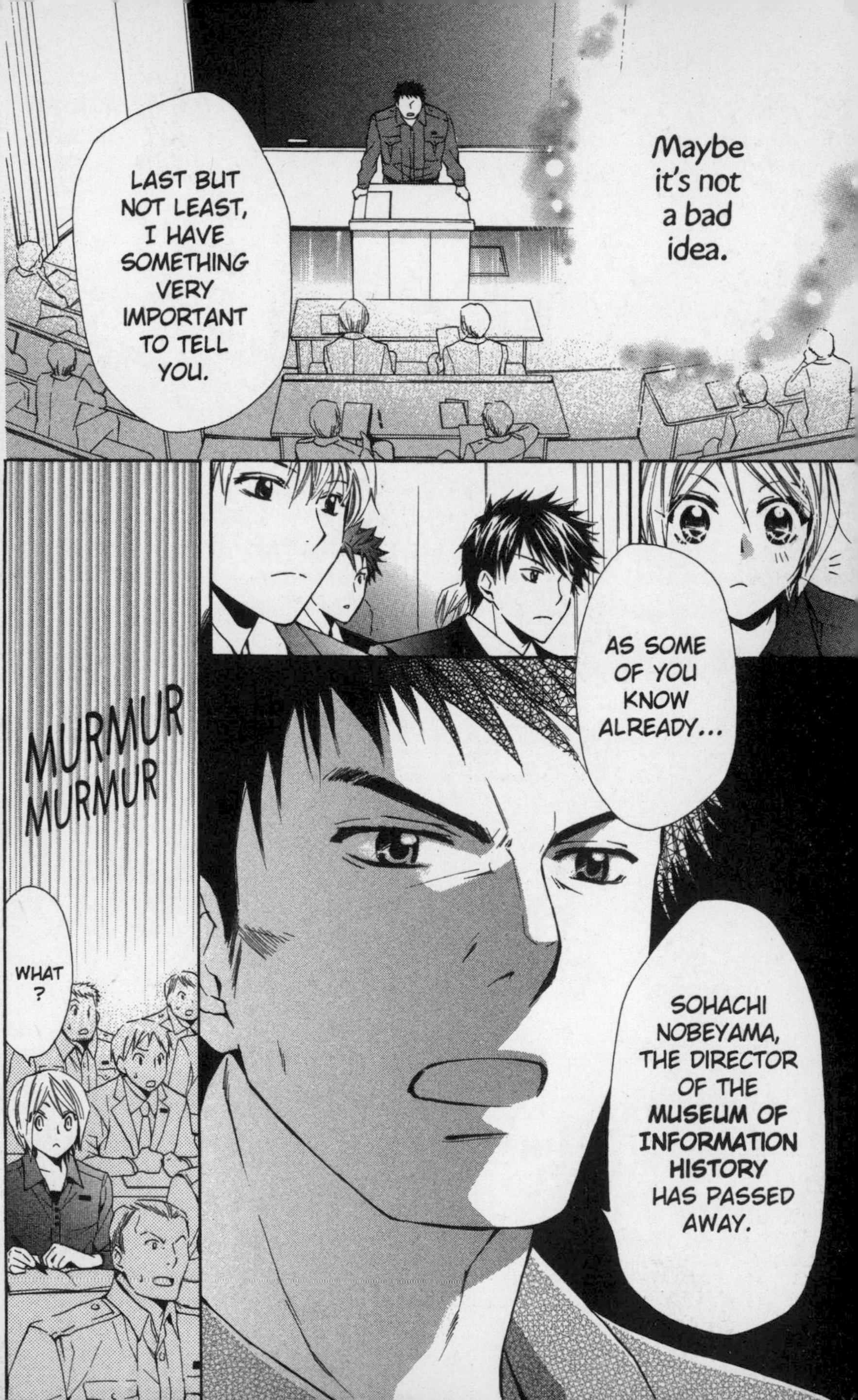
Maybe it's not a bad idea.
LAST BUT NOT LEAST, I HAVE SOMETHING VERY IMPORTANT TO TELL YOU.
AS SOME OF YOU KNOW ALREADY...
SOHACHI NOBEYAMA, THE DIRECTOR OF THE MUSEUM OF INFORMATION HISTORY HAS PASSED AWAY.
MURMUR MURMUR
WHAT?

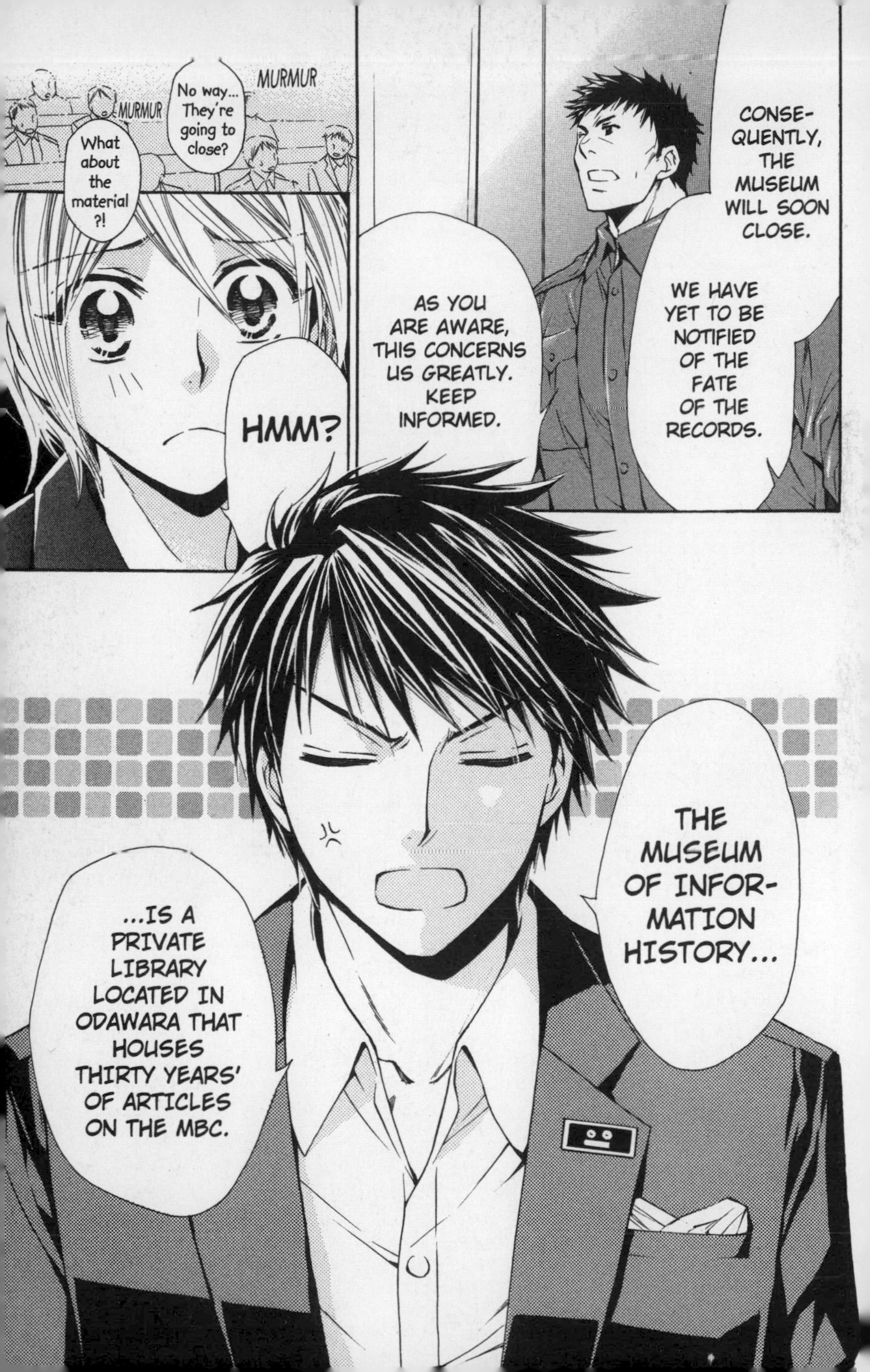
CONSEQUENTLY, THE MUSEUM WILL SOON CLOSE.
WE HAVE YET TO BE NOTIFIED OF THE FATE OF THE RECORDS.
AS YOU ARE AWARE, THIS CONCERNS US GREATLY. KEEP INFORMED.
MURMUR
No way... They're going to close?
MURMUR
What about the material?!
HMM?
THE MUSEUM OF INFORMATION HISTORY...
...IS A PRIVATE LIBRARY LOCATED IN ODAWARA THAT HOUSES THIRTY YEARS' OF ARTICLES ON THE MBC.

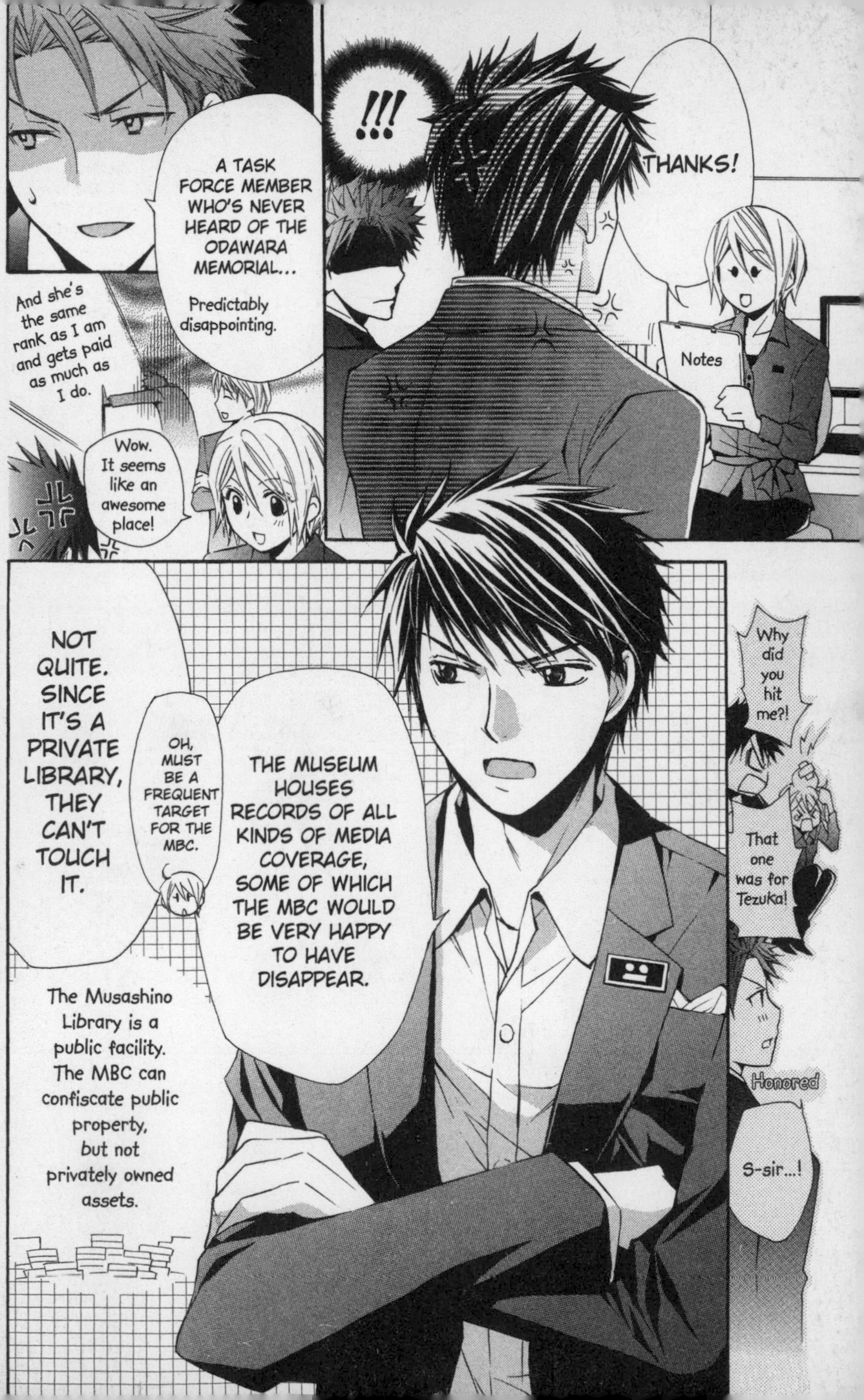
!!!
THANKS!
Notes
A TASK FORCE MEMBER WHO'S NEVER HEARD OF THE ODAWARA MEMORIAL...
Predictably disappointing.
And she's the same rank as I am and gets paid as much as I do.
Wow. It seems like an awesome place!
Why did you hit me?!
That one was for Tezuka!
Honored
S-sir...!
THE MUSEUM HOUSES RECORDS OF ALL KINDS OF MEDIA COVERAGE, SOME OF WHICH THE MBC WOULD BE VERY HAPPY TO HAVE DISAPPEAR.
OH, MUST BE A FREQUENT TARGET FOR THE MBC.
NOT QUITE. SINCE IT'S A PRIVATE LIBRARY, THEY CAN'T TOUCH IT.
The Musashino Library is a public facility. The MBC can confiscate public property, but not privately owned assets.

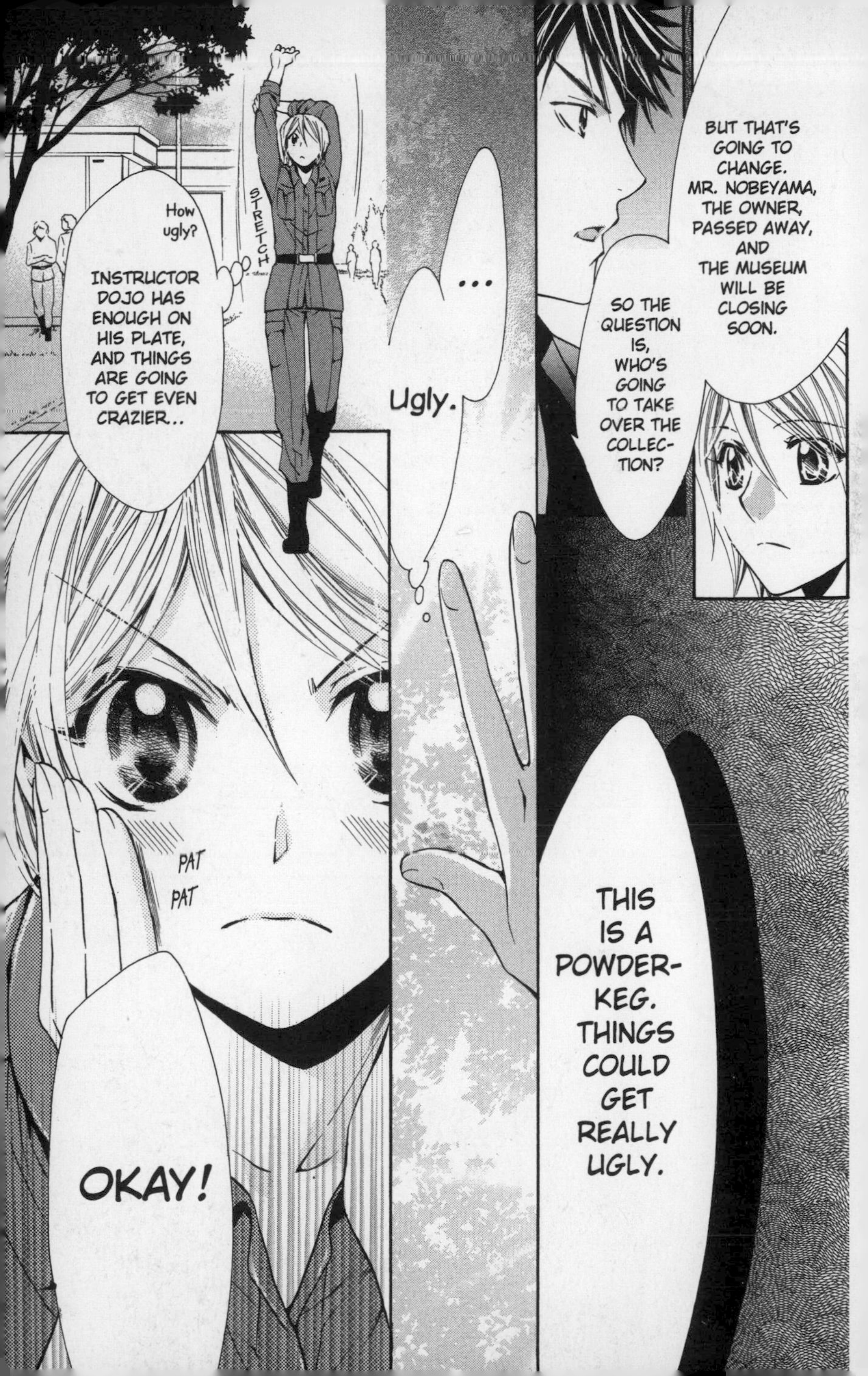
BUT THAT'S GOING TO CHANGE. MR. NOBEYAMA, THE OWNER, PASSED AWAY, AND THE MUSEUM WILL BE CLOSING SOON.
SO THE QUESTION IS, WHO'S GOING TO TAKE OVER THE COLLECTION?
THIS IS A POWDER-KEG. THINGS COULD GET REALLY UGLY.
...
Ugly.
STRETCH
How ugly?
INSTRUCTOR DOJO HAS ENOUGH ON HIS PLATE, AND THINGS ARE GOING TO GET EVEN CRAZIER...
PAT
PAT
OKAY!

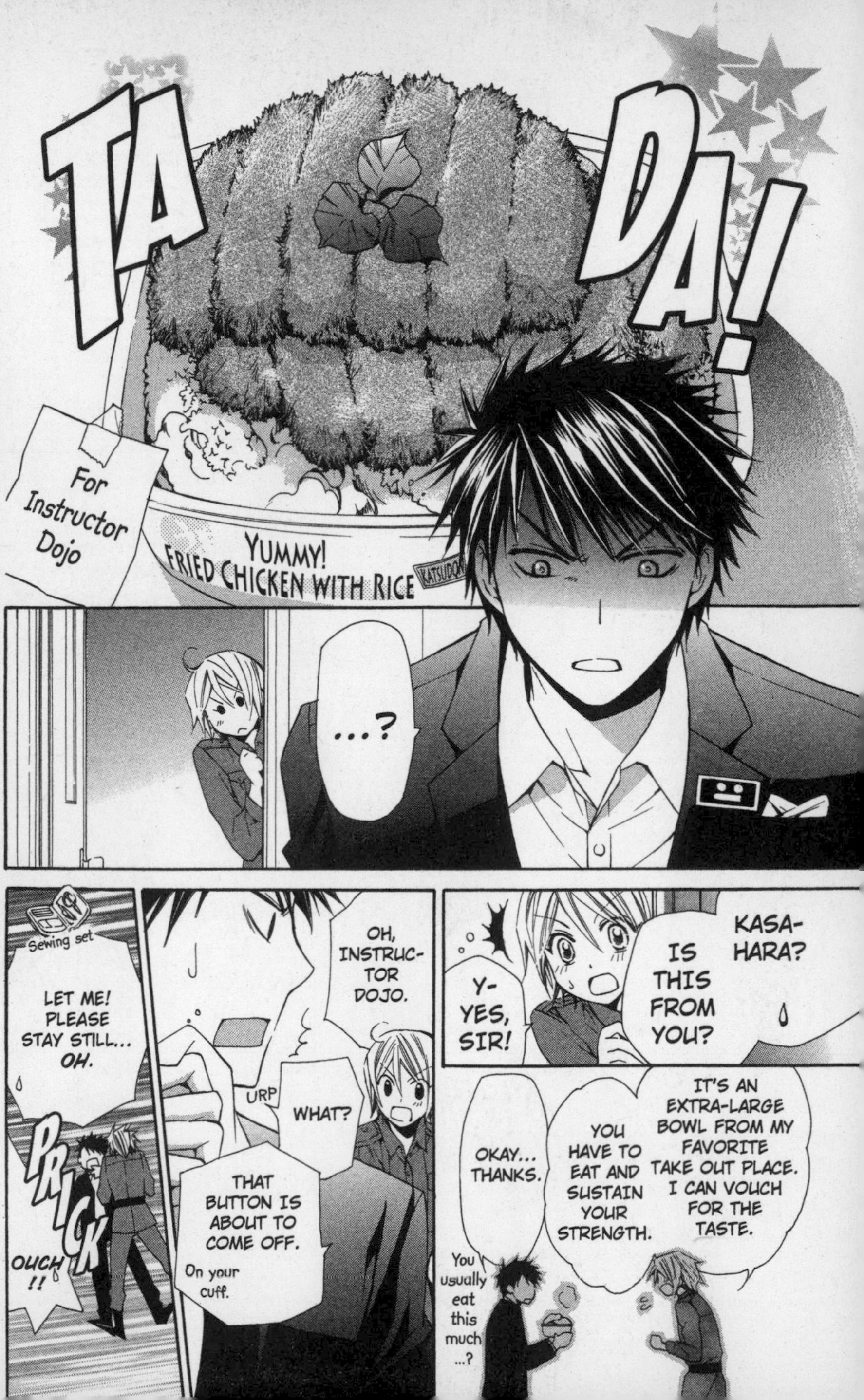

TA DA!
For Instructor Dojo
YUMMY! FRIED CHICKEN WITH RICE
KATSUDON
...?
KASA-HARA? IS THIS FROM YOU?
Y-YES, SIR!
IT'S AN EXTRA-LARGE BOWL FROM MY FAVORITE TAKE OUT PLACE. I CAN VOUCH FOR THE TASTE.
YOU HAVE TO EAT AND SUSTAIN YOUR STRENGTH.
OKAY... THANKS.
You usually eat this much ...?
OH, INSTRUCTOR DOJO.
WHAT?
URP
THAT BUTTON IS ABOUT TO COME OFF.
On your cuff.
Sewing set
LET ME! PLEASE STAY STILL... OH.
PRICK
OUCH!!

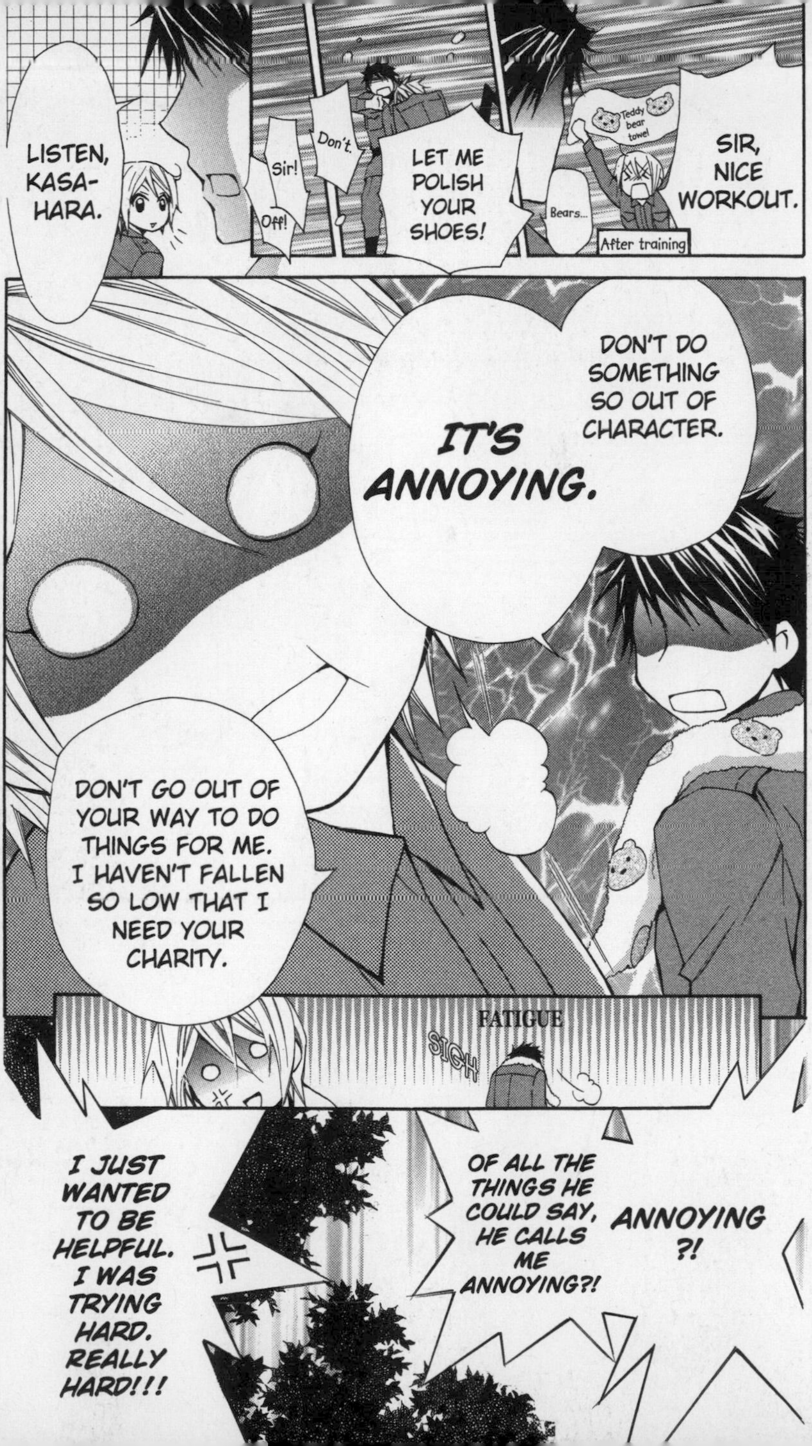
SIR, NICE WORKOUT.
After training
Teddy bear towel
Bears...
LET ME POLISH YOUR SHOES!
Don't.
Sir!
Off!
LISTEN, KASA-HARA.
DON'T DO SOMETHING SO OUT OF CHARACTER.
IT'S ANNOYING.
DON'T GO OUT OF YOUR WAY TO DO THINGS FOR ME. I HAVEN'T FALLEN SO LOW THAT I NEED YOUR CHARITY.
FATIGUE
SIGH
ANNOYING?!
OF ALL THE THINGS HE COULD SAY, HE CALLS ME ANNOYING?!
I JUST WANTED TO BE HELPFUL. I WAS TRYING HARD. REALLY HARD!!!

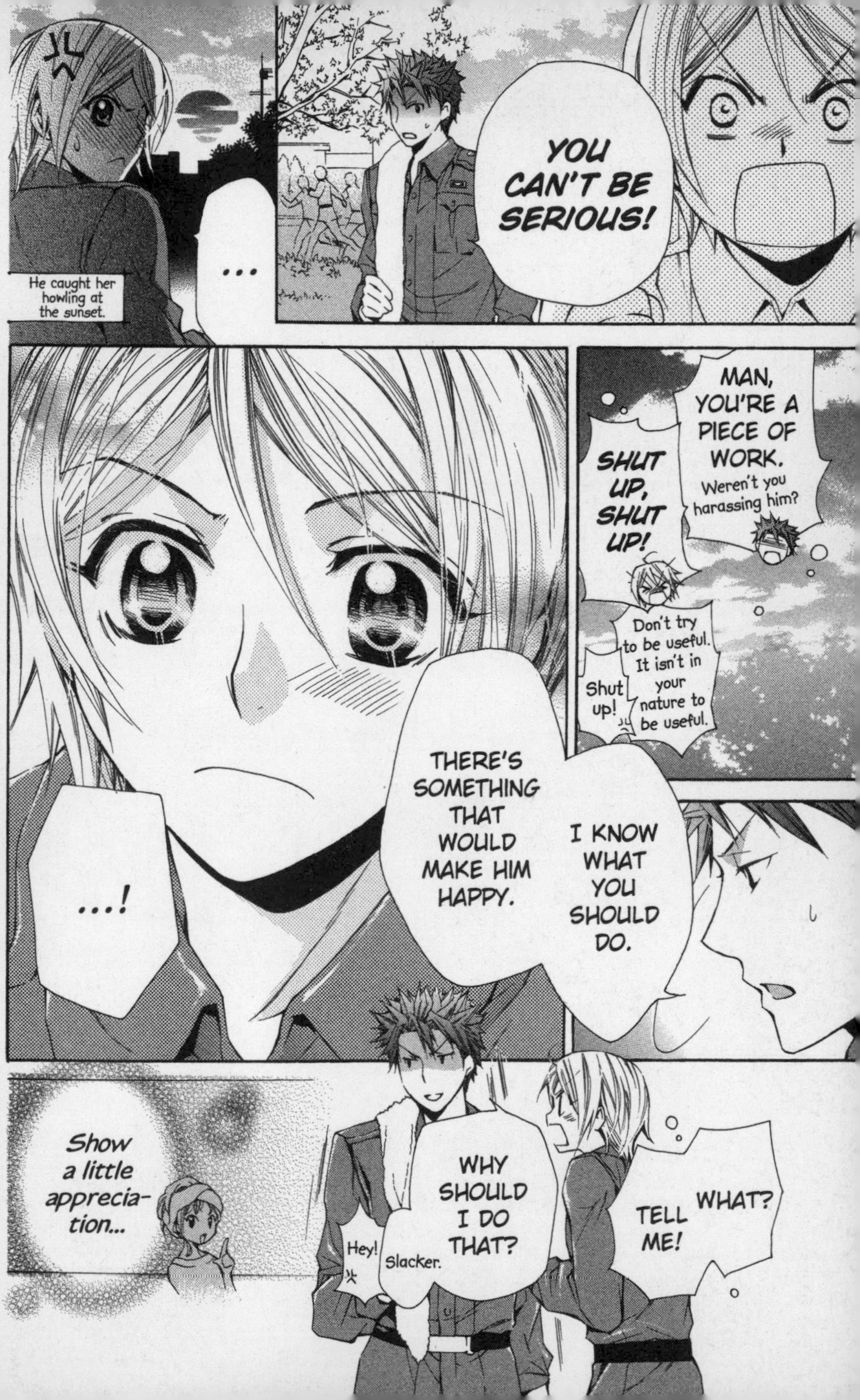
YOU CAN'T BE SERIOUS!
...
He caught her howling at the sunset.
MAN, YOU'RE A PIECE OF WORK.
Weren't you harassing him?
SHUT UP, SHUT UP!
Don't try to be useful. It isn't in your nature to be useful.
Shut up!
I KNOW WHAT YOU SHOULD DO.
THERE'S SOMETHING THAT WOULD MAKE HIM HAPPY.
...!
WHAT?
TELL ME!
WHY SHOULD I DO THAT?
Slacker.
Hey!
Show a little apprecia-tion...

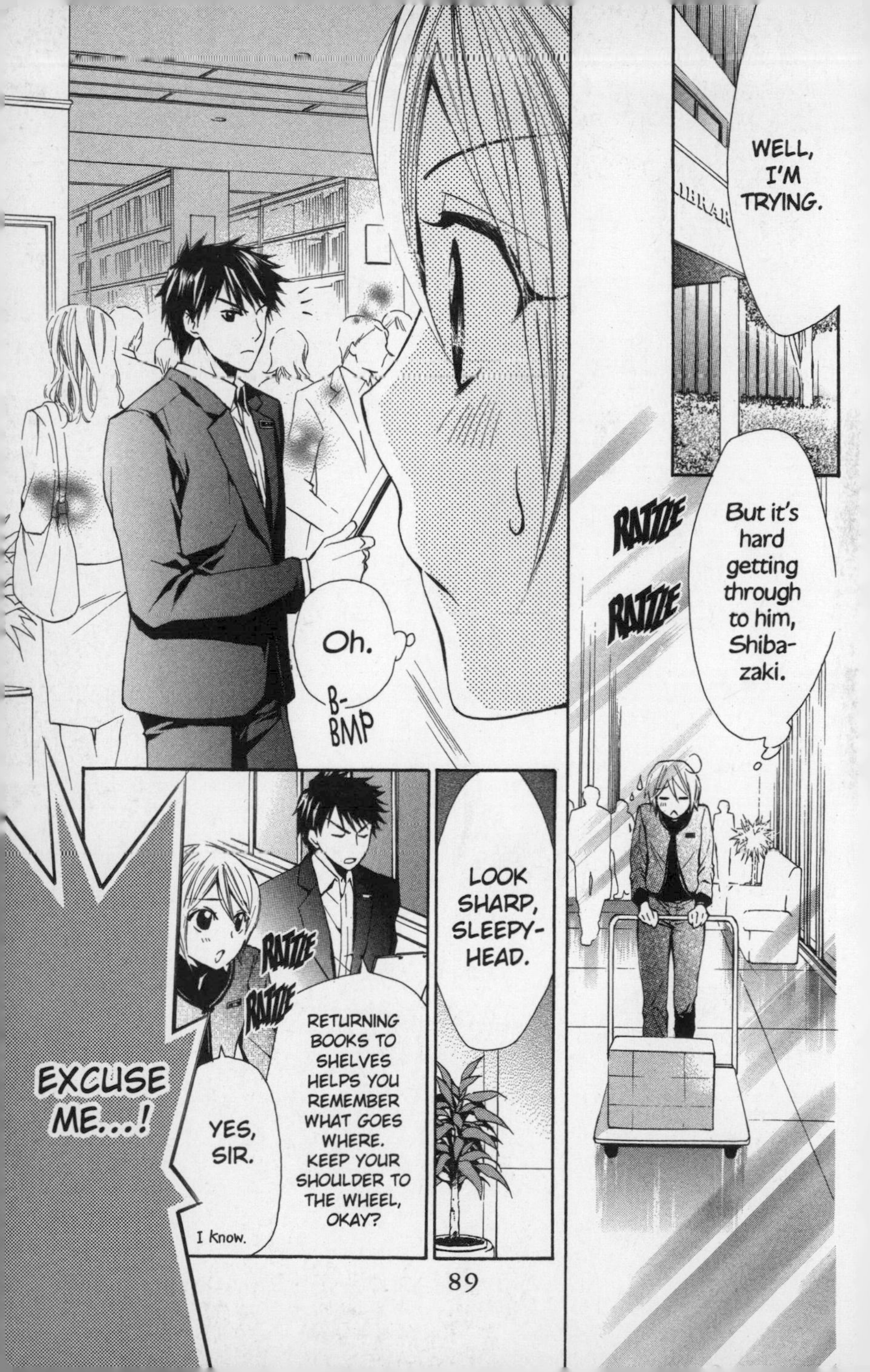
LIBRAR
WELL, I'M TRYING.
RATTLE
RATTLE
But it's hard getting through to him, Shiba-zaki.
Oh.
B-BMP
LOOK SHARP, SLEEPY-HEAD.
RATTLE
RATTLE
RETURNING BOOKS TO SHELVES HELPS YOU REMEMBER WHAT GOES WHERE. KEEP YOUR SHOULDER TO THE WHEEL, OKAY?
YES, SIR.
I know.
EXCUSE ME...!

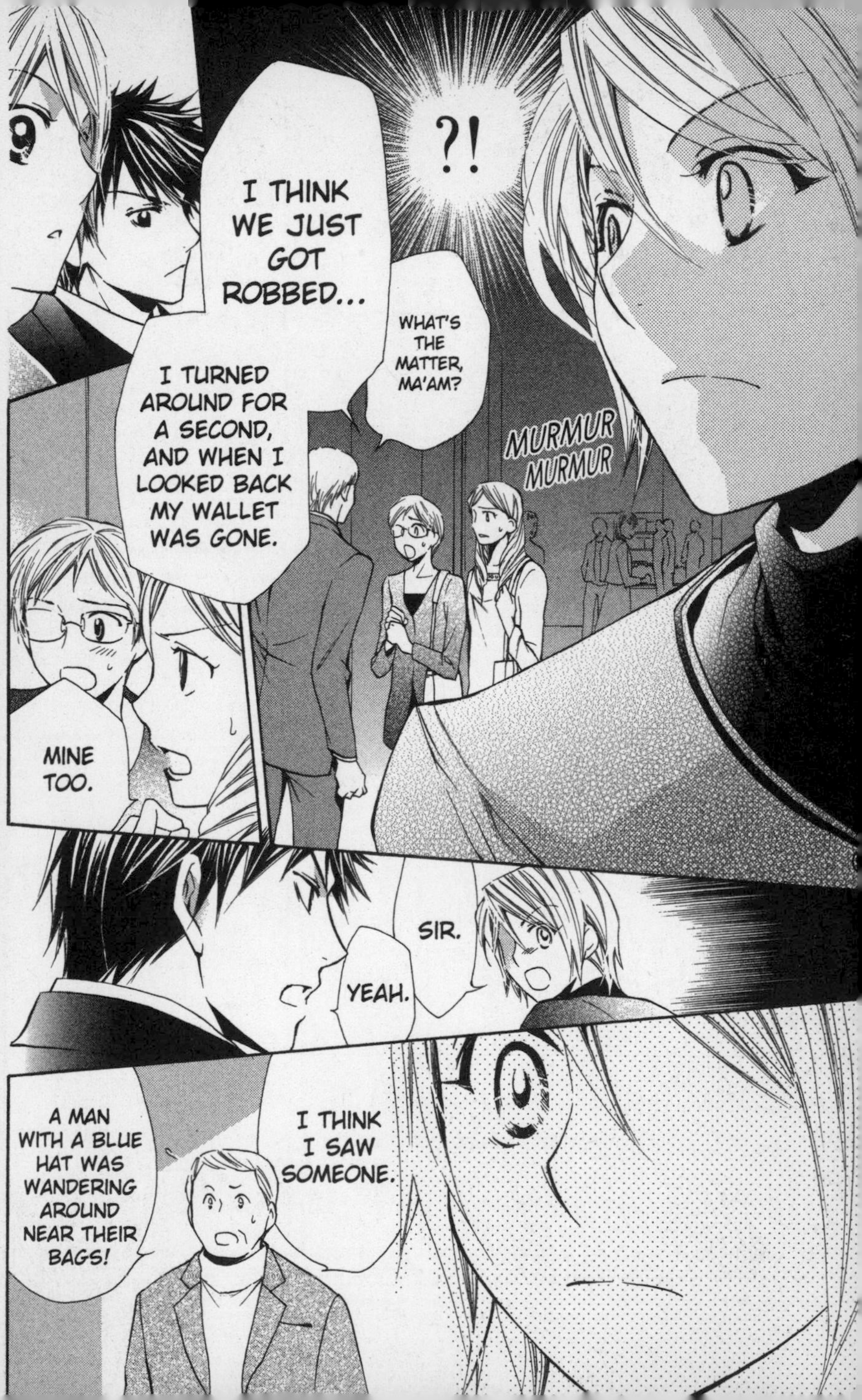
?!
I THINK WE JUST GOT ROBBED...
MURMUR MURMUR
WHAT'S THE MATTER, MA'AM?
I TURNED AROUND FOR A SECOND, AND WHEN I LOOKED BACK MY WALLET WAS GONE.
MINE TOO.
SIR.
YEAH.
I THINK I SAW SOMEONE.
A MAN WITH A BLUE HAT WAS WANDERING AROUND NEAR THEIR BAGS!

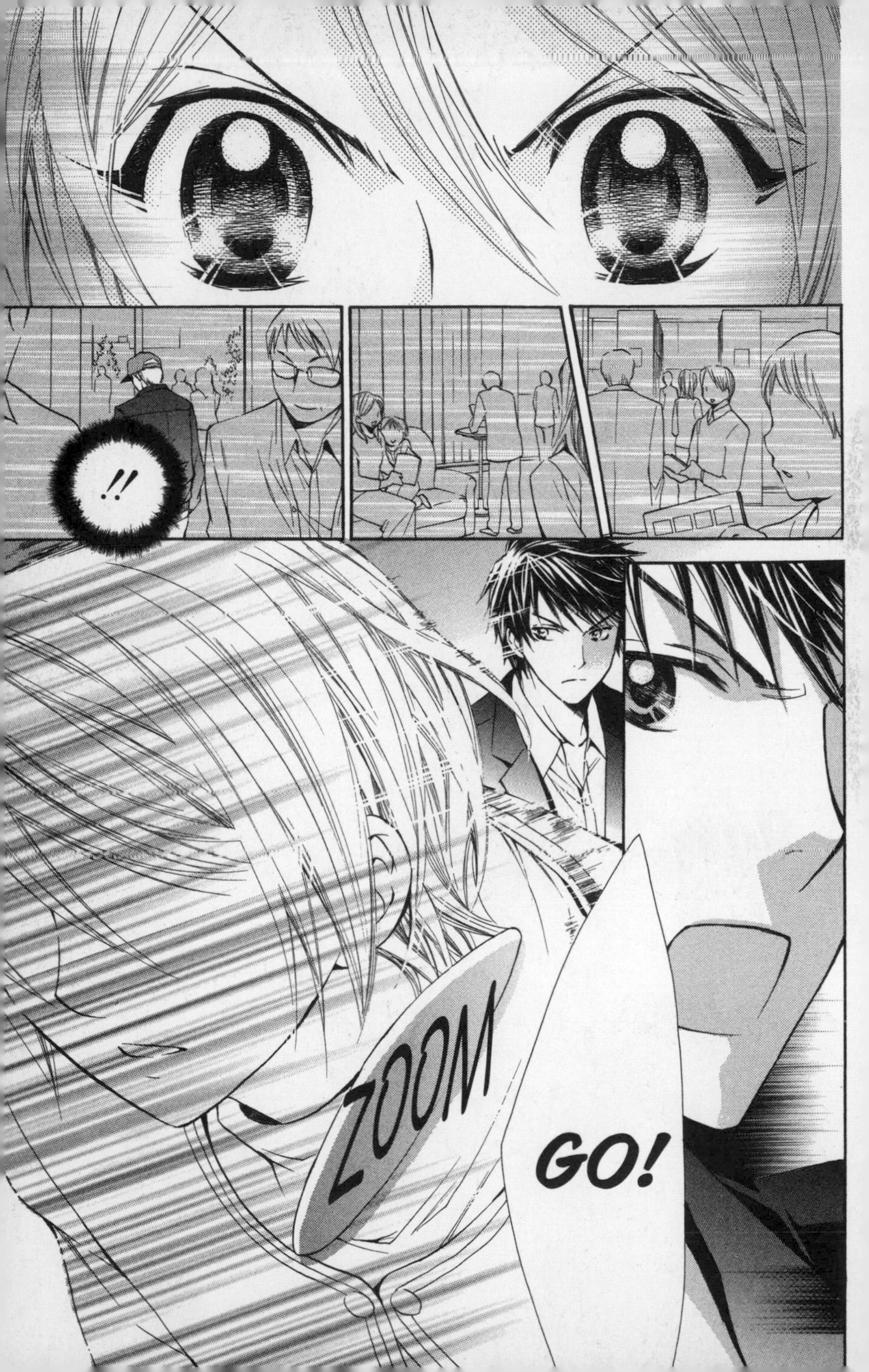
!!
GO!
ZOOM

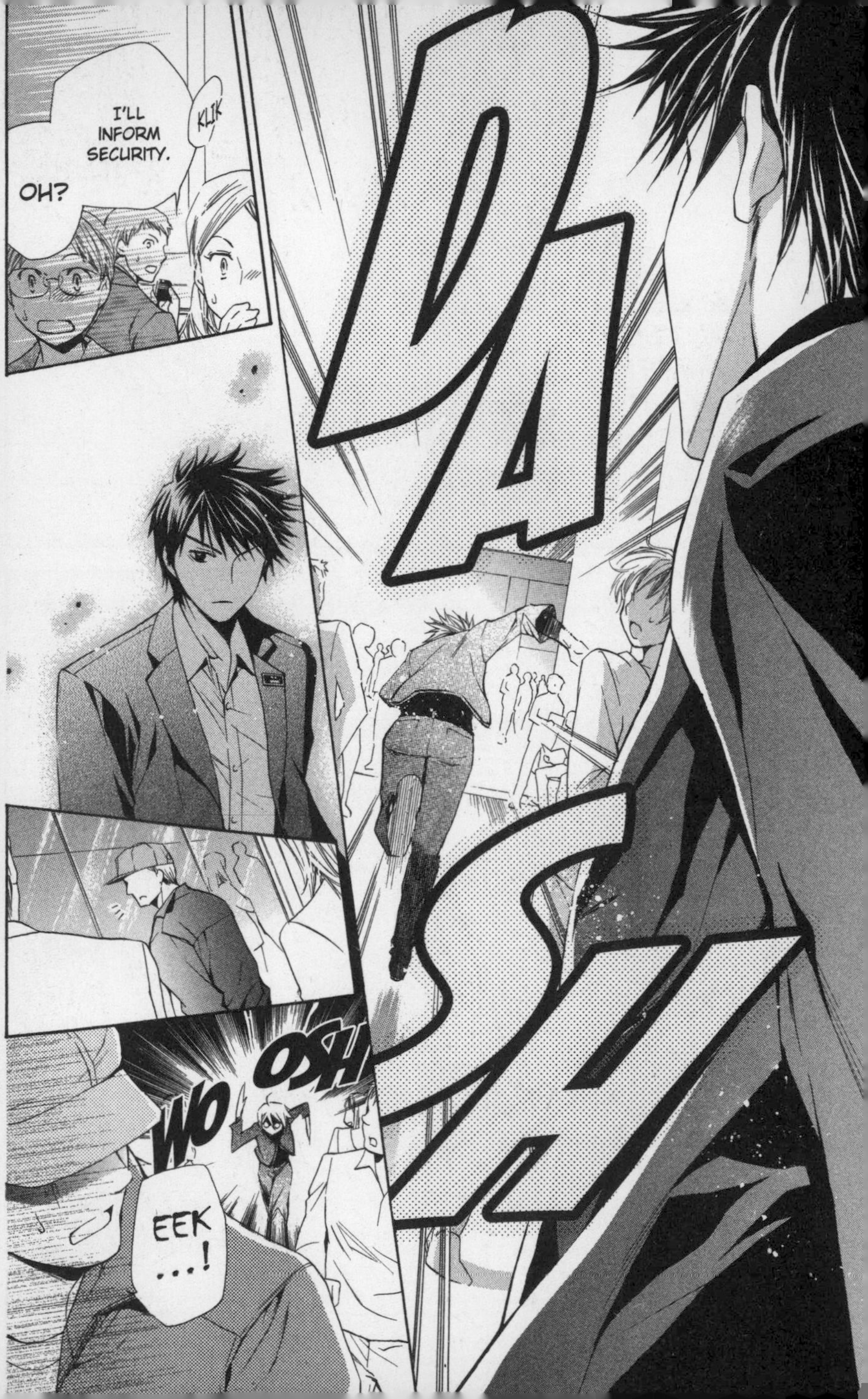
DASH
KLIK
I'LL INFORM SECURITY.
OH?
WOOSH
EEK ...!

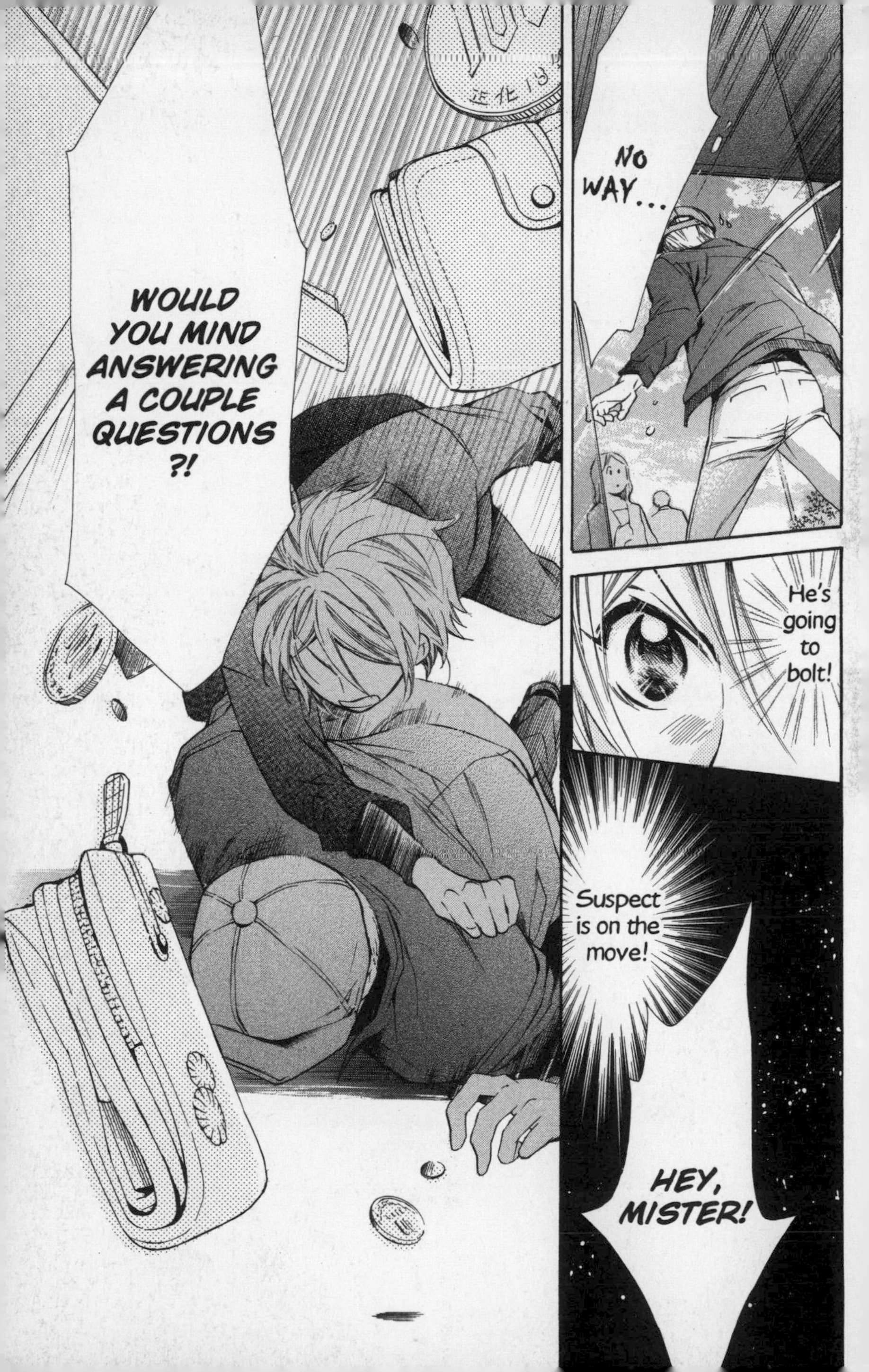
NO WAY...
He's going to bolt!
Suspect is on the move!
HEY, MISTER!
WOULD YOU MIND ANSWERING A COUPLE QUESTIONS ?!

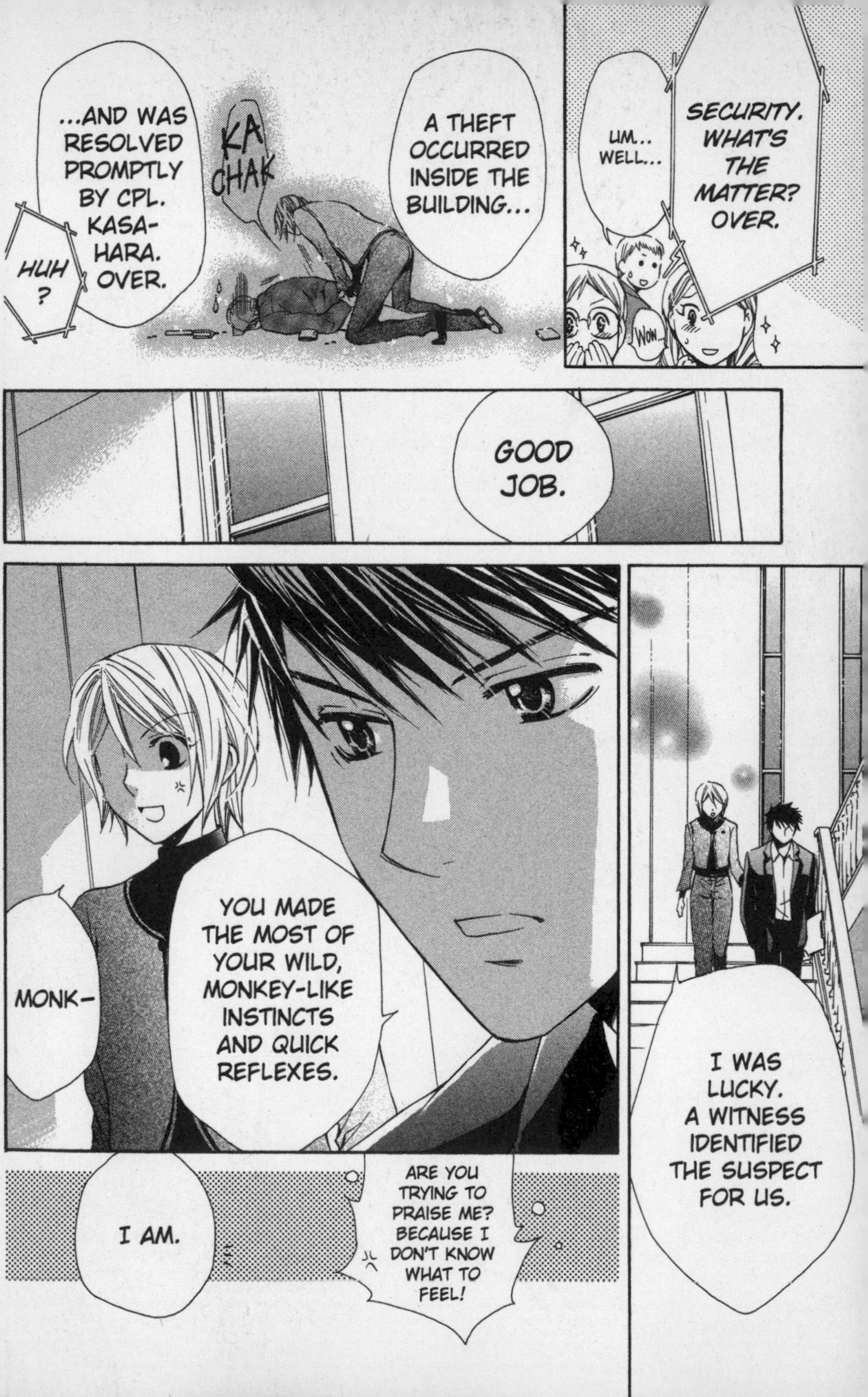
SECURITY. WHAT'S THE MATTER? OVER.
UM... WELL...
WOW...
A THEFT OCCURRED INSIDE THE BUILDING...
KA CHAK
...AND WAS RESOLVED PROMPTLY BY CPL. KASA-HARA. OVER.
HUH?
GOOD JOB.
I WAS LUCKY. A WITNESS IDENTIFIED THE SUSPECT FOR US.
YOU MADE THE MOST OF YOUR WILD, MONKEY-LIKE INSTINCTS AND QUICK REFLEXES.
MONK-
ARE YOU TRYING TO PRAISE ME? BECAUSE I DON'T KNOW WHAT TO FEEL!
I AM.

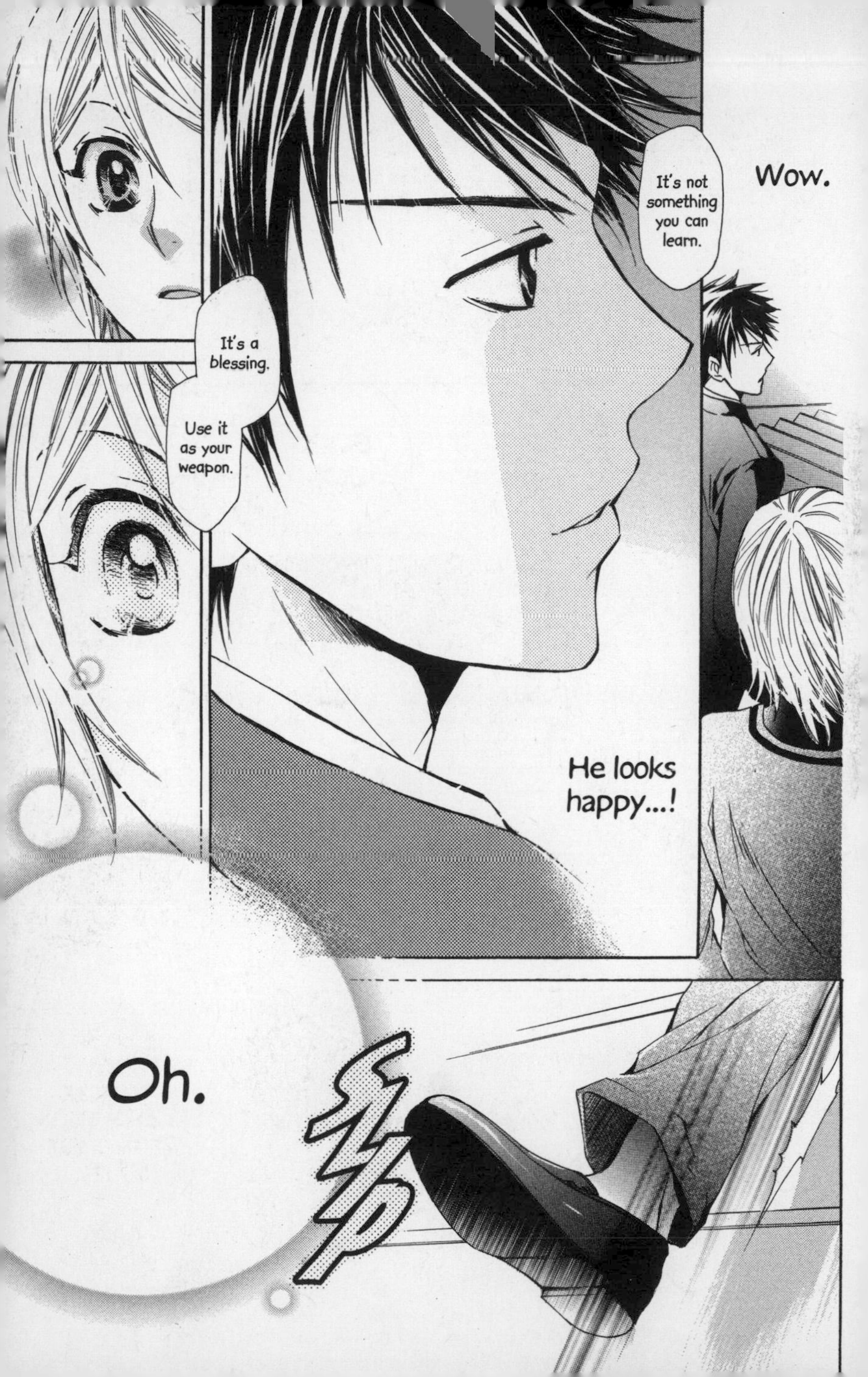
It's not something you can learn.
Wow.
It's a blessing.
Use it as your weapon.
He looks happy...!
SLIP
Oh.

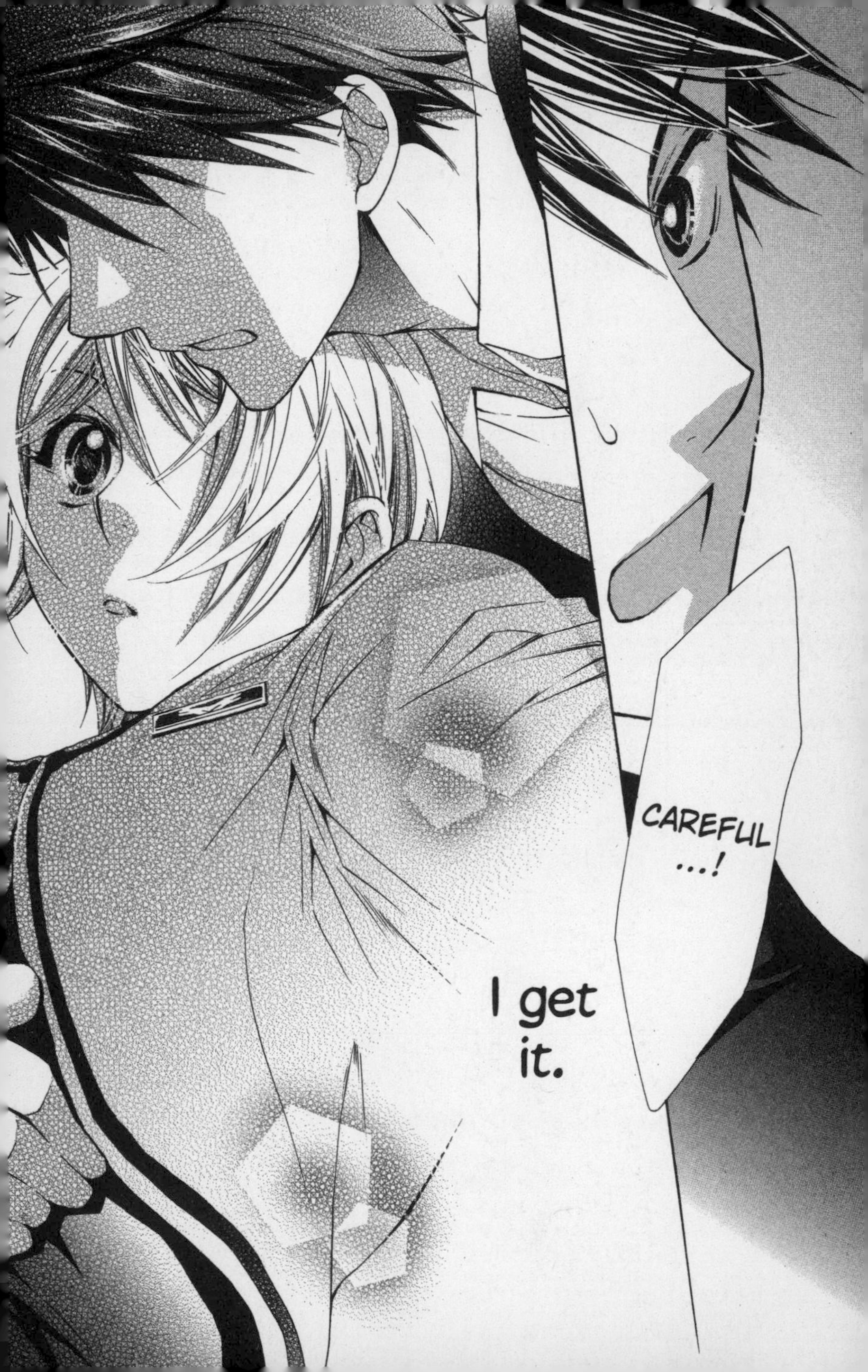
CAREFUL ...!
I get it.

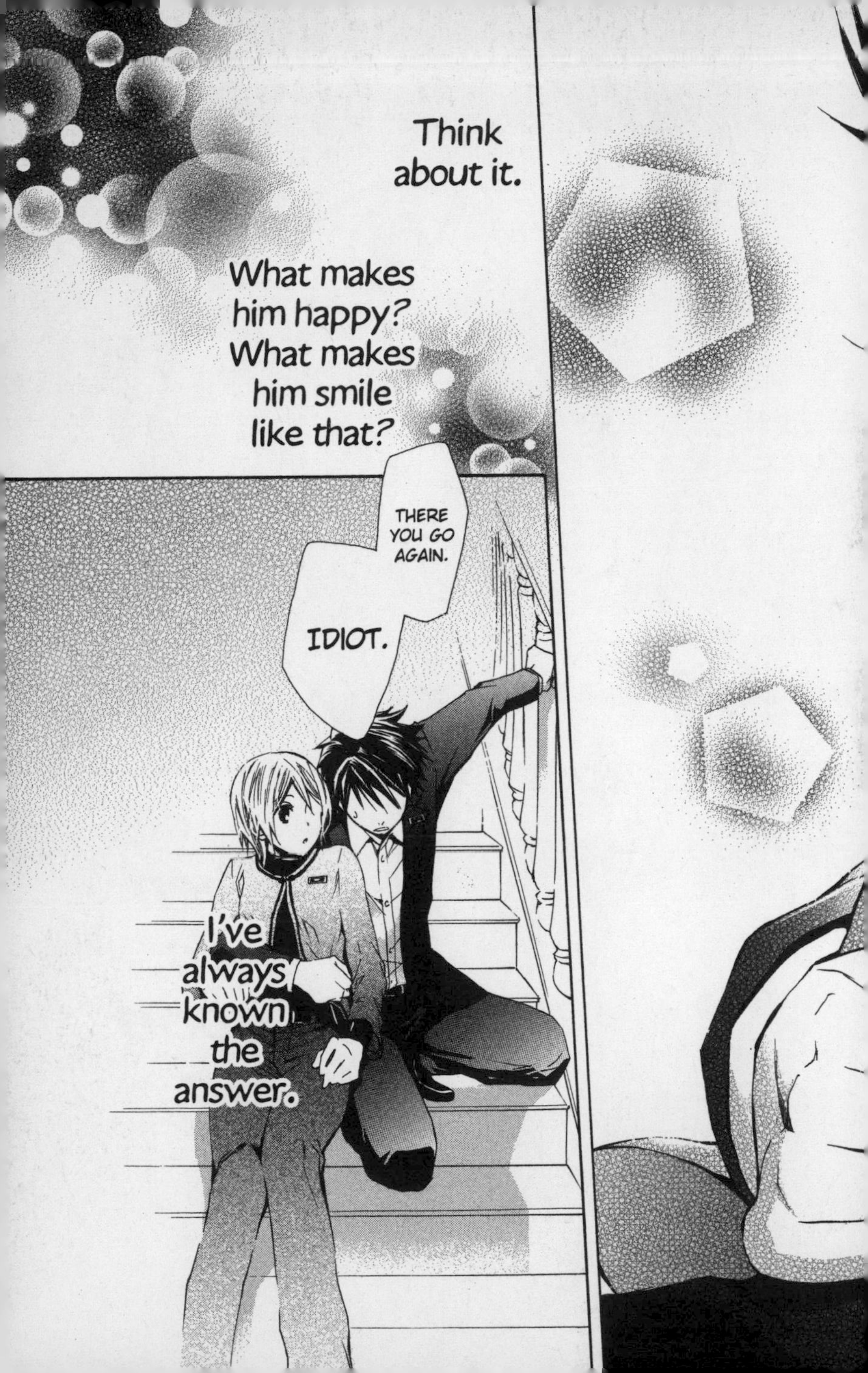
Think about it.
What makes him happy? What makes him smile like that?
THERE YOU GO AGAIN.
IDIOT.
I've always known the answer.

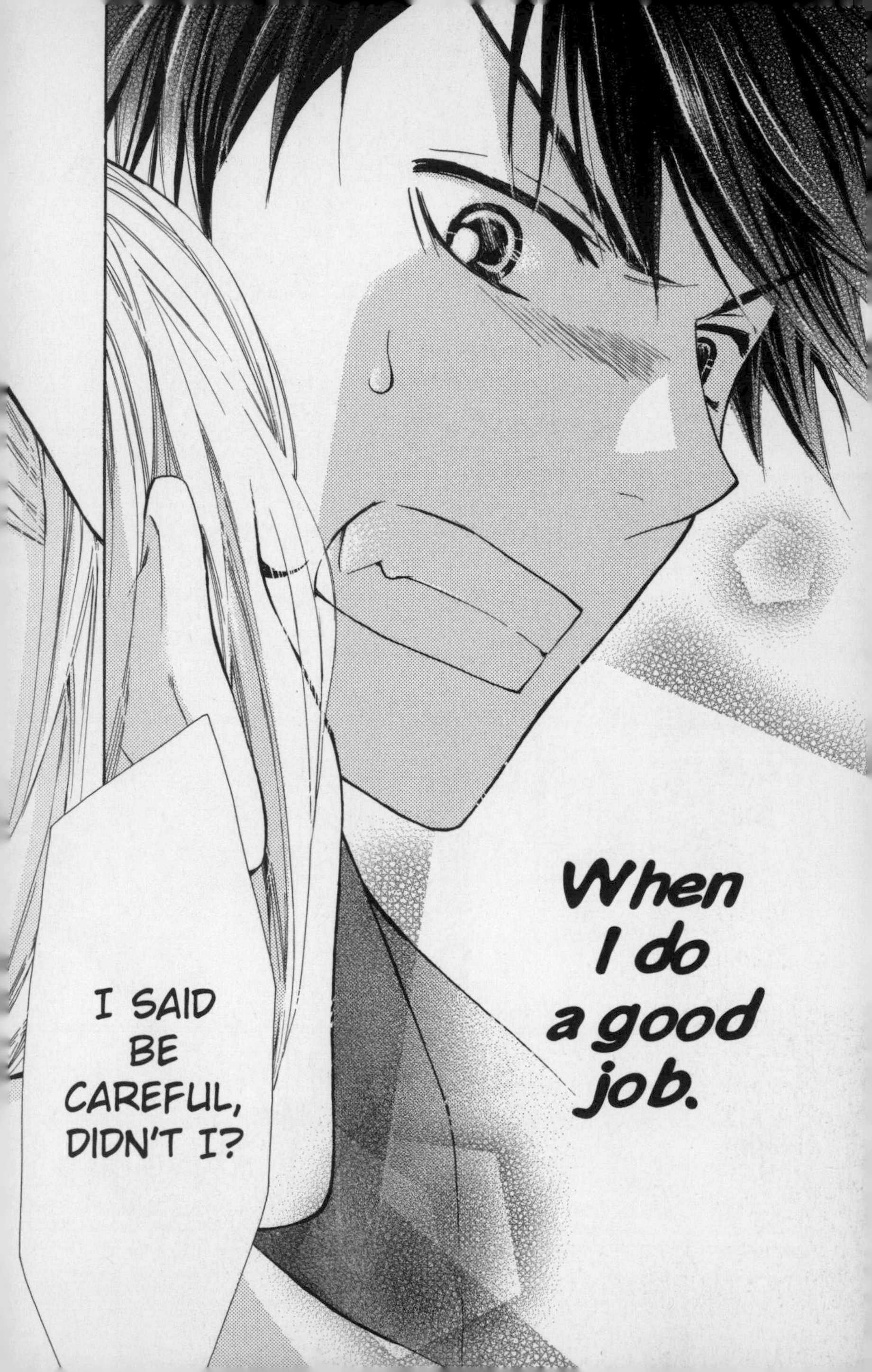
When I do a good job.
I SAID BE CAREFUL, DIDN'T I?

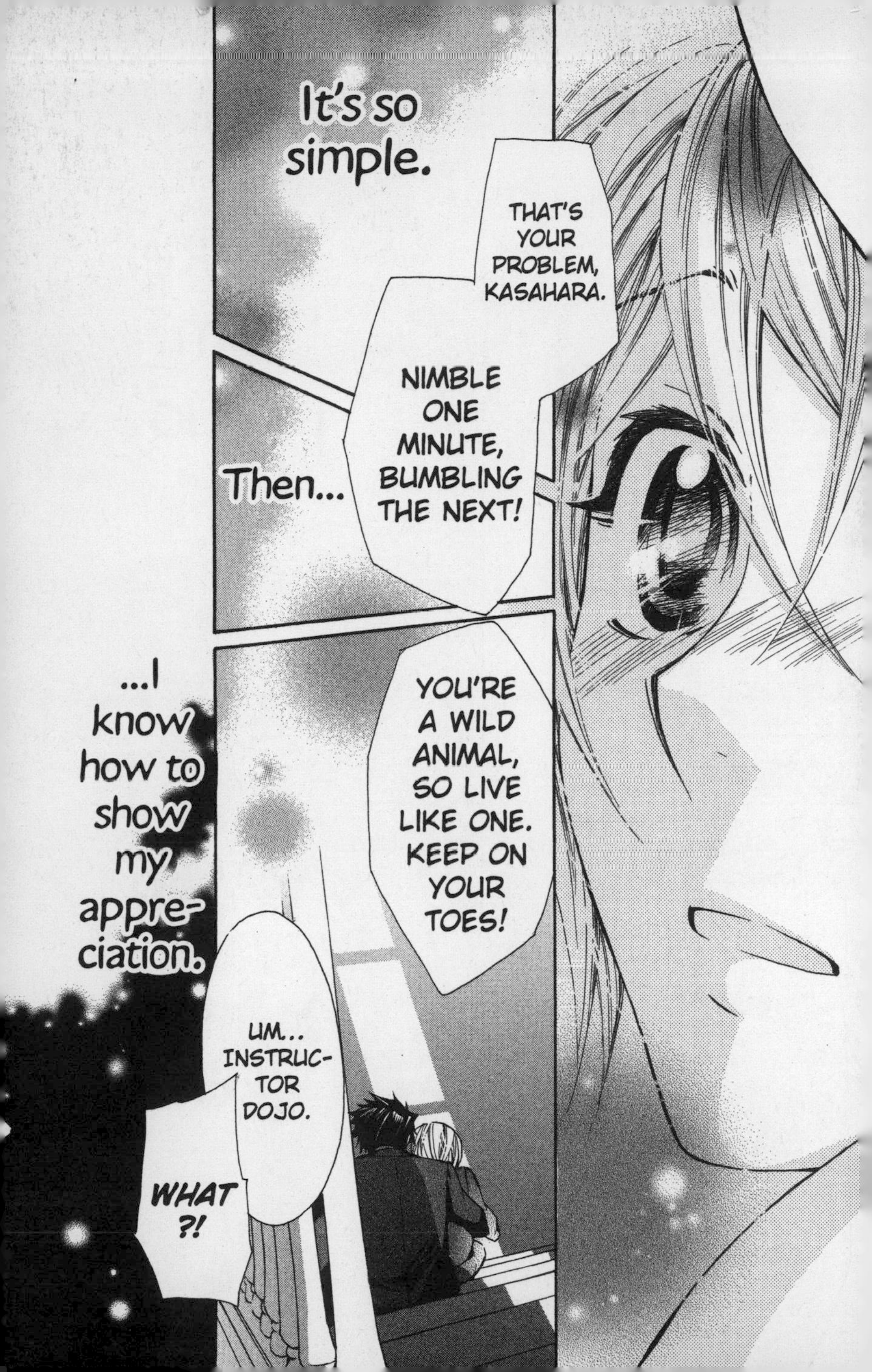
THAT'S YOUR PROBLEM, KASAHARA.
NIMBLE ONE MINUTE, BUMBLING THE NEXT!
YOU'RE A WILD ANIMAL, SO LIVE LIKE ONE. KEEP ON YOUR TOES!
It's so simple.
Then...
...I know how to show my appre-ciation.
UM... INSTRUC-TOR DOJO.
WHAT?!

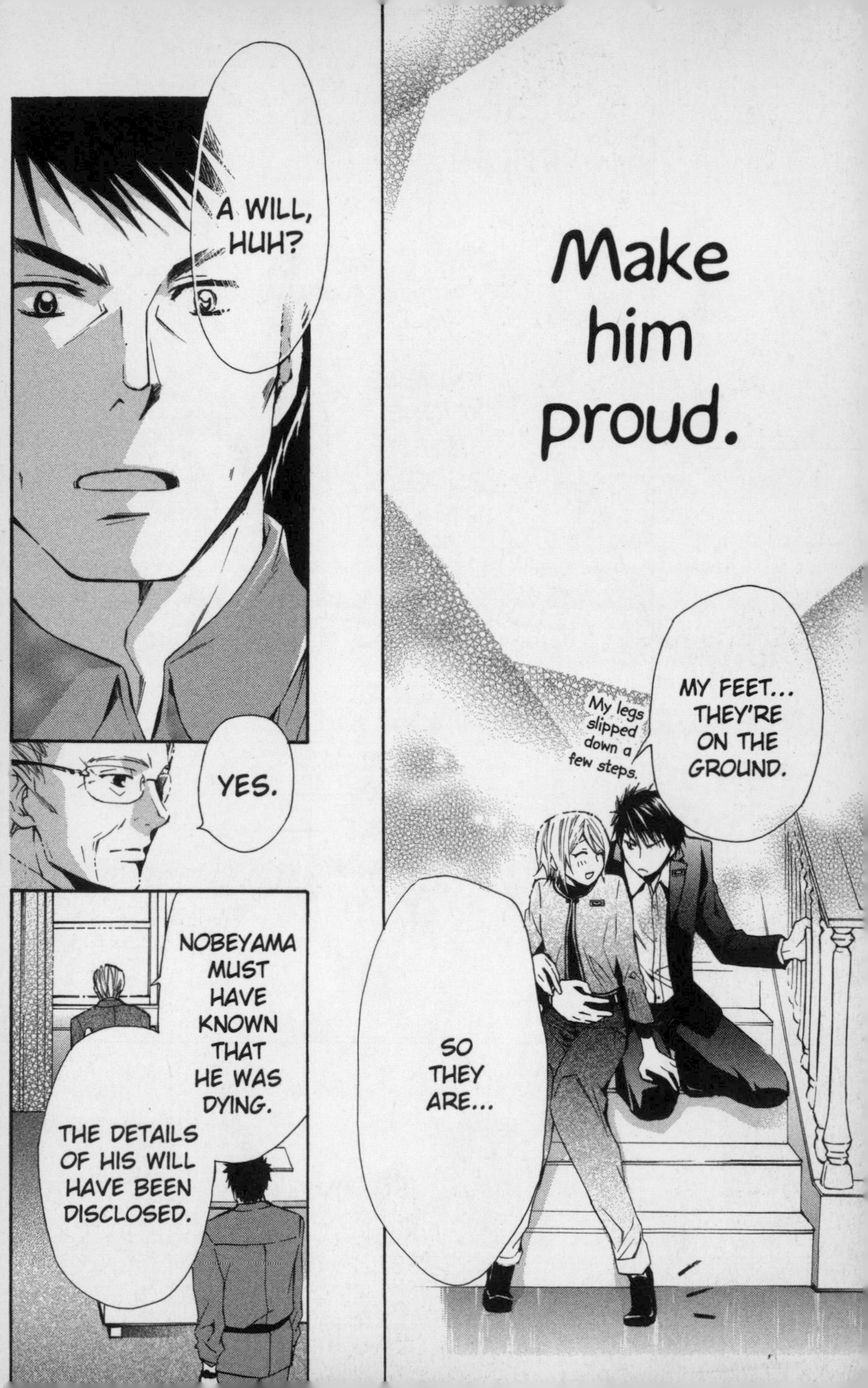
Make him proud.
MY FEET... THEY'RE ON THE GROUND.
My legs slipped down a few steps.
SO THEY ARE...
A WILL, HUH?
YES.
NOBEYAMA MUST HAVE KNOWN THAT HE WAS DYING.
THE DETAILS OF HIS WILL HAVE BEEN DISCLOSED.

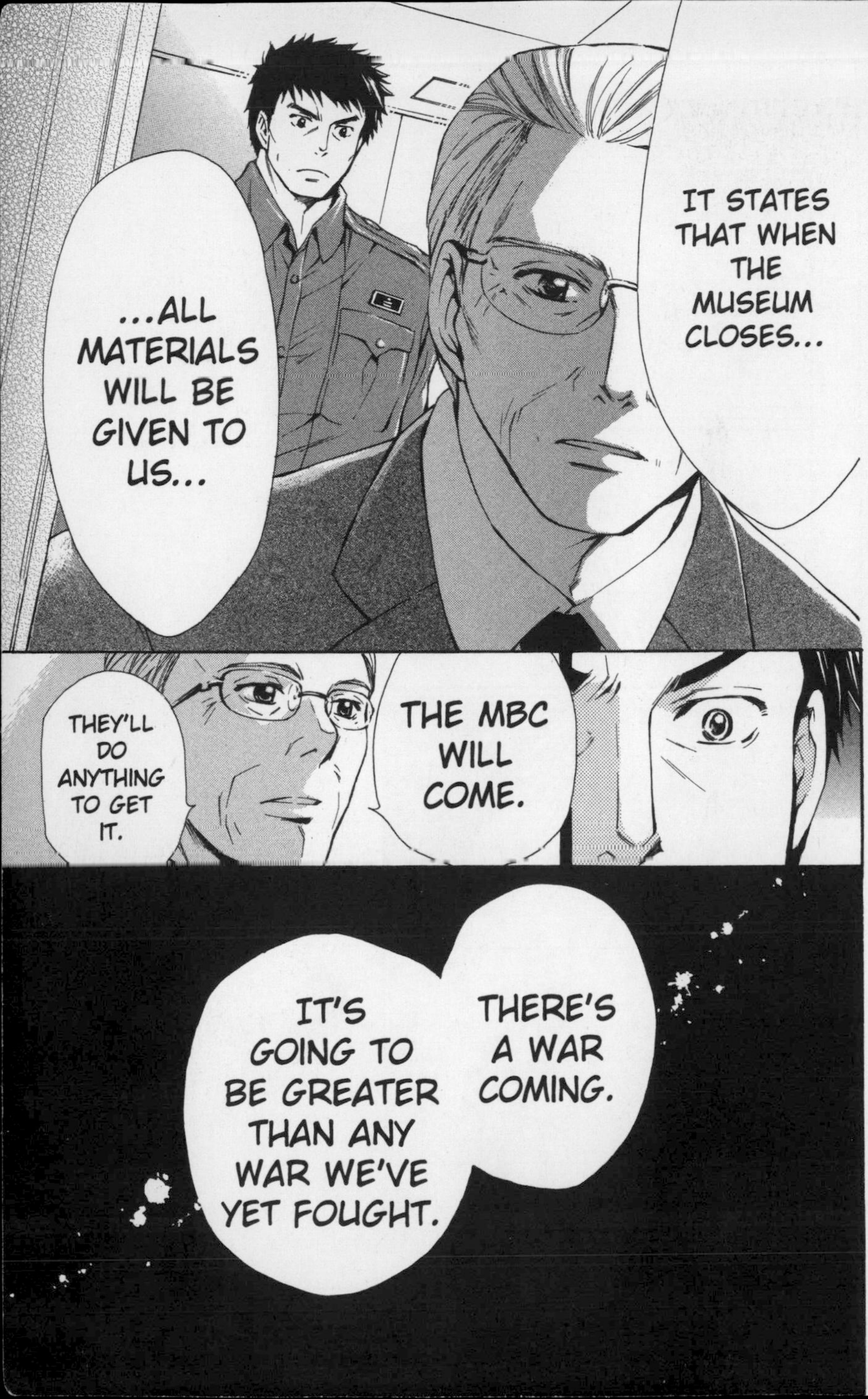
IT STATES THAT WHEN THE MUSEUM CLOSES...
...ALL MATERIALS WILL BE GIVEN TO US...
THE MBC WILL COME.
THEY'LL DO ANYTHING TO GET IT.
THERE'S A WAR COMING.
IT'S GOING TO BE GREATER THAN ANY WAR WE'VE YET FOUGHT.

Secret admirer part 2

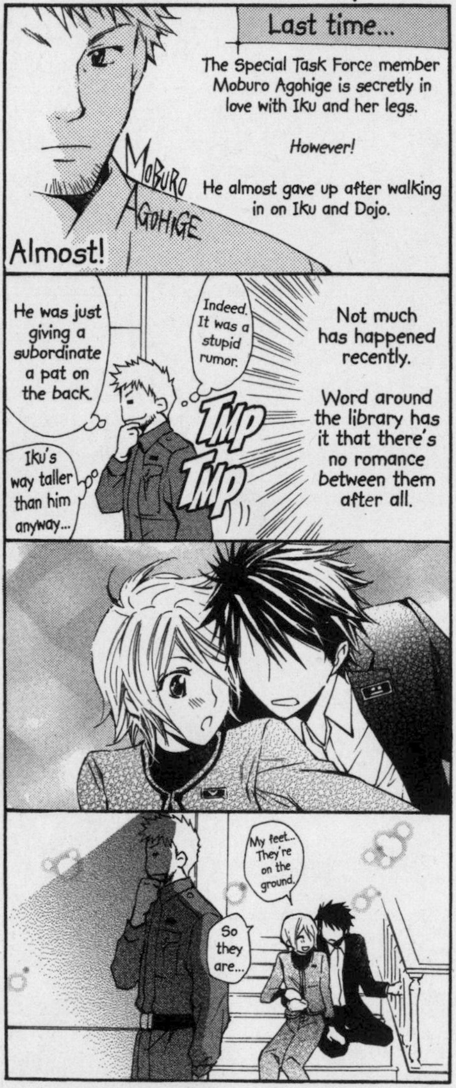
Last time...
The Special Task Force member Moburo Agohige is secretly in love with Iku and her legs.
However!
He almost gave up after walking in on Iku and Dojo.
MOBURO AGOHIGE
Almost!
Not much has happened recently.
Word around the library has it that there's no romance between them after all.
Indeed. It was a stupid rumor.
TMP TMP
He was just giving a subordinate a pat on the back.
Iku's way taller than him anyway...
My feet... They're on the ground.
So they are...

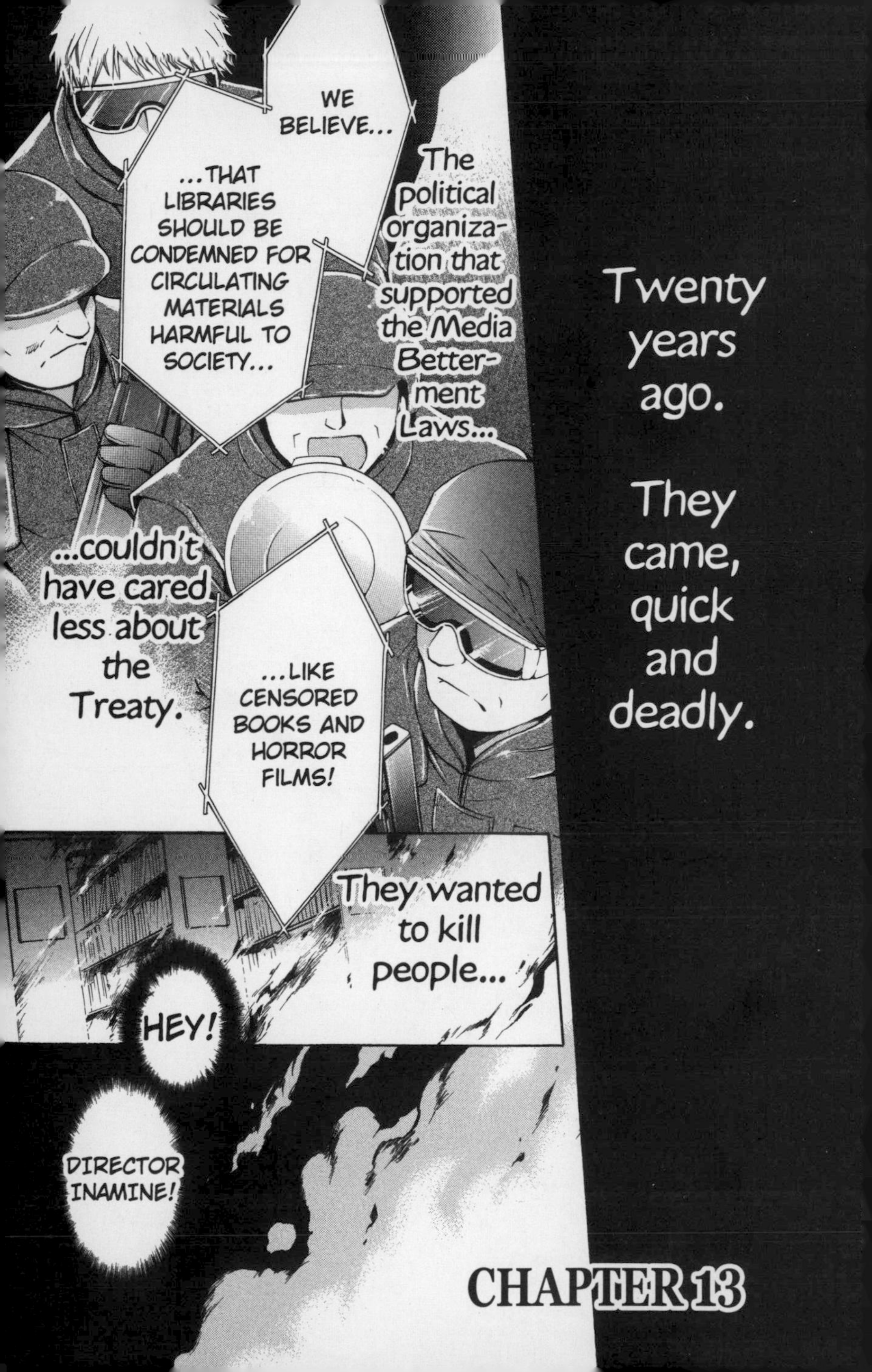
Twenty years ago.
They came, quick and deadly.
The political organization that supported the Media Betterment Laws...
...couldn't have cared less about the Treaty.
WE BELIEVE...
...THAT LIBRARIES SHOULD BE CONDEMNED FOR CIRCULATING MATERIALS HARMFUL TO SOCIETY...
...LIKE CENSORED BOOKS AND HORROR FILMS!
They wanted to kill people...
HEY!
DIRECTOR INAMINE!
CHAPTER 13

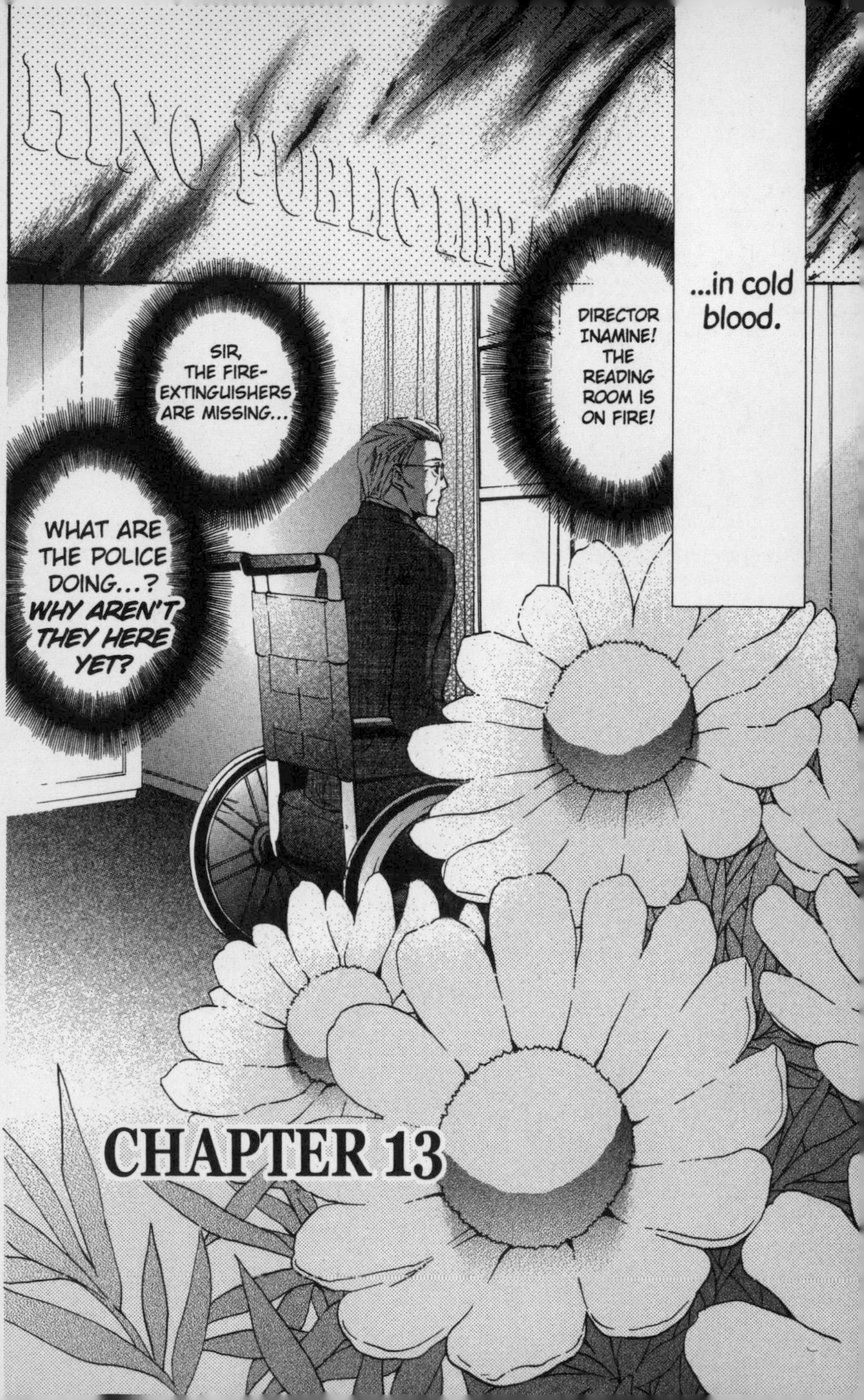
...in cold blood.
DIRECTOR INAMINE! THE READING ROOM IS ON FIRE!
SIR, THE FIRE-EXTINGUISHERS ARE MISSING...
WHAT ARE THE POLICE DOING...? WHY AREN'T THEY HERE YET?
CHAPTER 13

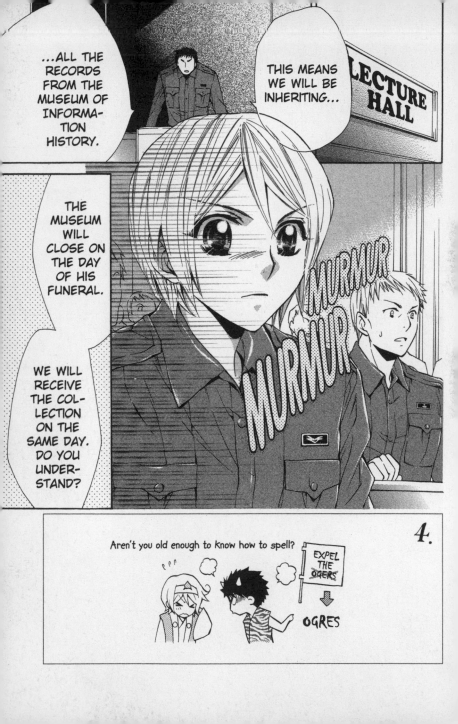

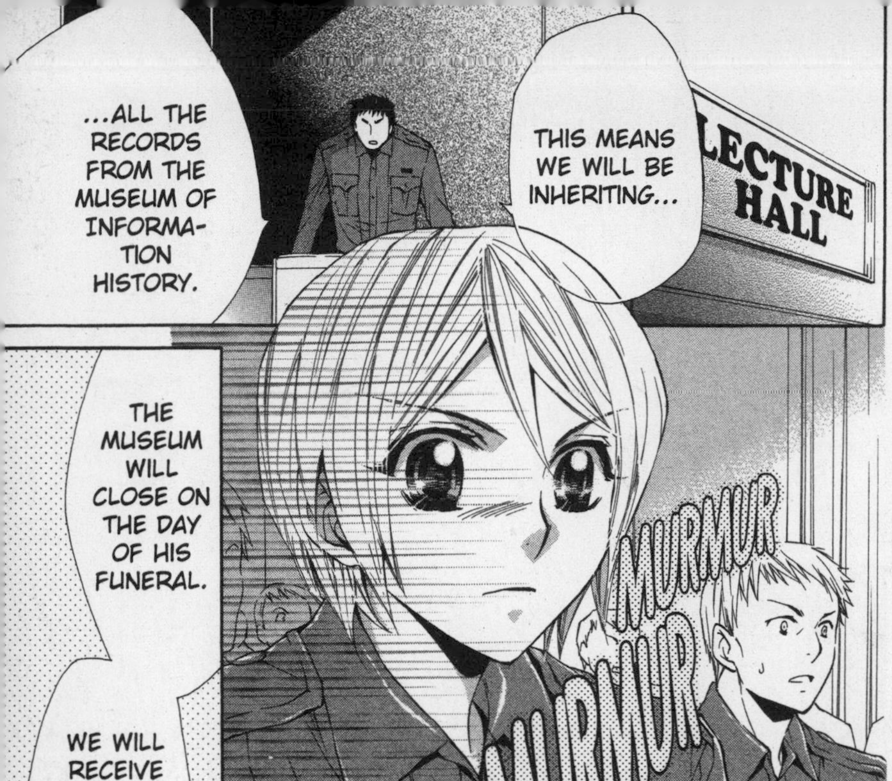
THIS MEANS WE WILL BE INHERITING...
LECTURE HALL
...ALL THE RECORDS FROM THE MUSEUM OF INFORMATION HISTORY.
MURMUR MURMUR
MURMUR
THE MUSEUM WILL CLOSE ON THE DAY OF HIS FUNERAL.
WE WILL RECEIVE THE COLLECTION ON THE SAME DAY. DO YOU UNDERSTAND?

4.

Aren't you old enough to know how to spell?

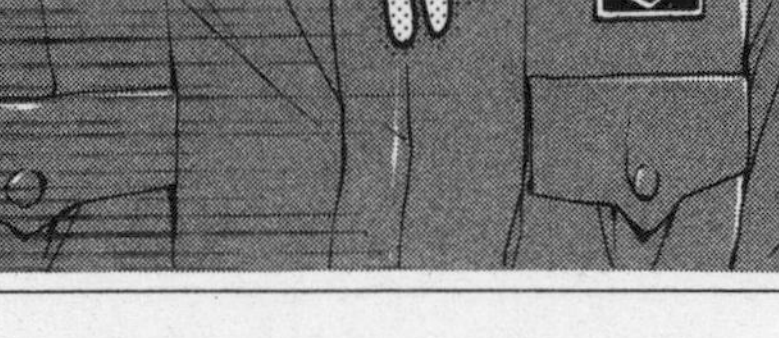
EXPEL THE OGERS
OGRES

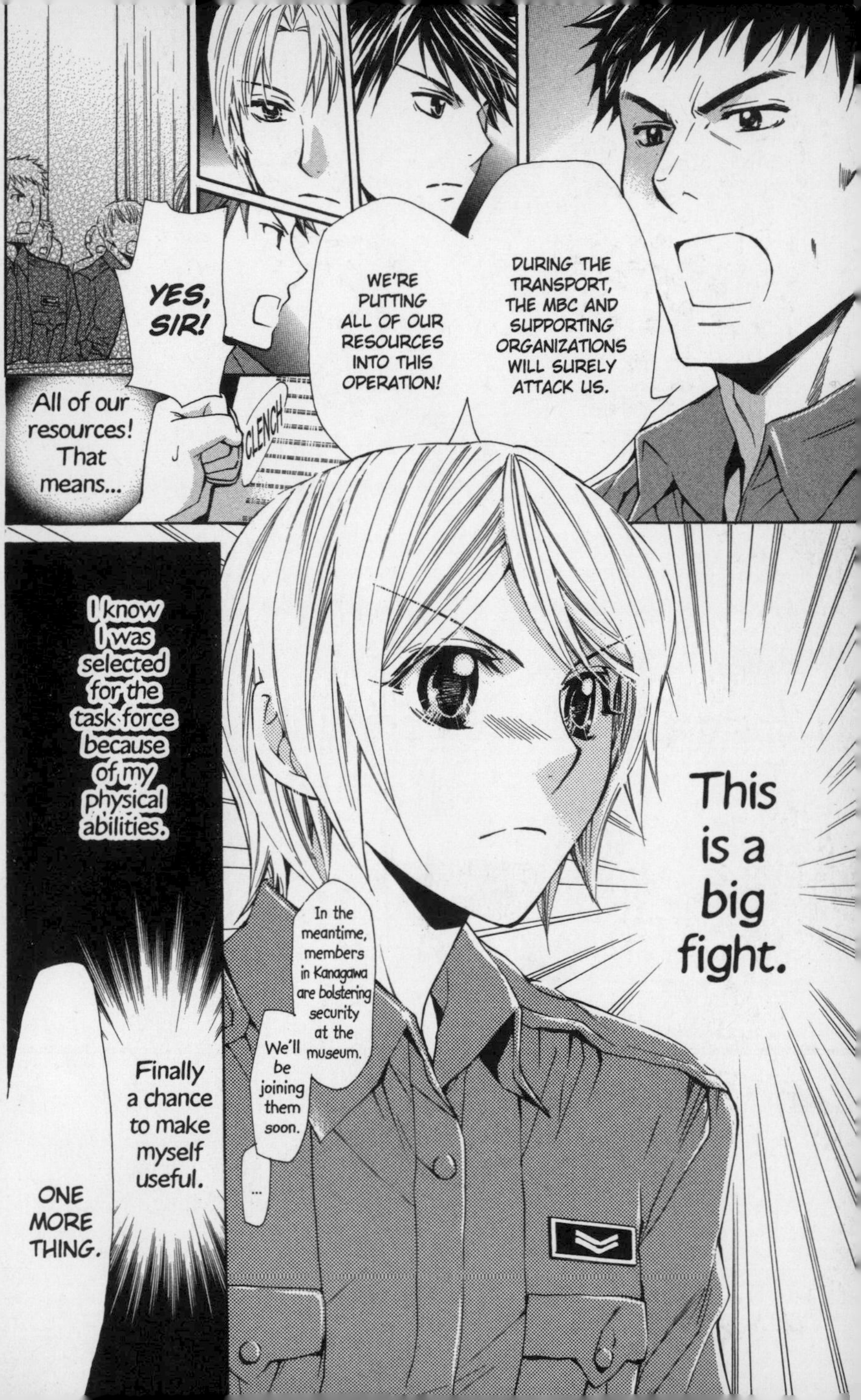
DURING THE TRANSPORT, THE MBC AND SUPPORTING ORGANIZATIONS WILL SURELY ATTACK US.
WE'RE PUTTING ALL OF OUR RESOURCES INTO THIS OPERATION!
YES, SIR!
CLENCH
All of our resources! That means...
This is a big fight.
I know I was selected for the task force because of my physical abilities.
In the meantime, members in Kanagawa are bolstering security at the museum.
We'll be joining them soon.
...
Finally a chance to make myself useful.
ONE MORE THING.

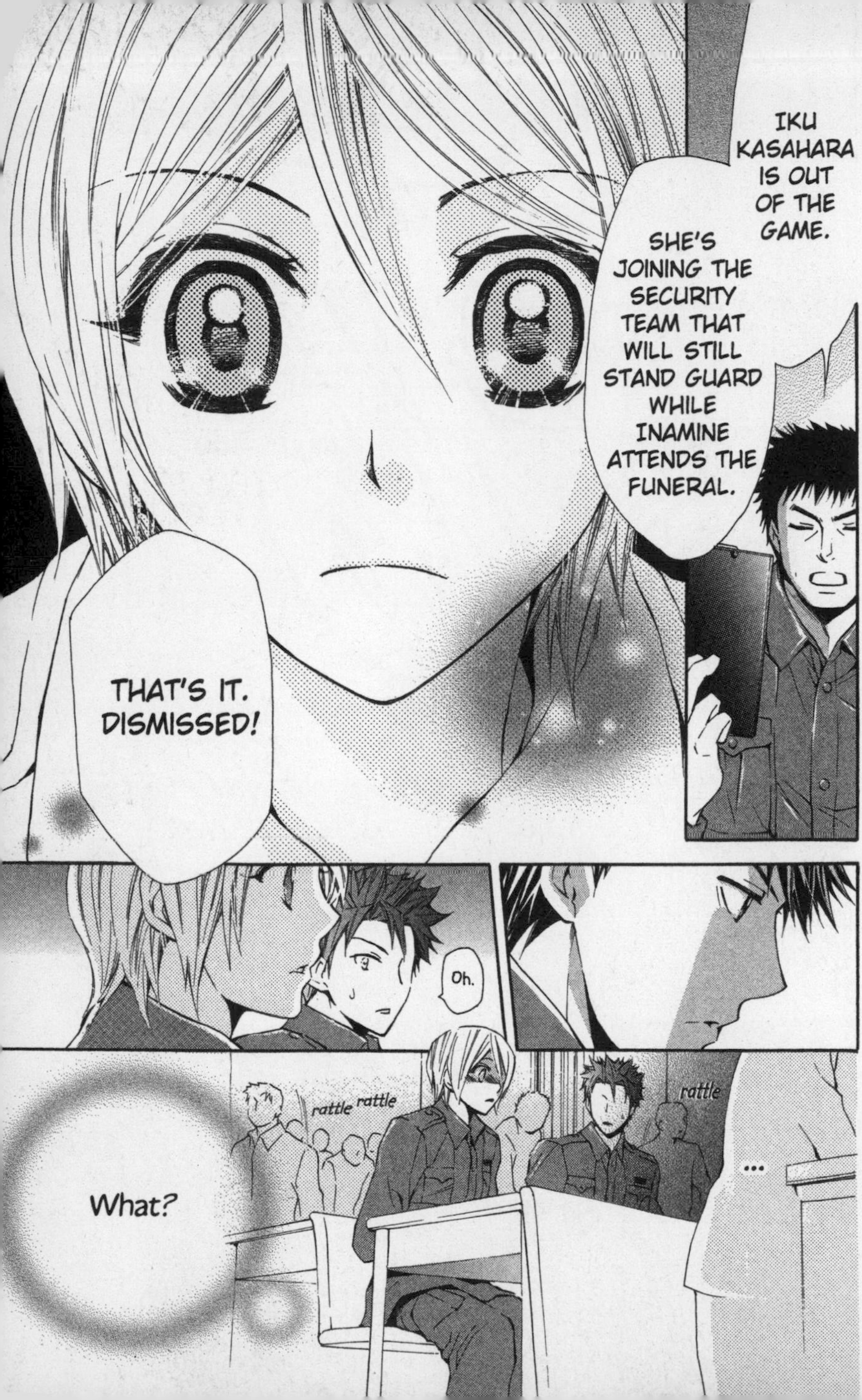
IKU KASAHARA IS OUT OF THE GAME.
SHE'S JOINING THE SECURITY TEAM THAT WILL STILL STAND GUARD WHILE INAMINE ATTENDS THE FUNERAL.
THAT'S IT. DISMISSED!
Oh.
...
rattle
rattle rattle
What?

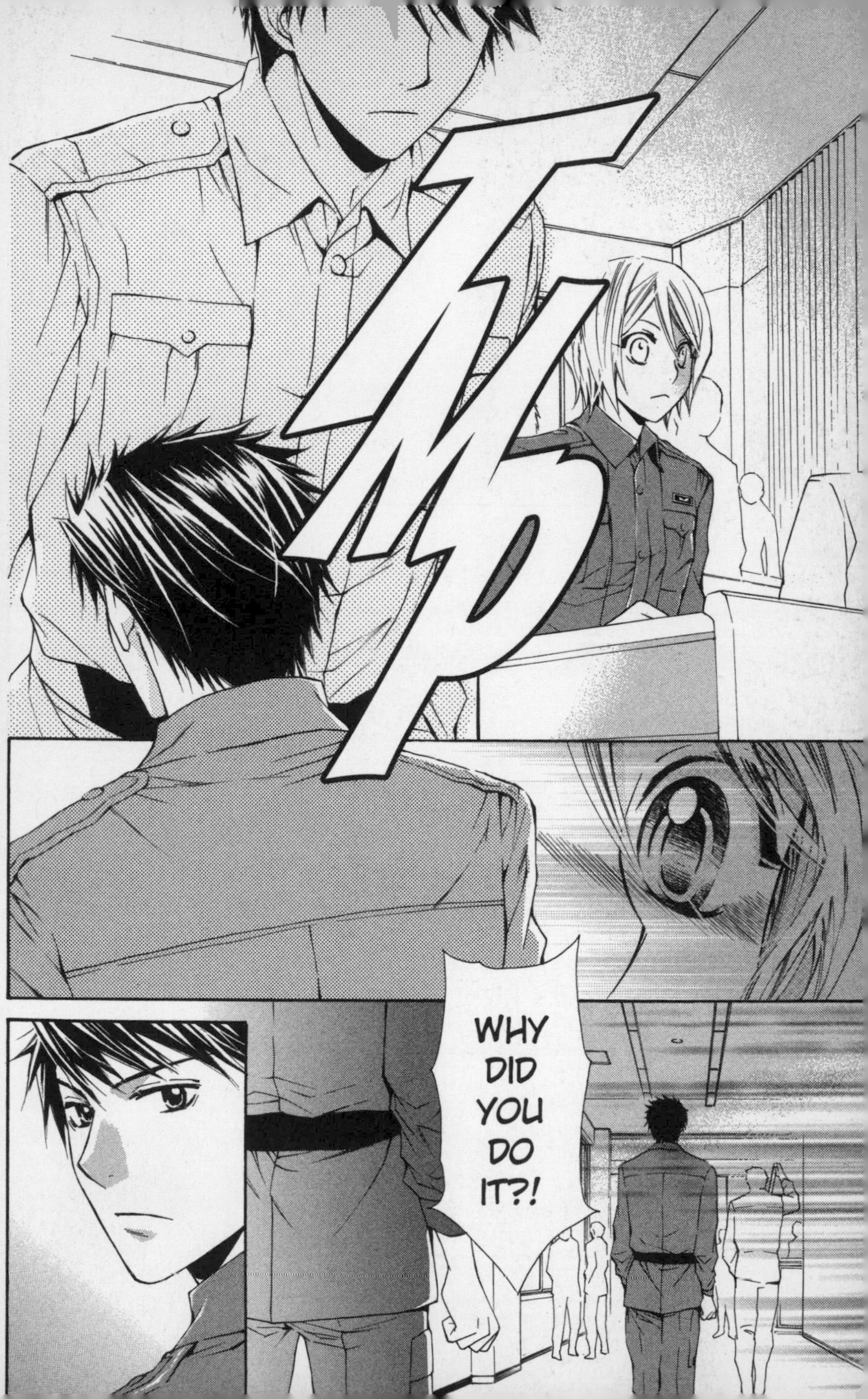
TMP
WHY DID YOU DO IT?!

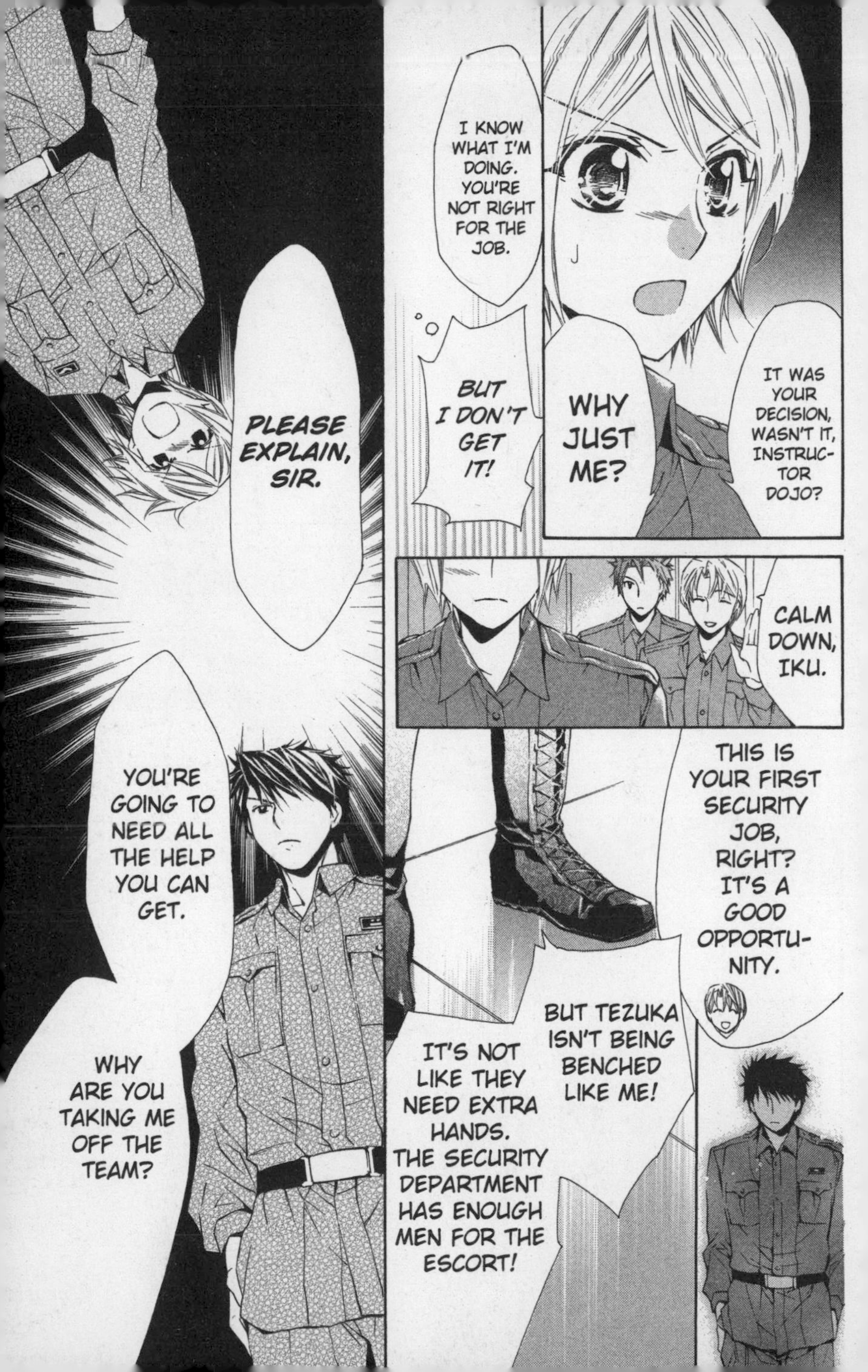

IT WAS YOUR DECISION, WASN'T IT, INSTRUCTOR DOJO?
WHY JUST ME?
I KNOW WHAT I'M DOING. YOU'RE NOT RIGHT FOR THE JOB.
BUT I DON'T GET IT!
CALM DOWN, IKU.
THIS IS YOUR FIRST SECURITY JOB, RIGHT? IT'S A GOOD OPPORTUNITY.
BUT TEZUKA ISN'T BEING BENCHED LIKE ME!
IT'S NOT LIKE THEY NEED EXTRA HANDS. THE SECURITY DEPARTMENT HAS ENOUGH MEN FOR THE ESCORT!
PLEASE EXPLAIN, SIR.
YOU'RE GOING TO NEED ALL THE HELP YOU CAN GET.
WHY ARE YOU TAKING ME OFF THE TEAM?

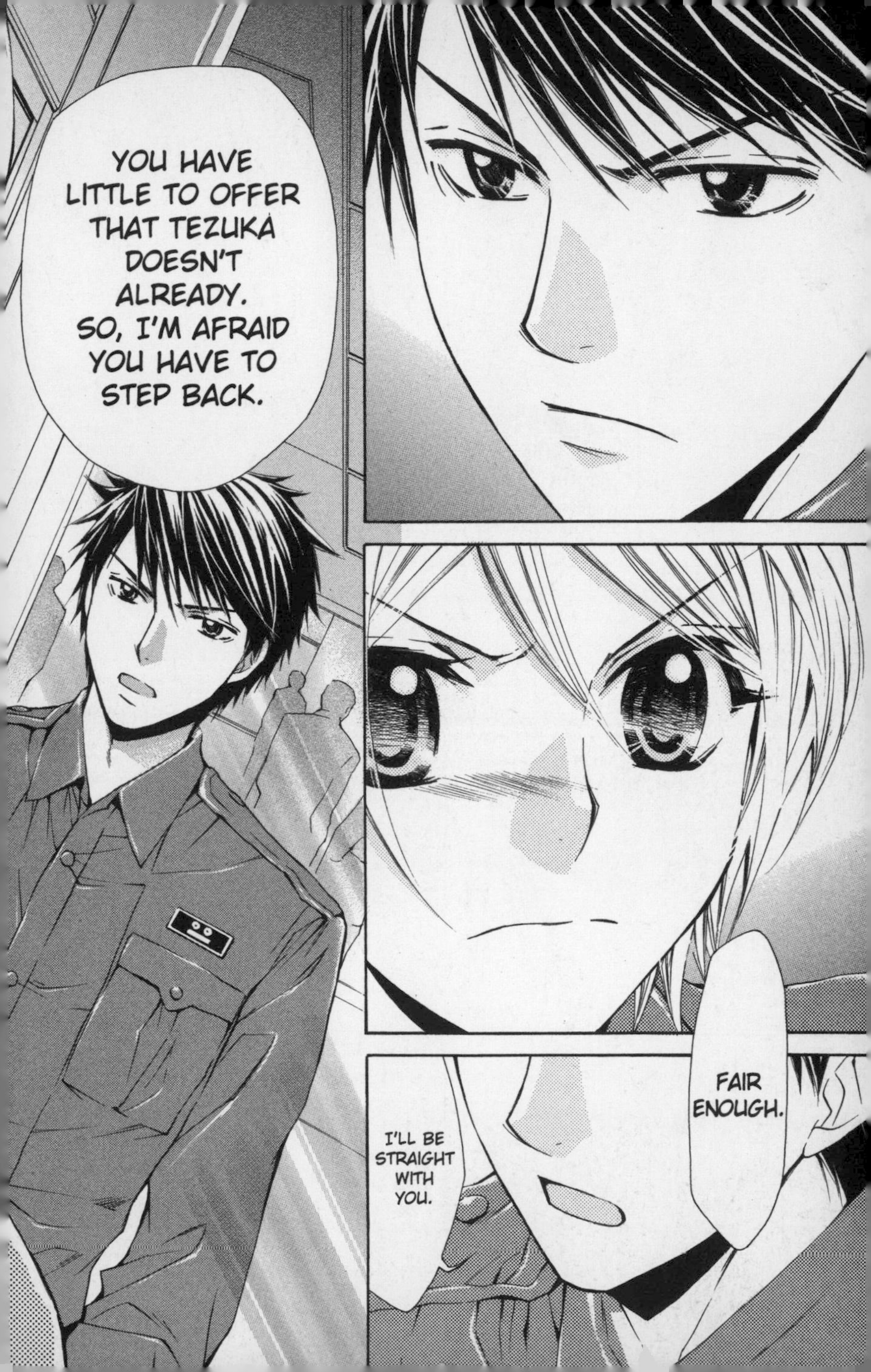
FAIR ENOUGH.
I'LL BE STRAIGHT WITH YOU.
YOU HAVE LITTLE TO OFFER THAT TEZUKA DOESN'T ALREADY. SO, I'M AFRAID YOU HAVE TO STEP BACK.

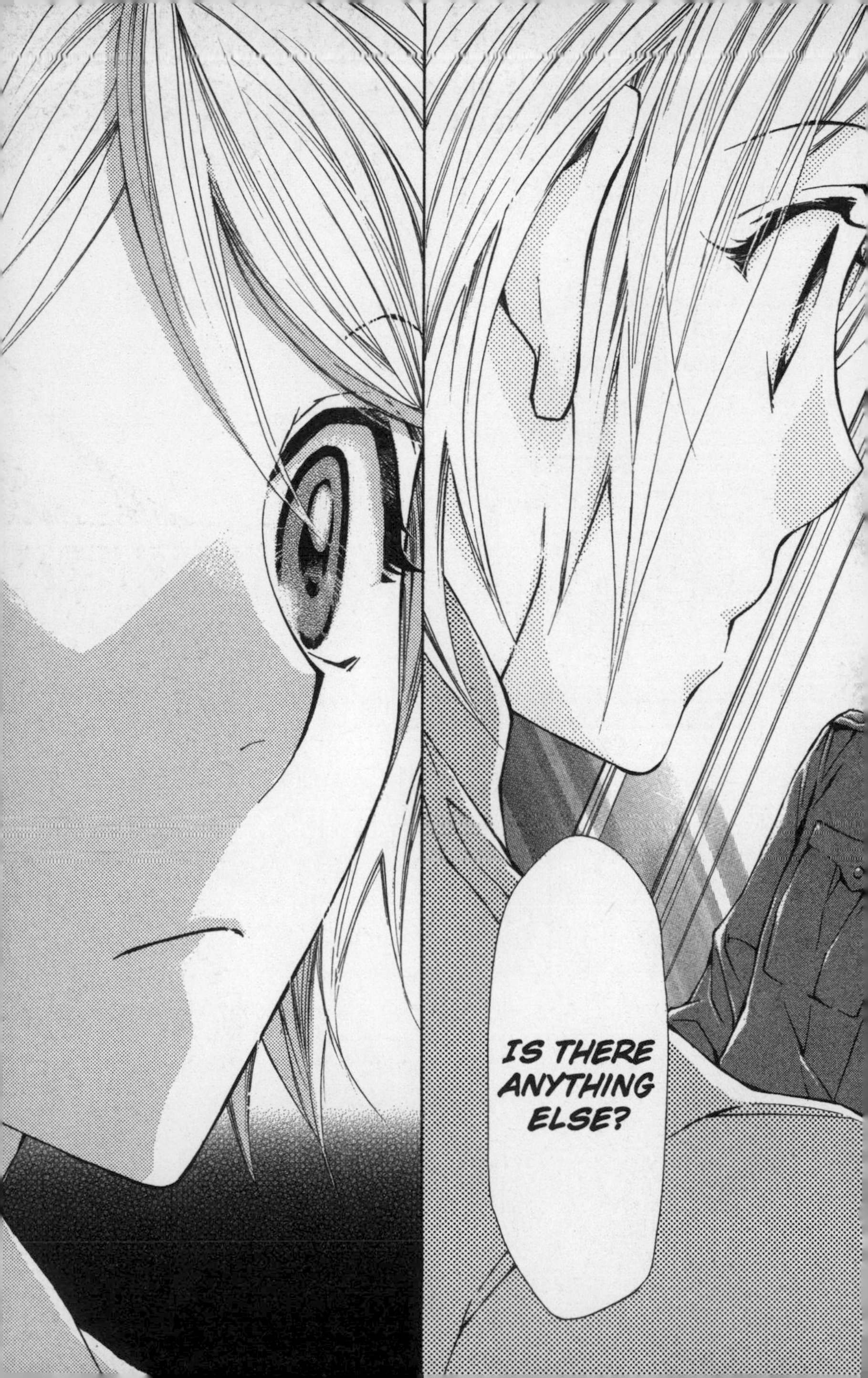
IS THERE ANYTHING ELSE?

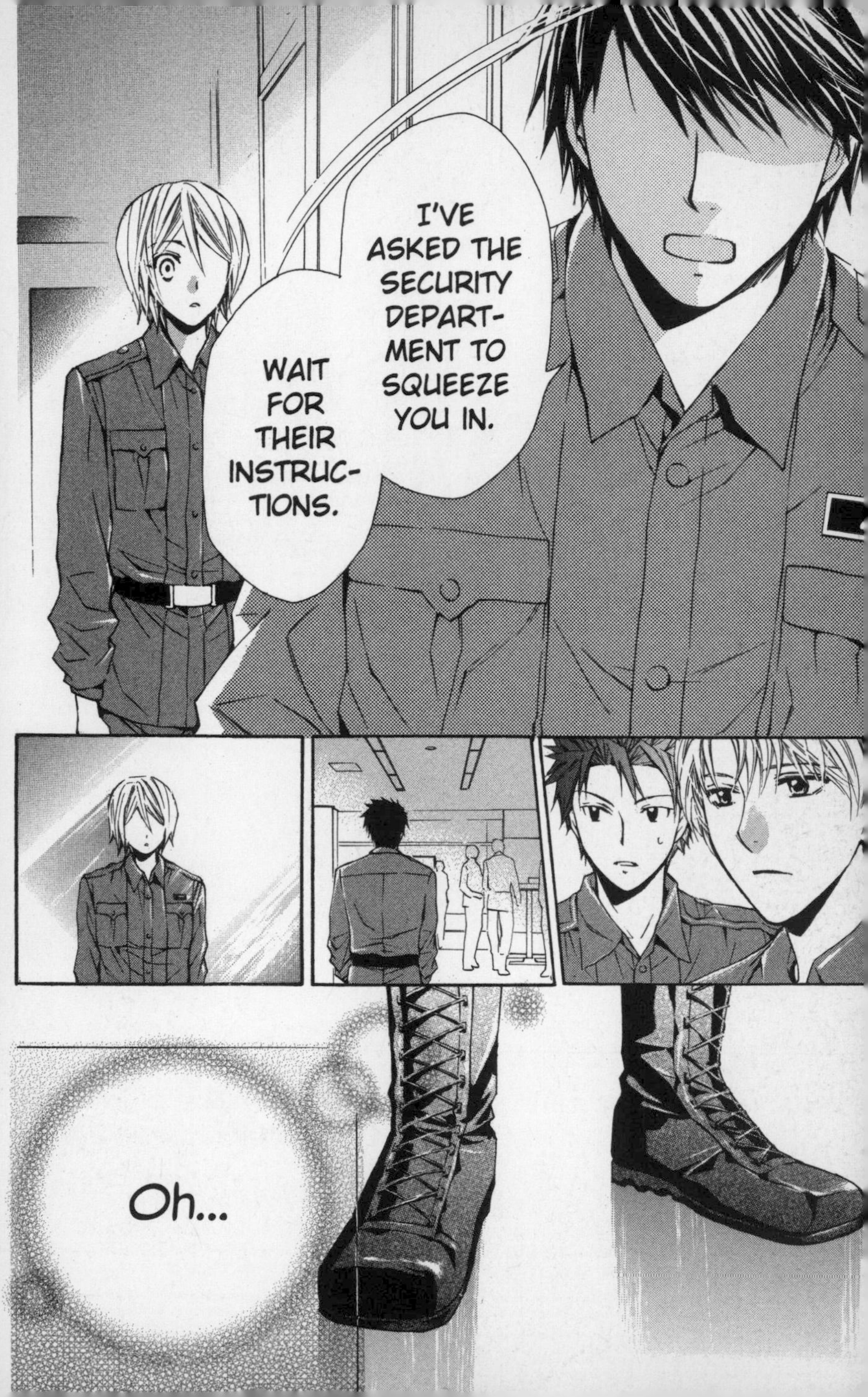
I'VE ASKED THE SECURITY DEPARTMENT TO SQUEEZE YOU IN.
WAIT FOR THEIR INSTRUCTIONS.
Oh...

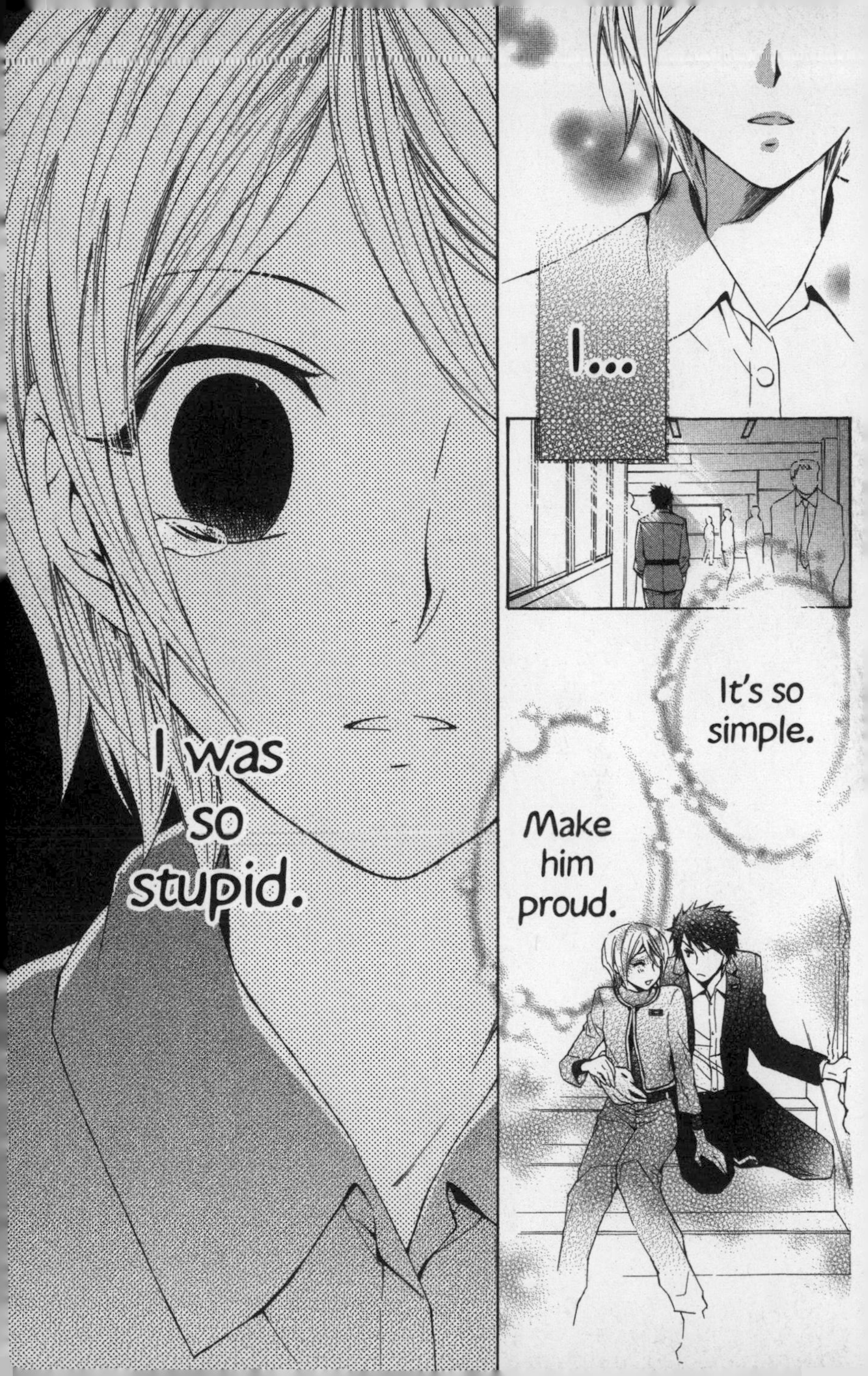
I...
It's so simple.
Make him proud.
I was so stupid.

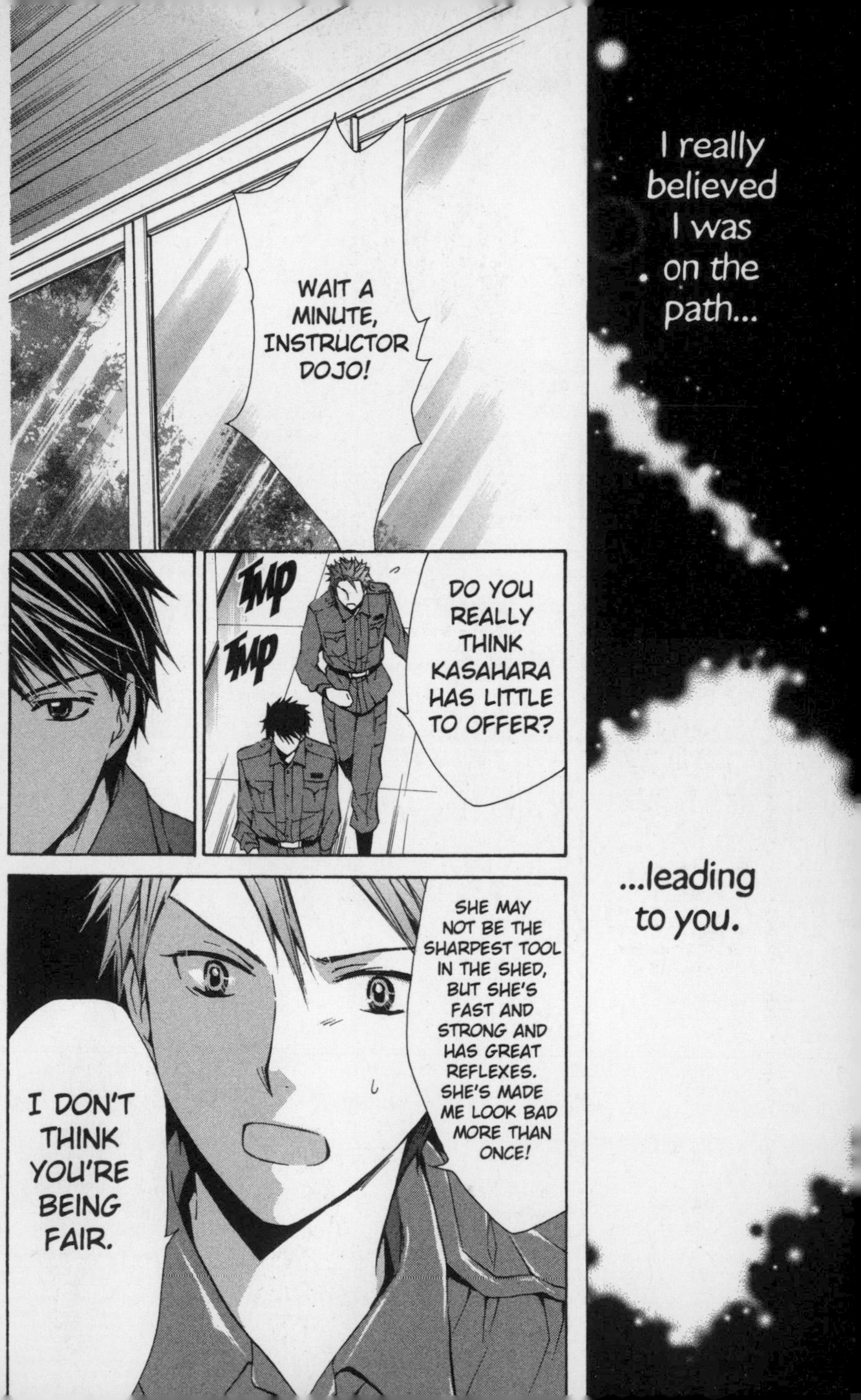
I really believed I was on the path...
...leading to you.
WAIT A MINUTE, INSTRUCTOR DOJO!
DO YOU REALLY THINK KASAHARA HAS LITTLE TO OFFER?
TMP
TMP
SHE MAY NOT BE THE SHARPEST TOOL IN THE SHED, BUT SHE'S FAST AND STRONG AND HAS GREAT REFLEXES. SHE'S MADE ME LOOK BAD MORE THAN ONCE!
I DON'T THINK YOU'RE BEING FAIR.

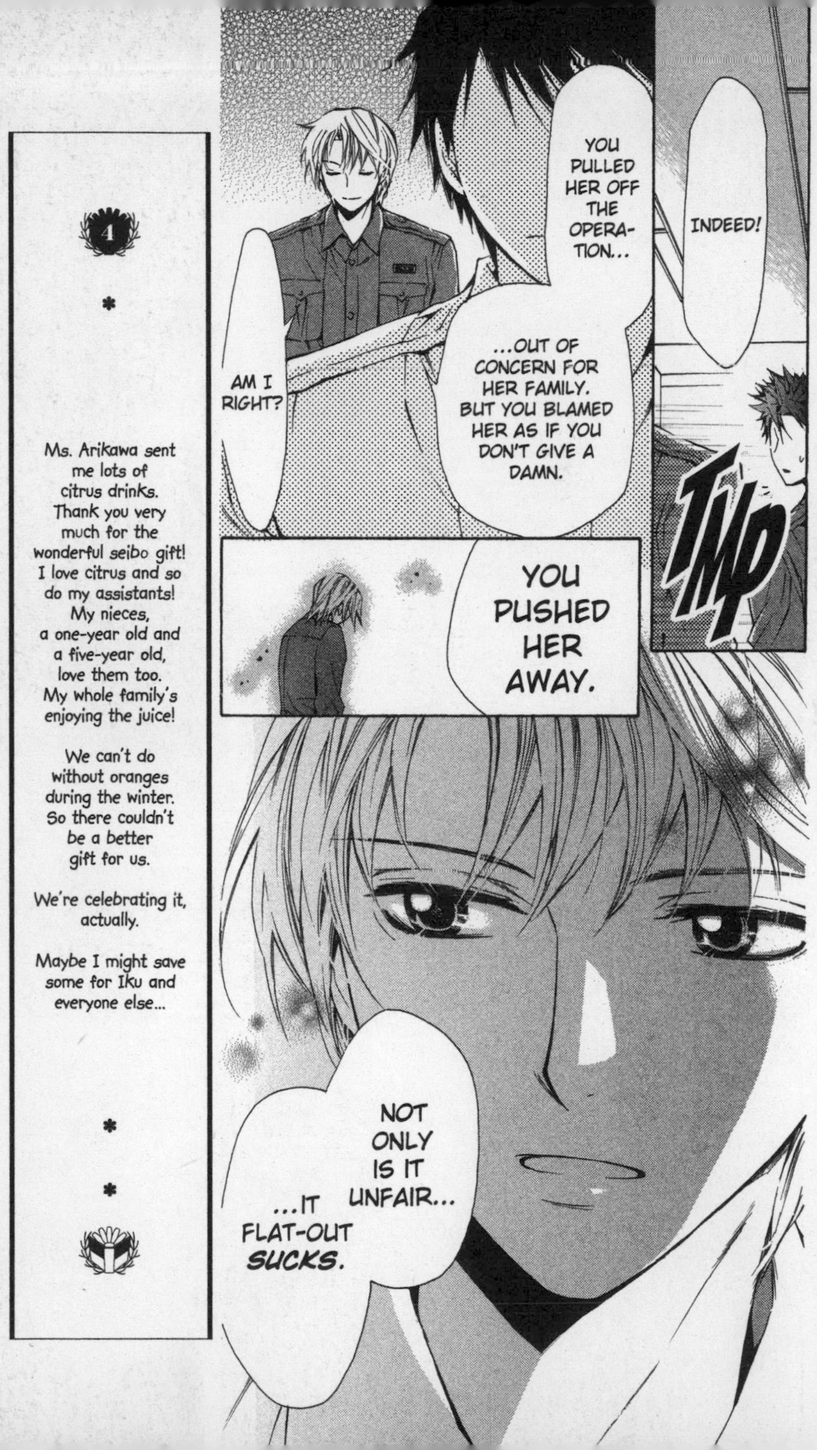
INDEED!
TMP
YOU PULLED HER OFF THE OPERATION...
...OUT OF CONCERN FOR HER FAMILY. BUT YOU BLAMED HER AS IF YOU DON'T GIVE A DAMN.
AM I RIGHT?
YOU PUSHED HER AWAY.
NOT ONLY IS IT UNFAIR...
...IT FLAT-OUT SUCKS.

4

*

Ms. Arikawa sent me lots of citrus drinks. Thank you very much for the wonderful seibo gift! I love citrus and so do my assistants! My nieces, a one-year old and a five-year old, love them too. My whole family's enjoying the juice!

We can't do without oranges during the winter. So there couldn't be a better gift for us.

We're celebrating it, actually.

Maybe I might save some for Iku and everyone else...

*

*

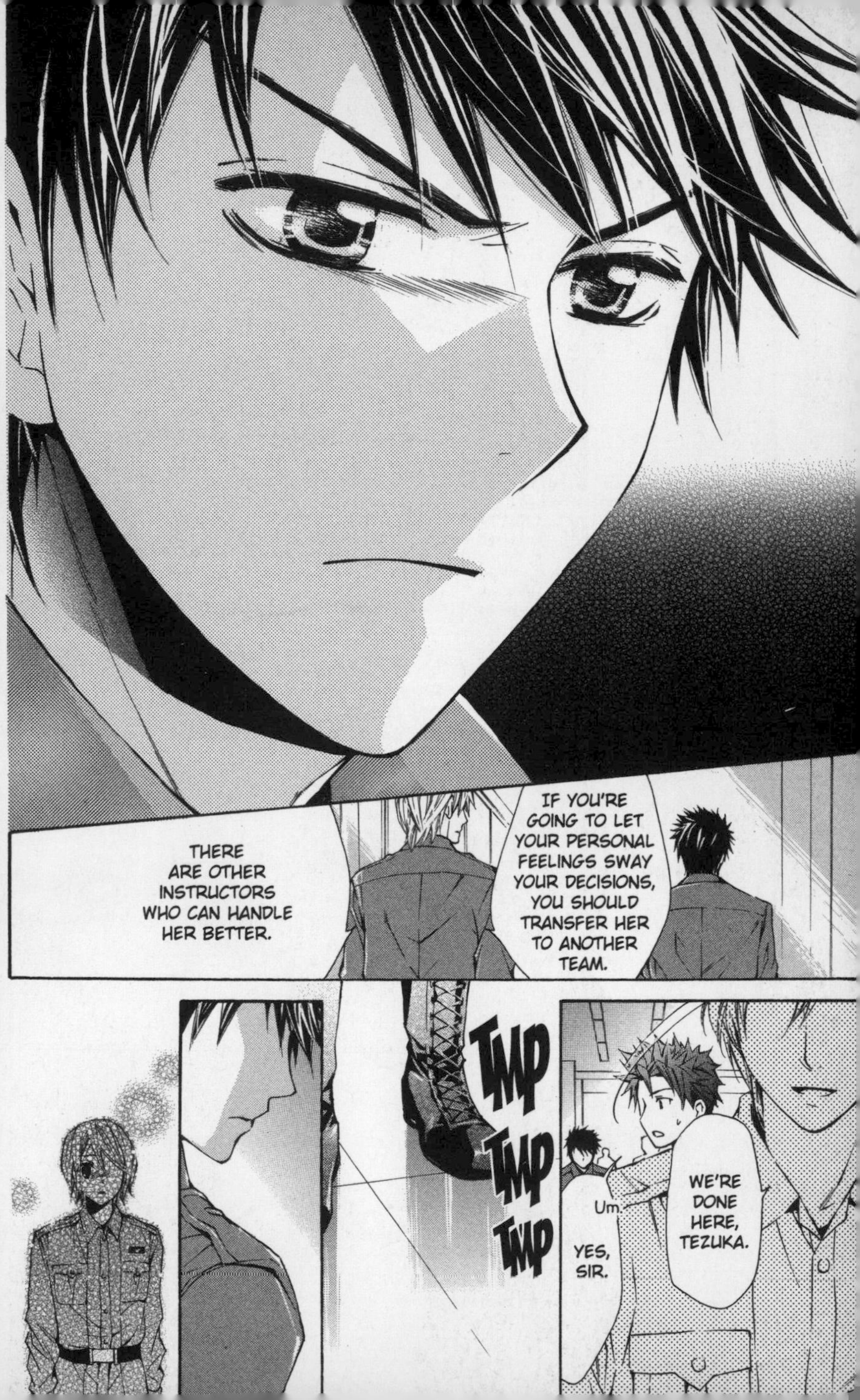
IF YOU'RE GOING TO LET YOUR PERSONAL FEELINGS SWAY YOUR DECISIONS, YOU SHOULD TRANSFER HER TO ANOTHER TEAM.
THERE ARE OTHER INSTRUCTORS WHO CAN HANDLE HER BETTER.
WE'RE DONE HERE, TEZUKA.
Um.
YES, SIR.
TMP TMP TMP

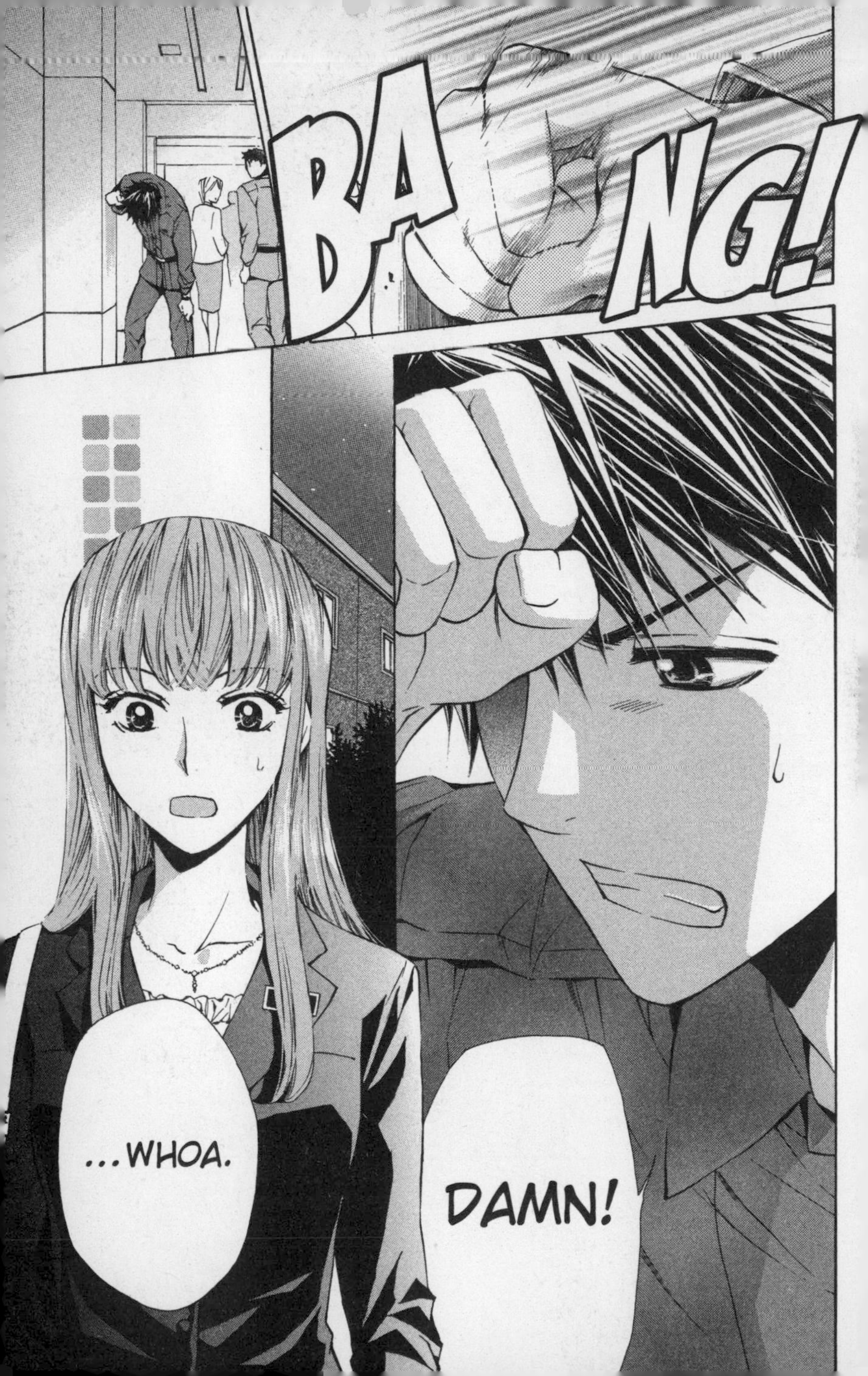
BANG!
DAMN!
...WHOA.

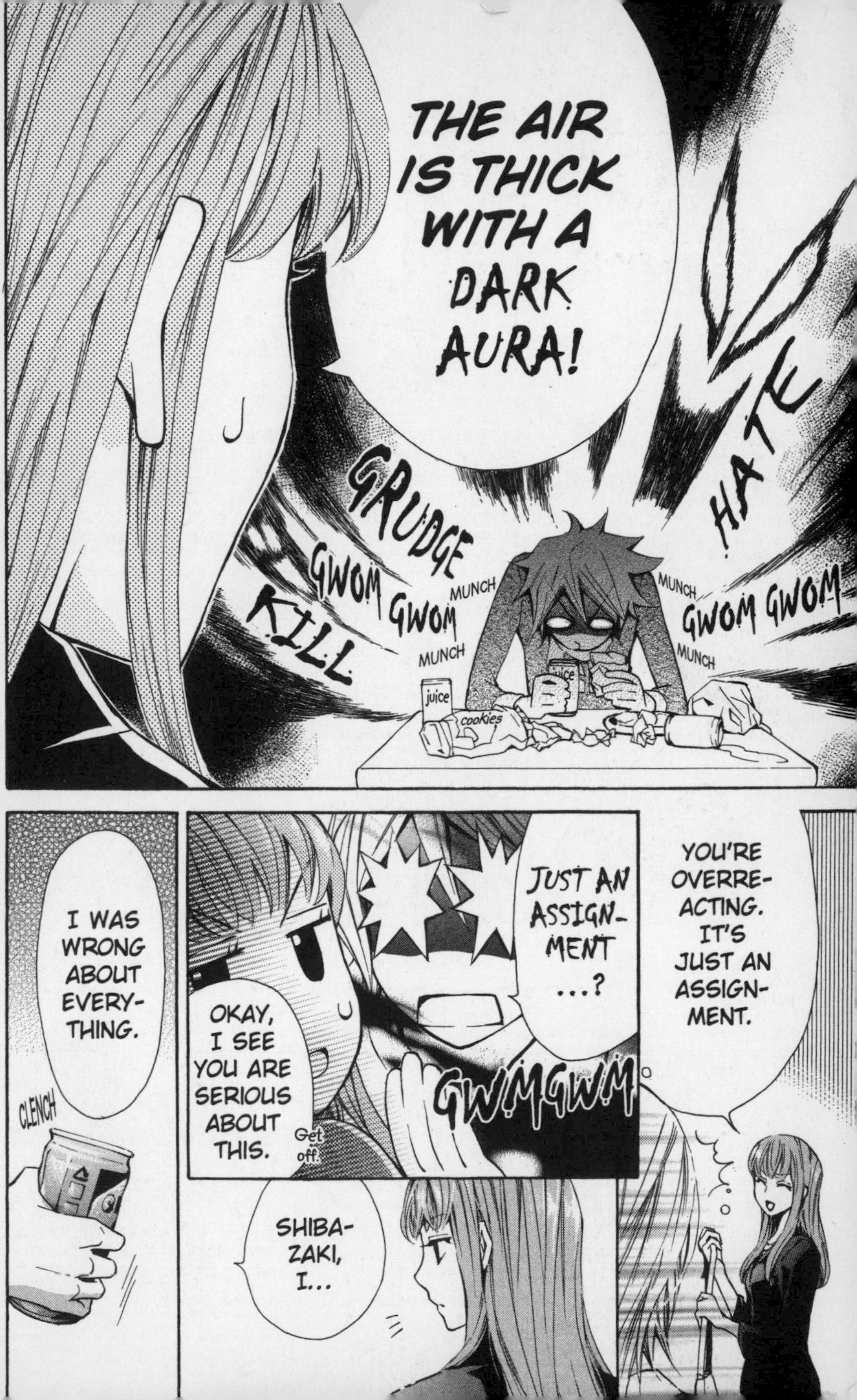
THE AIR IS THICK WITH A DARK AURA!
HATE
GRUDGE
GWOM GWOM
MUNCH
MUNCH
GWOM GWOM
KILL
MUNCH
MUNCH
juice
juice
cookies
YOU'RE OVERRE-ACTING. IT'S JUST AN ASSIGN-MENT.
JUST AN ASSIGN-MENT ...?
GWMGWM
OKAY, I SEE YOU ARE SERIOUS ABOUT THIS.
Get off.
SHIBA-ZAKI, I...
I WAS WRONG ABOUT EVERY-THING.
CLENCH

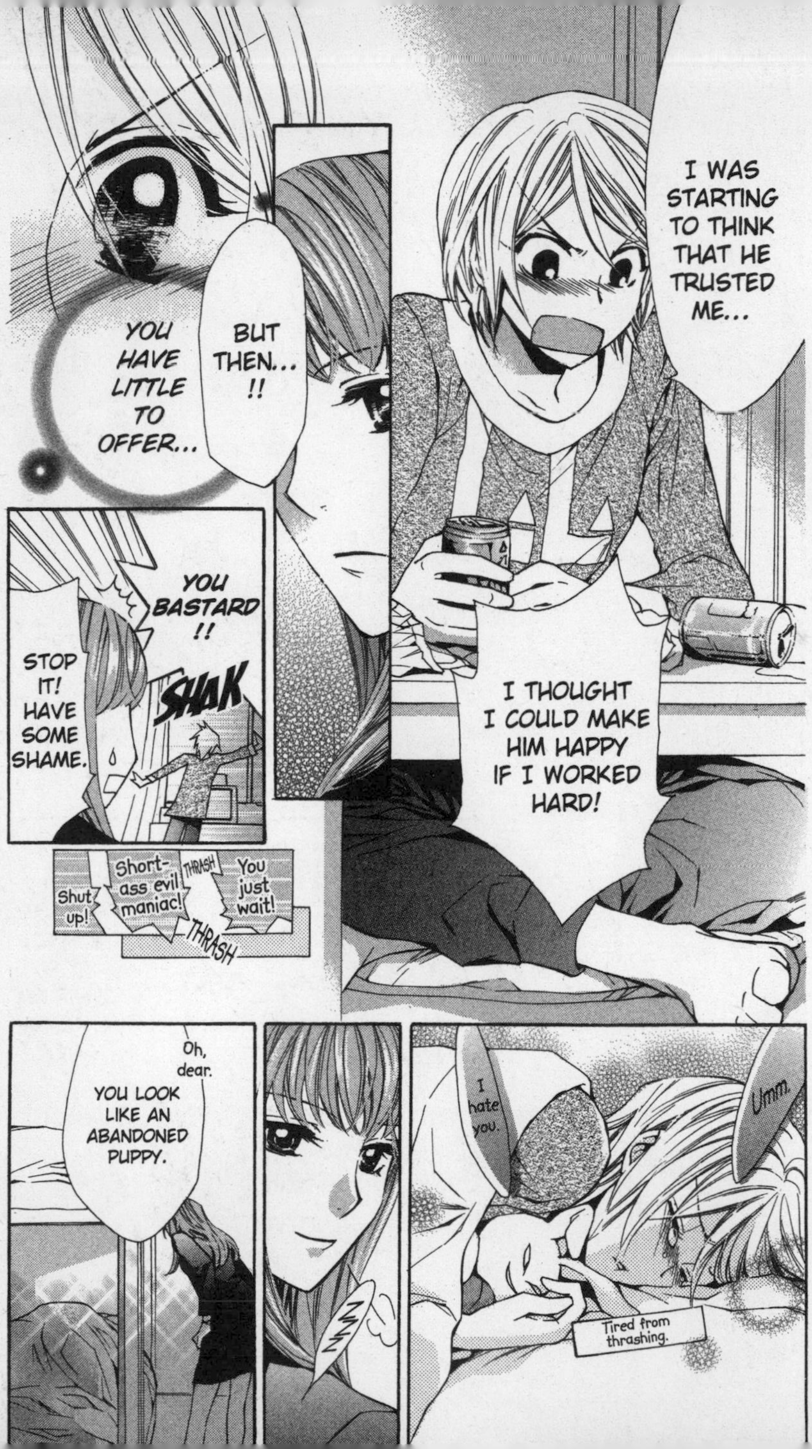

I WAS STARTING TO THINK THAT HE TRUSTED ME...
I THOUGHT I COULD MAKE HIM HAPPY IF I WORKED HARD!
BUT THEN... !!
YOU HAVE LITTLE TO OFFER...
YOU BASTARD !!
SHAK
STOP IT! HAVE SOME SHAME.
You just wait!
THRASH
Short-ass evil maniac!
Shut up!
THRASH
Umm.
I hate you.
Tired from thrashing.
Oh, dear.
YOU LOOK LIKE AN ABANDONED PUPPY.

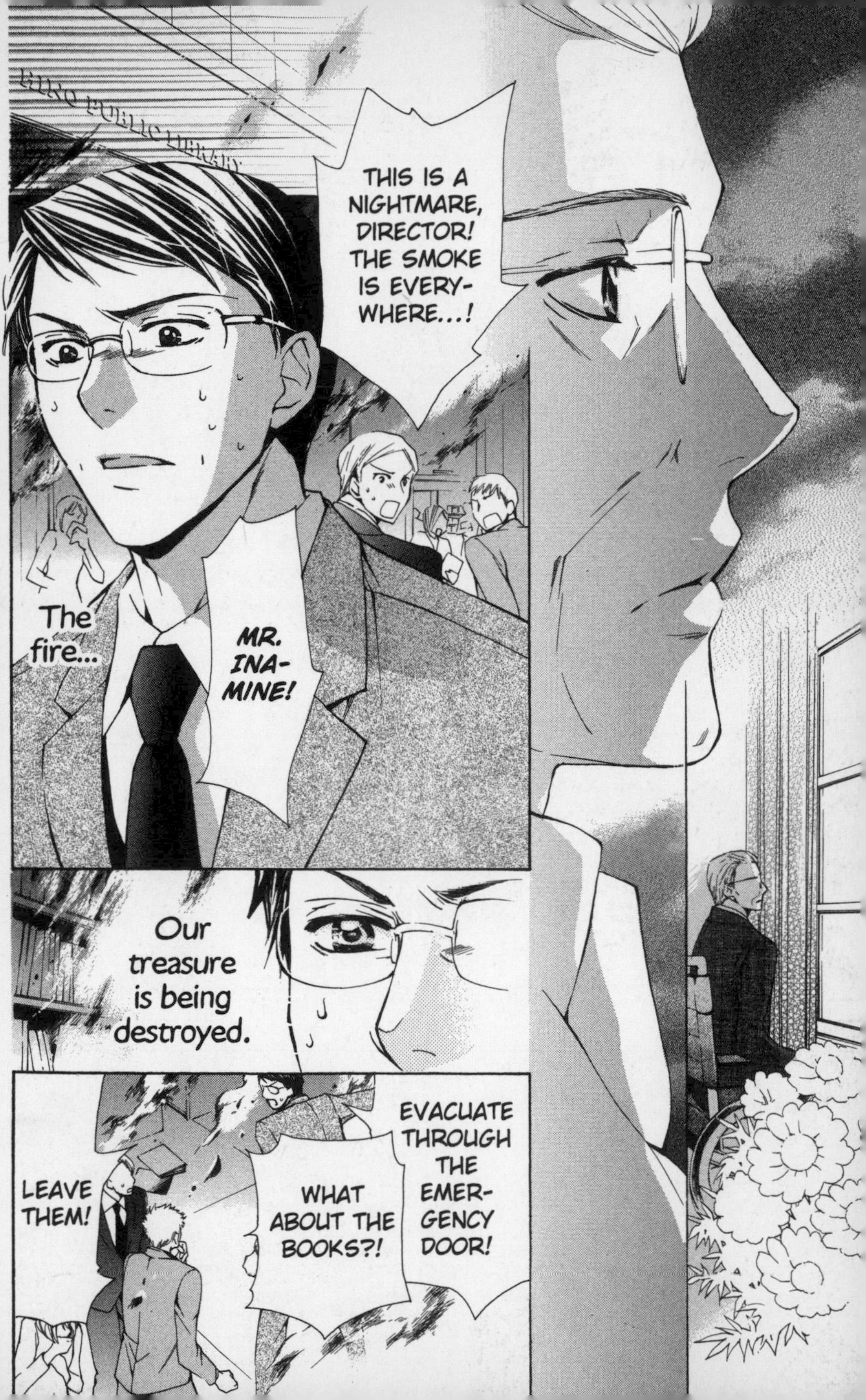
THIS IS A NIGHTMARE, DIRECTOR! THE SMOKE IS EVERY-WHERE...!
MR. INA-MINE!
The fire...
Our treasure is being destroyed.
EVACUATE THROUGH THE EMER-GENCY DOOR!
WHAT ABOUT THE BOOKS?!
LEAVE THEM!

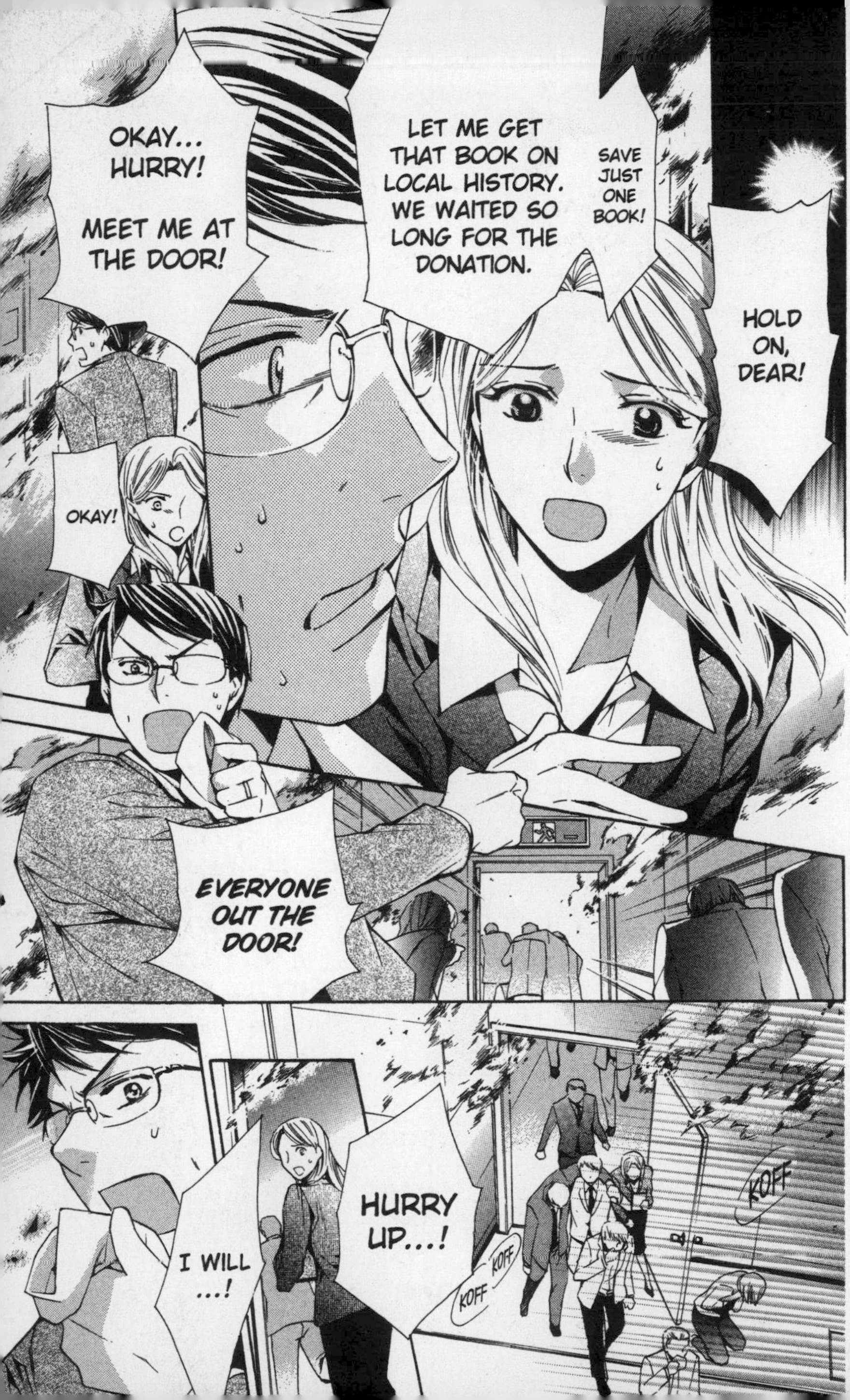
HOLD ON, DEAR!
SAVE JUST ONE BOOK!
LET ME GET THAT BOOK ON LOCAL HISTORY. WE WAITED SO LONG FOR THE DONATION.
OKAY... HURRY!
MEET ME AT THE DOOR!
OKAY!
EVERYONE OUT THE DOOR!
KOFF
KOFF
KOFF
HURRY UP...!
I WILL ...!

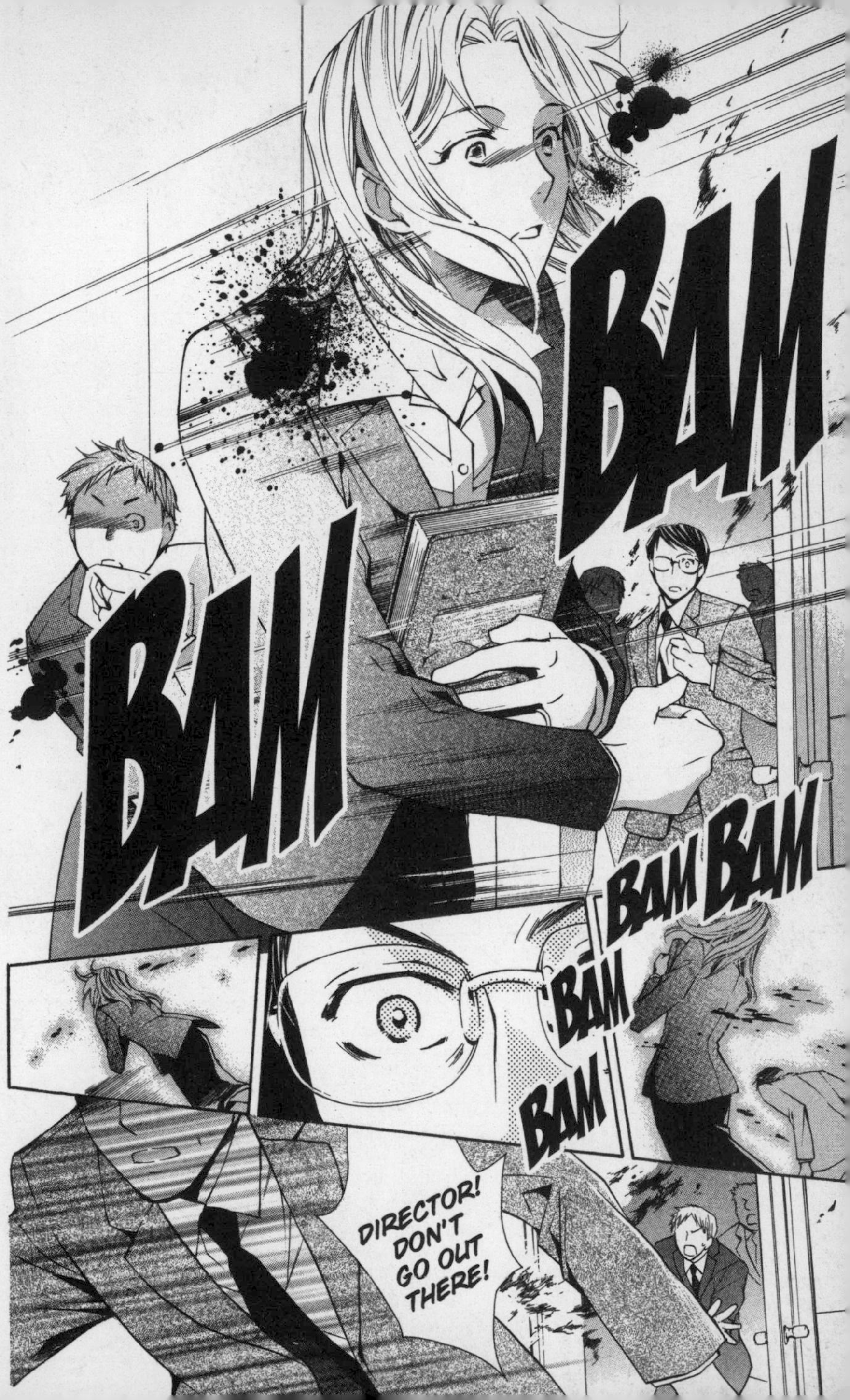
BAM
BAM
BAM BAM
BAM
BAM
BAM
DIRECTOR! DON'T GO OUT THERE!

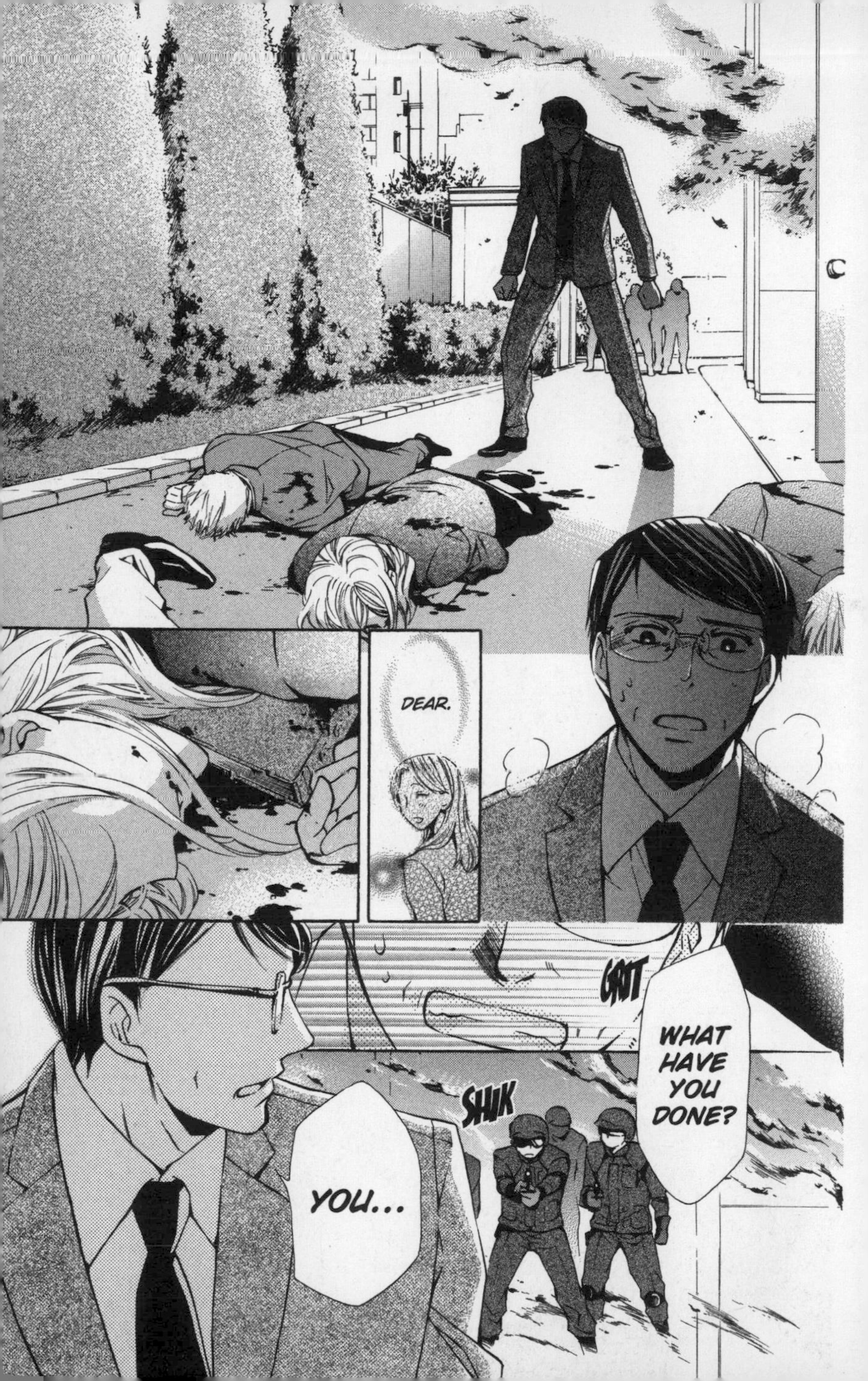
DEAR.
GRIT
WHAT HAVE YOU DONE?
SHUK
YOU...

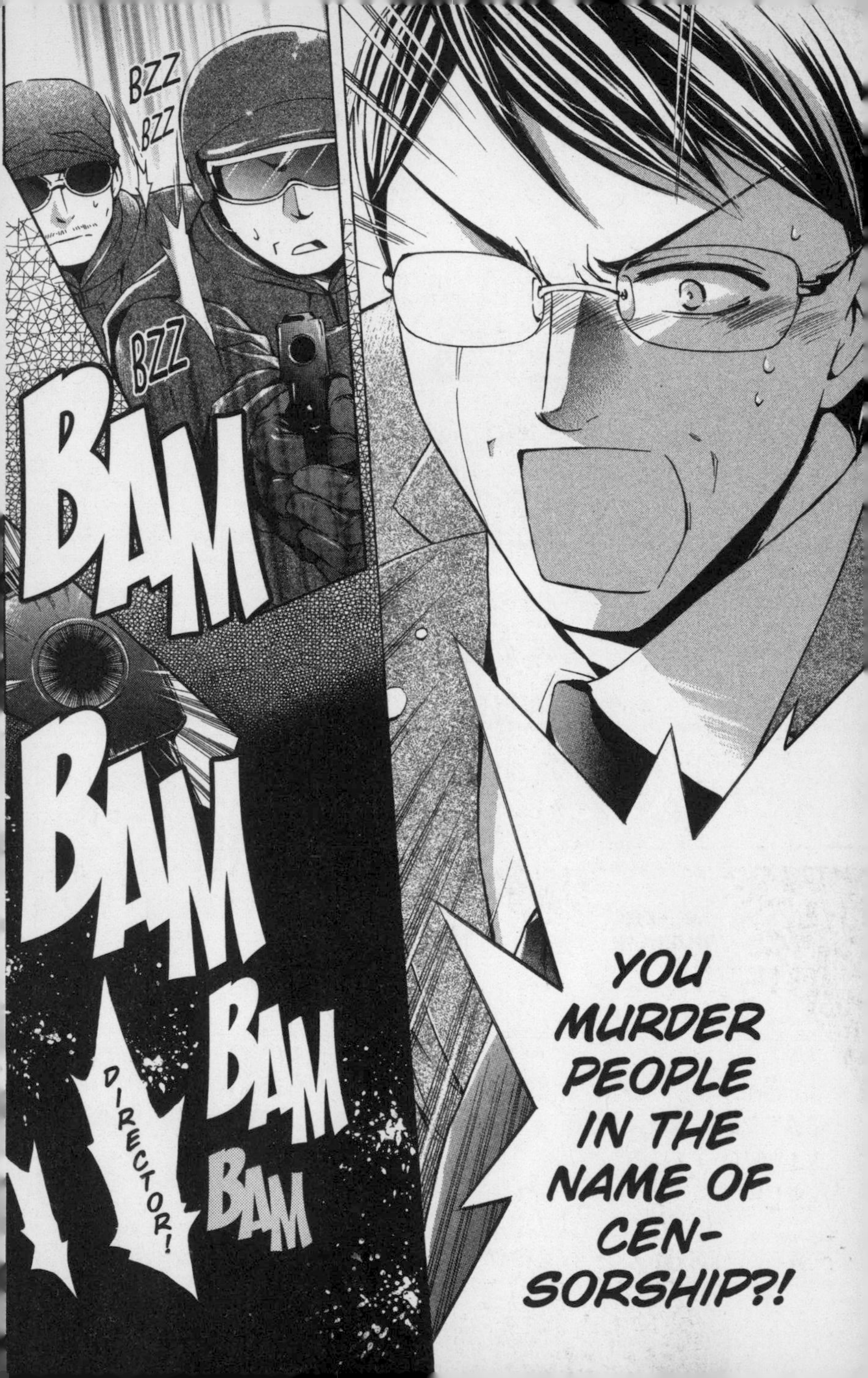
YOU MURDER PEOPLE IN THE NAME OF CEN-SORSHIP?!
BZZ
BZZ
BZZ
BAM
BAM
DIRECTOR!
BAM
BAM

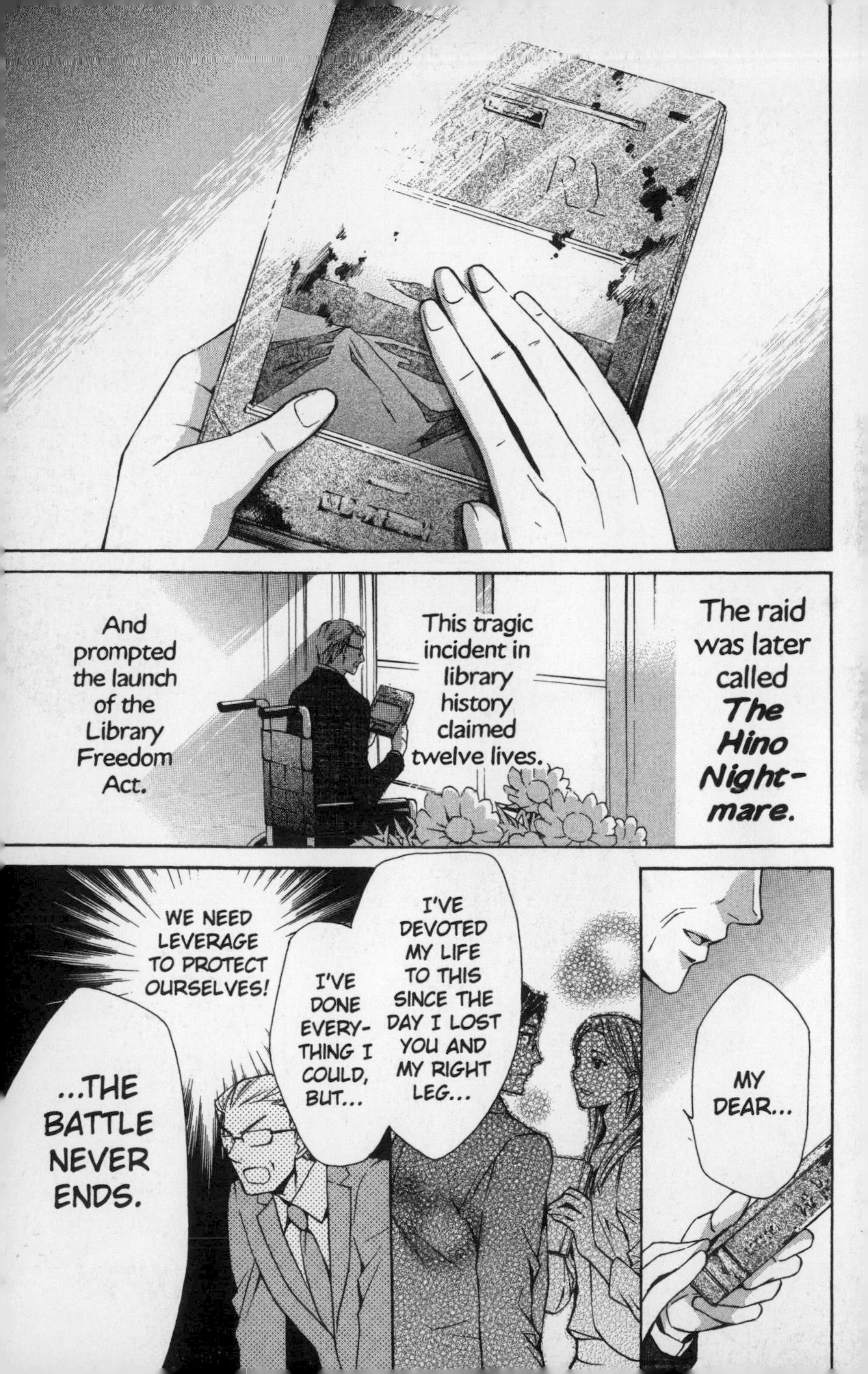
The raid was later called *The Hino Nightmare.*
This tragic incident in library history claimed twelve lives.
And prompted the launch of the Library Freedom Act.
MY DEAR...
I'VE DEVOTED MY LIFE TO THIS SINCE THE DAY I LOST YOU AND MY RIGHT LEG...
I'VE DONE EVERYTHING I COULD, BUT...
WE NEED LEVERAGE TO PROTECT OURSELVES!
...THE BATTLE NEVER ENDS.

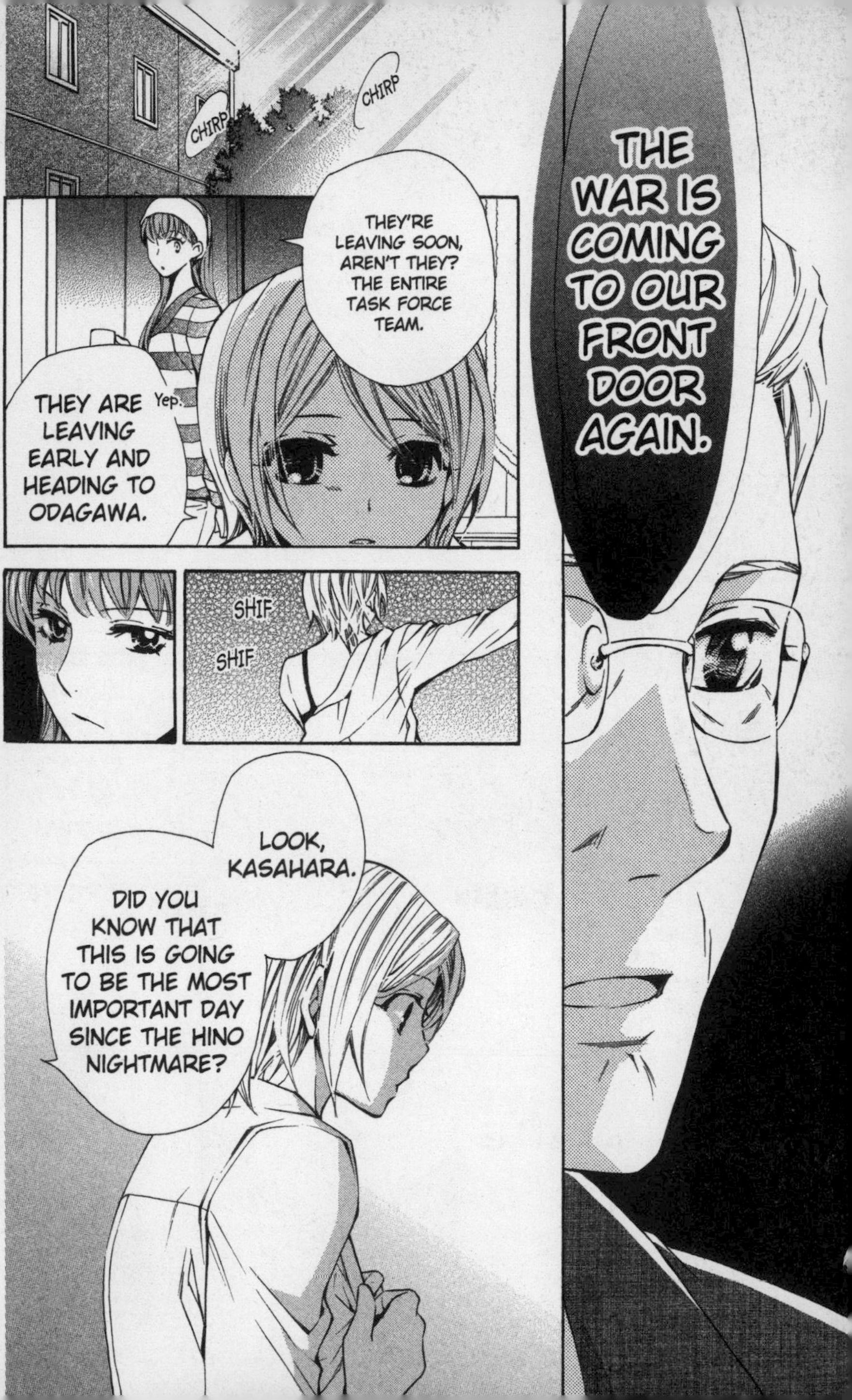
THE WAR IS COMING TO OUR FRONT DOOR AGAIN.
CHIRP
CHIRP
THEY'RE LEAVING SOON, AREN'T THEY? THE ENTIRE TASK FORCE TEAM.
Yep.
THEY ARE LEAVING EARLY AND HEADING TO ODAGAWA.
SHIF
SHIF
LOOK, KASAHARA.
DID YOU KNOW THAT THIS IS GOING TO BE THE MOST IMPORTANT DAY SINCE THE HINO NIGHTMARE?

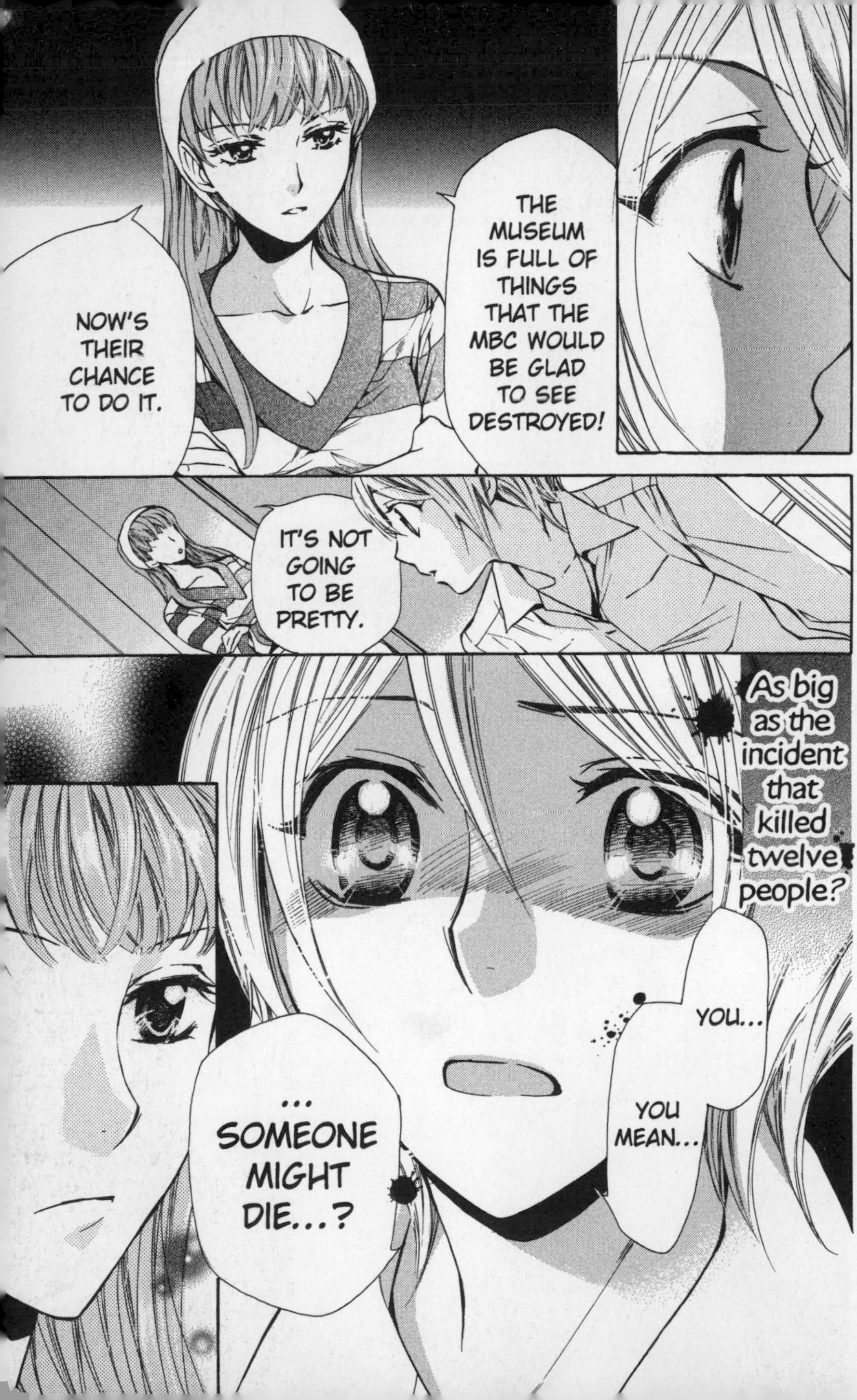
THE MUSEUM IS FULL OF THINGS THAT THE MBC WOULD BE GLAD TO SEE DESTROYED!
NOW'S THEIR CHANCE TO DO IT.
IT'S NOT GOING TO BE PRETTY.
As big as the incident that killed twelve people?
YOU...
YOU MEAN...
... SOMEONE MIGHT DIE...?

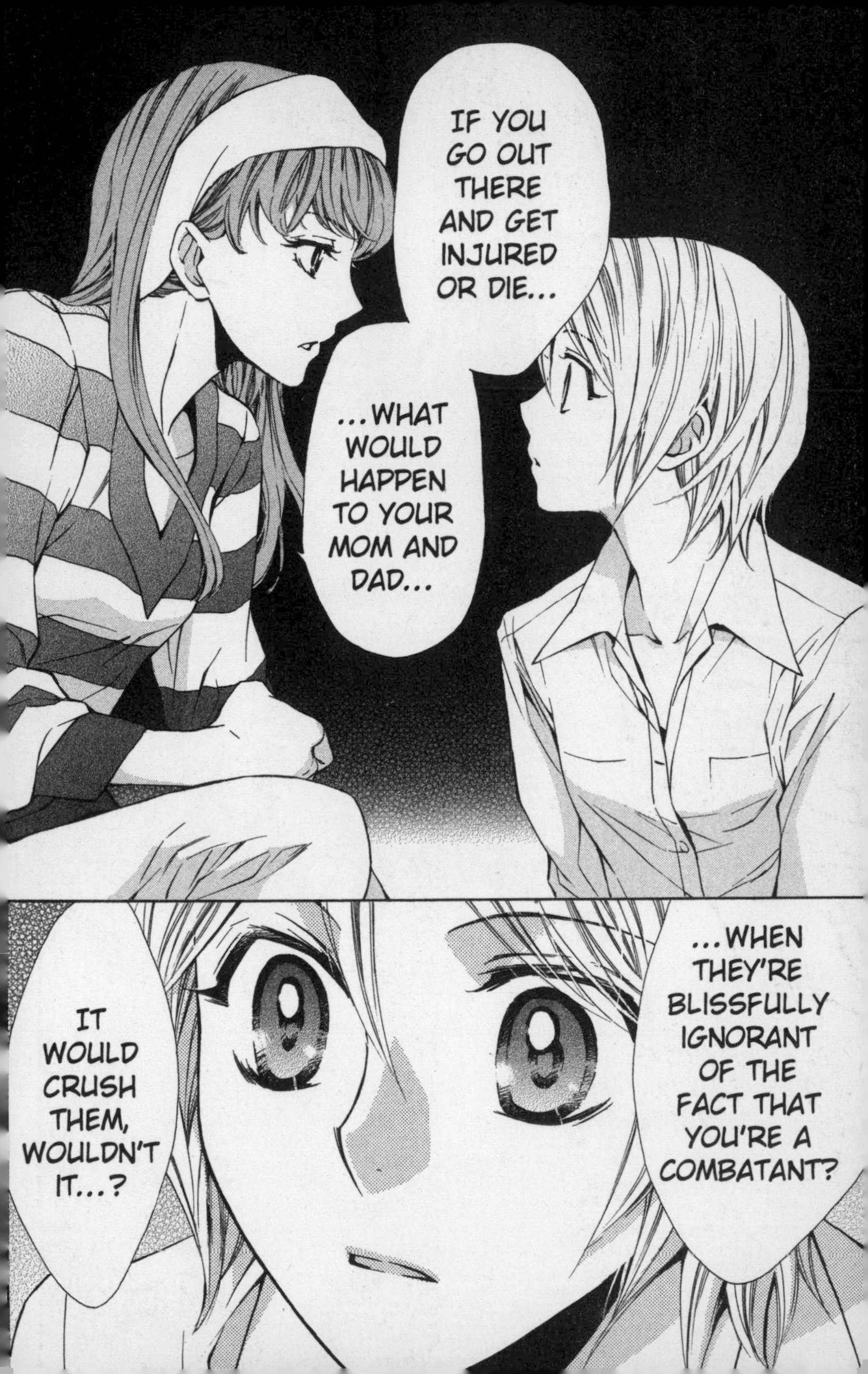
IF YOU GO OUT THERE AND GET INJURED OR DIE...
...WHAT WOULD HAPPEN TO YOUR MOM AND DAD...
...WHEN THEY'RE BLISSFULLY IGNORANT OF THE FACT THAT YOU'RE A COMBATANT?
IT WOULD CRUSH THEM, WOULDN'T IT...?

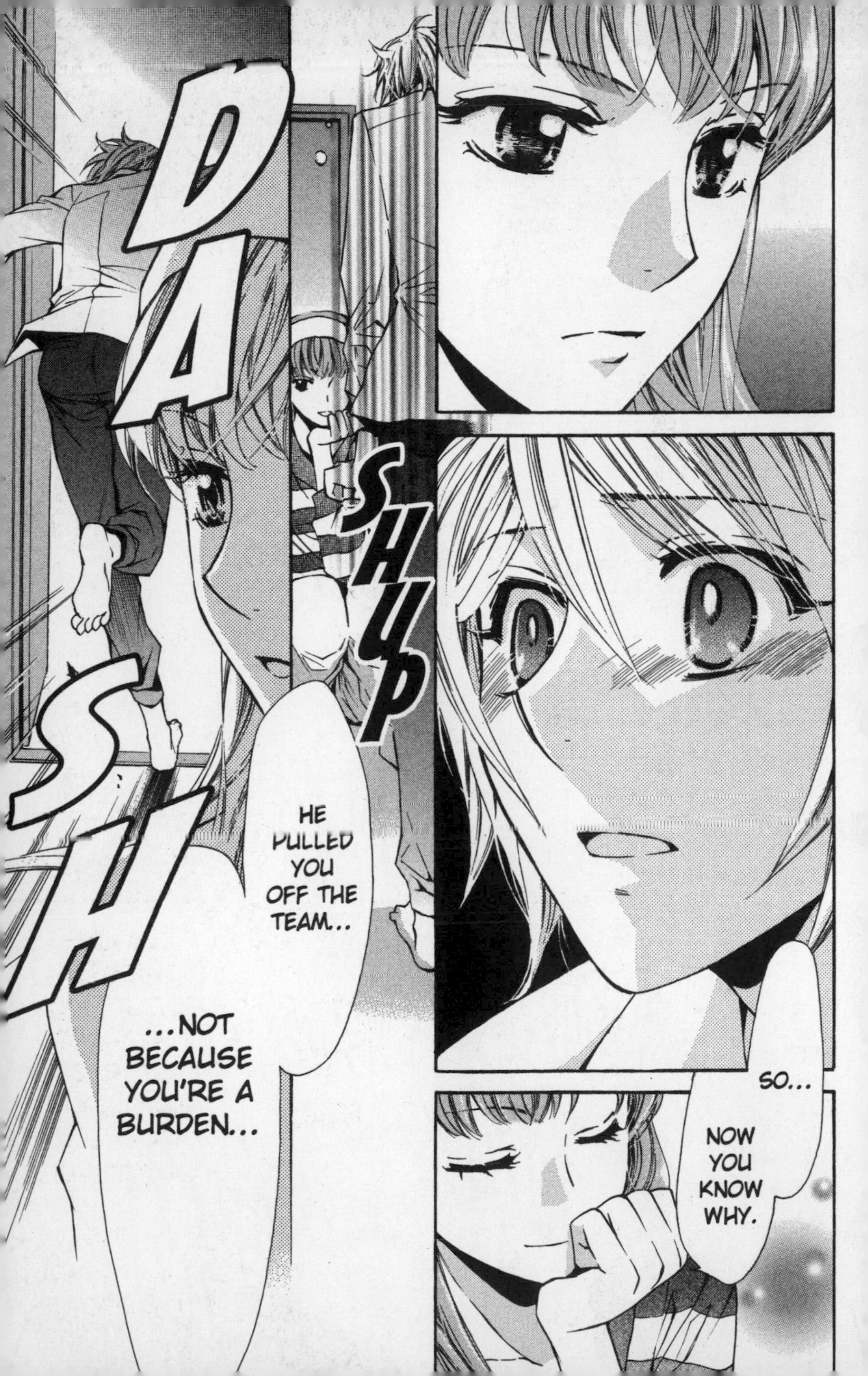
SO...
NOW YOU KNOW WHY.
SHUP
DASH
HE PULLED YOU OFF THE TEAM...
...NOT BECAUSE YOU'RE A BURDEN...

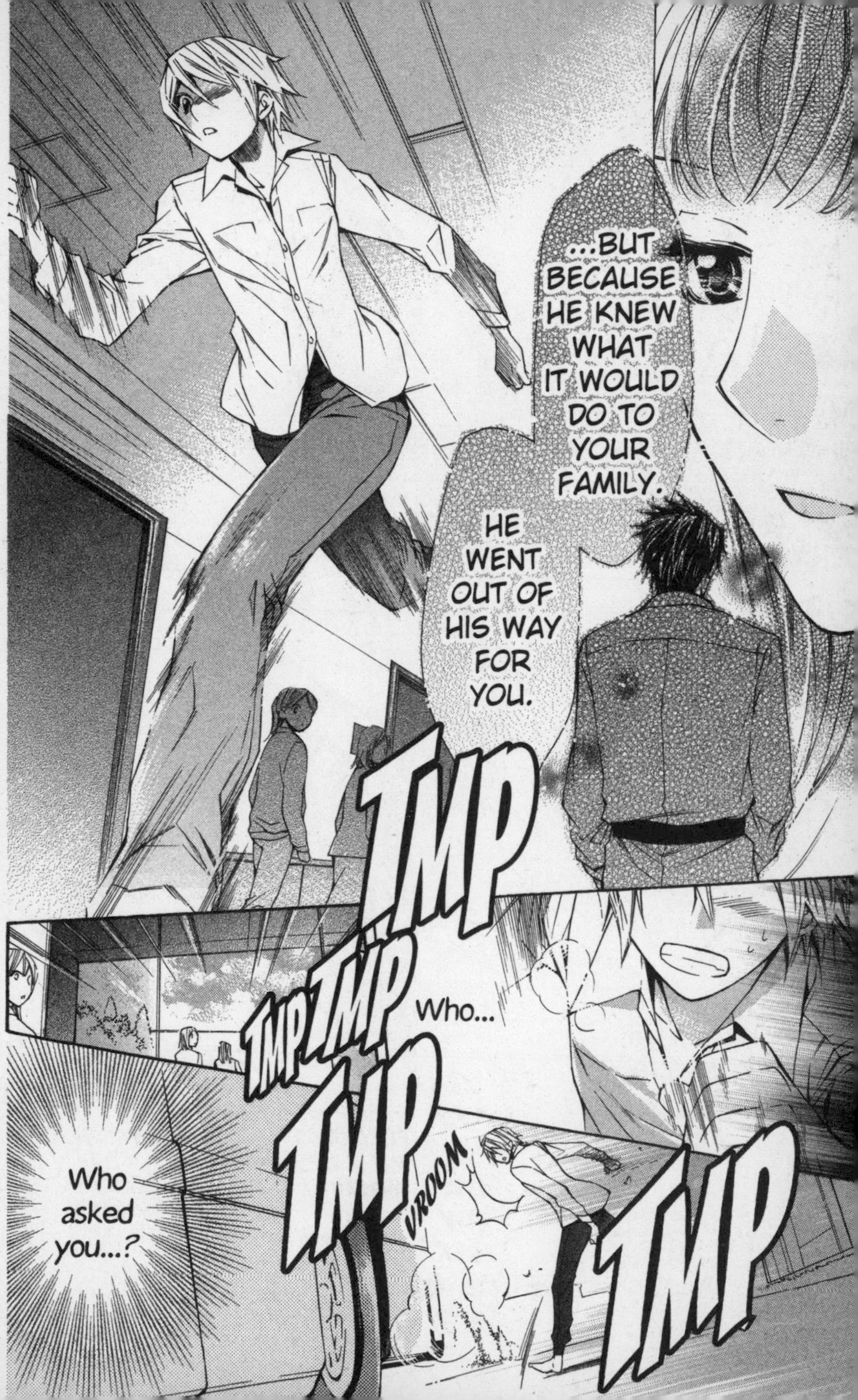
...BUT BECAUSE HE KNEW WHAT IT WOULD DO TO YOUR FAMILY.
HE WENT OUT OF HIS WAY FOR YOU.
TMP
TMP TMP
Who...
TMP
VROOM
Who asked you...?
TMP

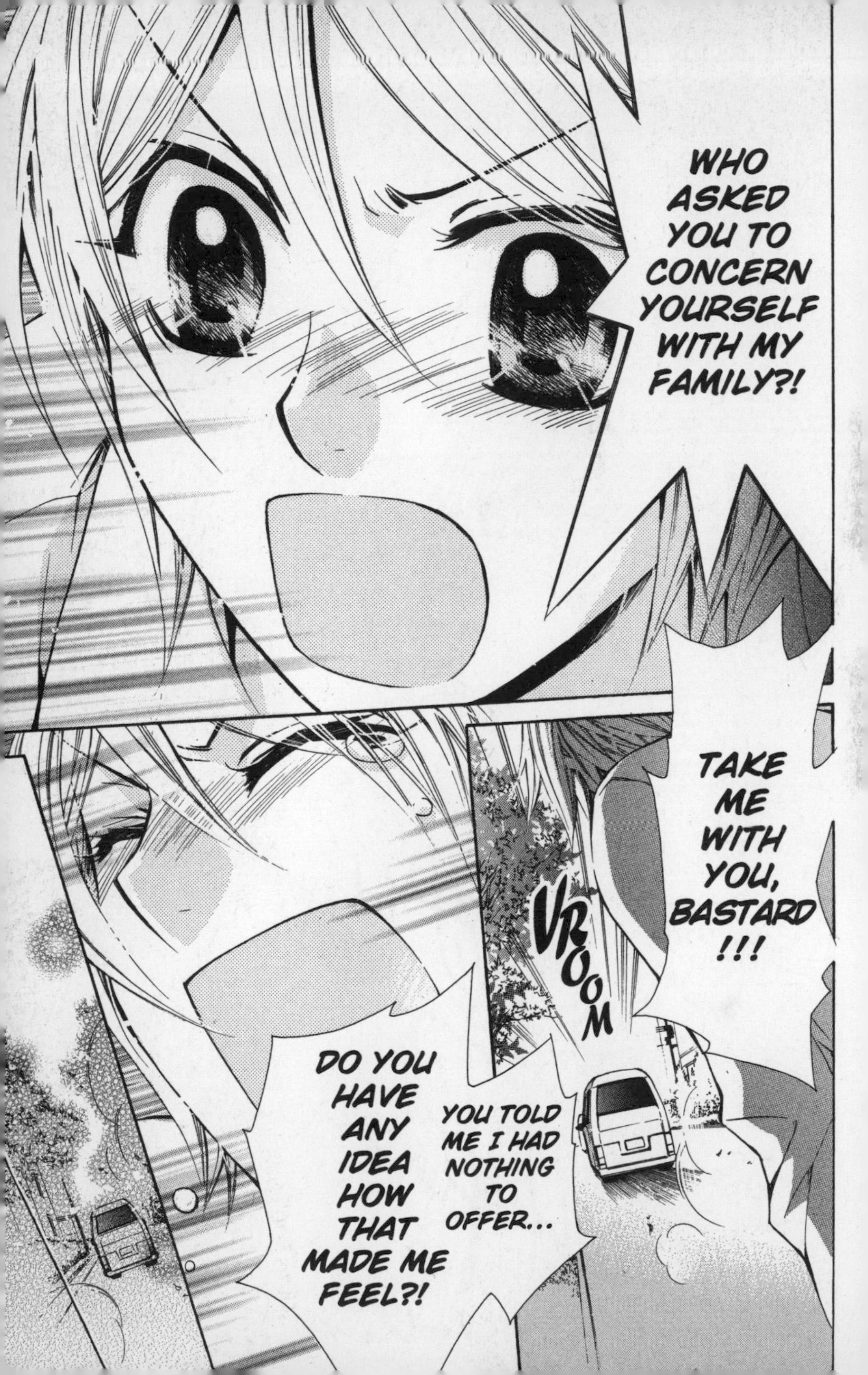
WHO ASKED YOU TO CONCERN YOURSELF WITH MY FAMILY?!
TAKE ME WITH YOU, BASTARD!!!
VROOM
YOU TOLD ME I HAD NOTHING TO OFFER...
DO YOU HAVE ANY IDEA HOW THAT MADE ME FEEL?!

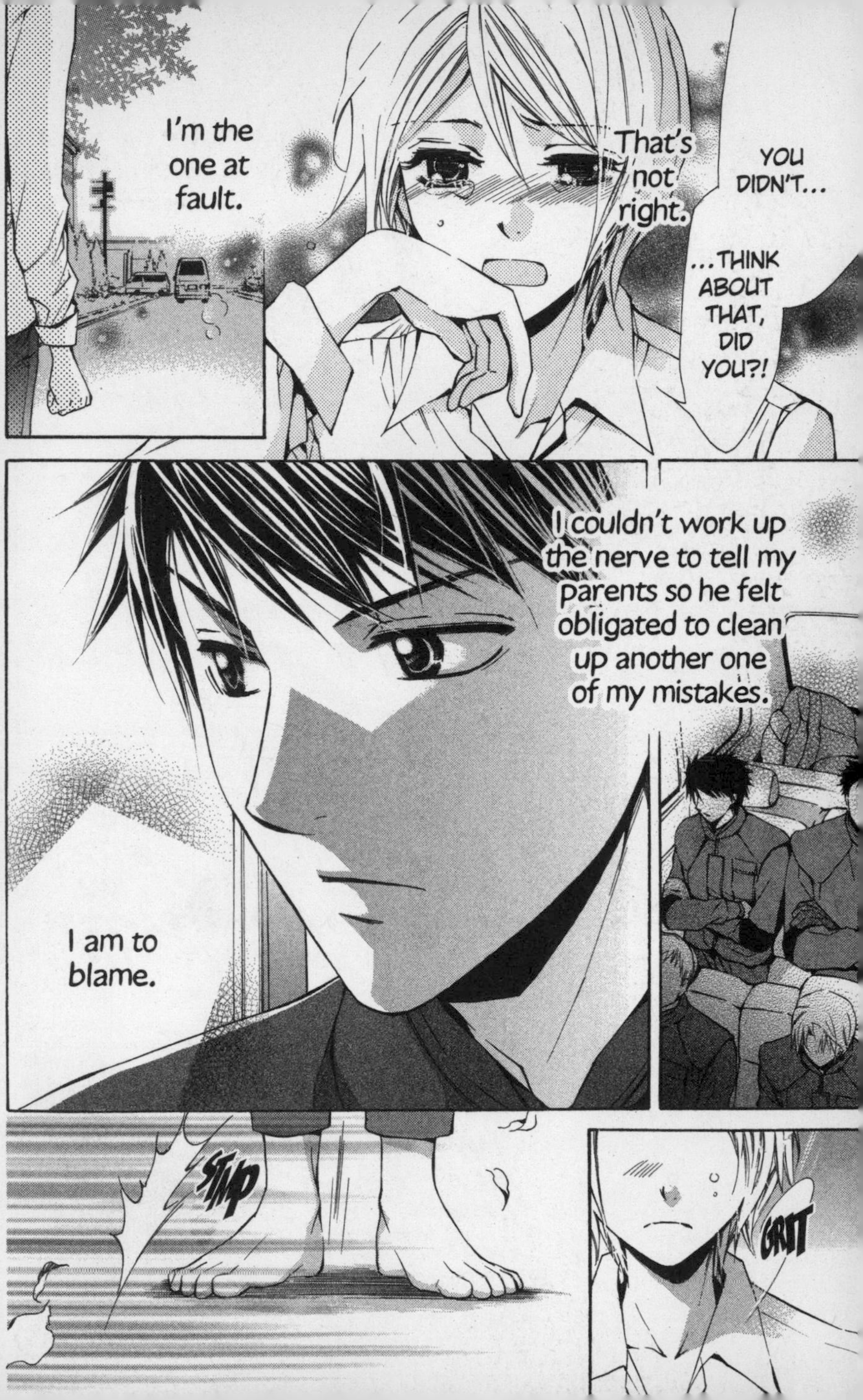
YOU DIDN'T...
...THINK ABOUT THAT, DID YOU?!
That's not right.
I'm the one at fault.
I couldn't work up the nerve to tell my parents so he felt obligated to clean up another one of my mistakes.
I am to blame.
GRIT
STAMP

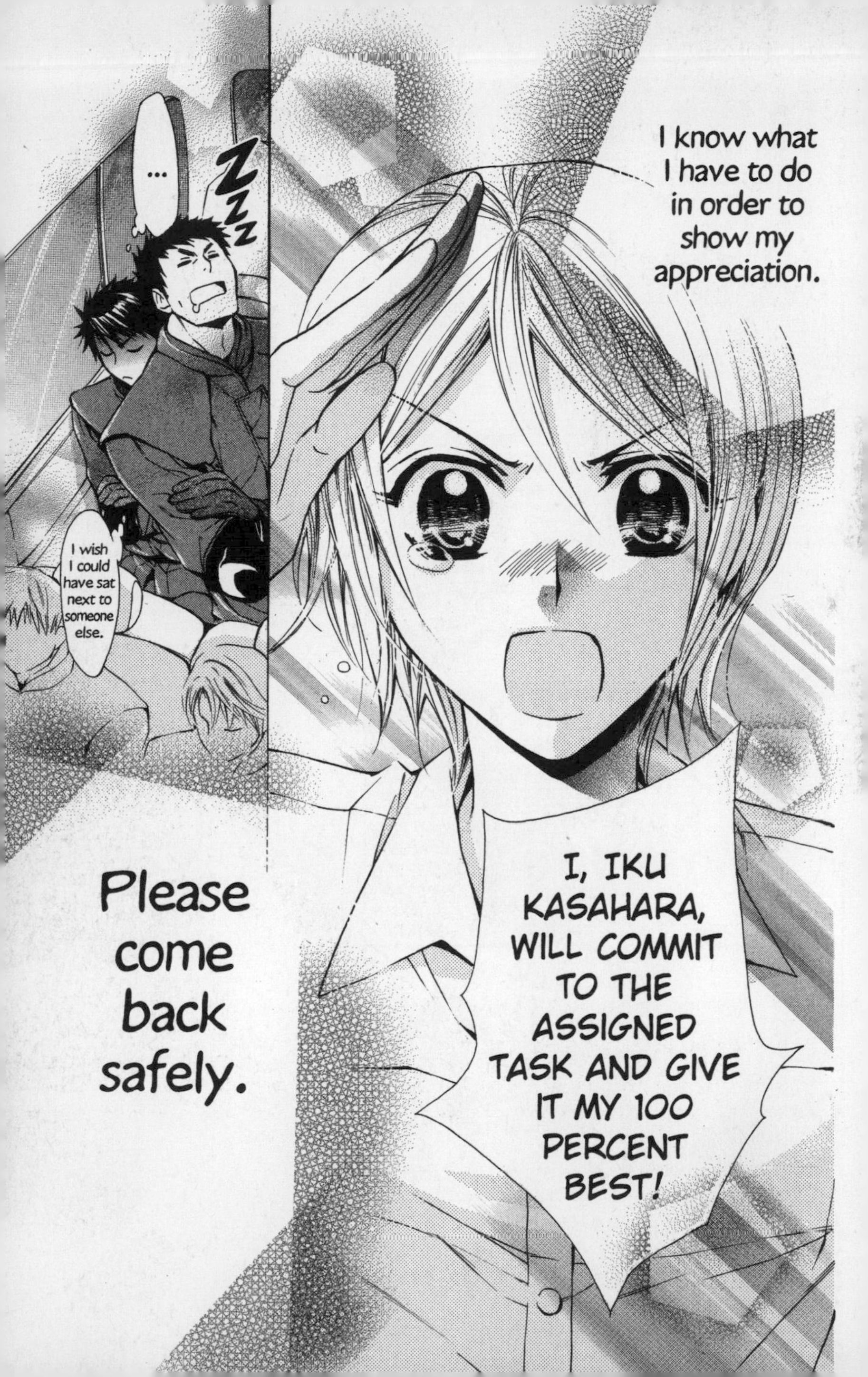
I know what I have to do in order to show my appreciation.
I, IKU KASAHARA, WILL COMMIT TO THE ASSIGNED TASK AND GIVE IT MY 100 PERCENT BEST!
...
ZZZ
I wish I could have sat next to someone else.
Please come back safely.

Big Bad Boss Genda

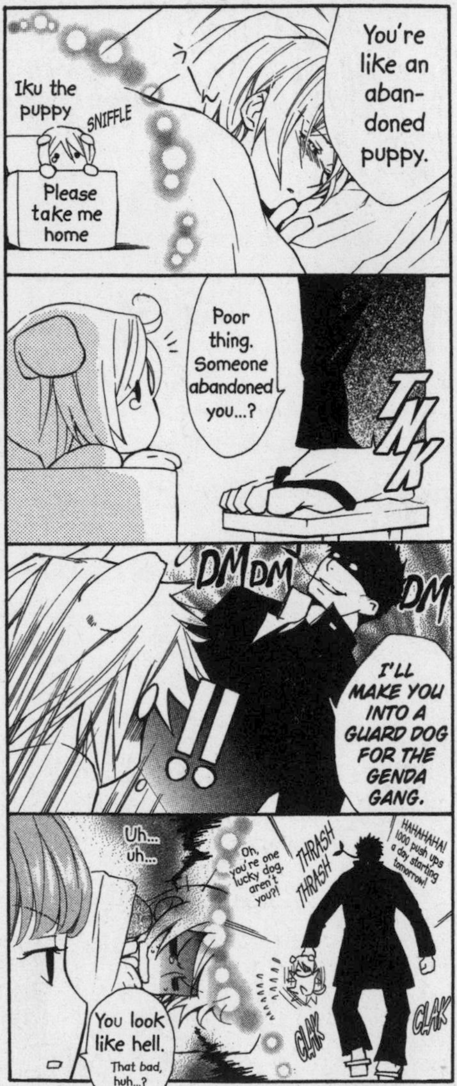
You're like an abandoned puppy.
Iku the puppy
SNIFFLE
Please take me home
TNK
Poor thing. Someone abandoned you...?
DM DM
DM
I'LL MAKE YOU INTO A GUARD DOG FOR THE GENDA GANG.
!!
HAHAHAHA! 1000 push ups a day starting tomorrow!
THRASH THRASH
Oh, you're one lucky dog, aren't you?!
Uh... uh...
CLAK
CLAK
You look like hell.
That bad, huh...?

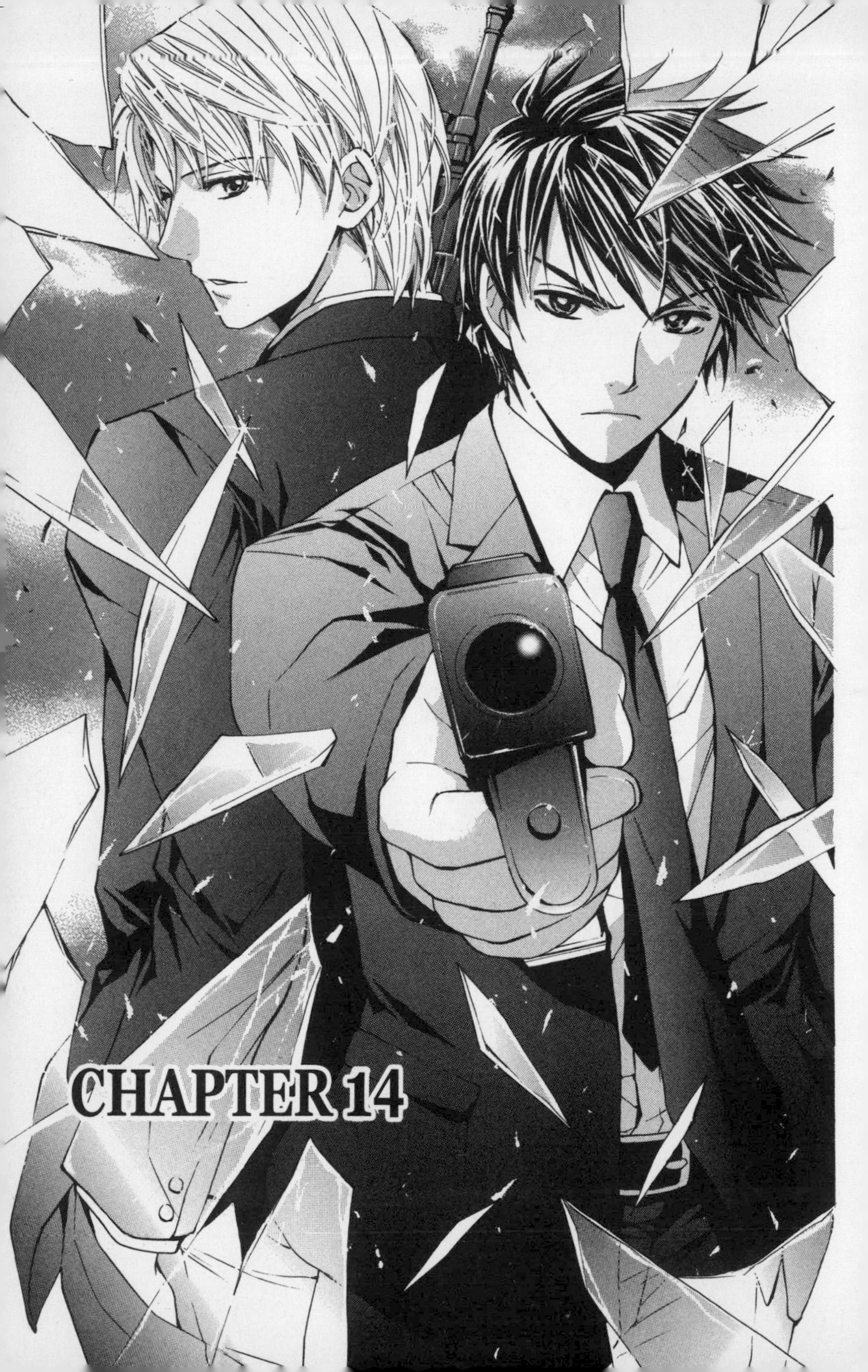
CHAPTER 14

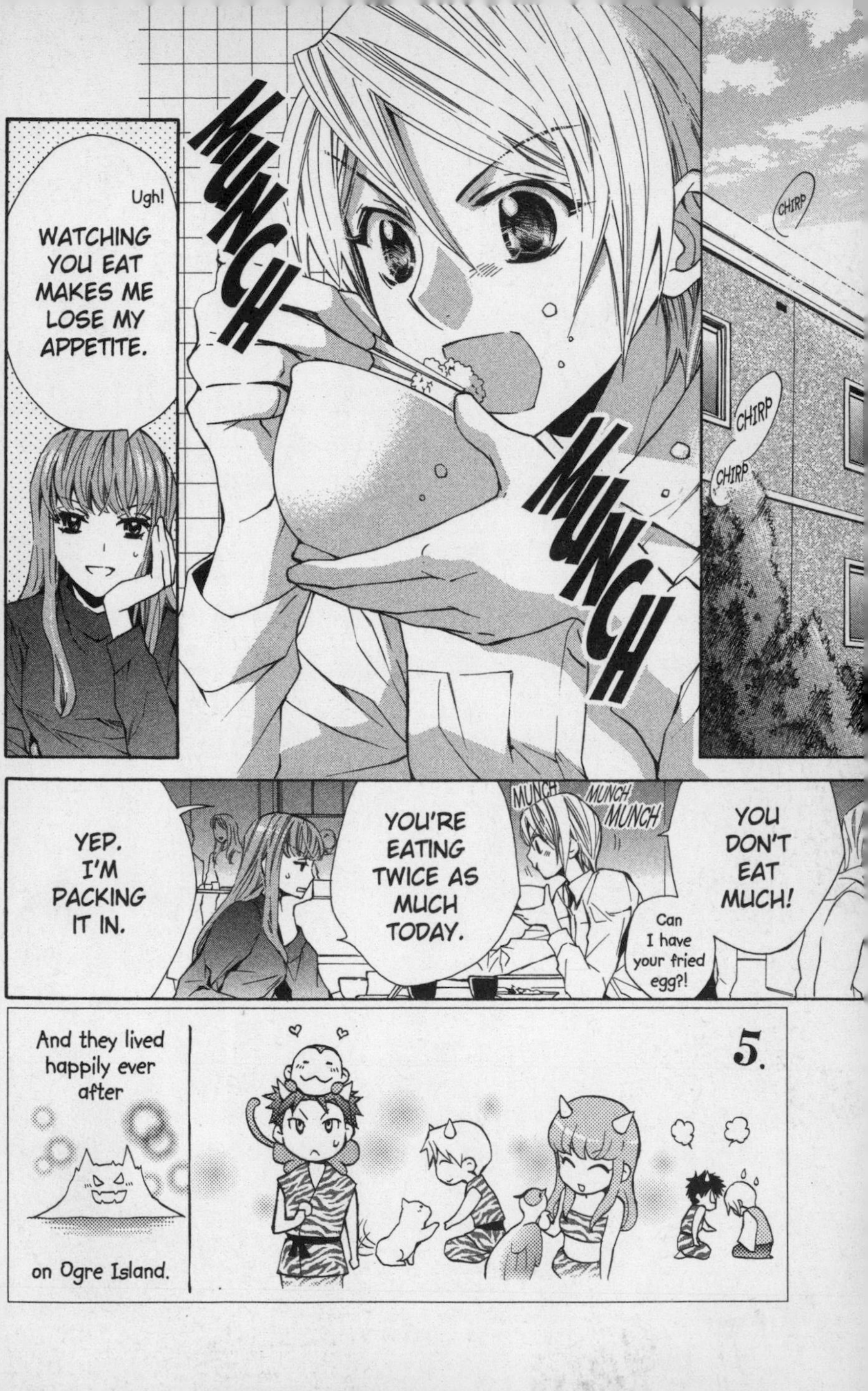

CHIRP
CHIRP
CHIRP
MUNCH
MUNCH
Ugh!
WATCHING YOU EAT MAKES ME LOSE MY APPETITE.
YOU DON'T EAT MUCH!
Can I have your fried egg?!
MUNCH
MUNCH MUNCH
YOU'RE EATING TWICE AS MUCH TODAY.
YEP. I'M PACKING IT IN.
5.
And they lived happily ever after
on Ogre Island.

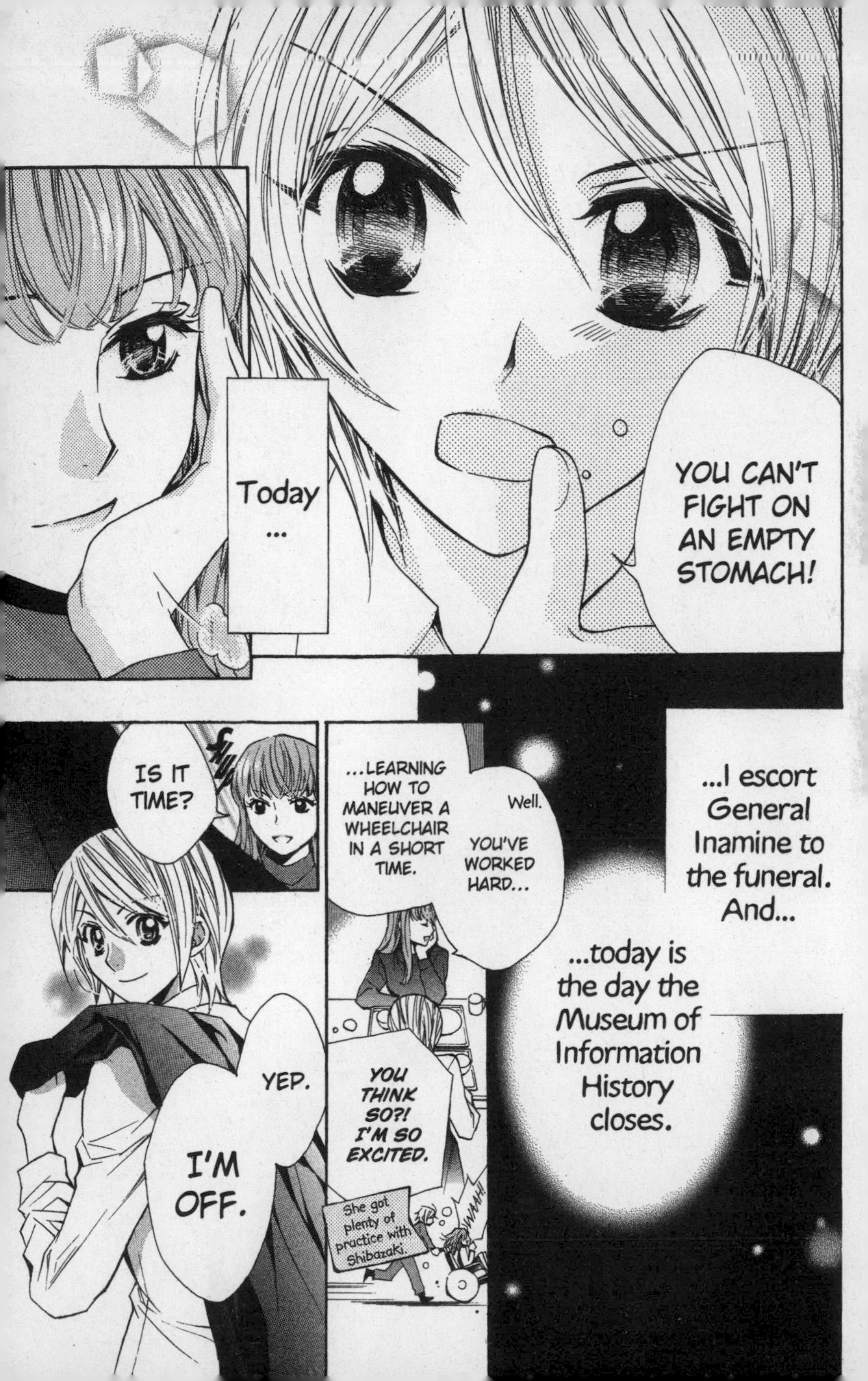
YOU CAN'T FIGHT ON AN EMPTY STOMACH!
Today ...
...I escort General Inamine to the funeral. And...
...today is the day the Museum of Information History closes.
Well.
YOU'VE WORKED HARD...
...LEARNING HOW TO MANEUVER A WHEELCHAIR IN A SHORT TIME.
YOU THINK SO?! I'M SO EXCITED.
WAAH!
She got plenty of practice with Shibazaki.
IS IT TIME?
YEP.
I'M OFF.

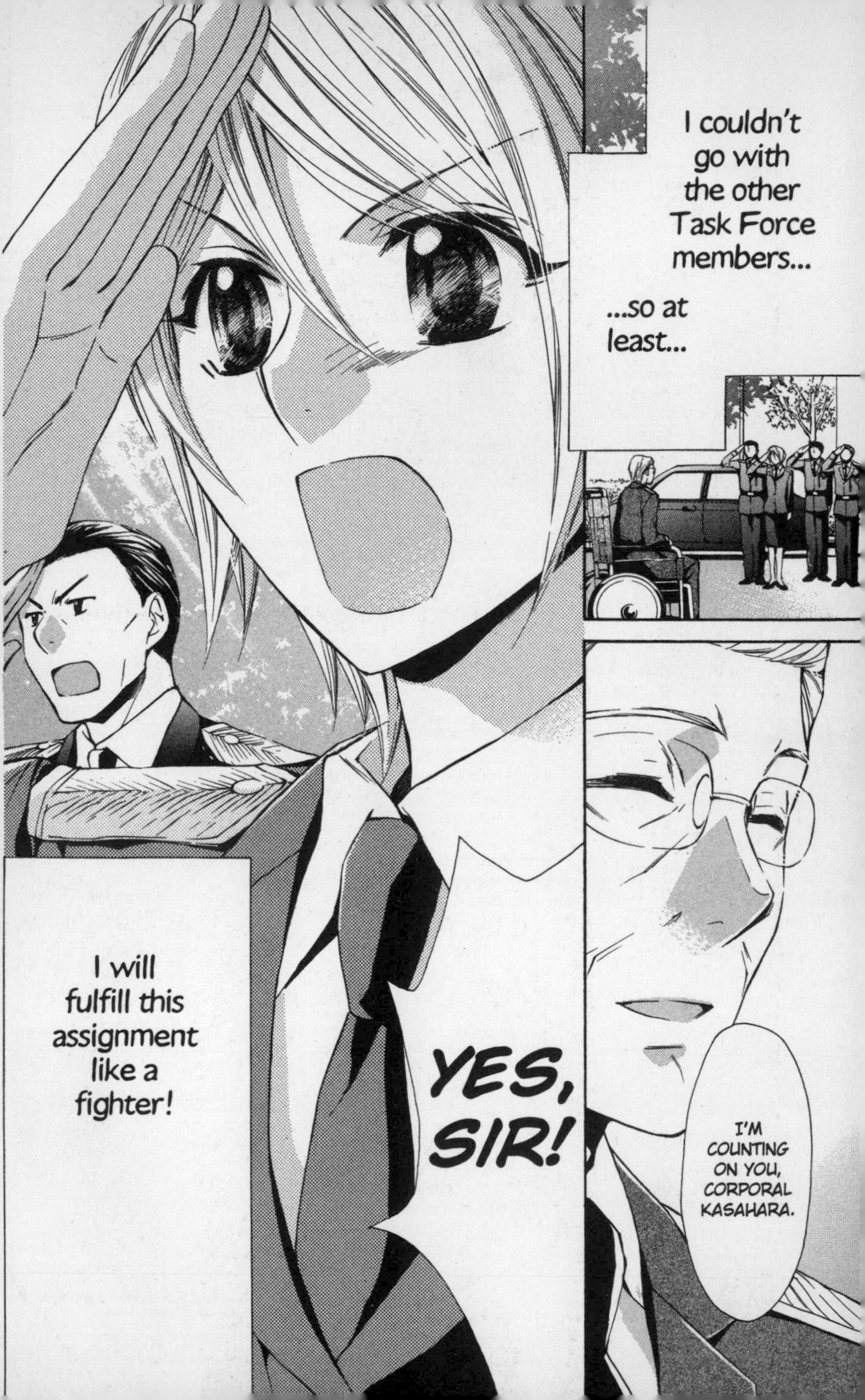
I couldn't go with the other Task Force members...
...so at least...
I'M COUNTING ON YOU, CORPORAL KASAHARA.
YES, SIR!
I will fulfill this assignment like a fighter!

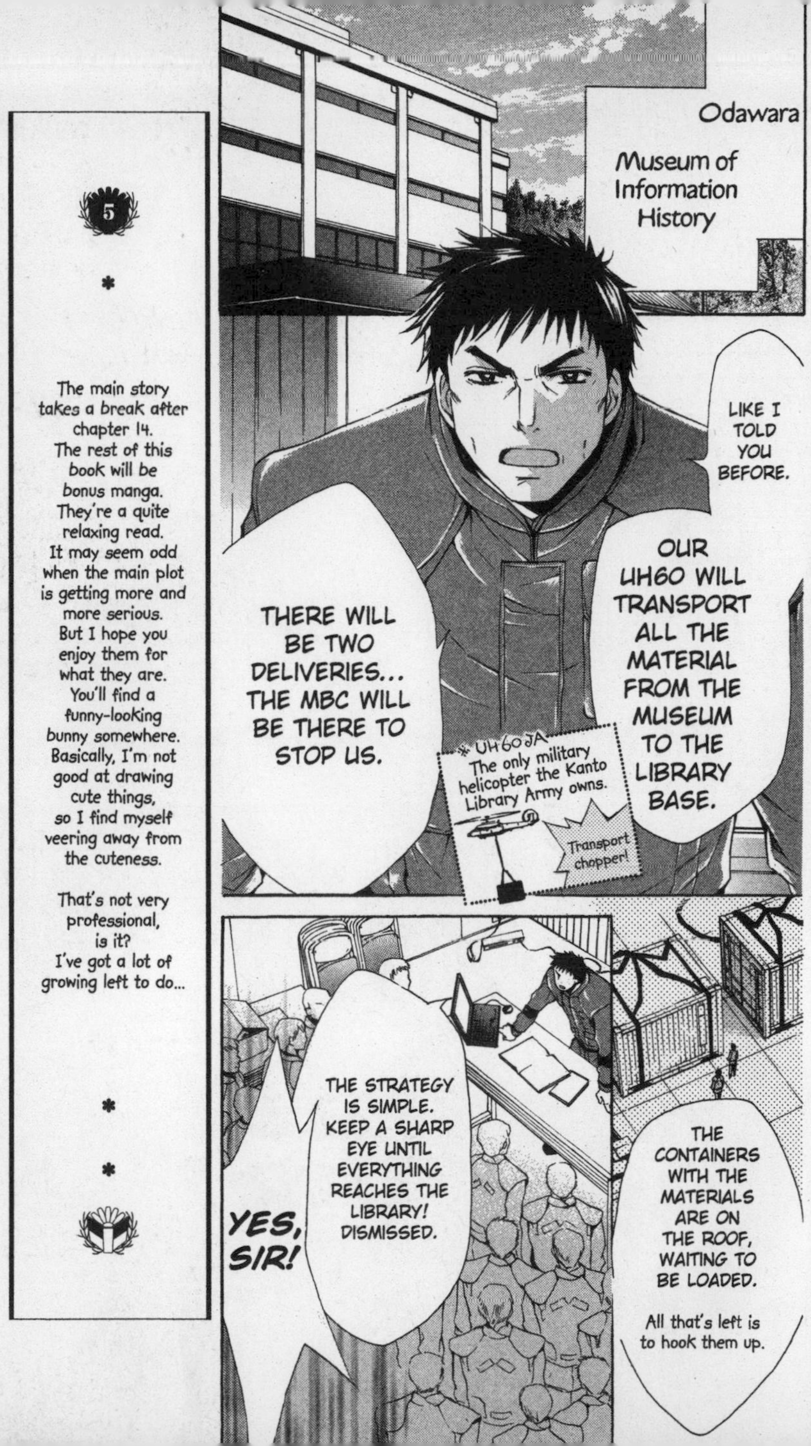
Odawara
Museum of Information History
LIKE I TOLD YOU BEFORE.
OUR UH60 WILL TRANSPORT ALL THE MATERIAL FROM THE MUSEUM TO THE LIBRARY BASE.
THERE WILL BE TWO DELIVERIES... THE MBC WILL BE THERE TO STOP US.
* UH60JA The only military helicopter the Kanto Library Army owns.
Transport chopper!
THE CONTAINERS WITH THE MATERIALS ARE ON THE ROOF, WAITING TO BE LOADED.
All that's left is to hook them up.
THE STRATEGY IS SIMPLE. KEEP A SHARP EYE UNTIL EVERYTHING REACHES THE LIBRARY! DISMISSED.
YES, SIR!

5

*

The main story takes a break after chapter 14. The rest of this book will be bonus manga. They're a quite relaxing read. It may seem odd when the main plot is getting more and more serious. But I hope you enjoy them for what they are. You'll find a funny-looking bunny somewhere. Basically, I'm not good at drawing cute things, so I find myself veering away from the cuteness.

That's not very professional, is it? I've got a lot of growing left to do...

*

*

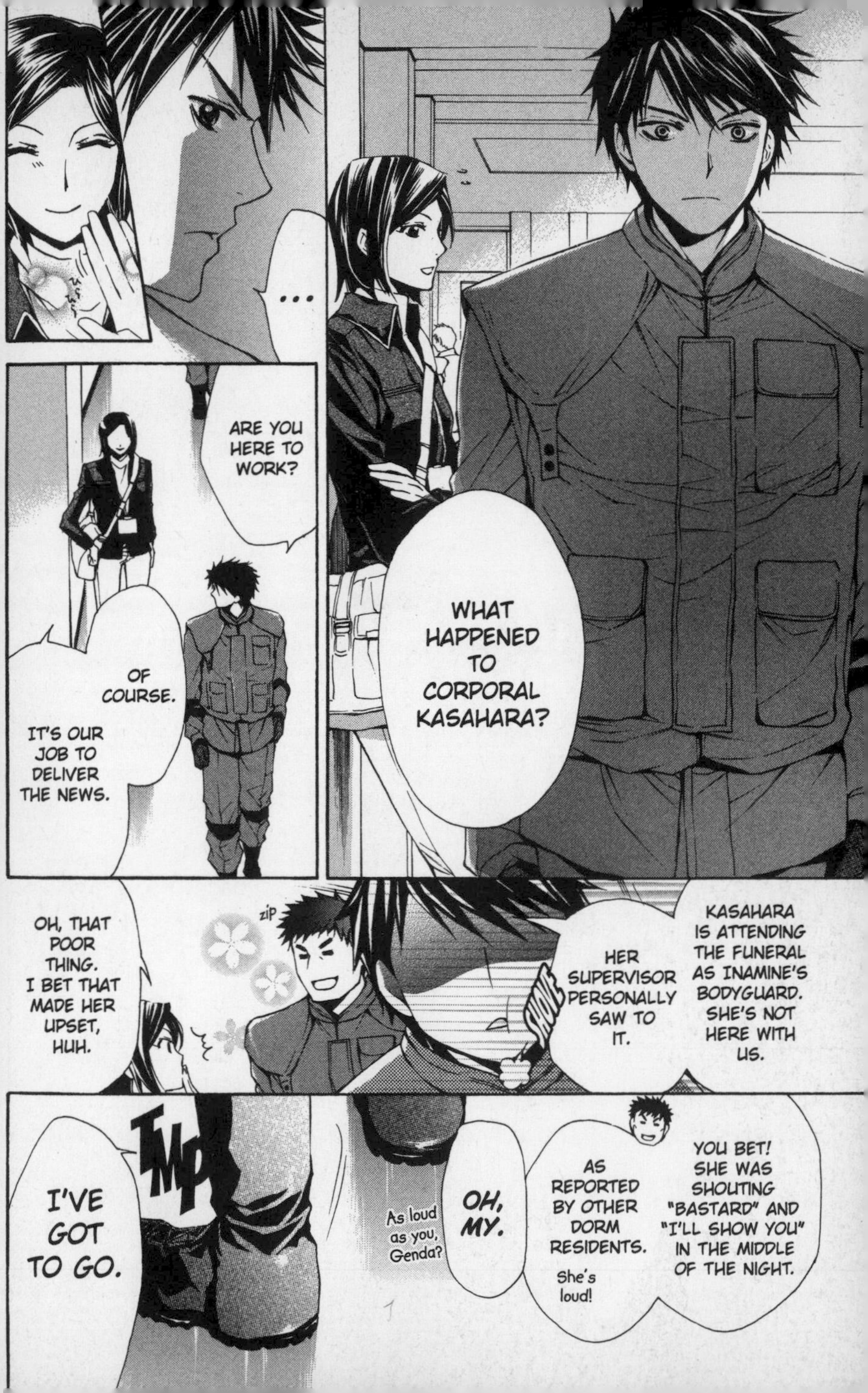
WHAT HAPPENED TO CORPORAL KASAHARA?
...
ARE YOU HERE TO WORK?
OF COURSE.
IT'S OUR JOB TO DELIVER THE NEWS.
KASAHARA IS ATTENDING THE FUNERAL AS INAMINE'S BODYGUARD. SHE'S NOT HERE WITH US.
HER SUPERVISOR PERSONALLY SAW TO IT.
SHOVE
zip
OH, THAT POOR THING. I BET THAT MADE HER UPSET, HUH.
YOU BET! SHE WAS SHOUTING "BASTARD" AND "I'LL SHOW YOU" IN THE MIDDLE OF THE NIGHT.
AS REPORTED BY OTHER DORM RESIDENTS.
She's loud!
OH, MY.
As loud as you, Genda?
TMP
I'VE GOT TO GO.

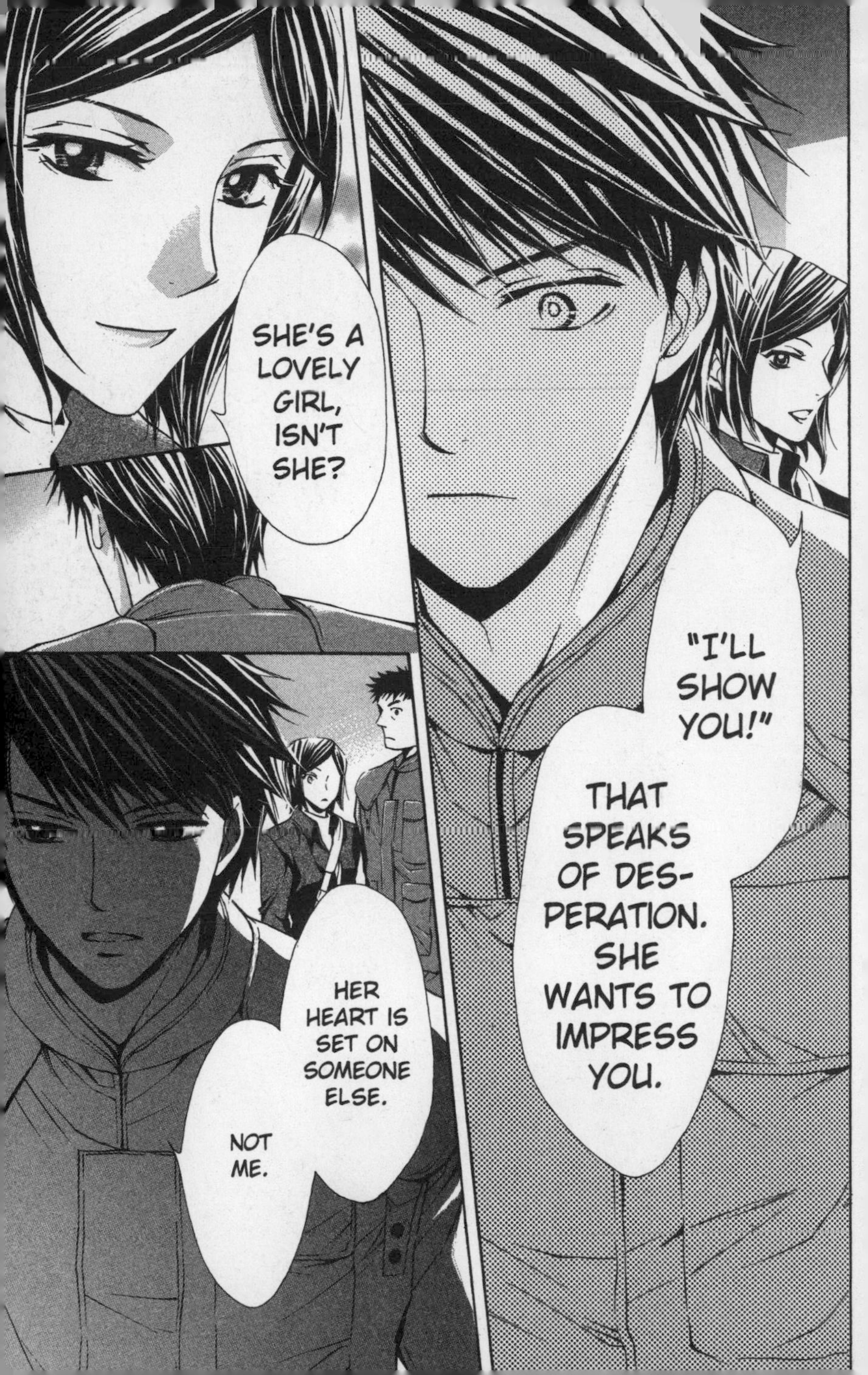
"I'LL SHOW YOU!"
THAT SPEAKS OF DES-PERATION. SHE WANTS TO IMPRESS YOU.
SHE'S A LOVELY GIRL, ISN'T SHE?
HER HEART IS SET ON SOMEONE ELSE.
NOT ME.

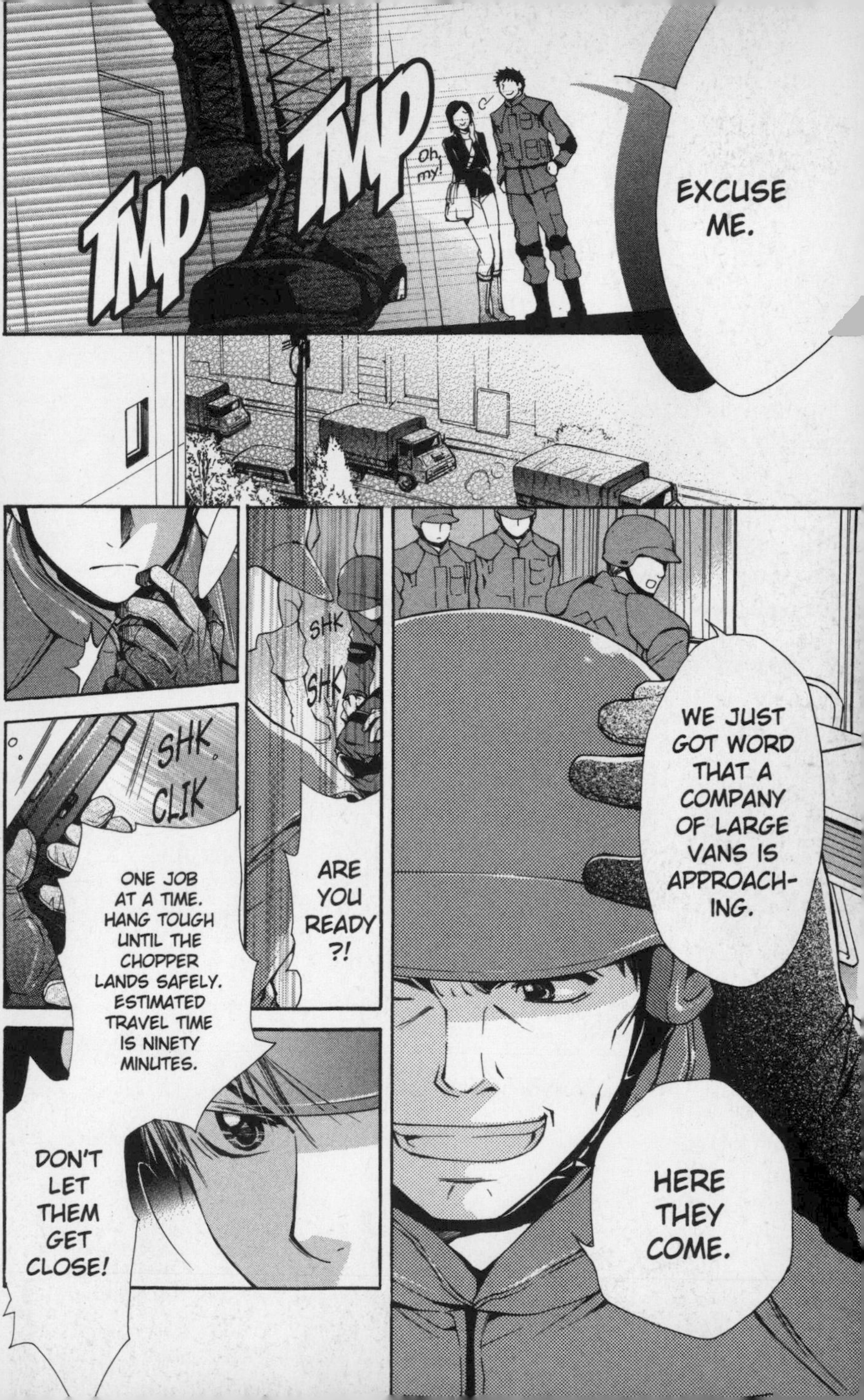
EXCUSE ME.
Oh, my!
TMP
TMP
WE JUST GOT WORD THAT A COMPANY OF LARGE VANS IS APPROACH-ING.
HERE THEY COME.
SHK
SHK
ARE YOU READY?!
SHK
CLIK
ONE JOB AT A TIME. HANG TOUGH UNTIL THE CHOPPER LANDS SAFELY. ESTIMATED TRAVEL TIME IS NINETY MINUTES.
DON'T LET THEM GET CLOSE!

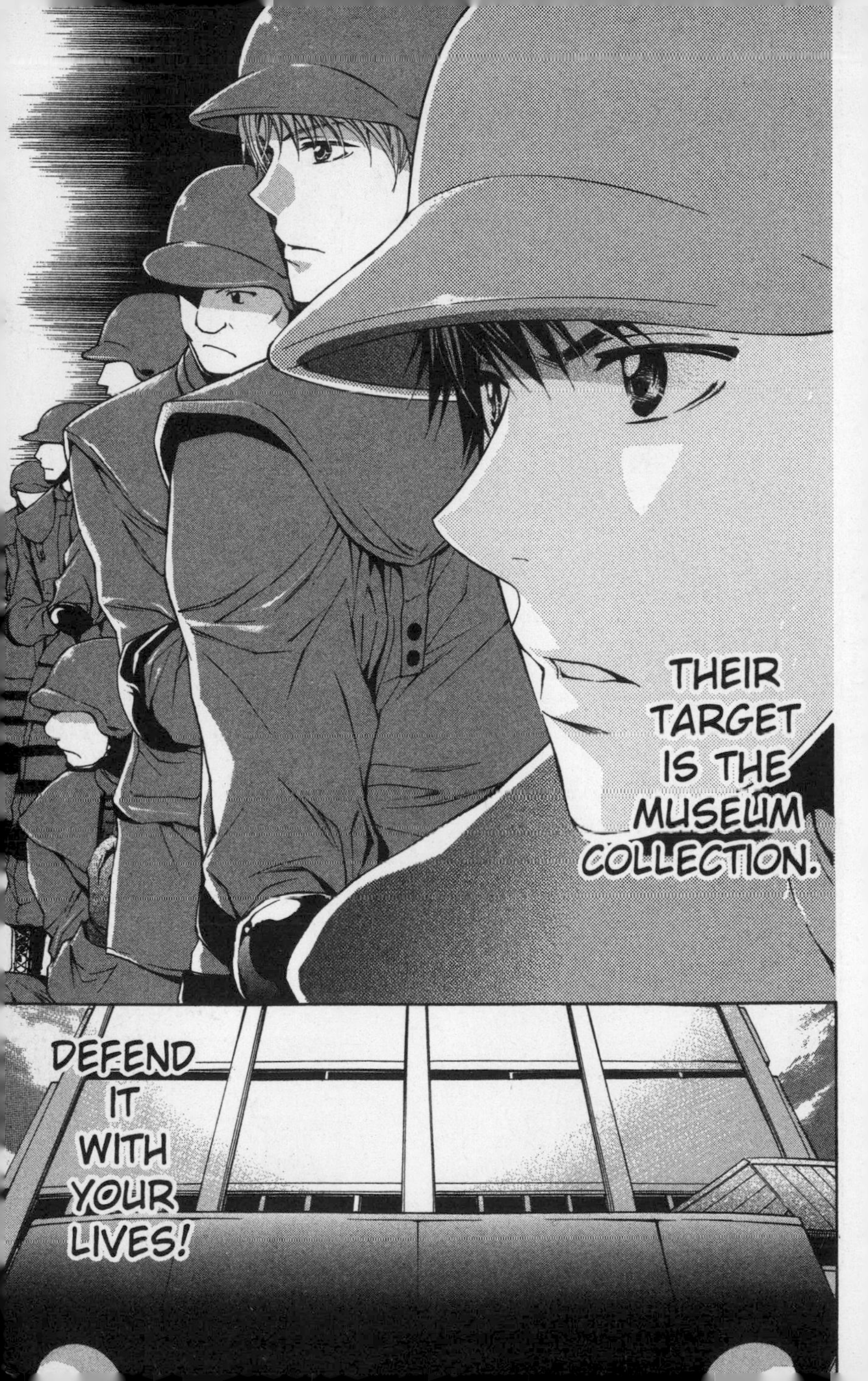
THEIR TARGET IS THE MUSEUM COLLECTION.
DEFEND IT WITH YOUR LIVES!

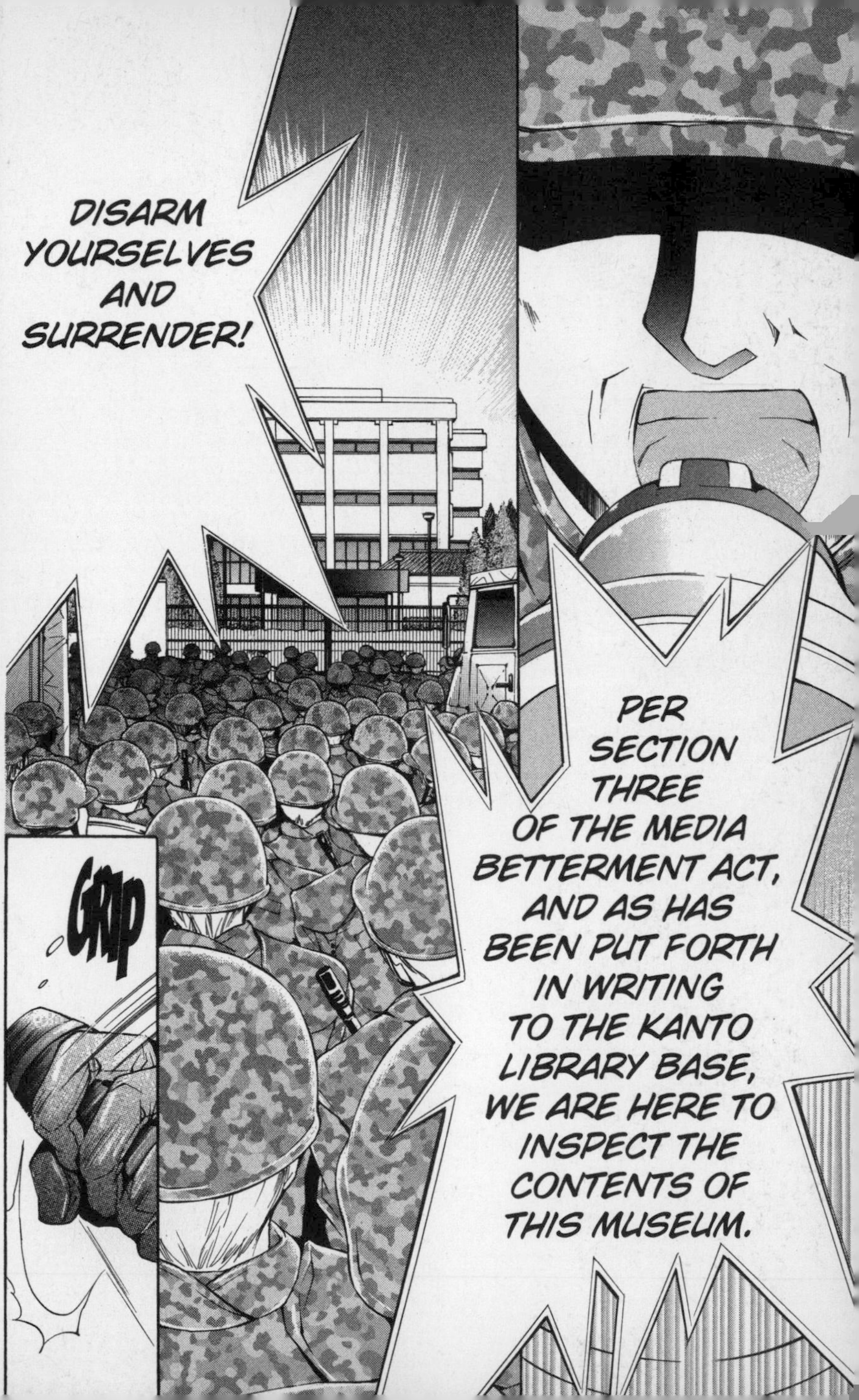
PER SECTION THREE OF THE MEDIA BETTERMENT ACT, AND AS HAS BEEN PUT FORTH IN WRITING TO THE KANTO LIBRARY BASE, WE ARE HERE TO INSPECT THE CONTENTS OF THIS MUSEUM.
DISARM YOURSELVES AND SURRENDER!
GRIP

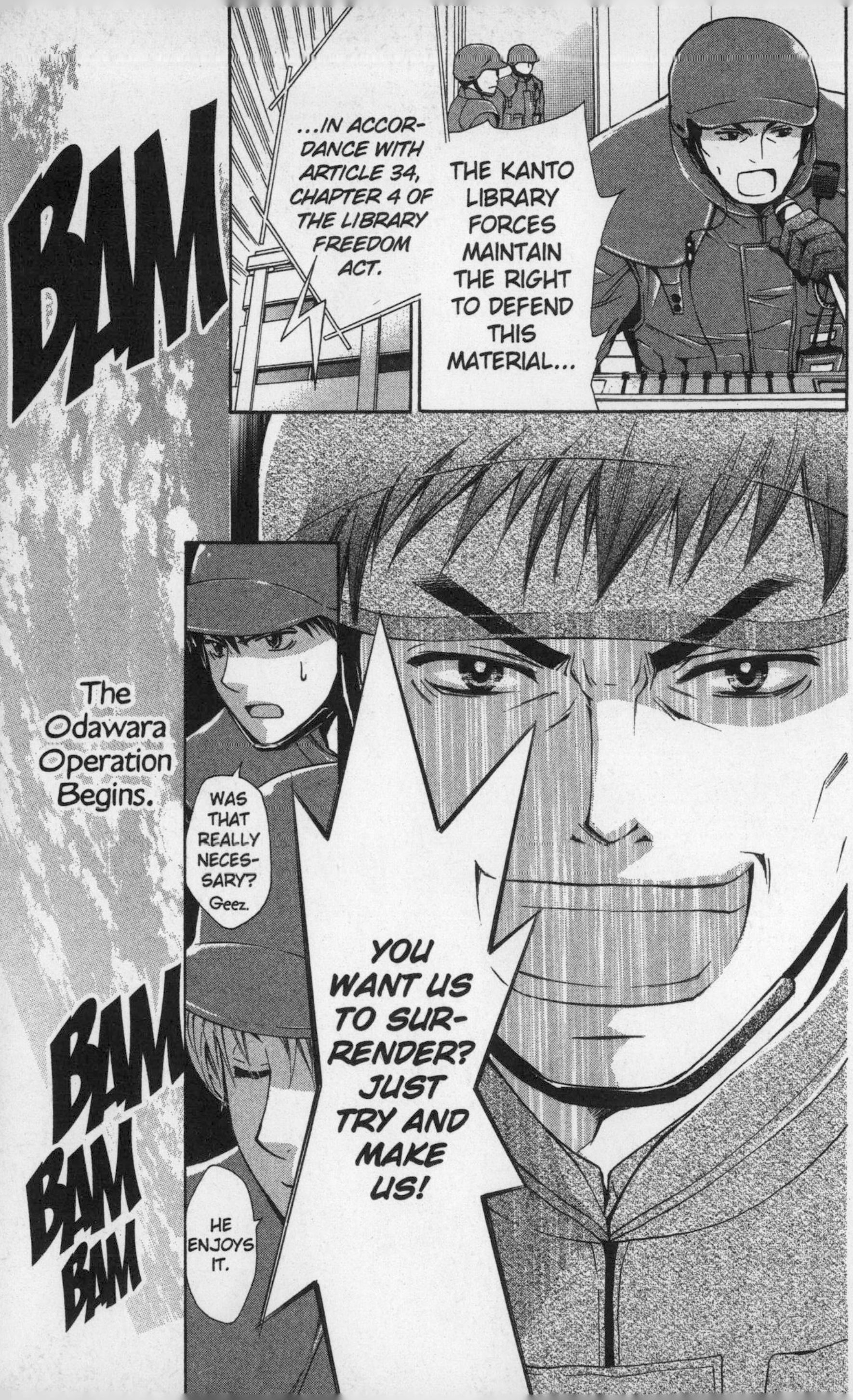
THE KANTO LIBRARY FORCES MAINTAIN THE RIGHT TO DEFEND THIS MATERIAL...
...IN ACCORDANCE WITH ARTICLE 34, CHAPTER 4 OF THE LIBRARY FREEDOM ACT.
BAM
YOU WANT US TO SURRENDER? JUST TRY AND MAKE US!
WAS THAT REALLY NECESSARY? Geez.
HE ENJOYS IT.
BAM BAM BAM
The Odawara Operation Begins.

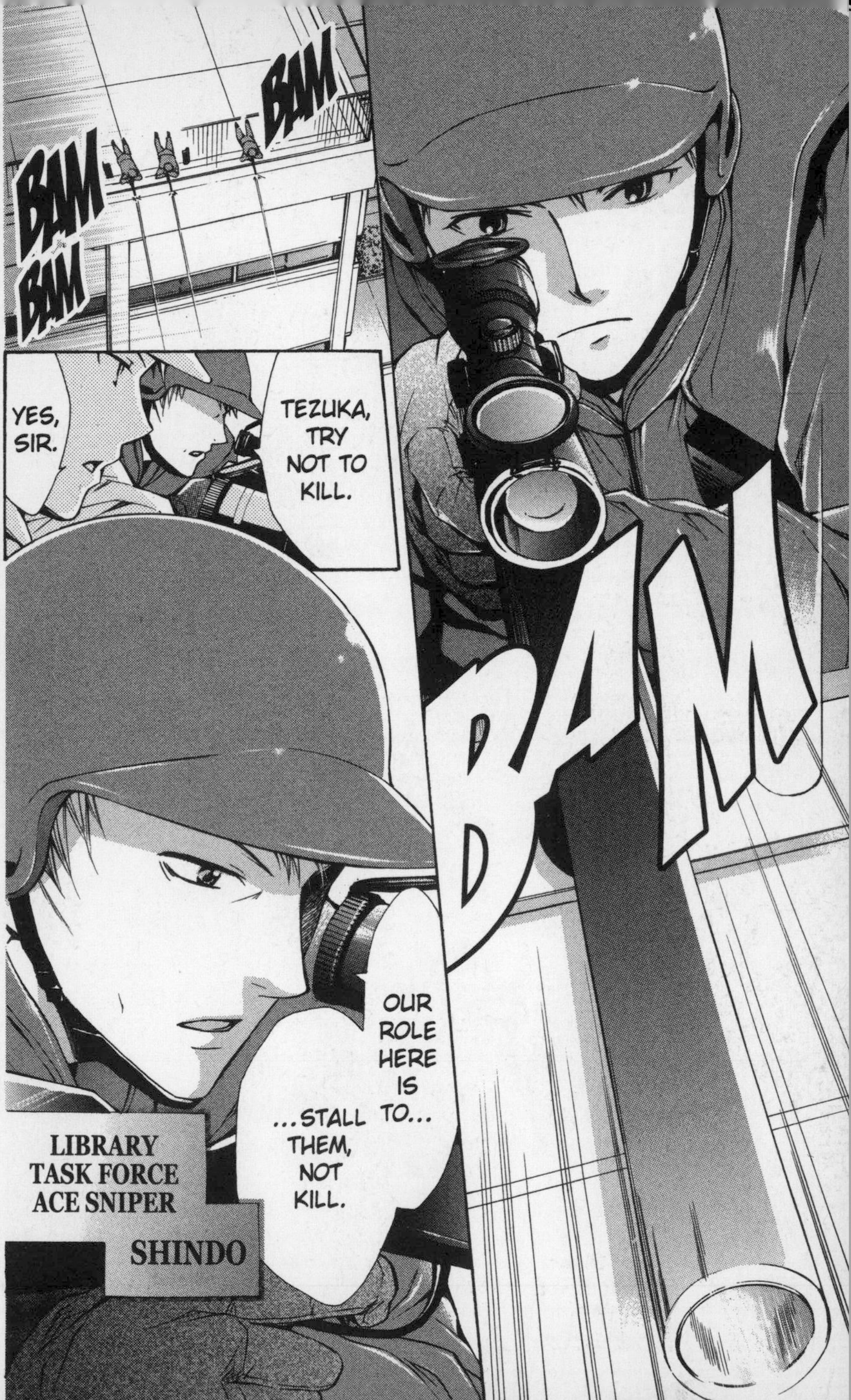
BAM
BAM
BAM
BAM
BAM
TEZUKA, TRY NOT TO KILL.
YES, SIR.
OUR ROLE HERE IS TO...
...STALL THEM, NOT KILL.
LIBRARY TASK FORCE ACE SNIPER
SHINDO

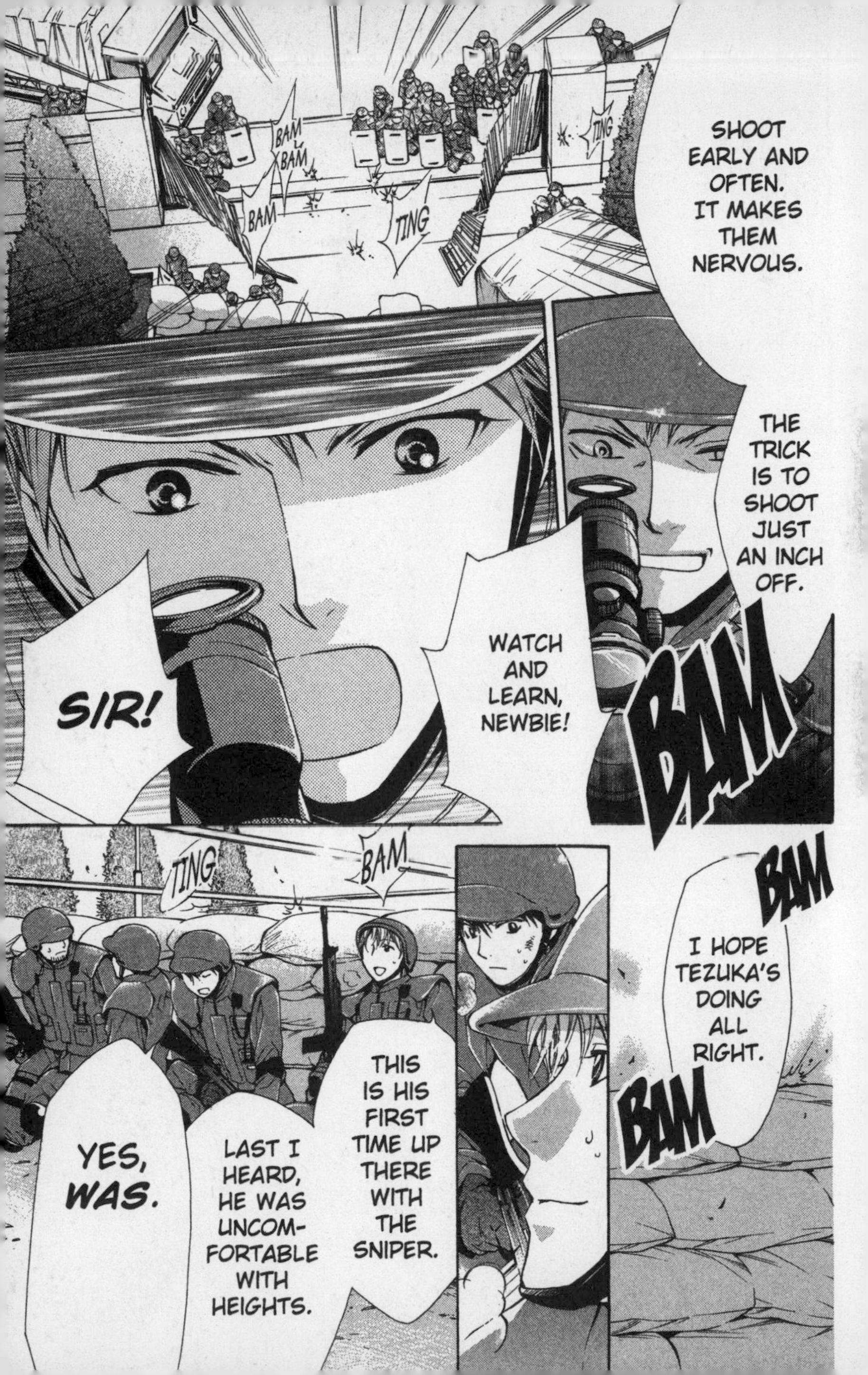
SHOOT EARLY AND OFTEN. IT MAKES THEM NERVOUS.
TING
BAM BAM
TING
BAM
THE TRICK IS TO SHOOT JUST AN INCH OFF.
BAM
WATCH AND LEARN, NEWBIE!
SIR!
BAM
I HOPE TEZUKA'S DOING ALL RIGHT.
BAM
BAM
TING
THIS IS HIS FIRST TIME UP THERE WITH THE SNIPER.
LAST I HEARD, HE WAS UNCOM-FORTABLE WITH HEIGHTS.
YES, *WAS*.

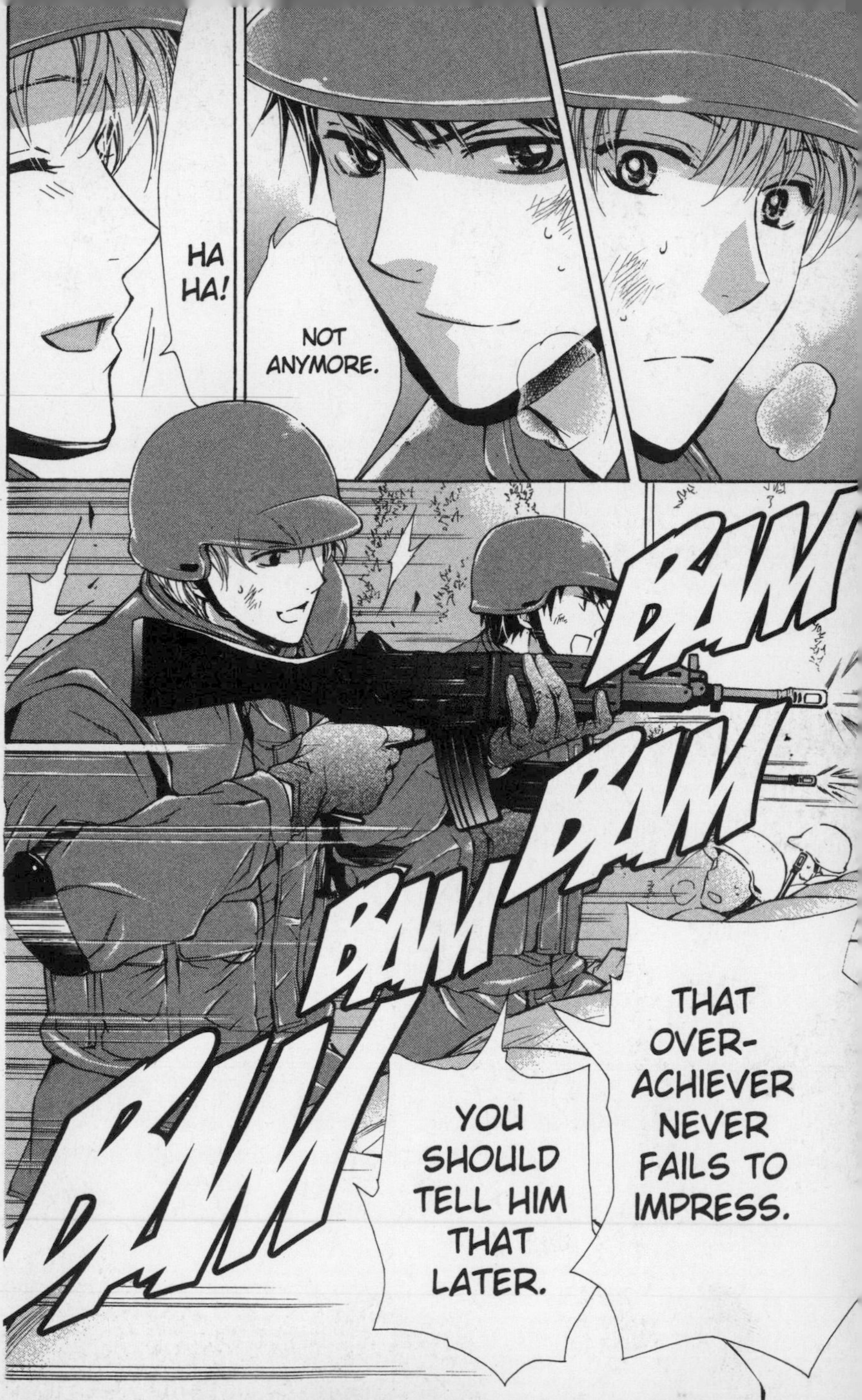
NOT ANYMORE.
HA HA!
BAM
BAM
BAM
BAM
THAT OVER-ACHIEVER NEVER FAILS TO IMPRESS.
YOU SHOULD TELL HIM THAT LATER.

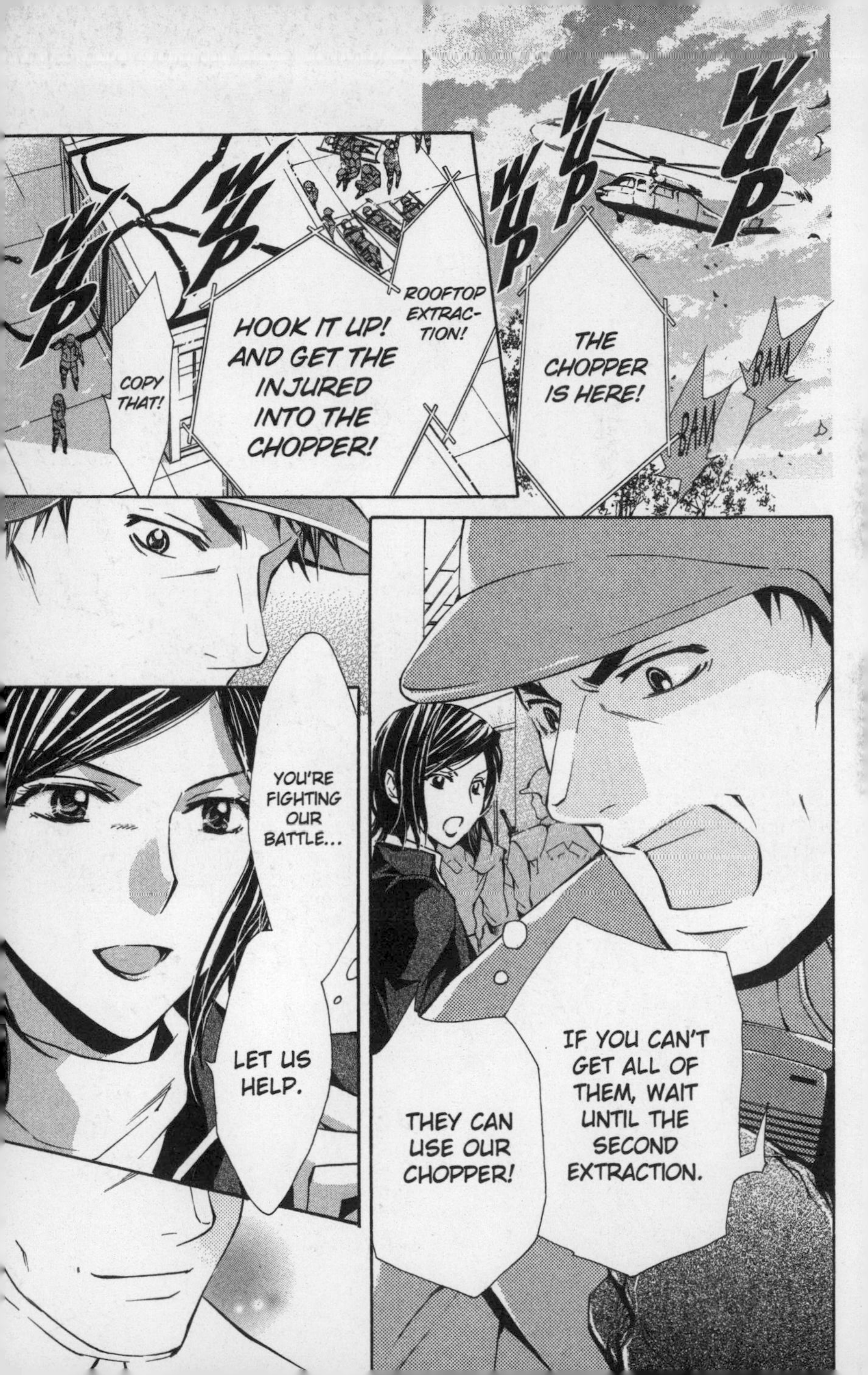
WUP
WUP
WUP
THE CHOPPER IS HERE!
BAM
BAM
ROOFTOP EXTRACTION!
HOOK IT UP! AND GET THE INJURED INTO THE CHOPPER!
WUP
WUP
COPY THAT!
IF YOU CAN'T GET ALL OF THEM, WAIT UNTIL THE SECOND EXTRACTION.
THEY CAN USE OUR CHOPPER!
YOU'RE FIGHTING OUR BATTLE...
LET US HELP.

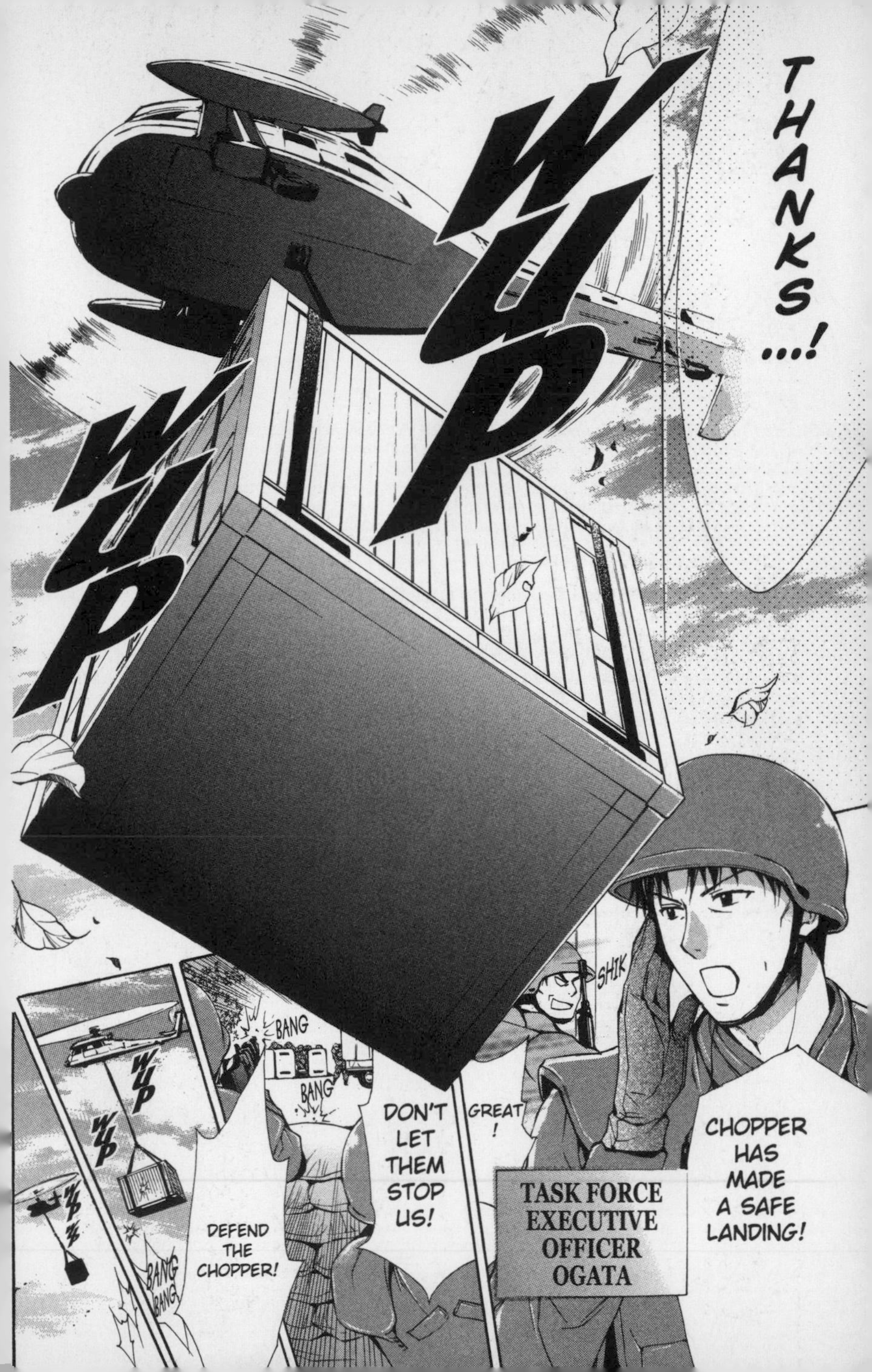
THANKS...!
WUP
WUP
SHIK
CHOPPER HAS MADE A SAFE LANDING!
TASK FORCE EXECUTIVE OFFICER OGATA
GREAT!
DON'T LET THEM STOP US!
BANG
BANG
DEFEND THE CHOPPER!
WUP
WUP
WUP
BANG
BANG

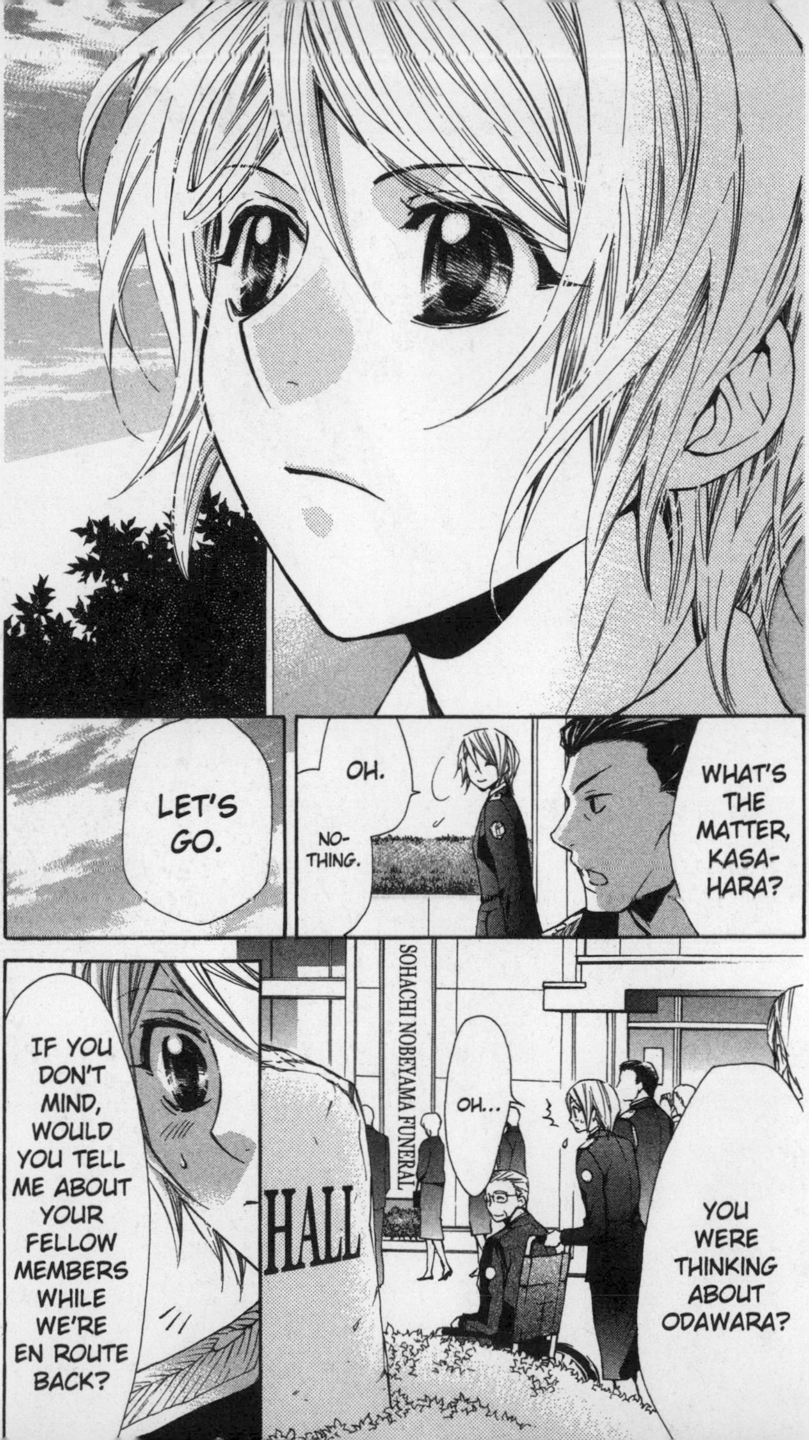
WHAT'S THE MATTER, KASAHARA?
OH.
NOTHING.
LET'S GO.
YOU WERE THINKING ABOUT ODAWARA?
OH...
SOHACHI NOBEYAMA FUNERAL HALL
IF YOU DON'T MIND, WOULD YOU TELL ME ABOUT YOUR FELLOW MEMBERS WHILE WE'RE EN ROUTE BACK?

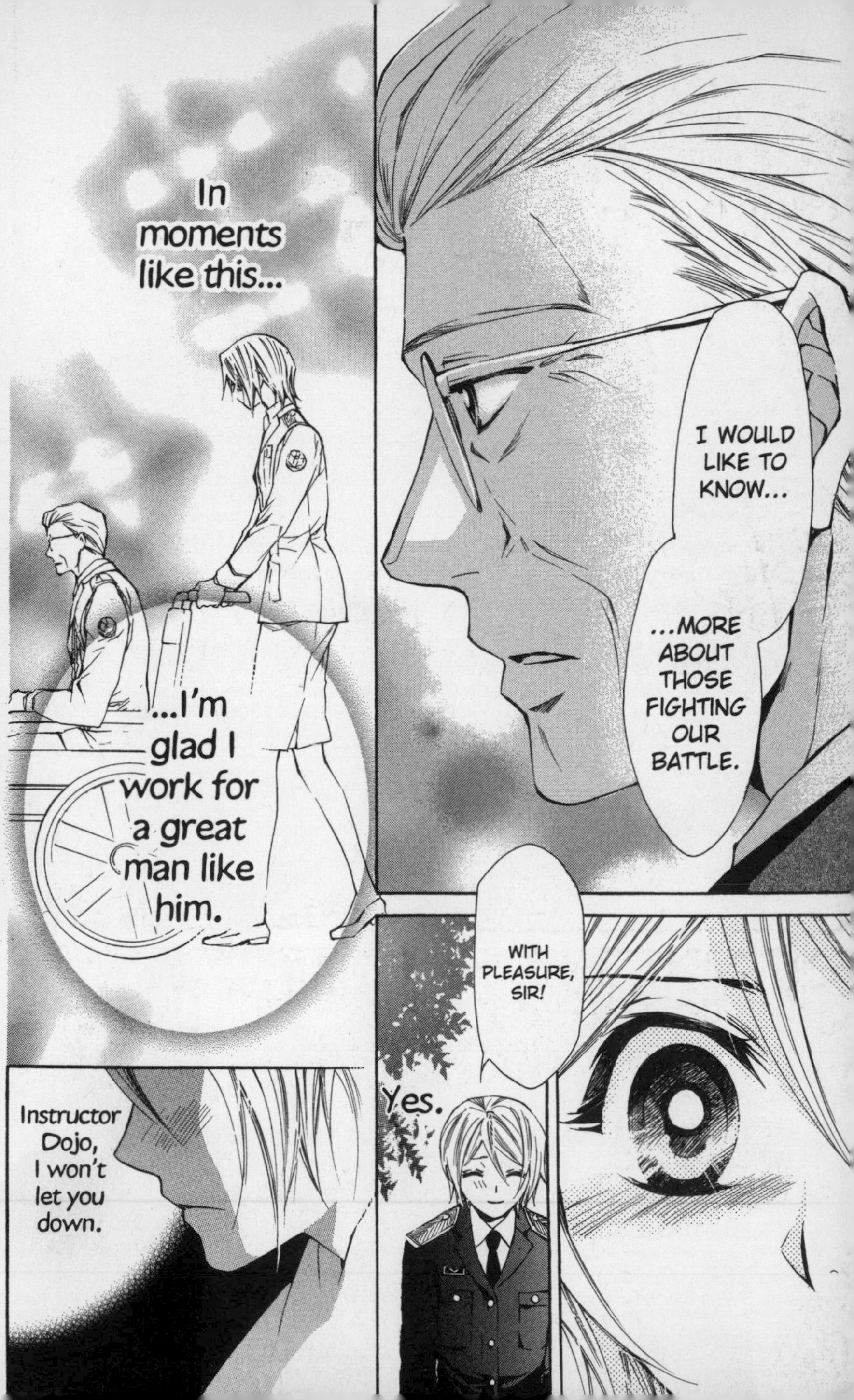
I WOULD LIKE TO KNOW...
...MORE ABOUT THOSE FIGHTING OUR BATTLE.
WITH PLEASURE, SIR!
Yes.
In moments like this...
...I'm glad I work for a great man like him.
Instructor Dojo, I won't let you down.

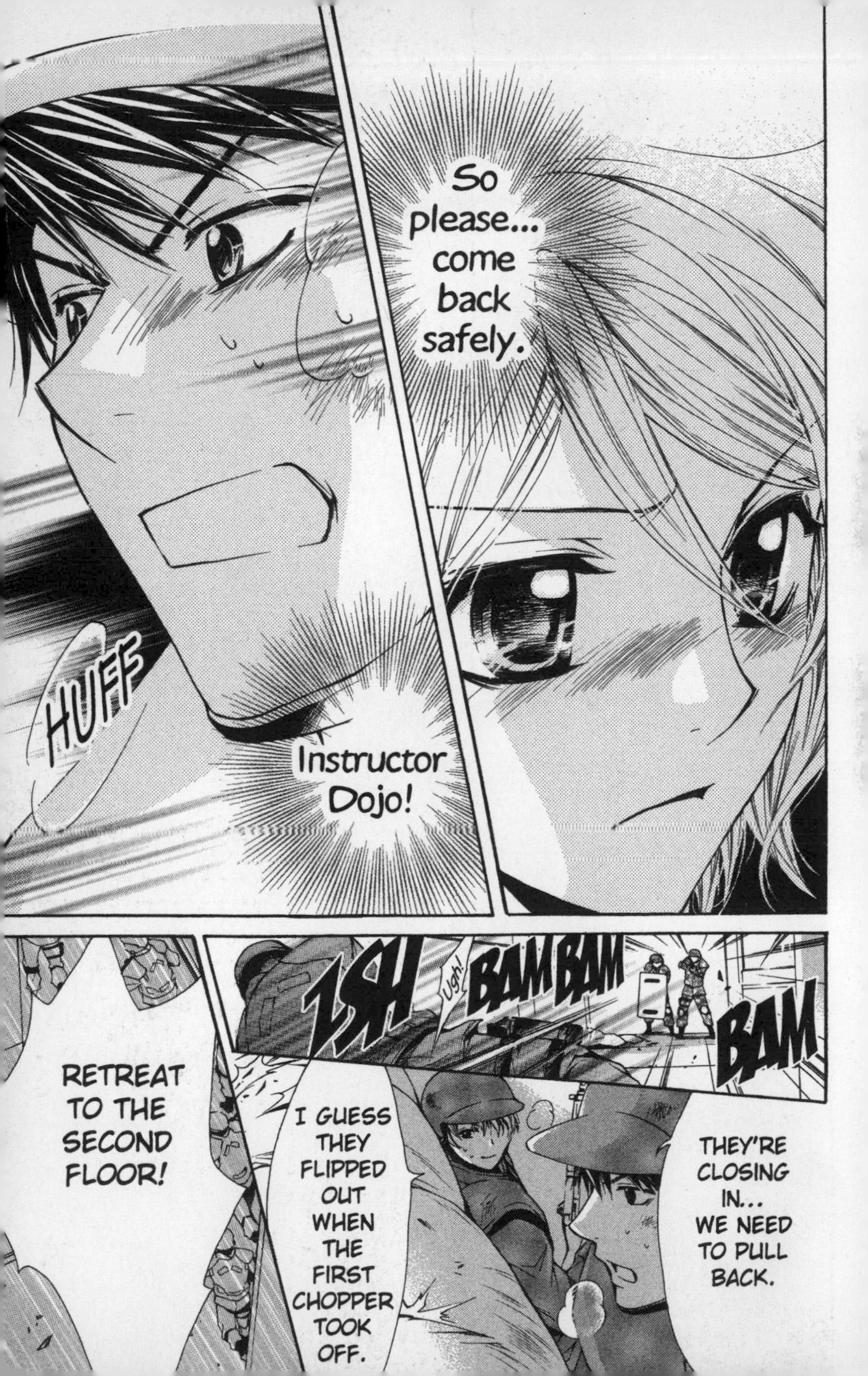
So please... come back safely.
Instructor Dojo!
HUFF
BAM
BAM BAM
Ugh!
ZSH
THEY'RE CLOSING IN... WE NEED TO PULL BACK.
I GUESS THEY FLIPPED OUT WHEN THE FIRST CHOPPER TOOK OFF.
RETREAT TO THE SECOND FLOOR!

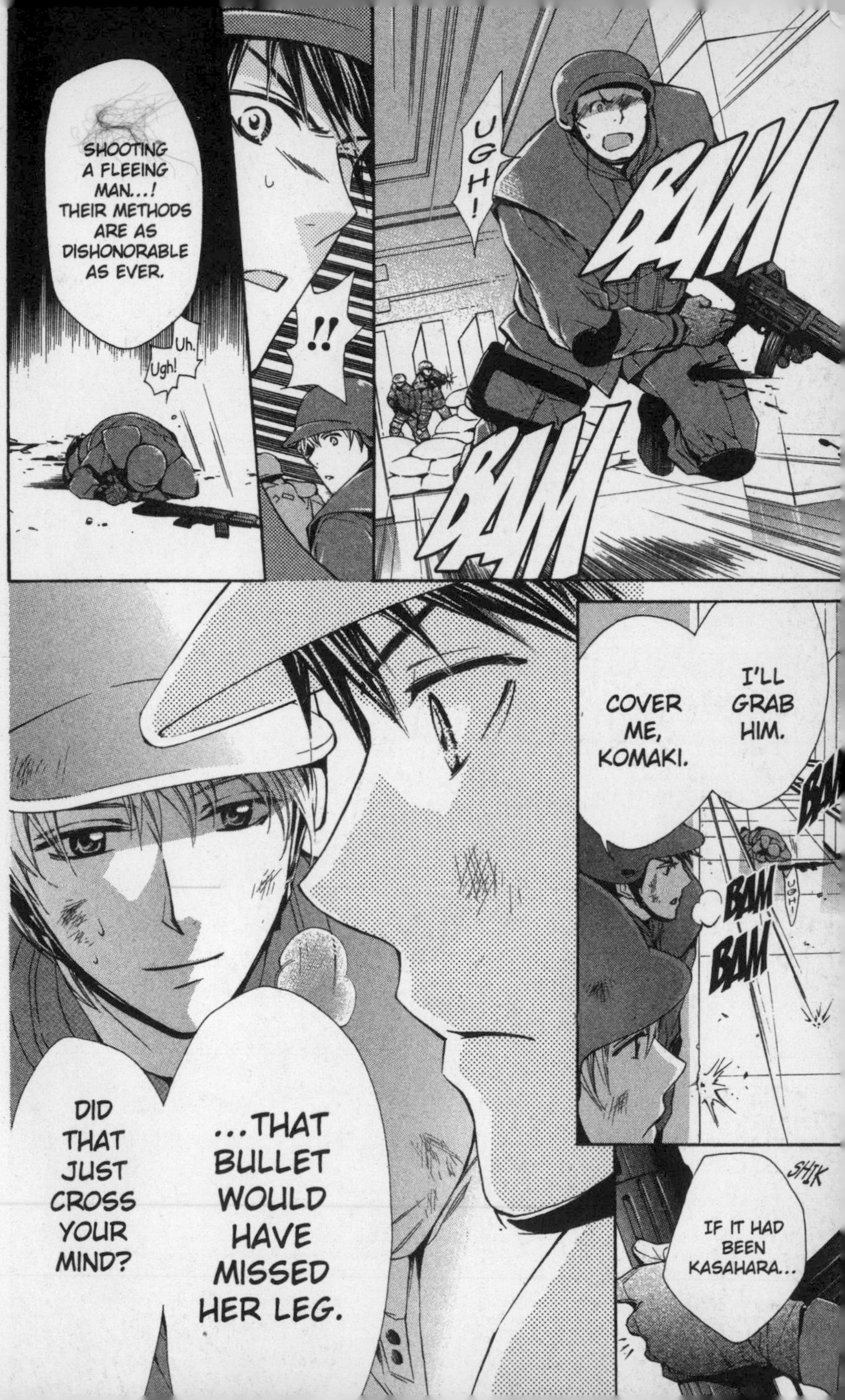
UGH!
BAM
BAM
SHOOTING A FLEEING MAN...! THEIR METHODS ARE AS DISHONORABLE AS EVER.
!!
Uh.
Ugh!
I'LL GRAB HIM.
COVER ME, KOMAKI.
BAM
UGH!
BAM
BAM
SHIK
IF IT HAD BEEN KASAHARA...
...THAT BULLET WOULD HAVE MISSED HER LEG.
DID THAT JUST CROSS YOUR MIND?

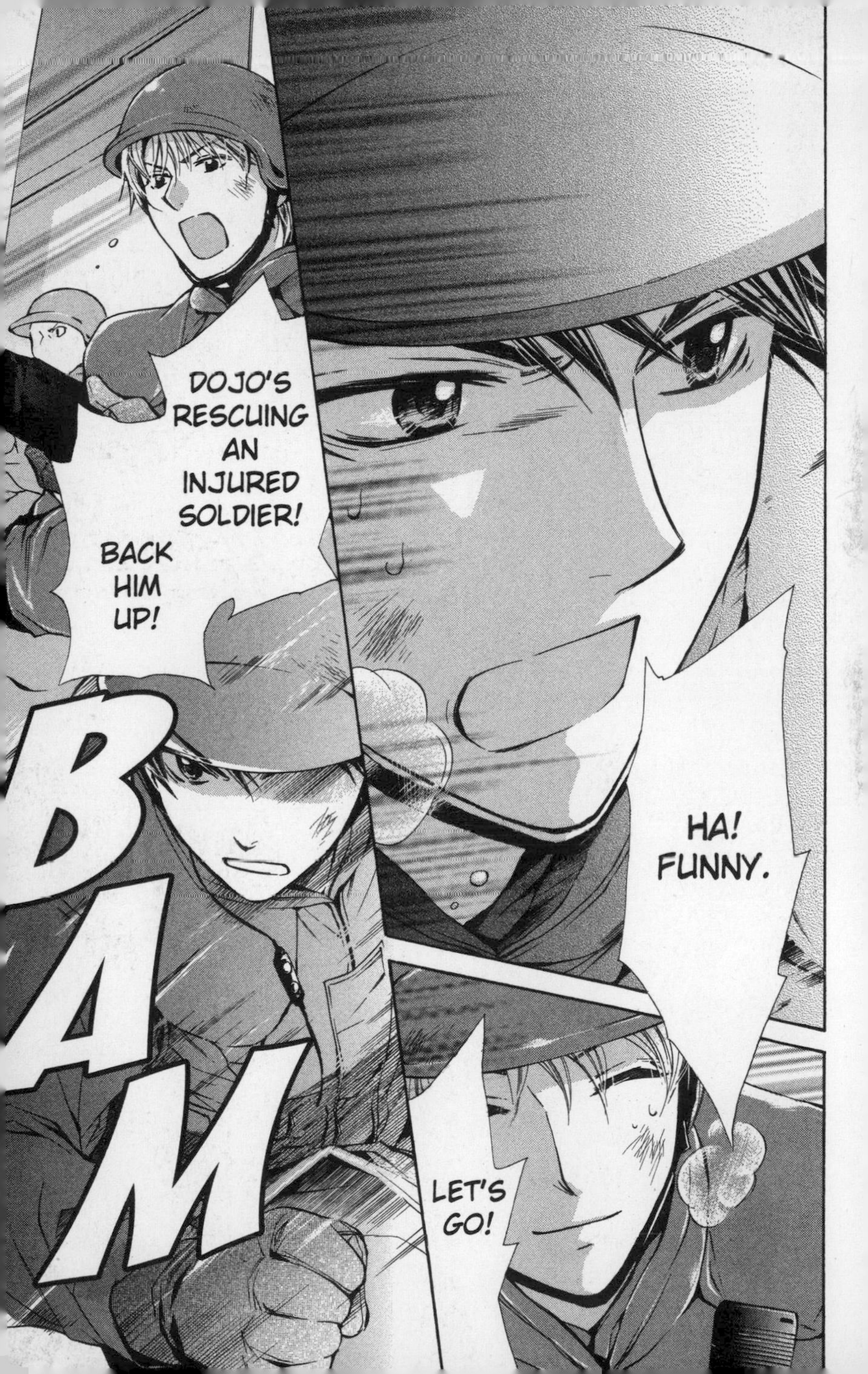
DOJO'S RESCUING AN INJURED SOLDIER!
BACK HIM UP!
BAM
HA! FUNNY.
LET'S GO!

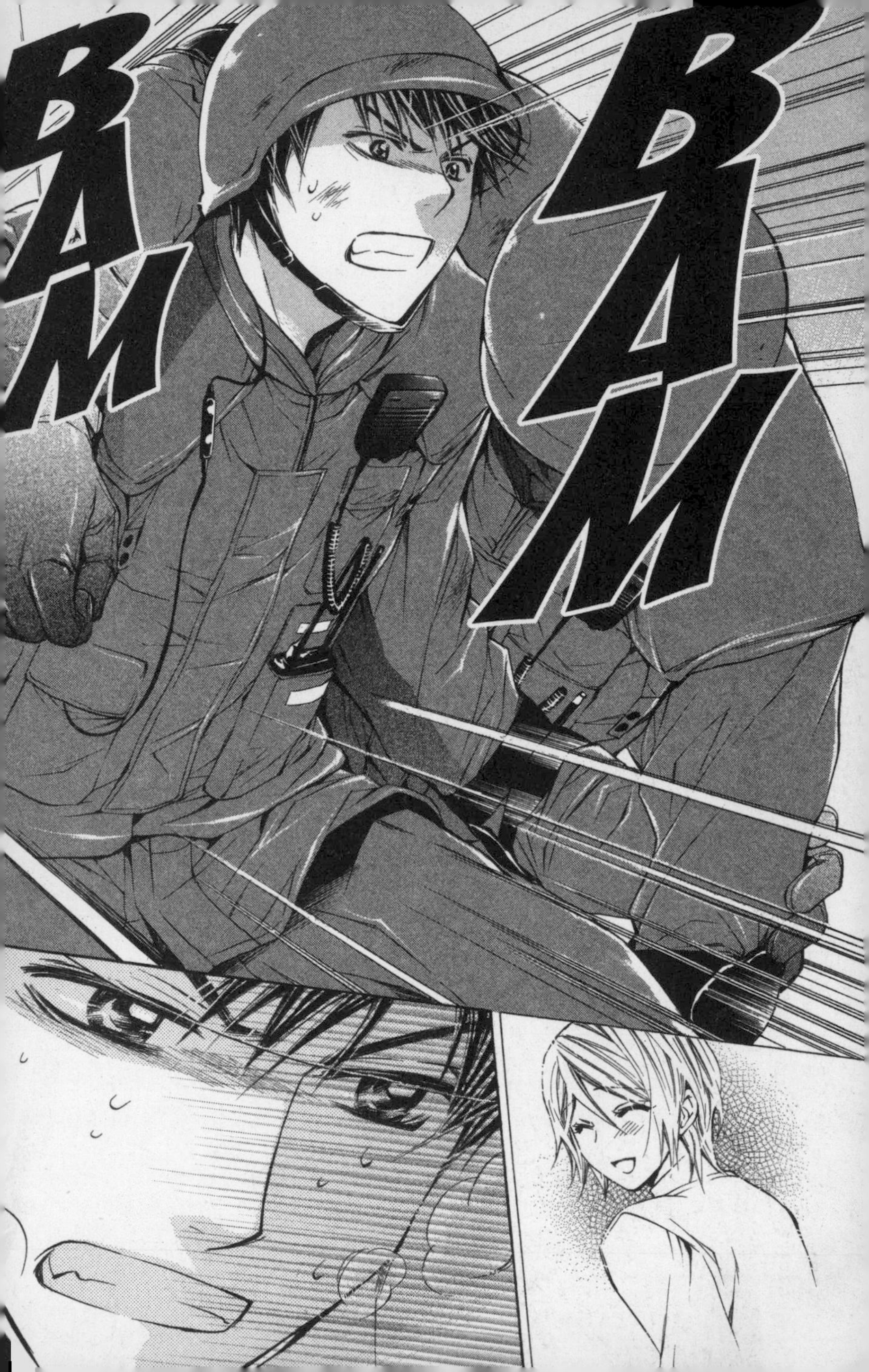
BAM
BAM

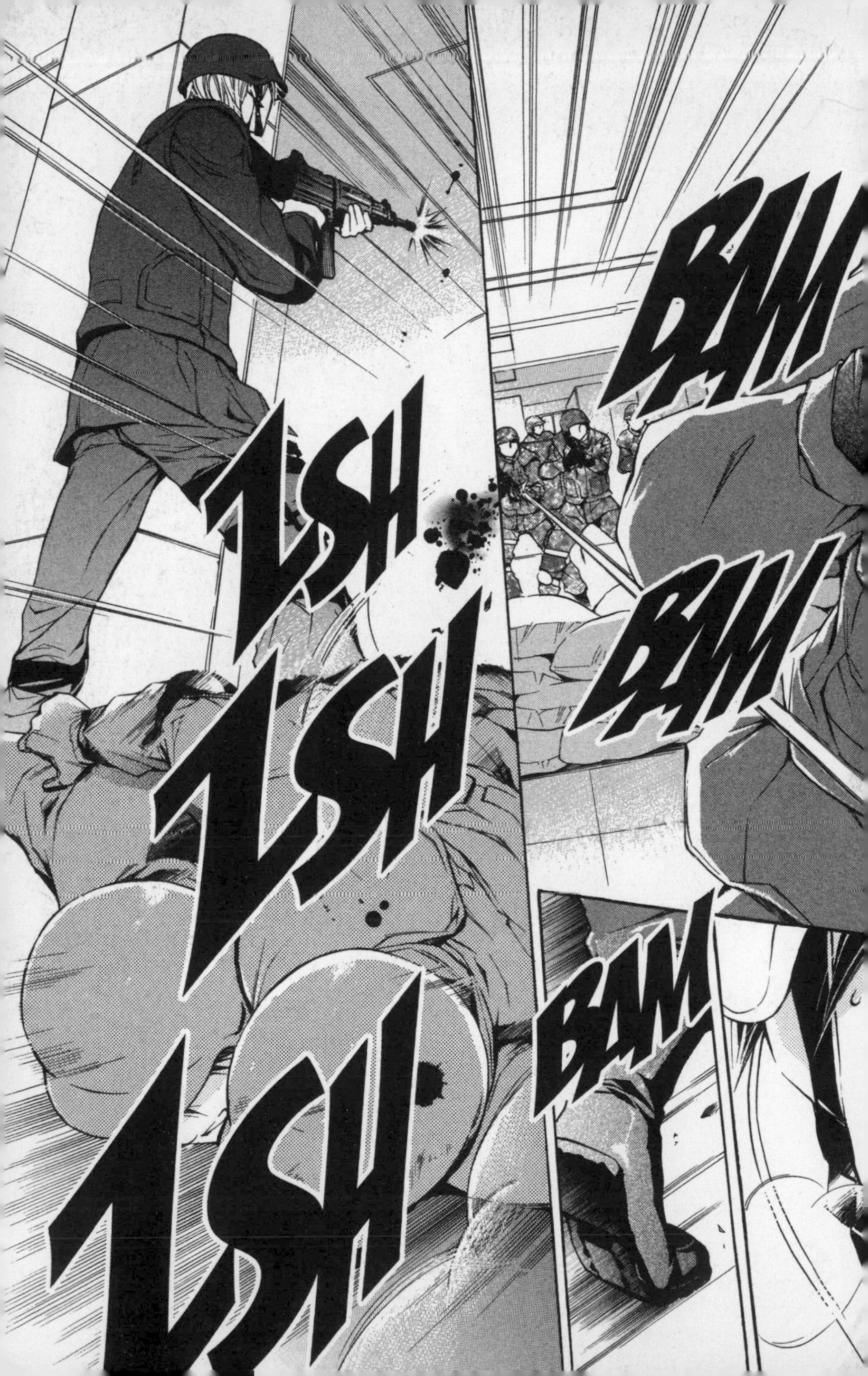
BAM
BAM
BAM
ZSH
ZSH
ZSH

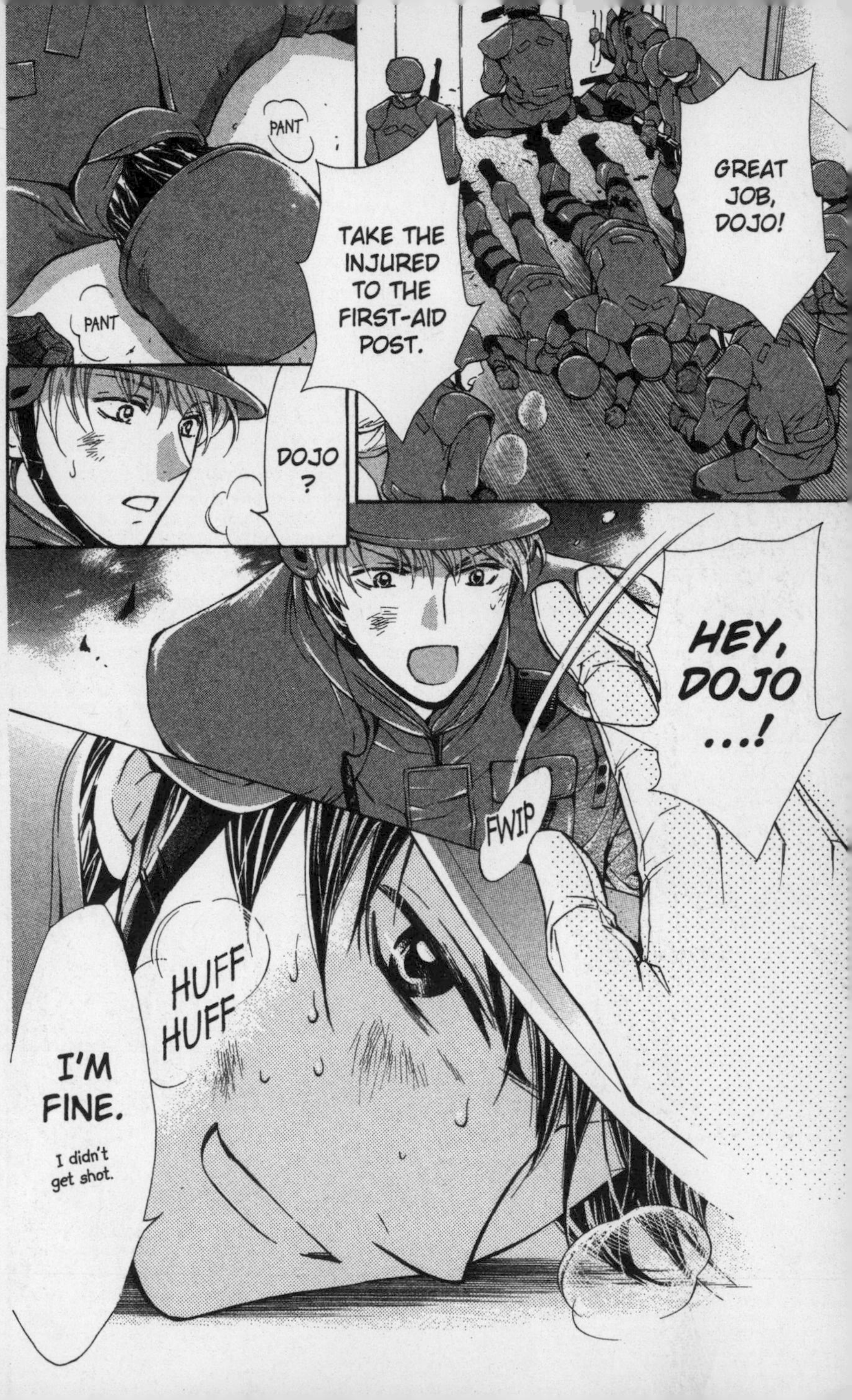
GREAT JOB, DOJO!
TAKE THE INJURED TO THE FIRST-AID POST.
PANT
PANT
DOJO ?
HEY, DOJO ...!
FWIP
HUFF HUFF
I'M FINE.
I didn't get shot.

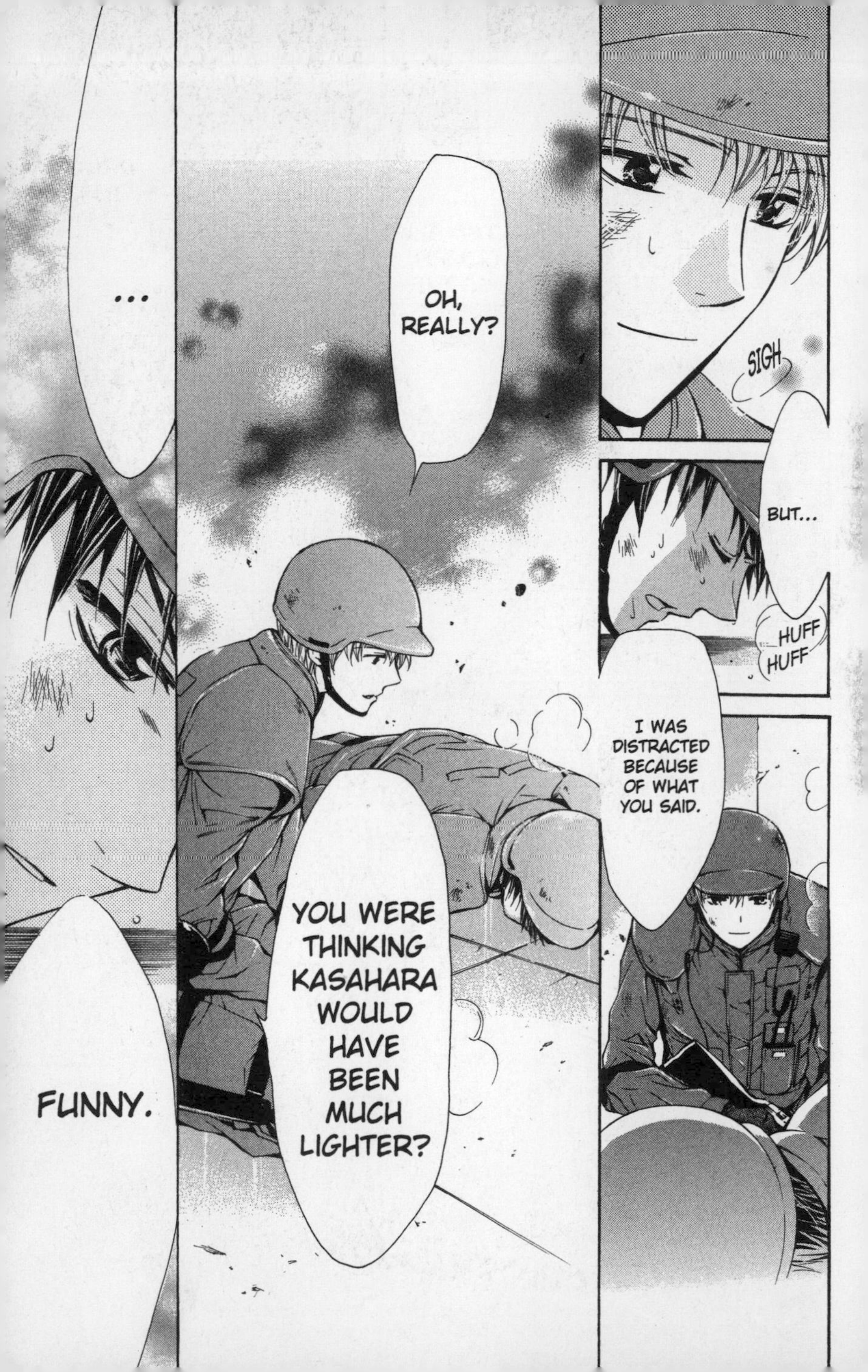
SIGH
BUT...
HUFF HUFF
I WAS DISTRACTED BECAUSE OF WHAT YOU SAID.
OH, REALLY?
YOU WERE THINKING KASAHARA WOULD HAVE BEEN MUCH LIGHTER?
...
FUNNY.

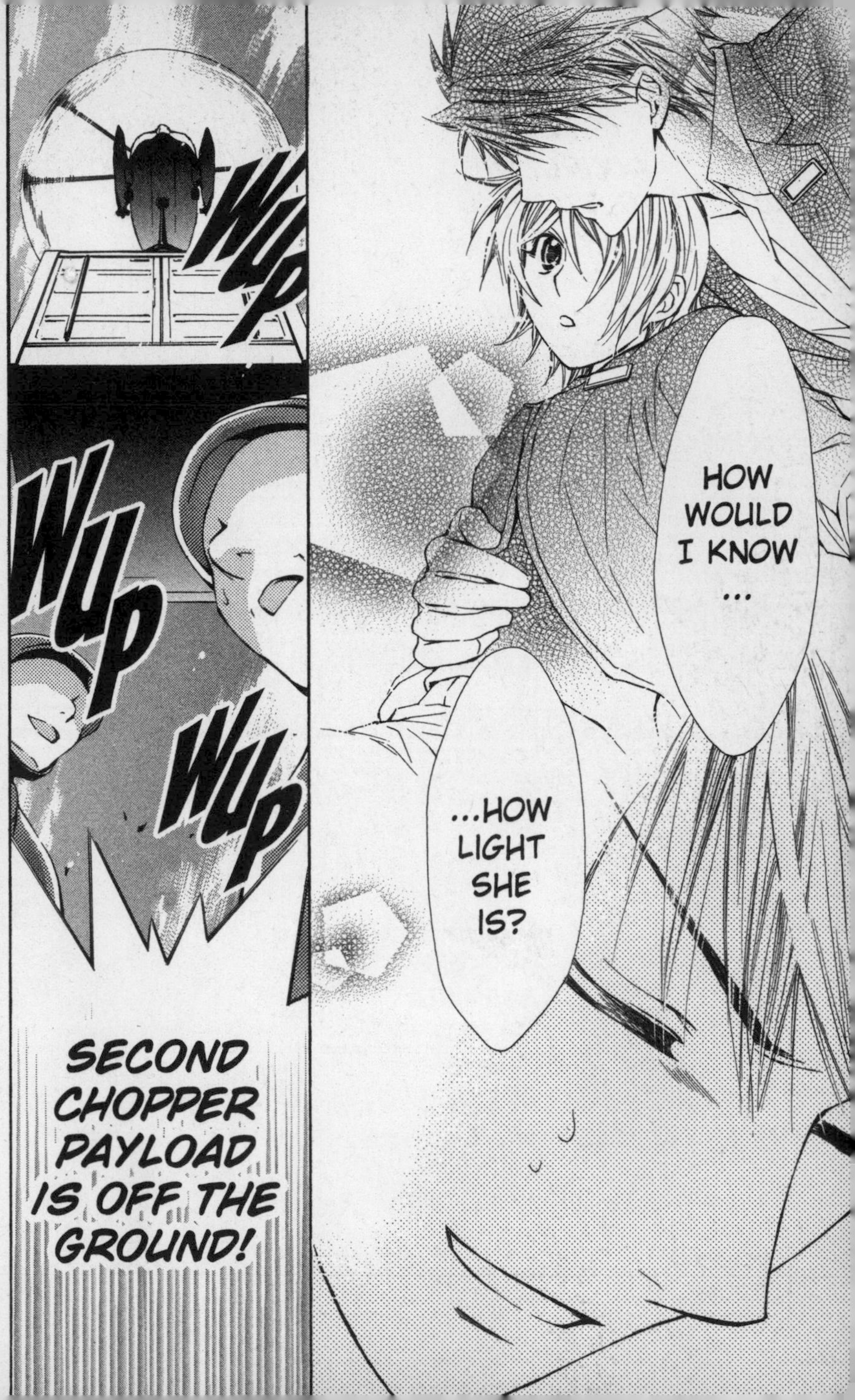
HOW WOULD I KNOW ...
...HOW LIGHT SHE IS?
WUP
WUP
WUP
SECOND CHOPPER PAYLOAD IS OFF THE GROUND!

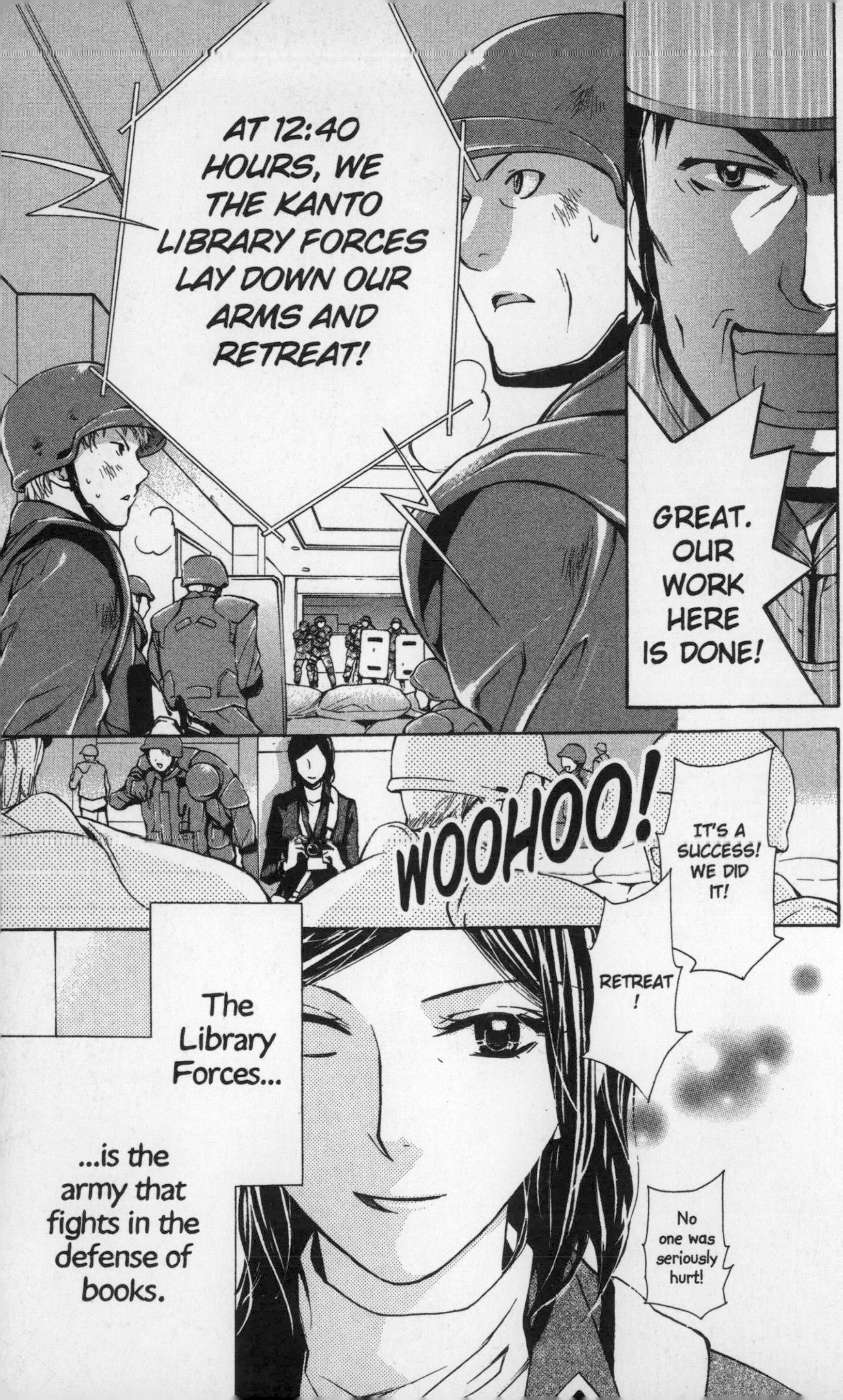
GREAT. OUR WORK HERE IS DONE!
AT 12:40 HOURS, WE THE KANTO LIBRARY FORCES LAY DOWN OUR ARMS AND RETREAT!
IT'S A SUCCESS! WE DID IT!
WOOHOO!
RETREAT!
No one was seriously hurt!
The Library Forces...
...is the army that fights in the defense of books.

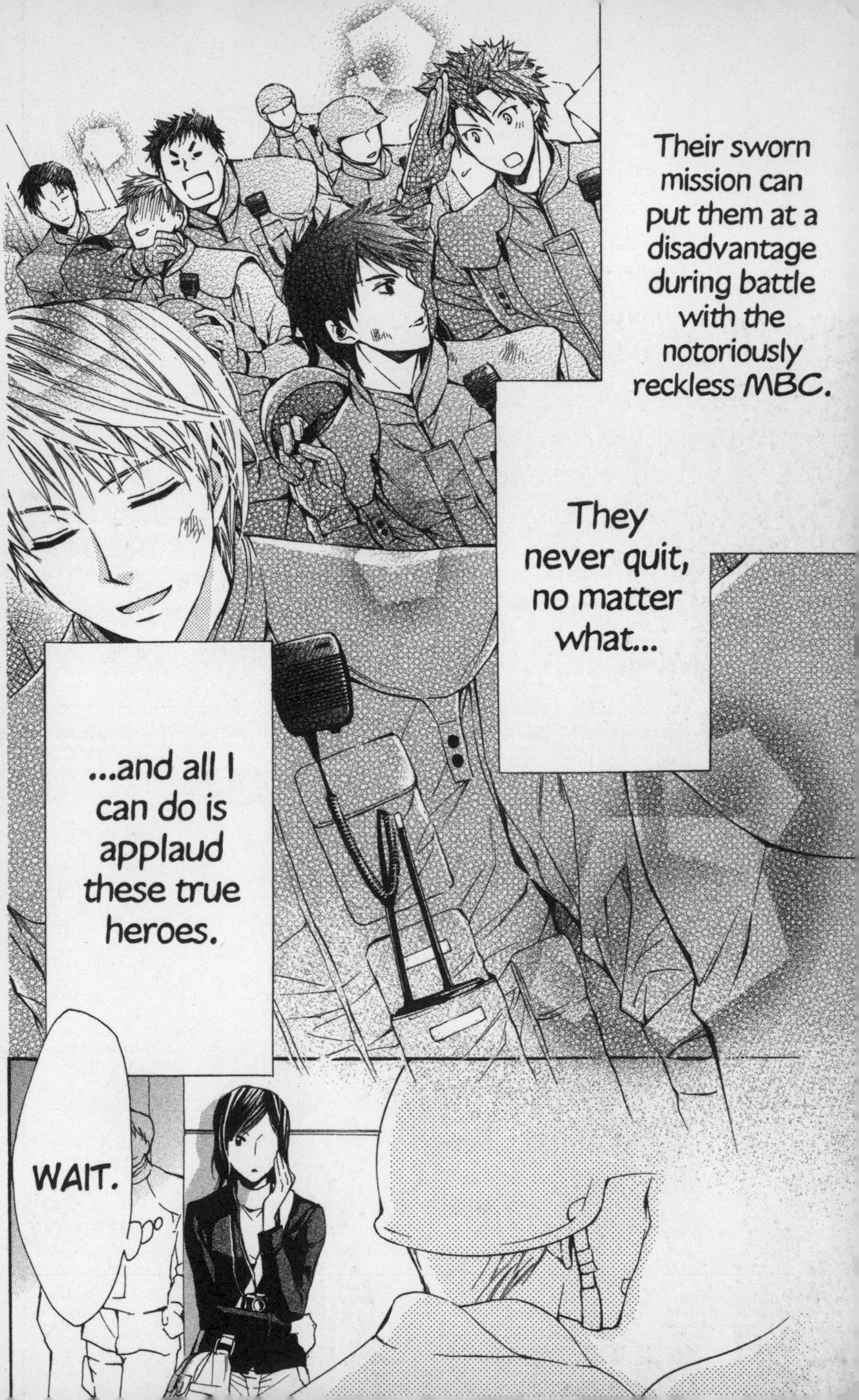
Their sworn mission can put them at a disadvantage during battle with the notoriously reckless MBC.
They never quit, no matter what...
...and all I can do is applaud these true heroes.
WAIT.

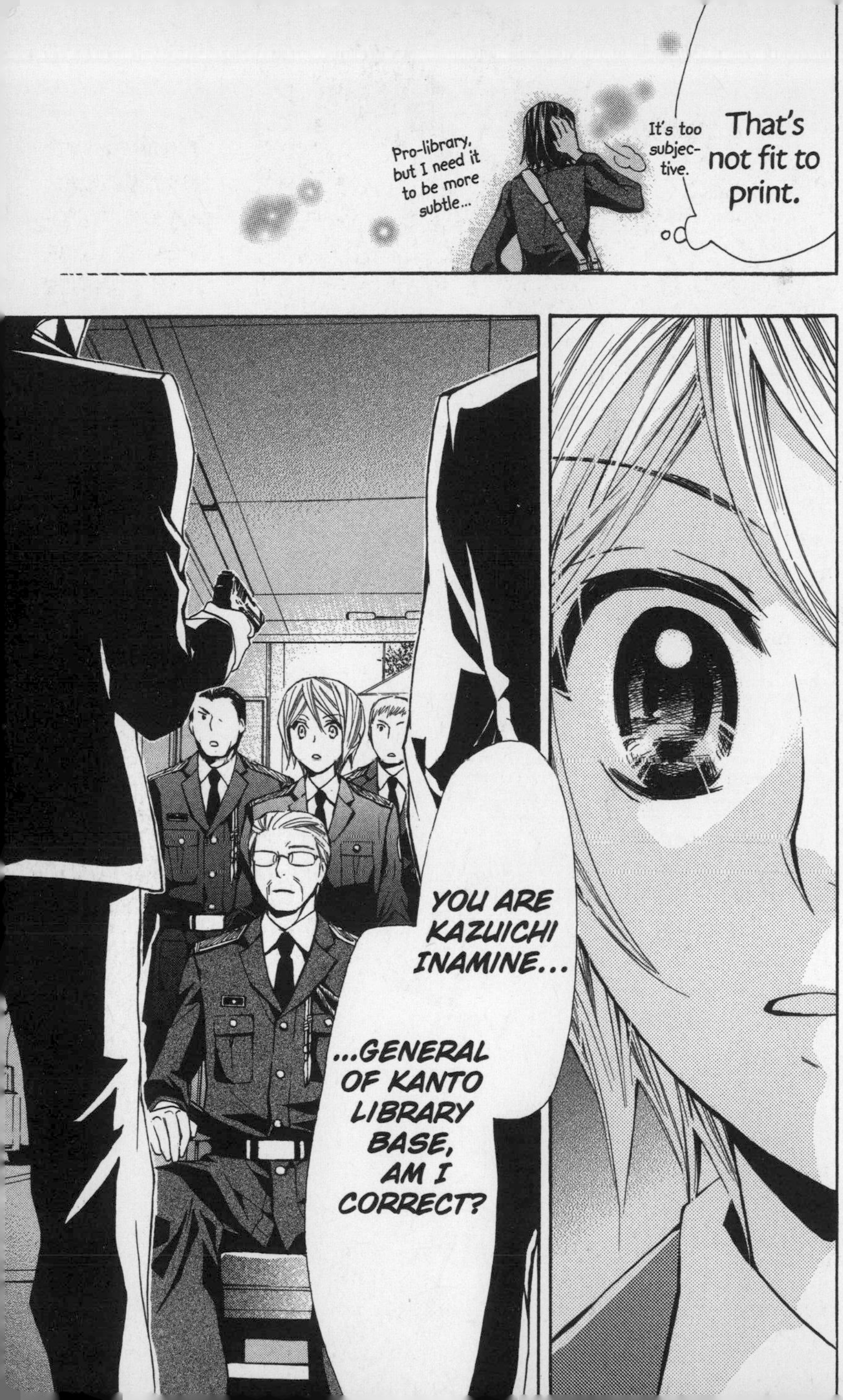
That's not fit to print.
It's too subjective.
Pro-library, but I need it to be more subtle...
YOU ARE KAZUICHI INAMINE...
...GENERAL OF KANTO LIBRARY BASE, AM I CORRECT?

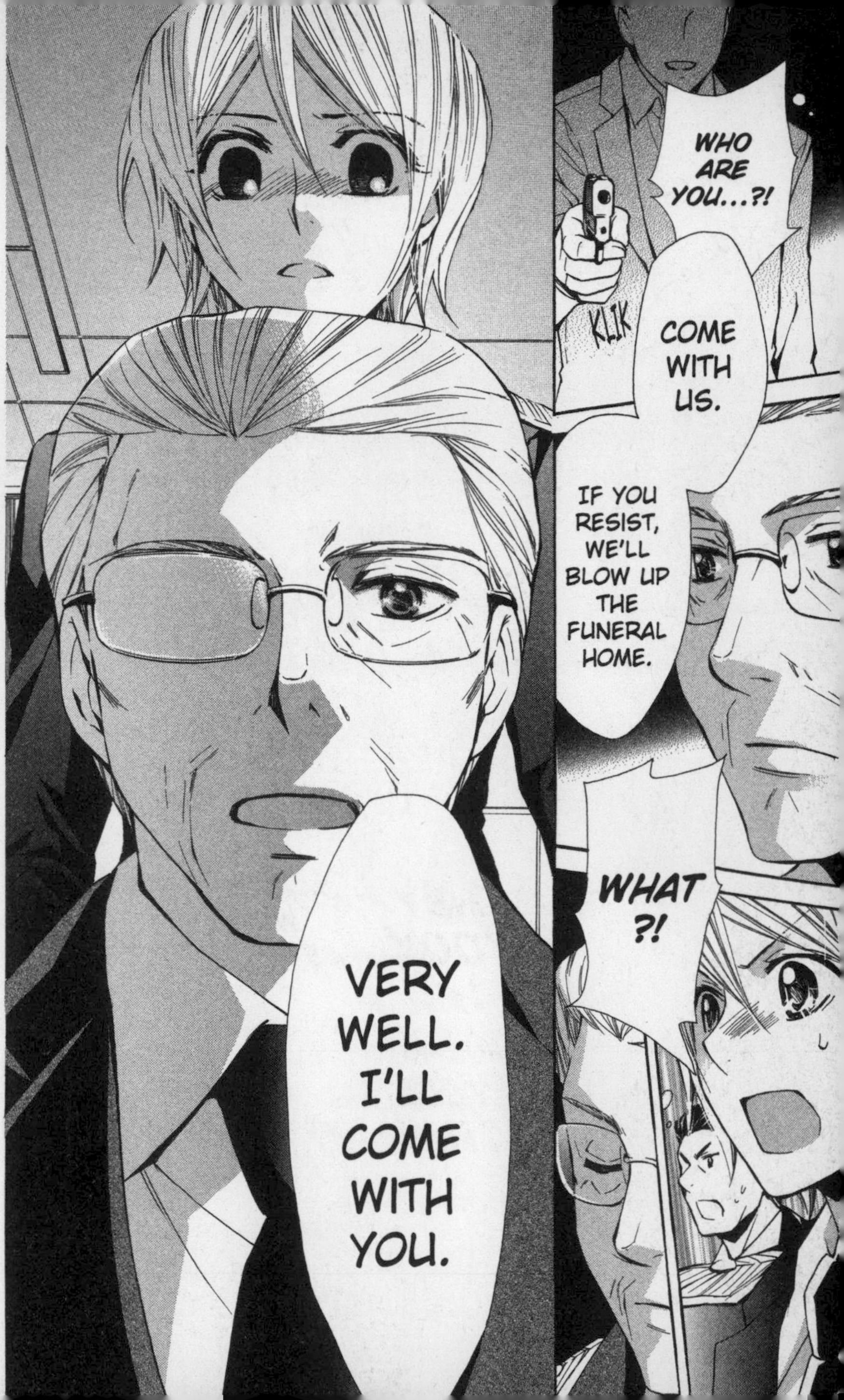
WHO ARE YOU...?!
KLIK
COME WITH US.
IF YOU RESIST, WE'LL BLOW UP THE FUNERAL HOME.
WHAT ?!
VERY WELL. I'LL COME WITH YOU.

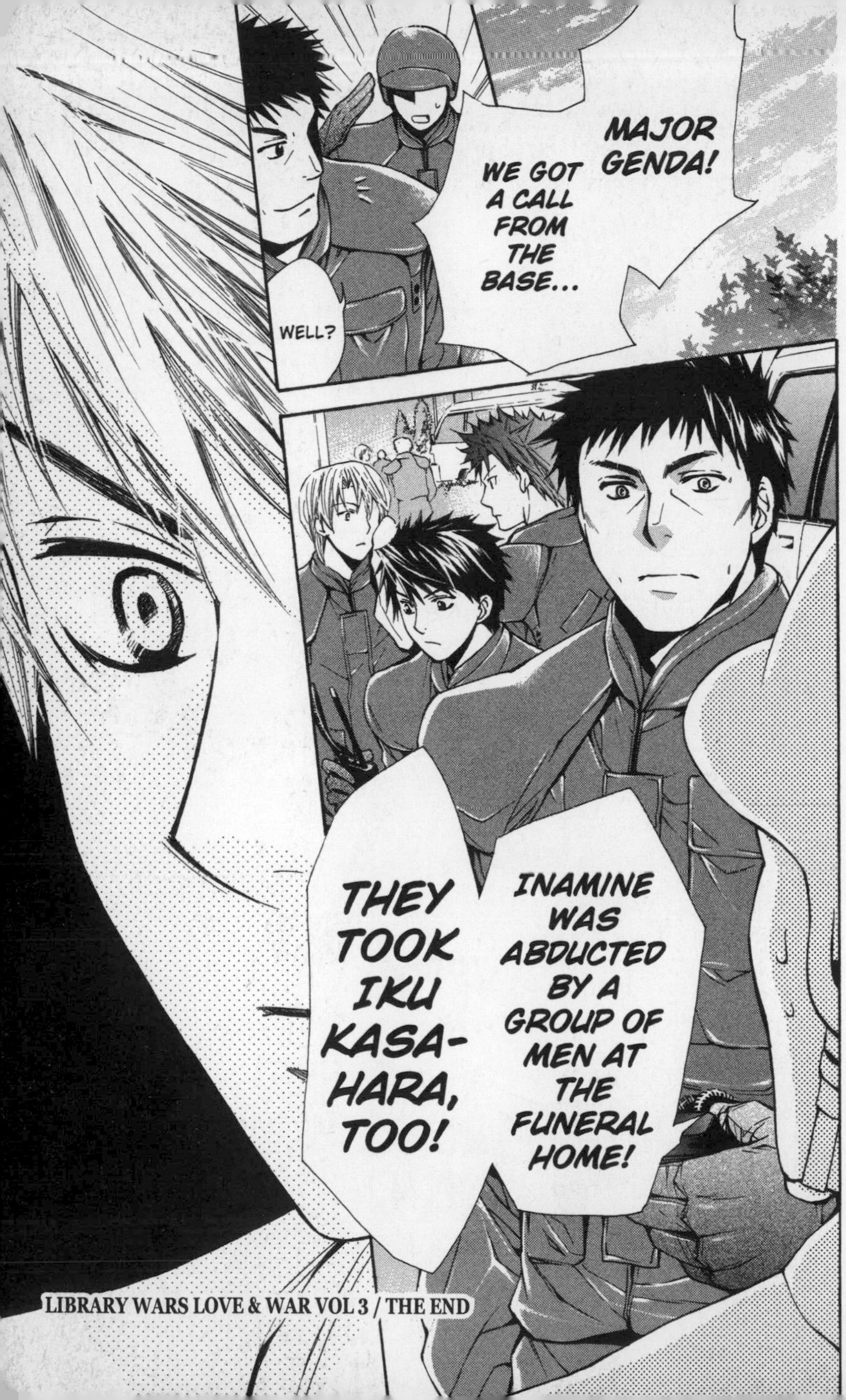
MAJOR GENDA!
WE GOT A CALL FROM THE BASE...
WELL?
INAMINE WAS ABDUCTED BY A GROUP OF MEN AT THE FUNERAL HOME!
THEY TOOK IKU KASAHARA, TOO!
LIBRARY WARS LOVE & WAR VOL 3 / THE END

Full of Memories

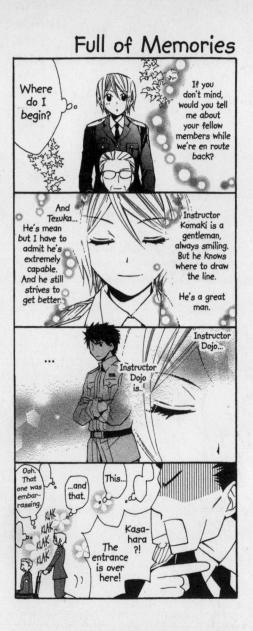

If you don't mind, would you tell me about your fellow members while we're en route back?
Where do I begin?
Instructor Komaki is a gentleman, always smiling. But he knows where to draw the line.
He's a great man.
And Tezuka... He's mean but I have to admit he's extremely capable. And he still strives to get better.
Instructor Dojo...
Instructor Dojo is..!
...
This...
...and that.
Ooh. That one was embar-rassing.
Kasa-hara ?!
The entrance is over here!
KLAK KLAK KLAK KLAK

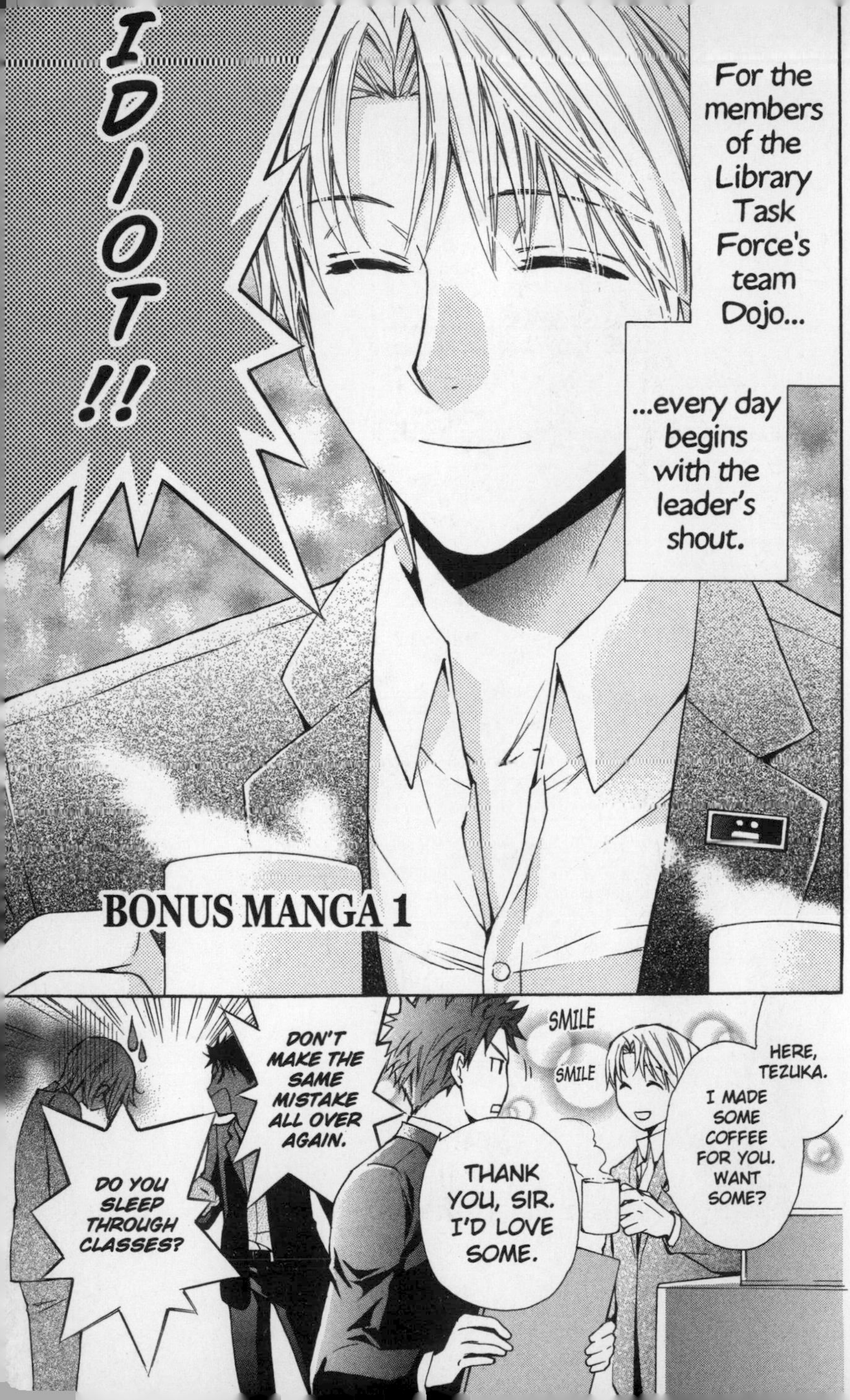
For the members of the Library Task Force's team Dojo...
...every day begins with the leader's shout.
IDIOT!!
BONUS MANGA 1
HERE, TEZUKA. I MADE SOME COFFEE FOR YOU. WANT SOME?
SMILE
SMILE
THANK YOU, SIR. I'D LOVE SOME.
DON'T MAKE THE SAME MISTAKE ALL OVER AGAIN.
DO YOU SLEEP THROUGH CLASSES?

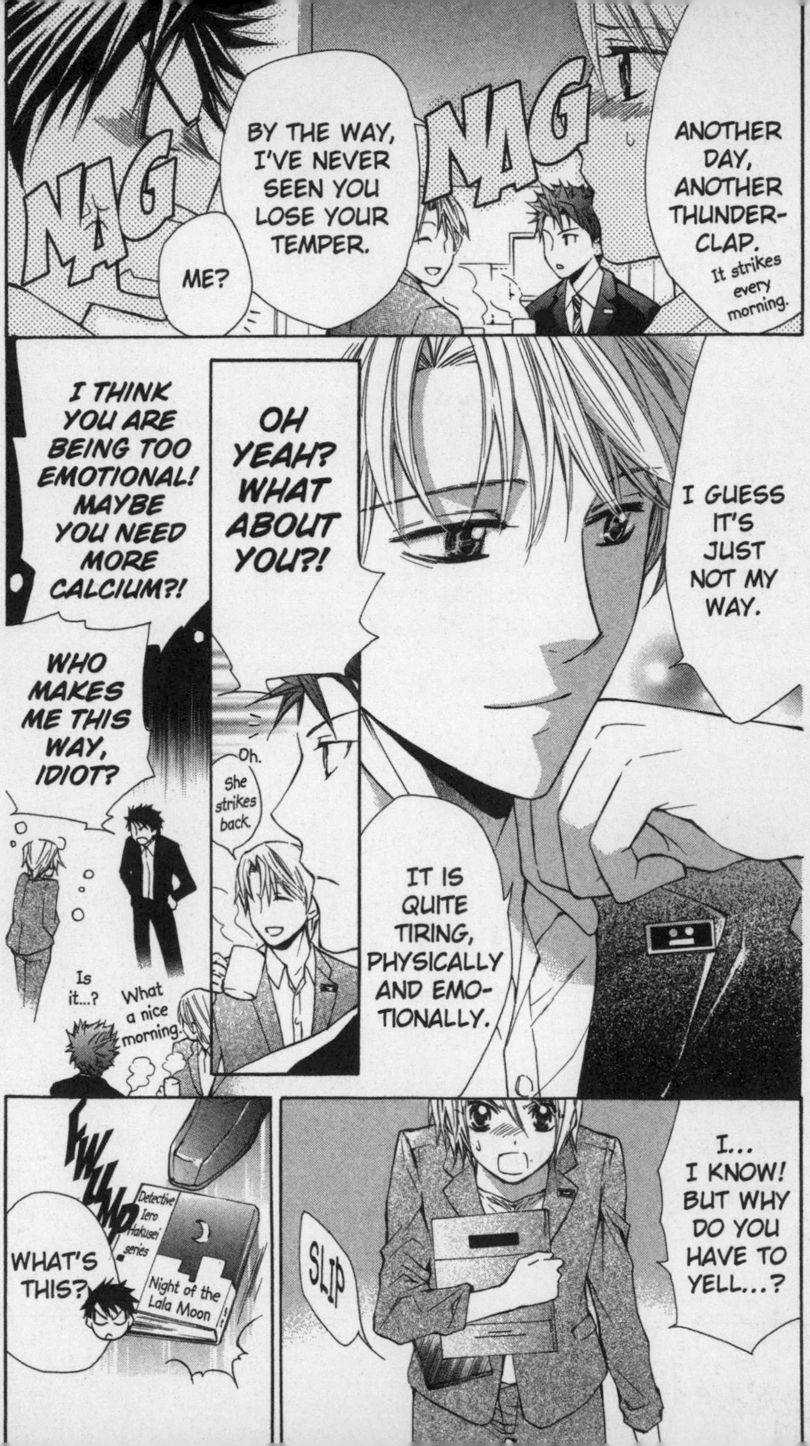
ANOTHER DAY, ANOTHER THUNDER-CLAP.
It strikes every morning.
NAG
NAG
BY THE WAY, I'VE NEVER SEEN YOU LOSE YOUR TEMPER.
ME?
I GUESS IT'S JUST NOT MY WAY.
IT IS QUITE TIRING, PHYSICALLY AND EMO-TIONALLY.
OH YEAH? WHAT ABOUT YOU?!
Oh. She strikes back.
I THINK YOU ARE BEING TOO EMOTIONAL! MAYBE YOU NEED MORE CALCIUM?!
WHO MAKES ME THIS WAY, IDIOT?
Is it...?
What a nice morning.
I... I KNOW! BUT WHY DO YOU HAVE TO YELL...?
SLIP
KWUMP
Detective Iero Hakusei series
Night of the Lala Moon
WHAT'S THIS?

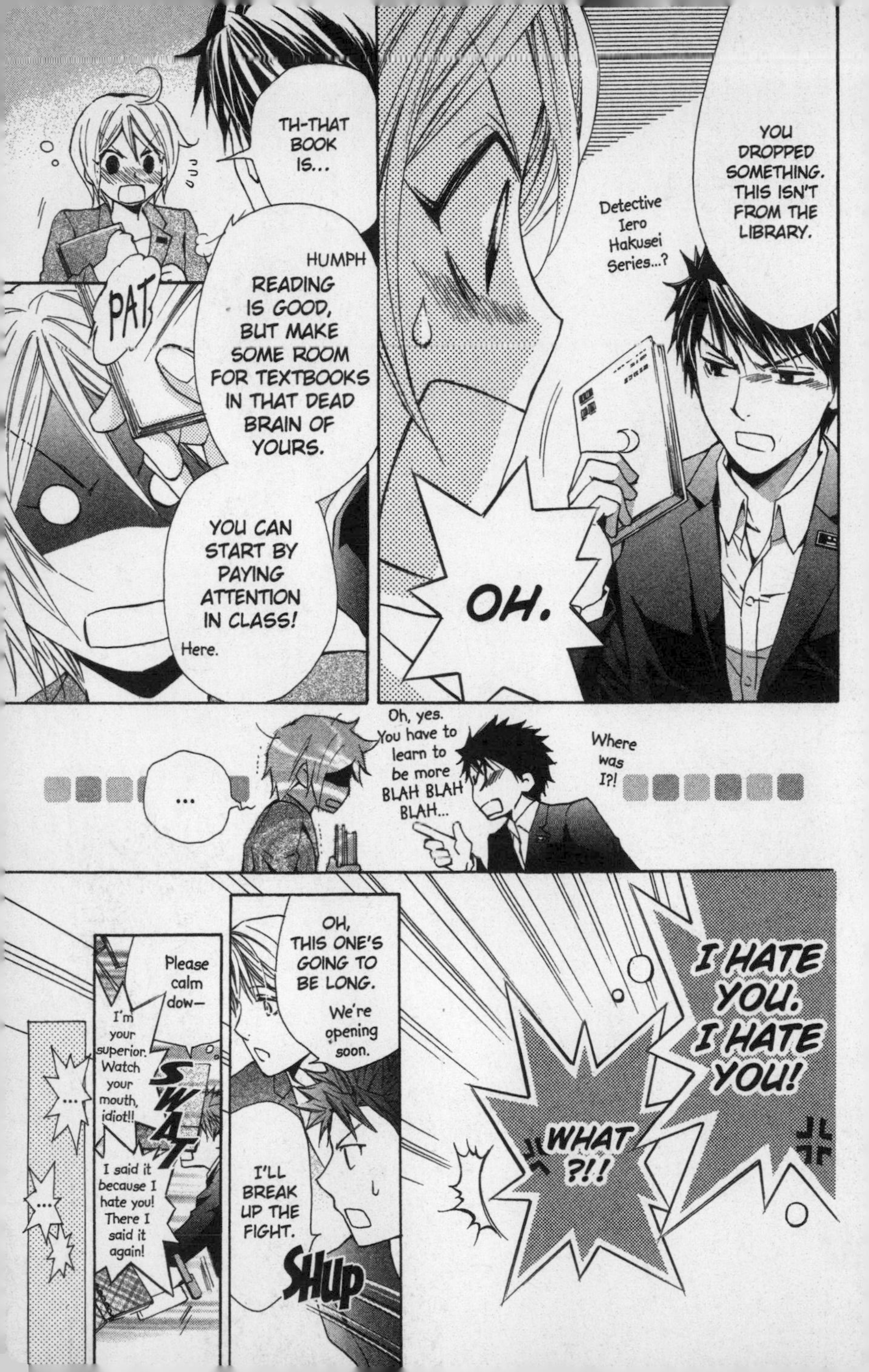
YOU DROPPED SOMETHING. THIS ISN'T FROM THE LIBRARY.
Detective Iero Hakusei Series...?
OH.
TH-THAT BOOK IS...
HUMPH
READING IS GOOD, BUT MAKE SOME ROOM FOR TEXTBOOKS IN THAT DEAD BRAIN OF YOURS.
PAT
YOU CAN START BY PAYING ATTENTION IN CLASS!
Here.
Where was I?!
Oh, yes. You have to learn to be more BLAH BLAH BLAH...
...
I HATE YOU. I HATE YOU!
WHAT ?!!
OH, THIS ONE'S GOING TO BE LONG.
We're opening soon.
I'LL BREAK UP THE FIGHT.
SHUP
Please calm dow—
I'm your superior. Watch your mouth, idiot!!
SWAT
I said it because I hate you! There I said it again!
...
...

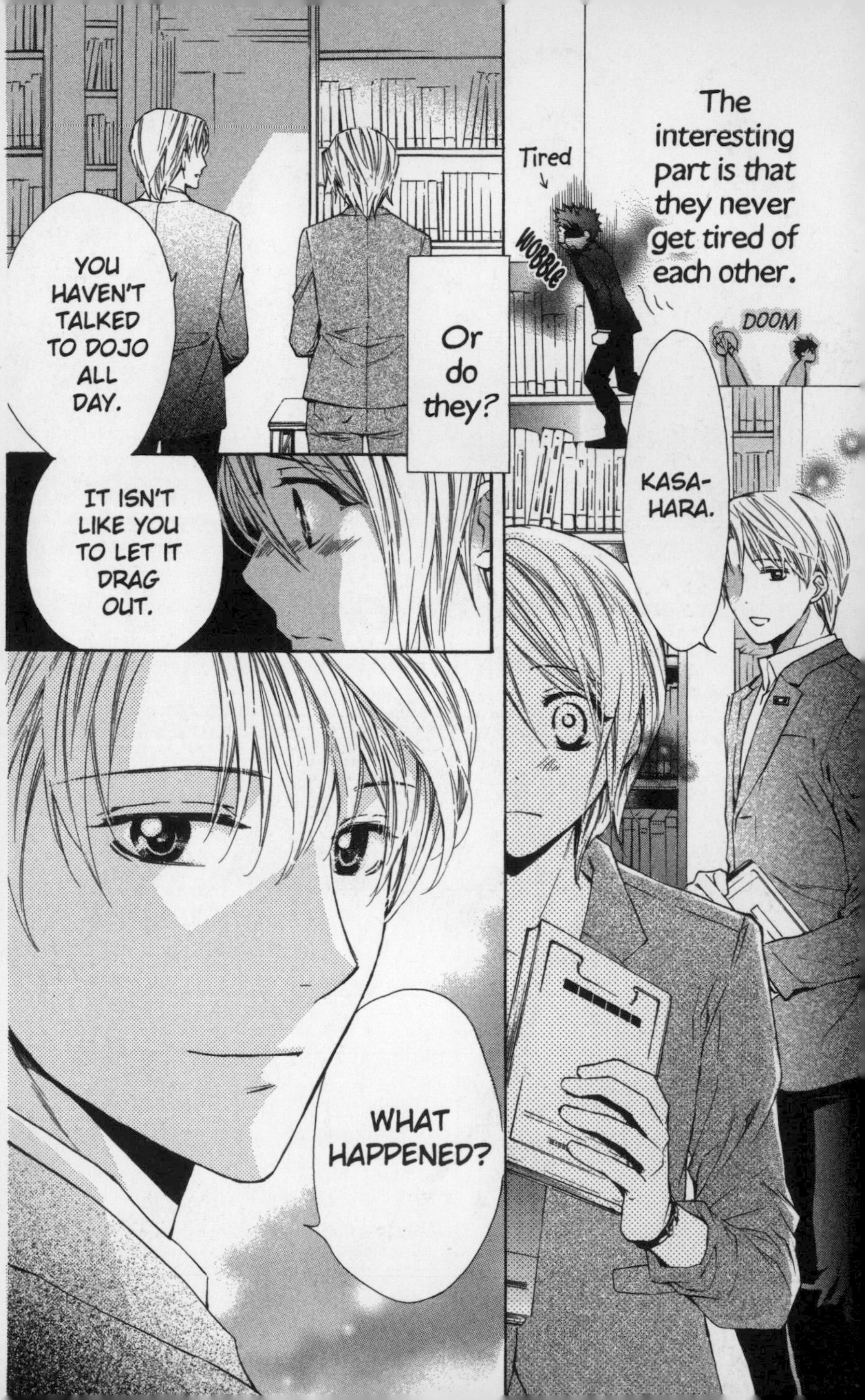

The interesting part is that they never get tired of each other.
Tired
WOBBLE
DOOM
KASA-HARA.
Or do they?
YOU HAVEN'T TALKED TO DOJO ALL DAY.
IT ISN'T LIKE YOU TO LET IT DRAG OUT.
WHAT HAPPENED?

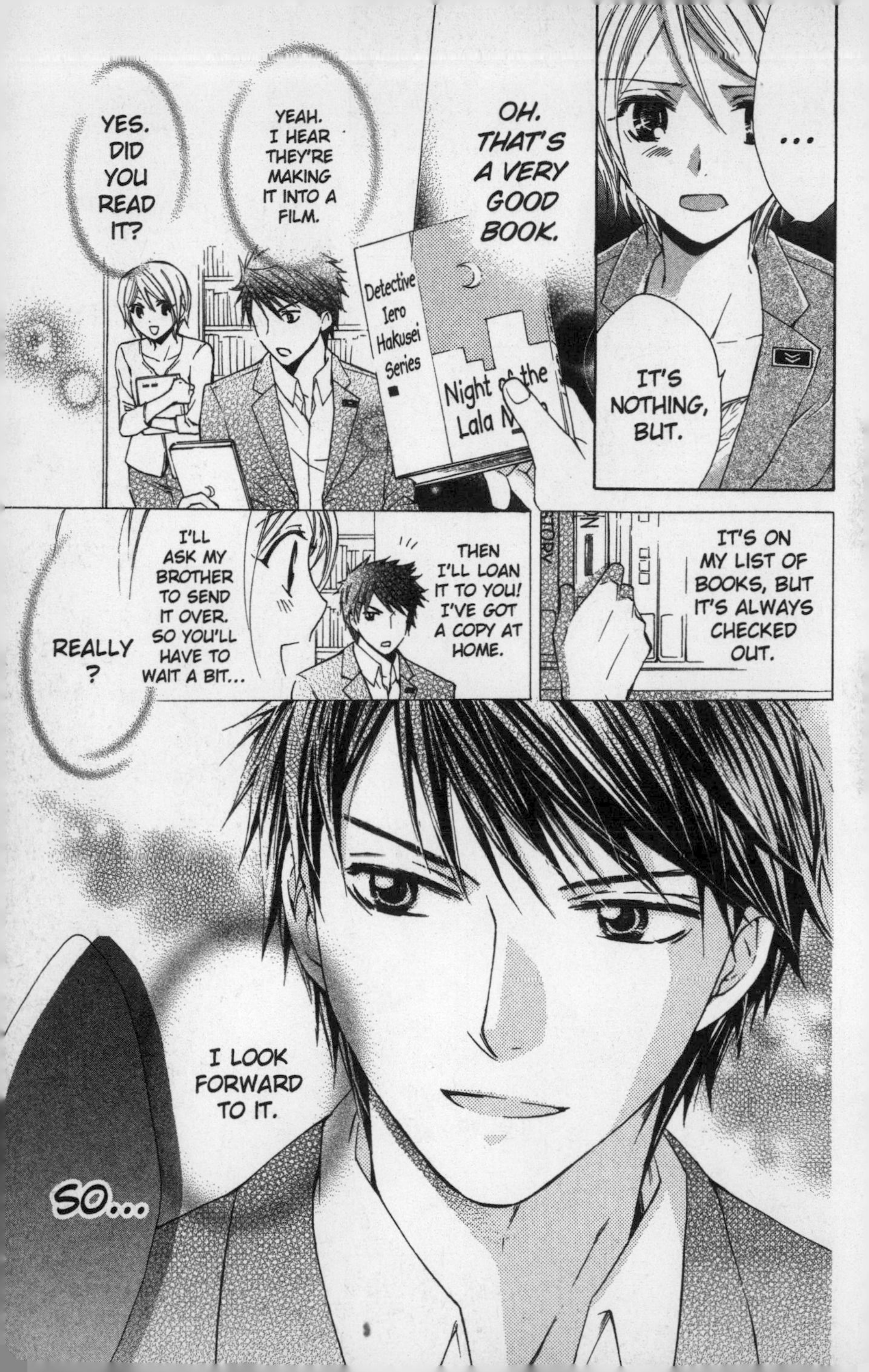
...
IT'S NOTHING, BUT.
OH. THAT'S A VERY GOOD BOOK.
Detective Iero Hakusei Series
YEAH. I HEAR THEY'RE MAKING IT INTO A FILM.
YES. DID YOU READ IT?
IT'S ON MY LIST OF BOOKS, BUT IT'S ALWAYS CHECKED OUT.
THEN I'LL LOAN IT TO YOU! I'VE GOT A COPY AT HOME.
I'LL ASK MY BROTHER TO SEND IT OVER. SO YOU'LL HAVE TO WAIT A BIT...
REALLY?
I LOOK FORWARD TO IT.
SO...

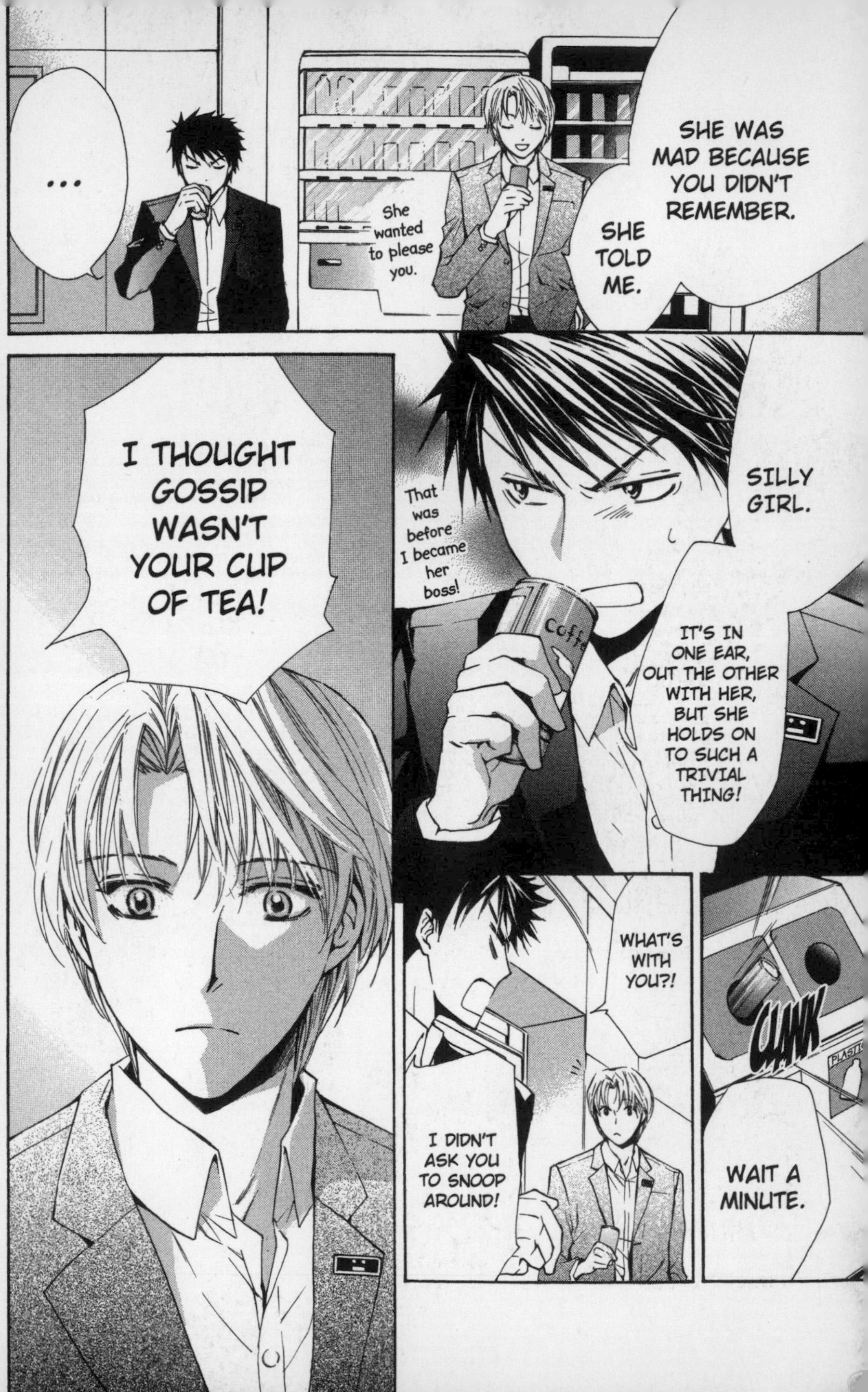
SHE WAS MAD BECAUSE YOU DIDN'T REMEMBER.
SHE TOLD ME.
She wanted to please you.
...
SILLY GIRL.
IT'S IN ONE EAR, OUT THE OTHER WITH HER, BUT SHE HOLDS ON TO SUCH A TRIVIAL THING!
That was before I became her boss!
CLANK
WAIT A MINUTE.
WHAT'S WITH YOU?!
I DIDN'T ASK YOU TO SNOOP AROUND!
I THOUGHT GOSSIP WASN'T YOUR CUP OF TEA!

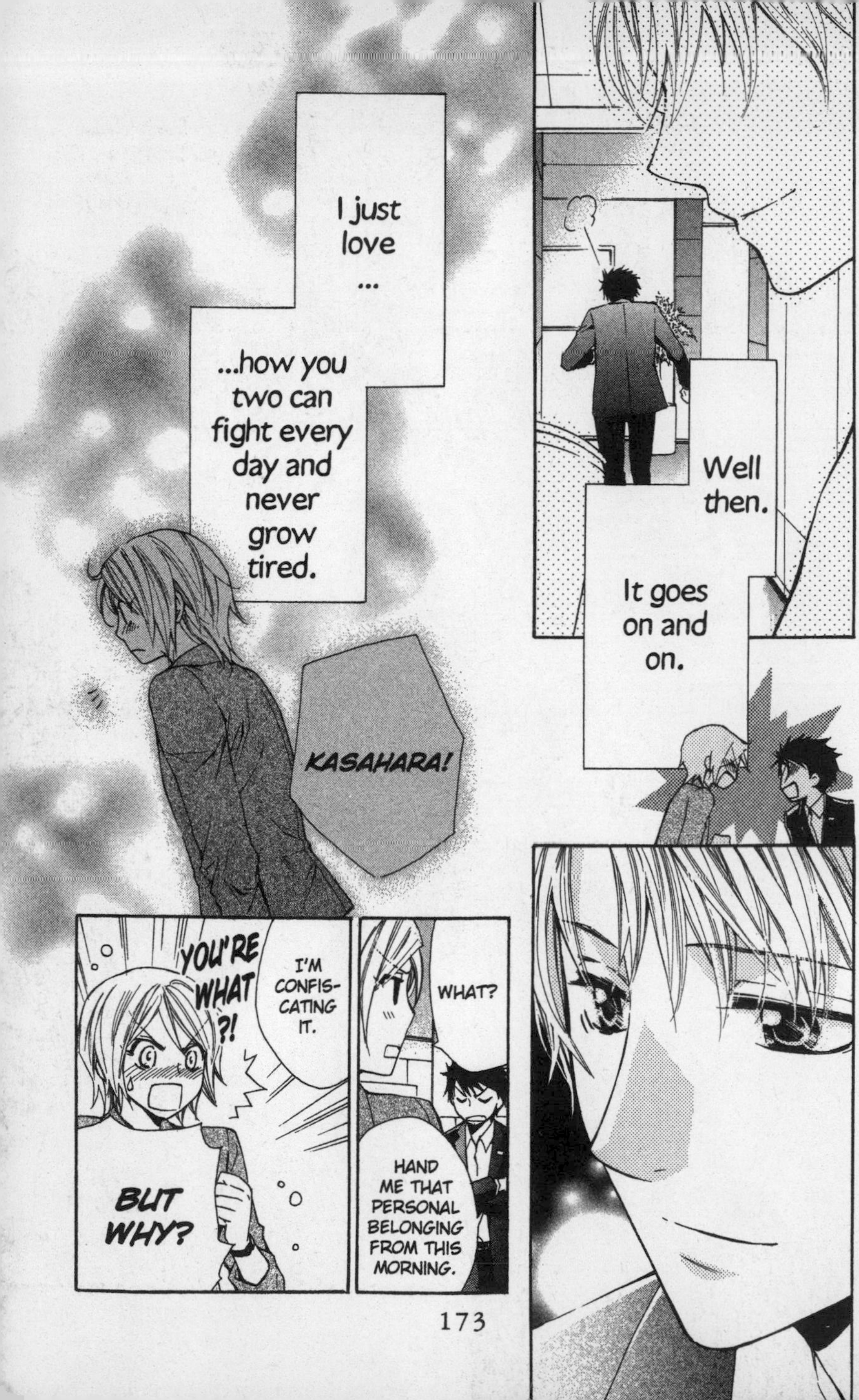
Well then.
It goes on and on.
I just love ...
...how you two can fight every day and never grow tired.
KASAHARA!
HAND ME THAT PERSONAL BELONGING FROM THIS MORNING.
WHAT?
I'M CONFIS-CATING IT.
YOU'RE WHAT ?!
BUT WHY?

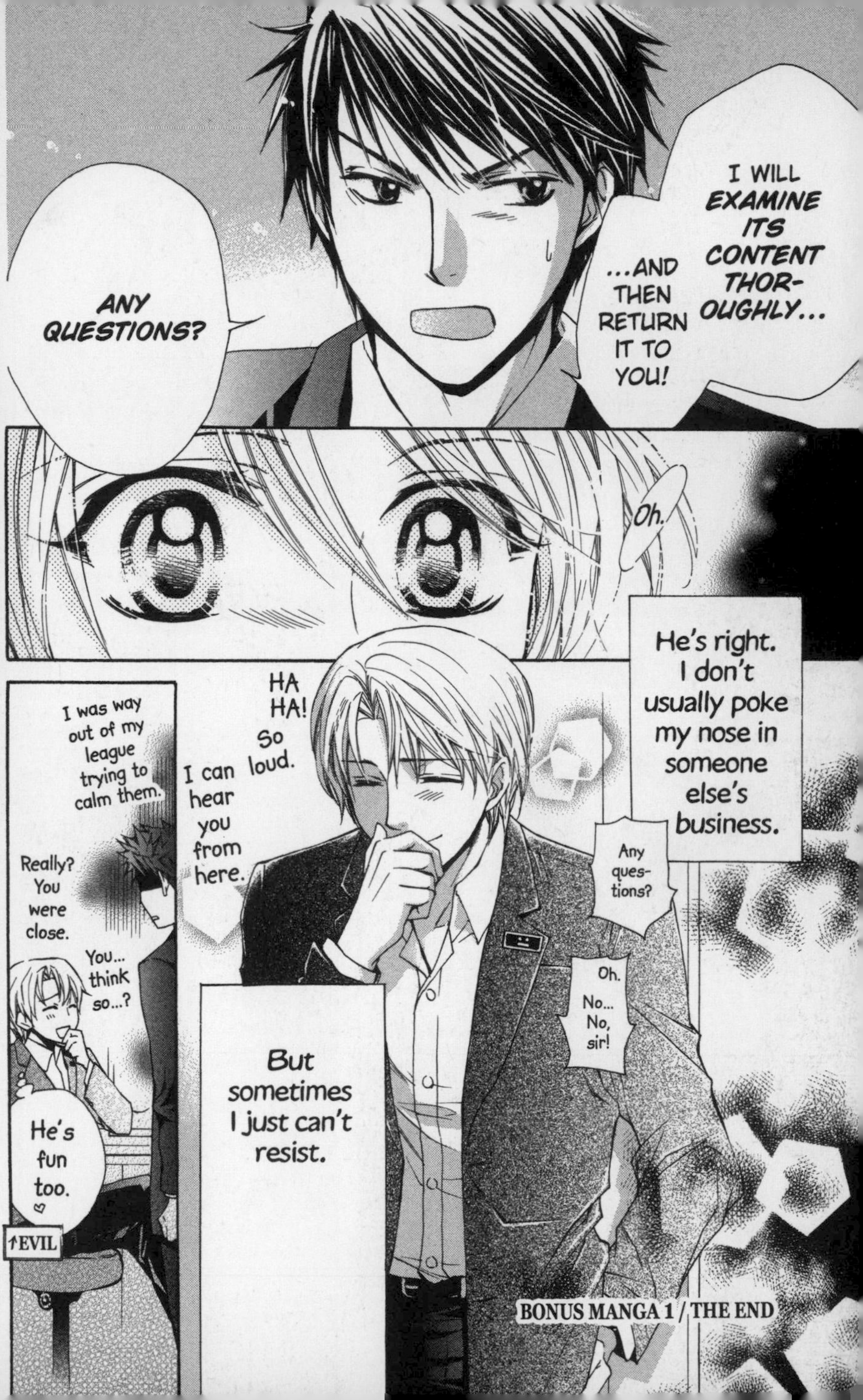
I WILL EXAMINE ITS CONTENT THOR-OUGHLY...
...AND THEN RETURN IT TO YOU!
ANY QUESTIONS?
Oh.
He's right. I don't usually poke my nose in someone else's business.
Any ques-tions?
Oh.
No... No, sir!
HA HA! So loud.
I can hear you from here.
But sometimes I just can't resist.
I was way out of my league trying to calm them.
Really? You were close.
You... think so...?
He's fun too. ♡
↑EVIL
BONUS MANGA 1 / THE END

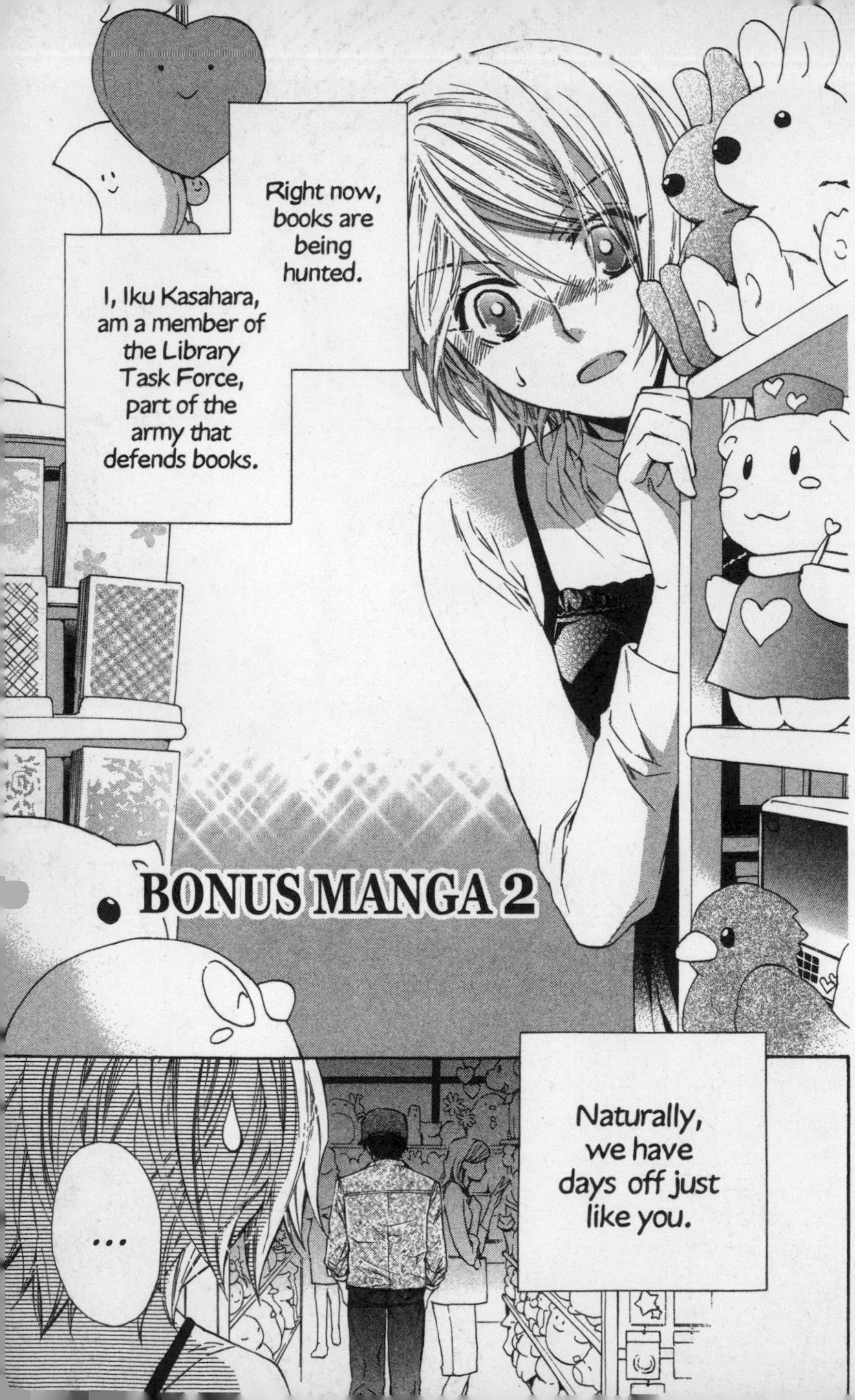
Right now, books are being hunted.
I, Iku Kasahara, am a member of the Library Task Force, part of the army that defends books.
BONUS MANGA 2
Naturally, we have days off just like you.
...

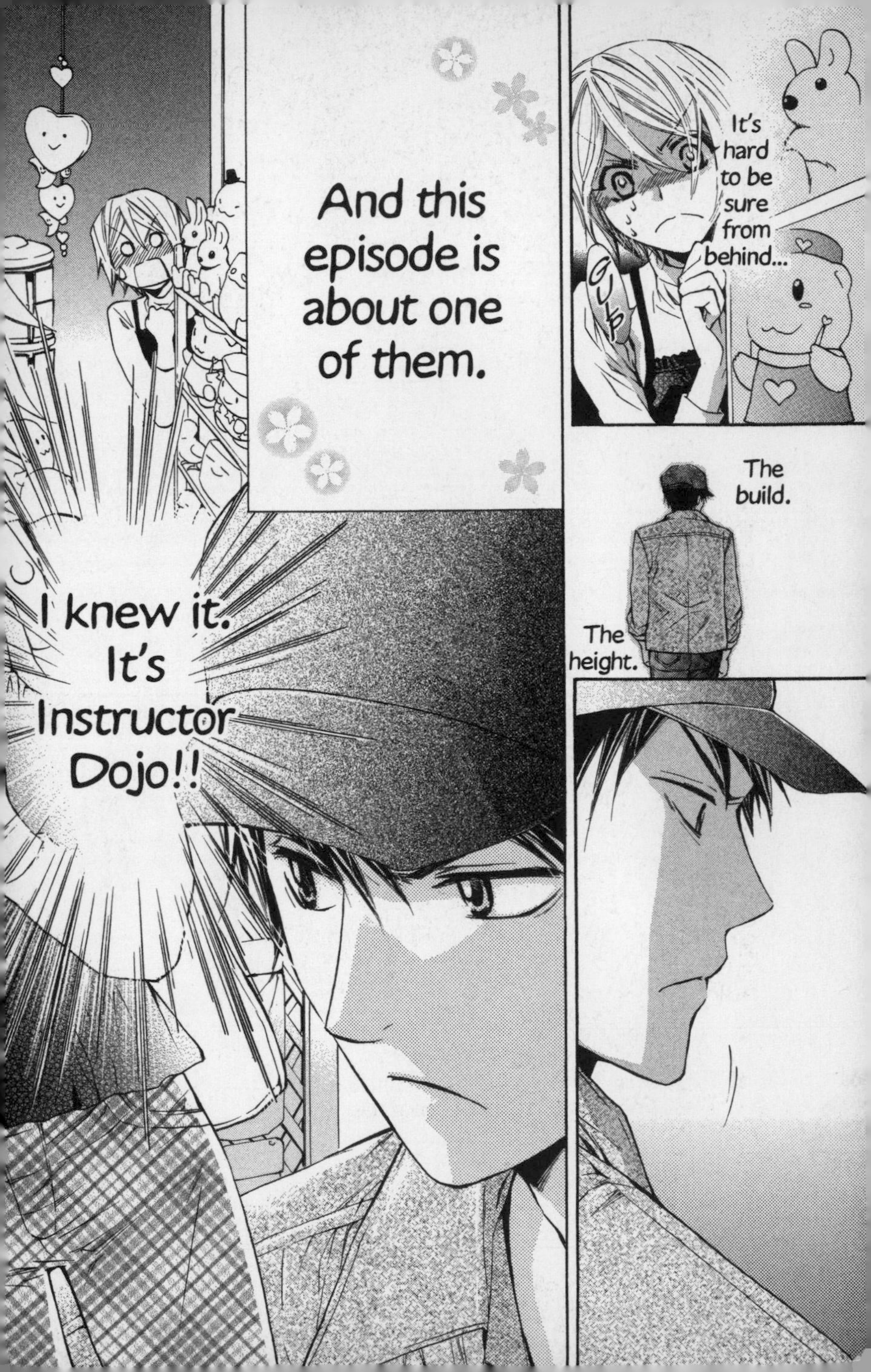
GULP
It's hard to be sure from behind...
The build.
The height.
And this episode is about one of them.
I knew it. It's Instructor Dojo!!

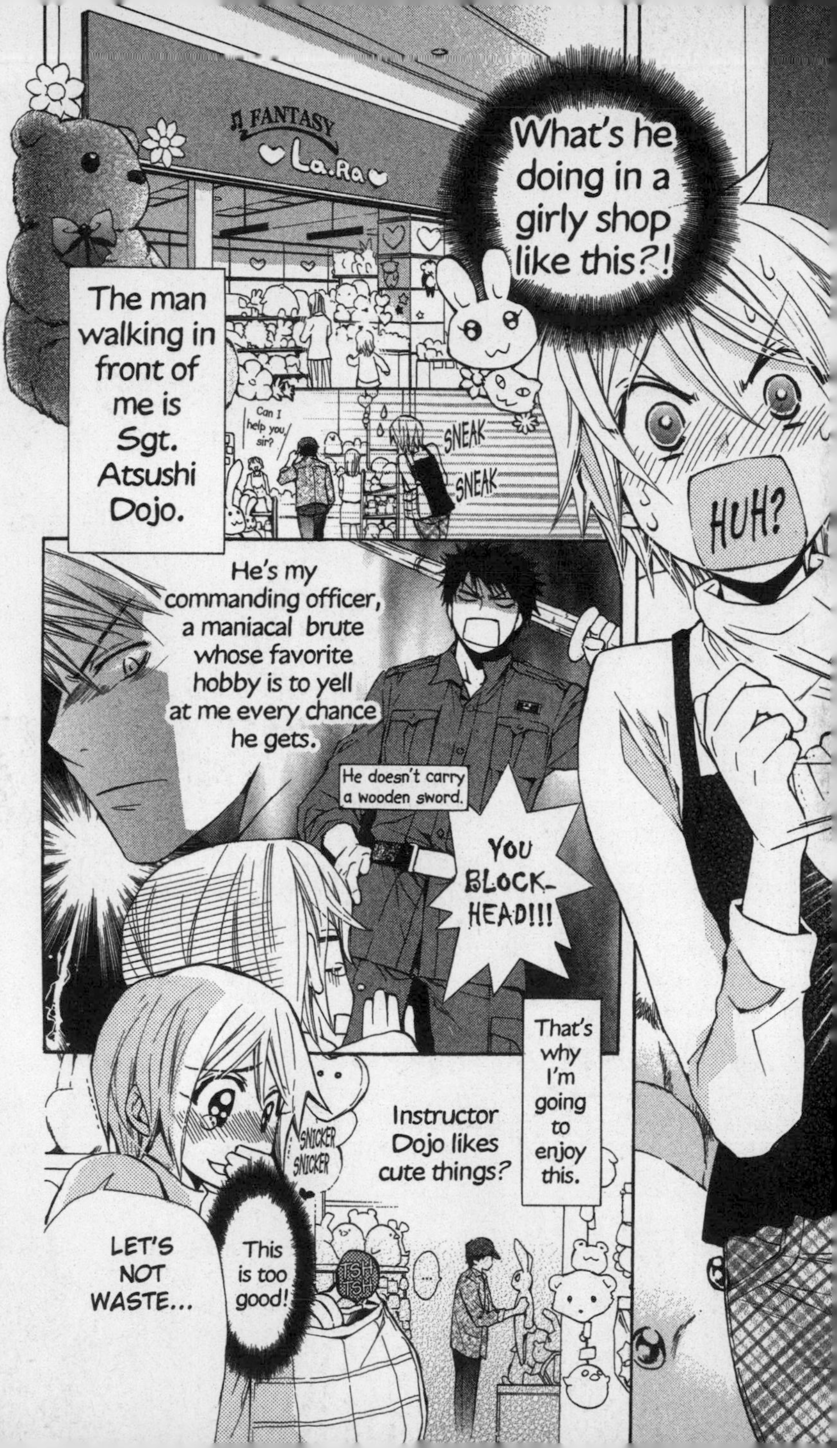
What's he doing in a girly shop like this?!
HUH?
FANTASY
La.Ra
The man walking in front of me is Sgt. Atsushi Dojo.
SNEAK
SNEAK
Can I help you, sir?
He's my commanding officer, a maniacal brute whose favorite hobby is to yell at me every chance he gets.
YOU BLOCK-HEAD!!!
He doesn't carry a wooden sword.
That's why I'm going to enjoy this.
Instructor Dojo likes cute things?
SNICKER SNICKER
...
TSH TSH
This is too good!
LET'S NOT WASTE...

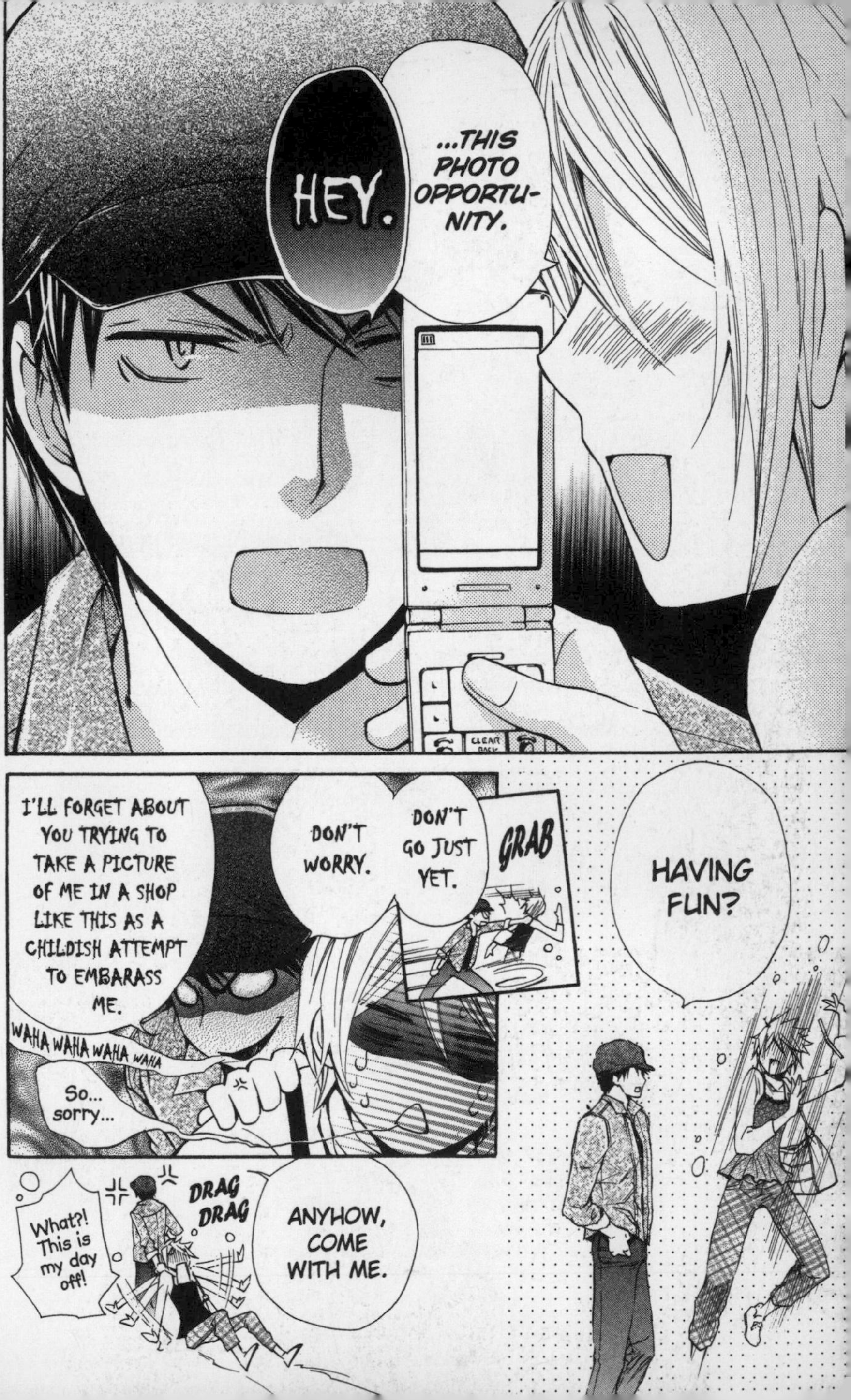
...THIS PHOTO OPPORTUNITY.
HEY.
HAVING FUN?
GRAB
DON'T GO JUST YET.
DON'T WORRY.
I'LL FORGET ABOUT YOU TRYING TO TAKE A PICTURE OF ME IN A SHOP LIKE THIS AS A CHILDISH ATTEMPT TO EMBARASS ME.
WAHA WAHA WAHA WAHA
So... sorry...
ANYHOW, COME WITH ME.
DRAG DRAG
What?! This is my day off!

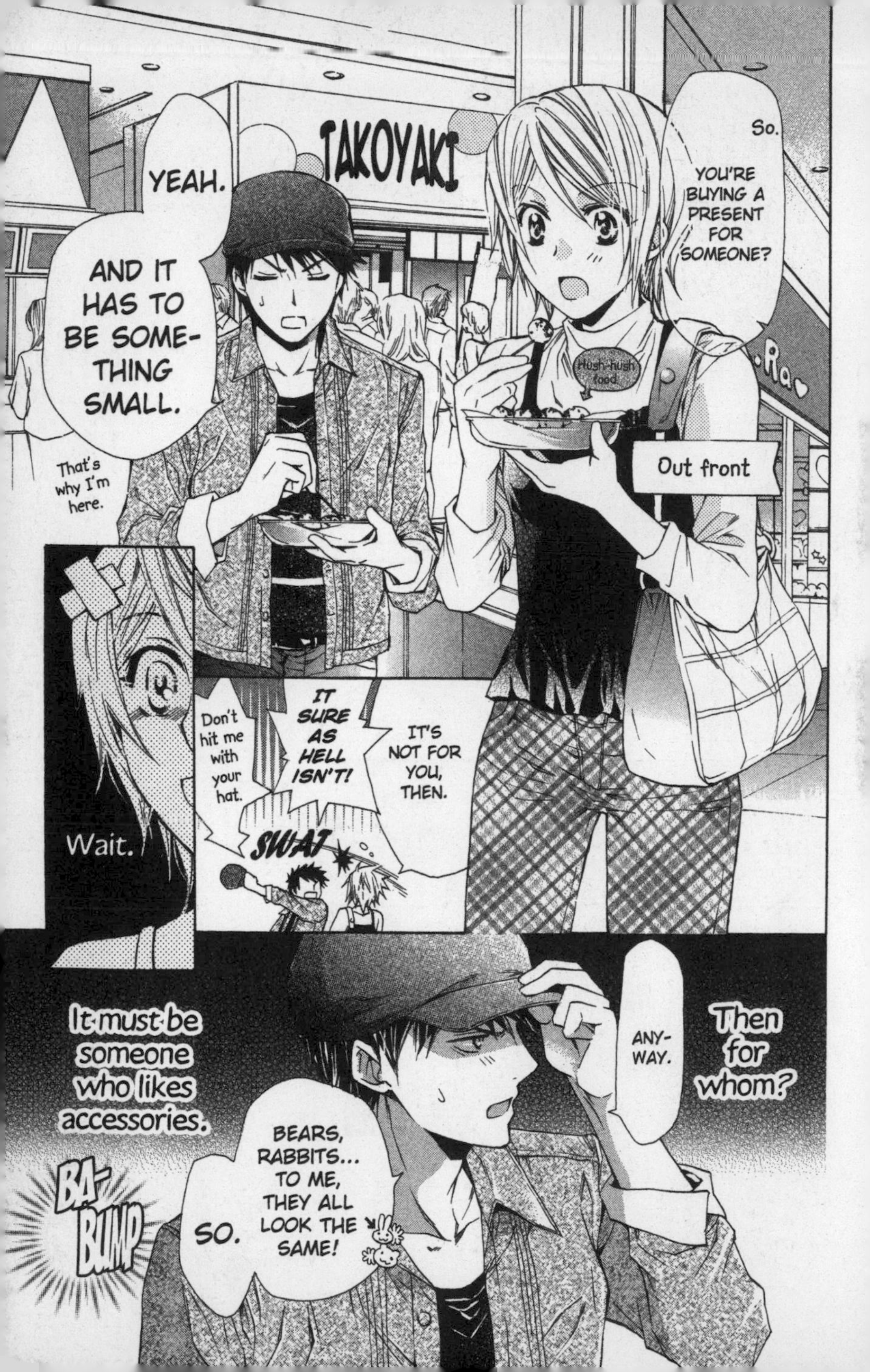
TAKOYAKI
So.
YOU'RE BUYING A PRESENT FOR SOMEONE?
Hush-hush food
Out front
YEAH.
AND IT HAS TO BE SOME-THING SMALL.
That's why I'm here.
IT'S NOT FOR YOU, THEN.
IT SURE AS HELL ISN'T!
Don't hit me with your hat.
SWAT
Wait.
Then for whom?
ANY-WAY.
BEARS, RABBITS... TO ME, THEY ALL LOOK THE SAME!
SO.
It must be someone who likes accessories.
BA-BUMP

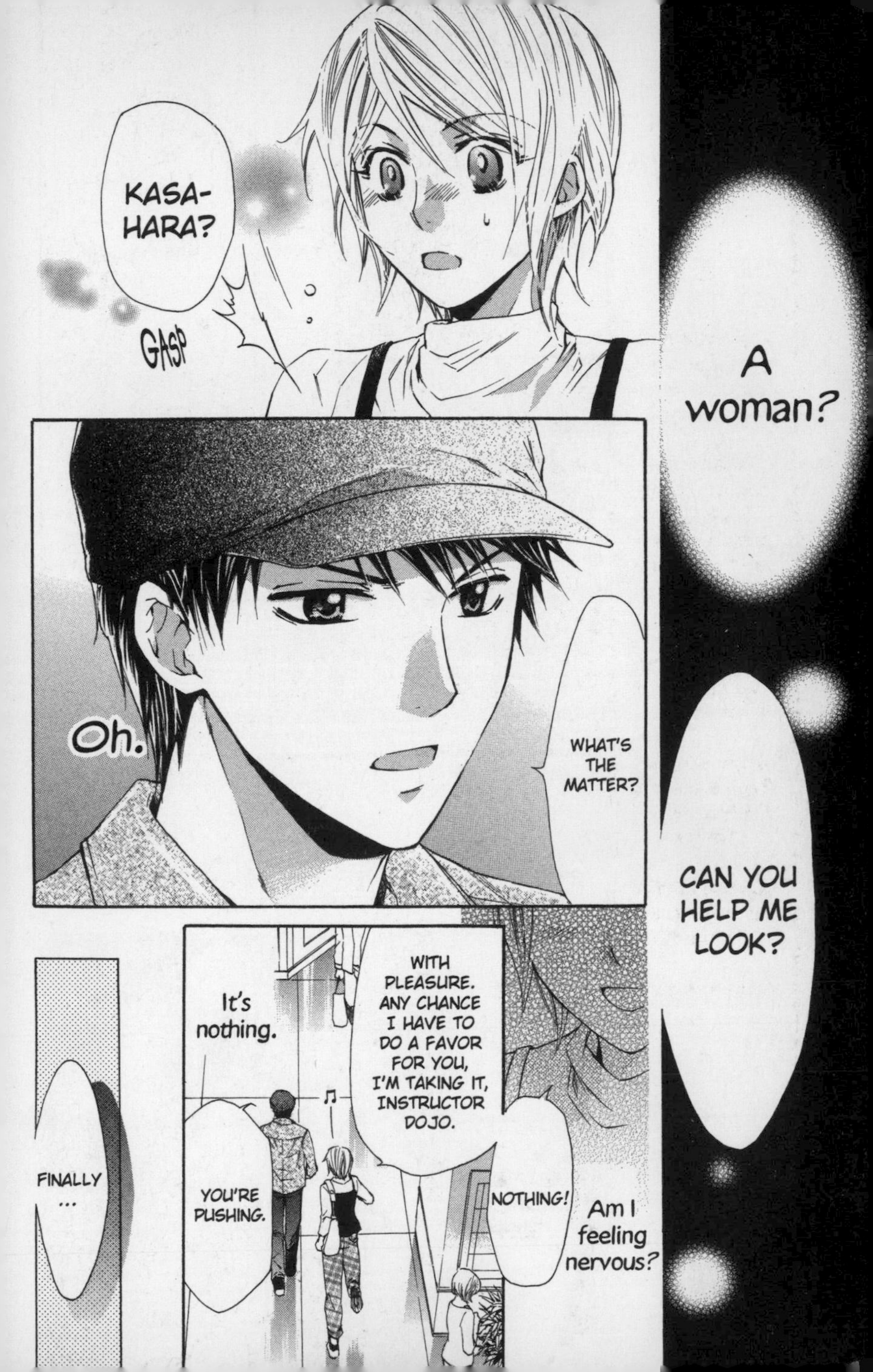
A woman?
CAN YOU HELP ME LOOK?
KASA-HARA?
GASP
WHAT'S THE MATTER?
Oh.
Am I feeling nervous?
NOTHING!
WITH PLEASURE. ANY CHANCE I HAVE TO DO A FAVOR FOR YOU, I'M TAKING IT, INSTRUCTOR DOJO.
It's nothing.
♫
YOU'RE PUSHING.
FINALLY ...

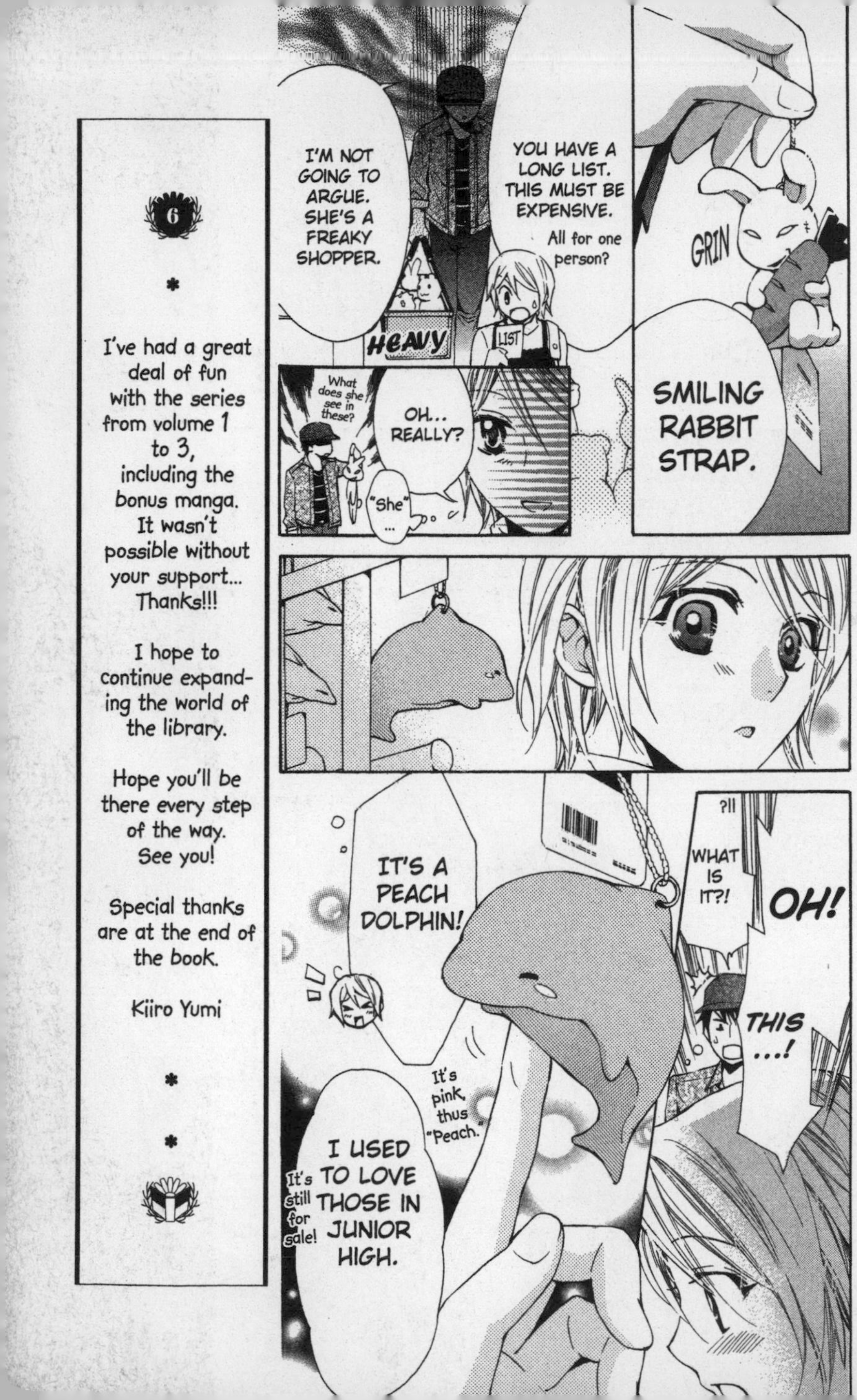
GRIN
SMILING RABBIT STRAP.
YOU HAVE A LONG LIST. THIS MUST BE EXPENSIVE.
All for one person?
I'M NOT GOING TO ARGUE. SHE'S A FREAKY SHOPPER.
HEAVY
LIST
OH... REALLY?
What does she see in these?
"She" ...
?!!
WHAT IS IT?!
OH!
THIS ...!
IT'S A PEACH DOLPHIN!
It's pink, thus "Peach."
I USED TO LOVE THOSE IN JUNIOR HIGH.
It's still for sale!

6

*

I've had a great deal of fun with the series from volume 1 to 3, including the bonus manga. It wasn't possible without your support... Thanks!!!

I hope to continue expanding the world of the library.

Hope you'll be there every step of the way. See you!

Special thanks are at the end of the book.

Kiiro Yumi

*

*

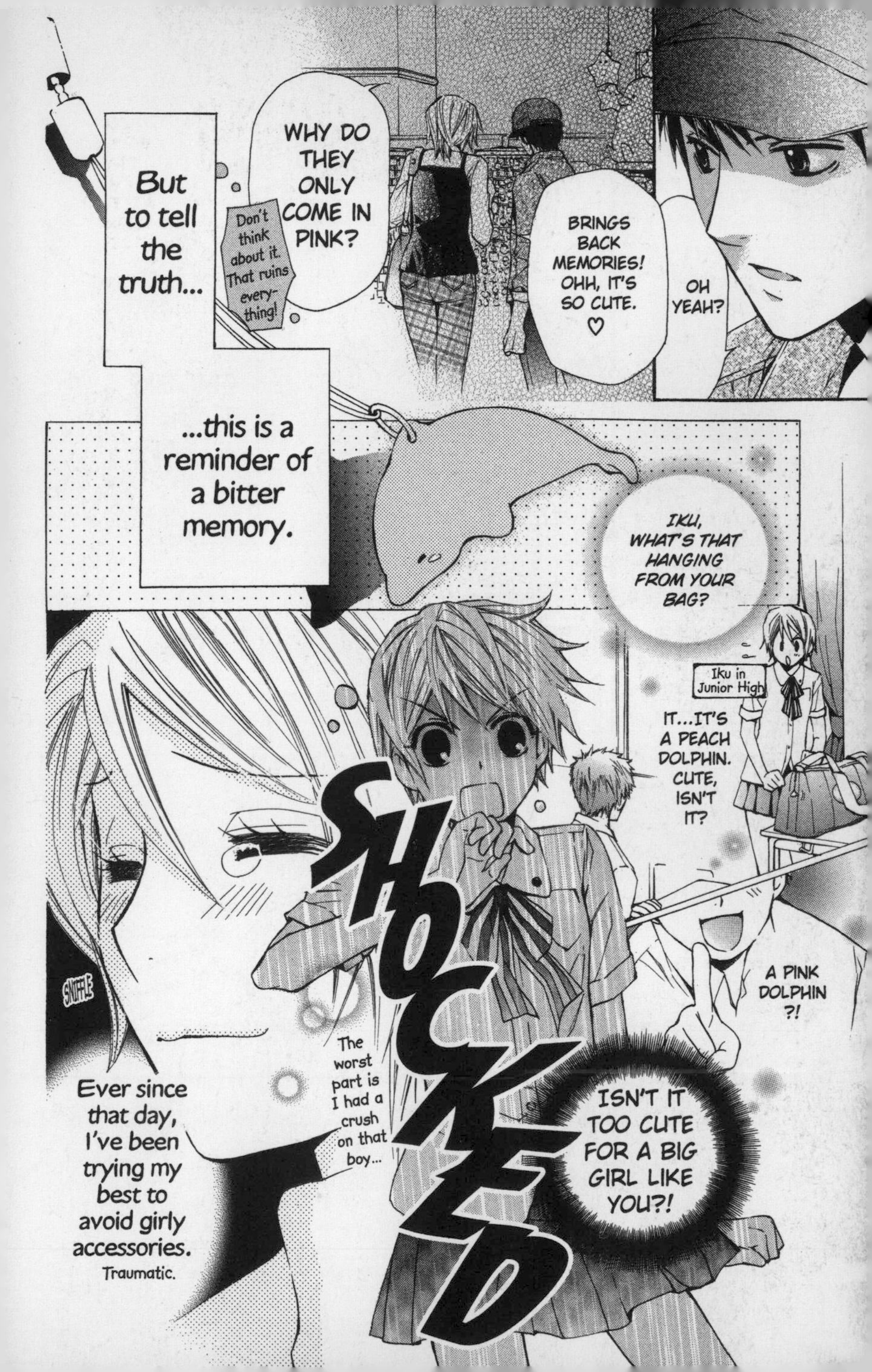
BRINGS BACK MEMORIES! OHH, IT'S SO CUTE. ♡
OH YEAH?
WHY DO THEY ONLY COME IN PINK?
Don't think about it. That ruins every-thing!
But to tell the truth...
...this is a reminder of a bitter memory.
IKU, WHAT'S THAT HANGING FROM YOUR BAG?
Iku in Junior High
IT...IT'S A PEACH DOLPHIN. CUTE, ISN'T IT?
A PINK DOLPHIN ?!
ISN'T IT TOO CUTE FOR A BIG GIRL LIKE YOU?!
SHOCKED
The worst part is I had a crush on that boy...
SNIFFLE
Ever since that day, I've been trying my best to avoid girly accessories.
Traumatic.

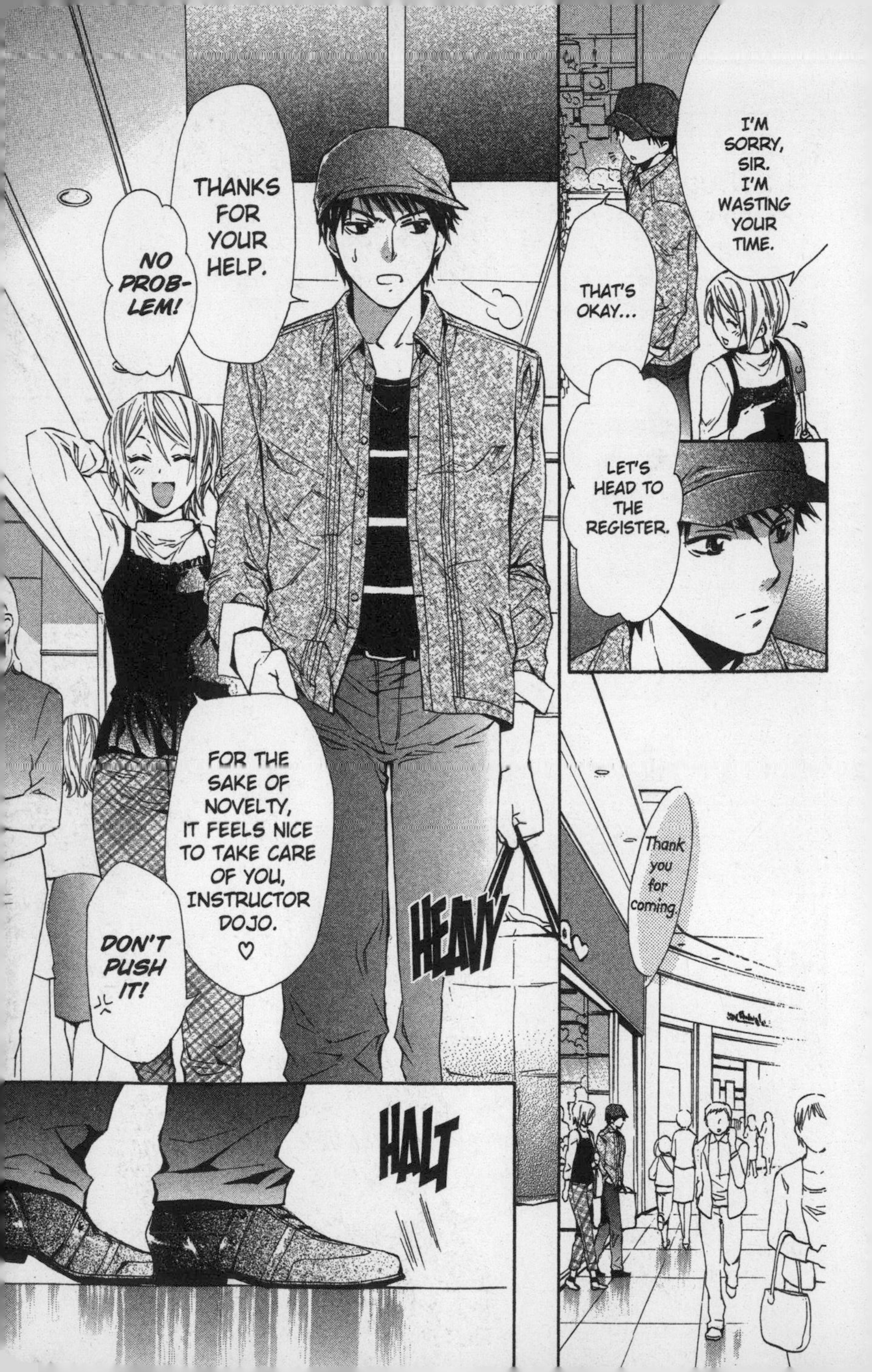
I'M SORRY, SIR. I'M WASTING YOUR TIME.
THAT'S OKAY...
LET'S HEAD TO THE REGISTER.
Thank you for coming.
THANKS FOR YOUR HELP.
NO PROB-LEM!
FOR THE SAKE OF NOVELTY, IT FEELS NICE TO TAKE CARE OF YOU, INSTRUCTOR DOJO. ♡
DON'T PUSH IT!
HEAVY
HALT

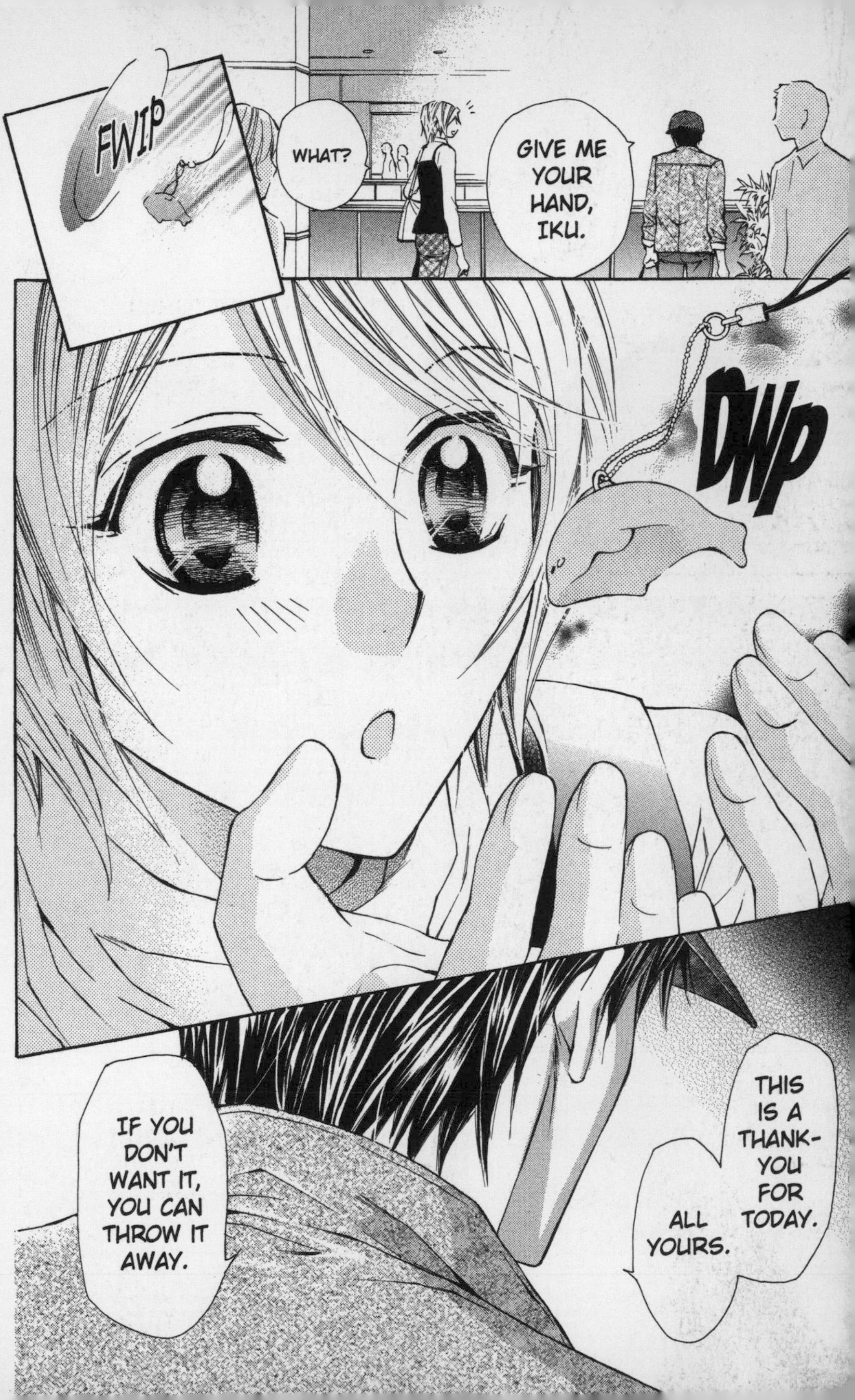
GIVE ME YOUR HAND, IKU.
WHAT?
FWIP
DWP
THIS IS A THANK-YOU FOR TODAY.
ALL YOURS.
IF YOU DON'T WANT IT, YOU CAN THROW IT AWAY.

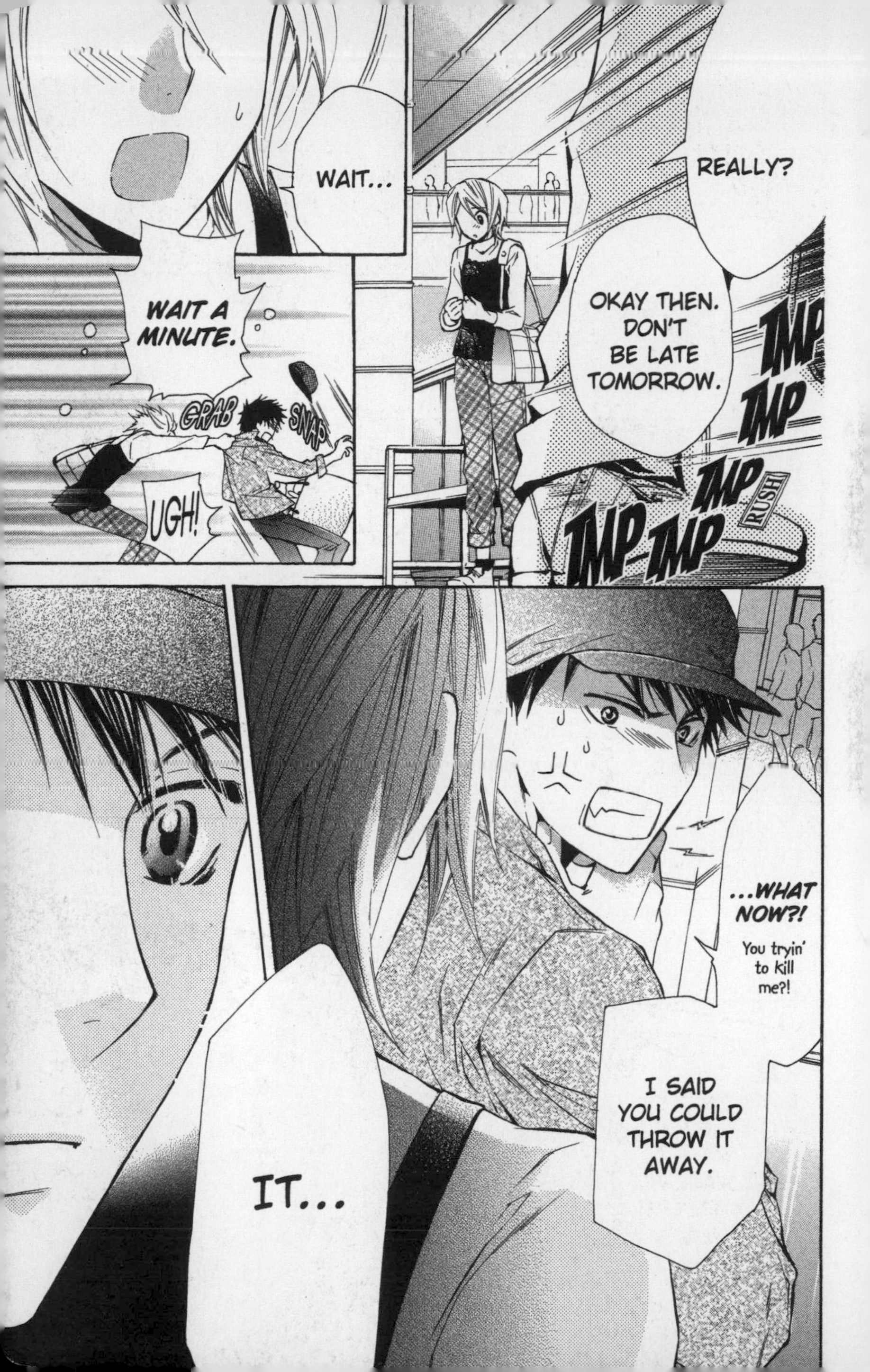
REALLY?
OKAY THEN. DON'T BE LATE TOMORROW.
TMP TMP TMP TMP-TMP-TMP
RUSH
WAIT...
WAIT A MINUTE.
SNAP
GRAB
UGH!
...WHAT NOW?!
You tryin' to kill me?!
I SAID YOU COULD THROW IT AWAY.
IT...

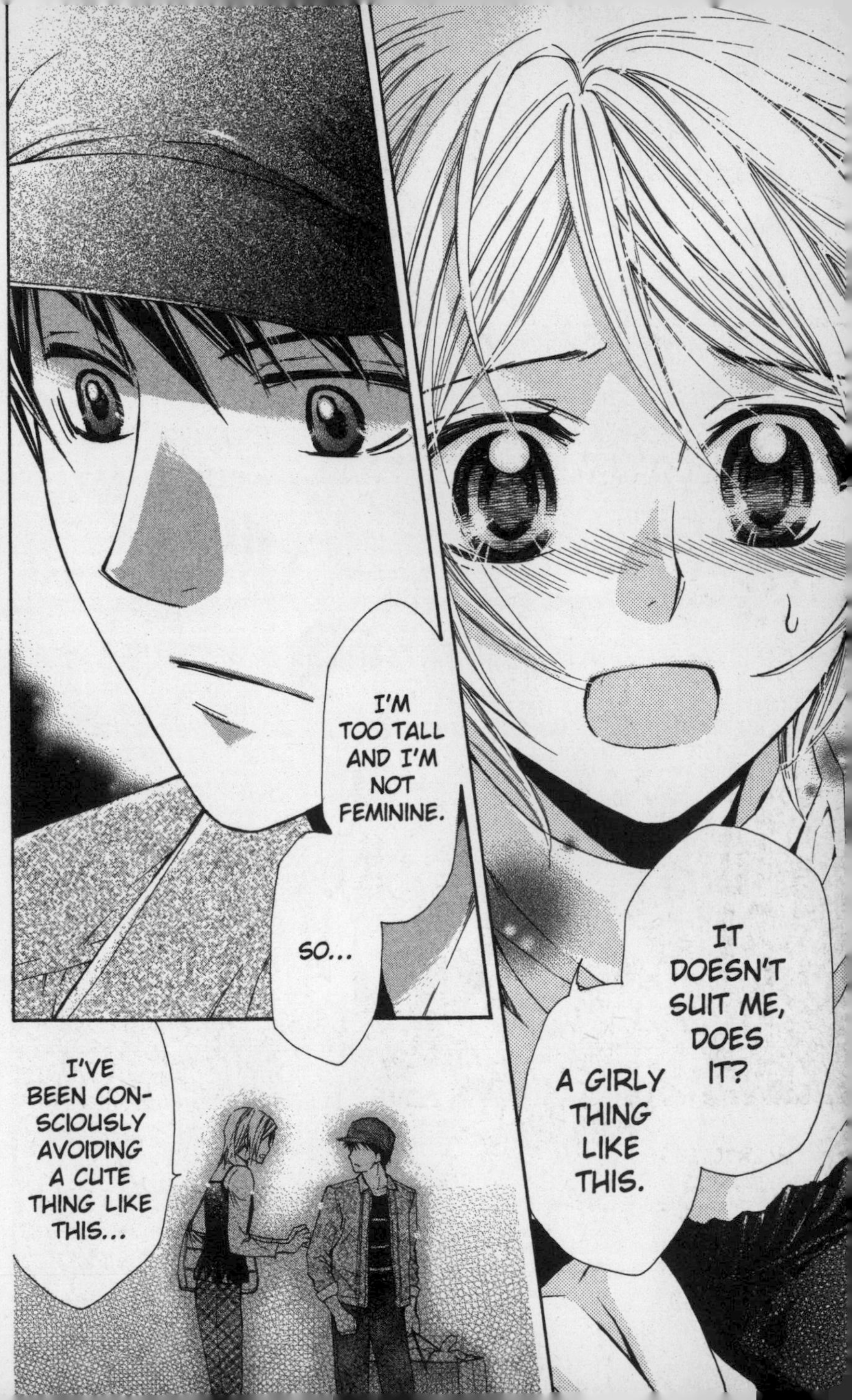
I'VE BEEN CON-SCIOUSLY AVOIDING A CUTE THING LIKE THIS...
I'M TOO TALL AND I'M NOT FEMININE.
SO...
IT DOESN'T SUIT ME, DOES IT?
A GIRLY THING LIKE THIS.

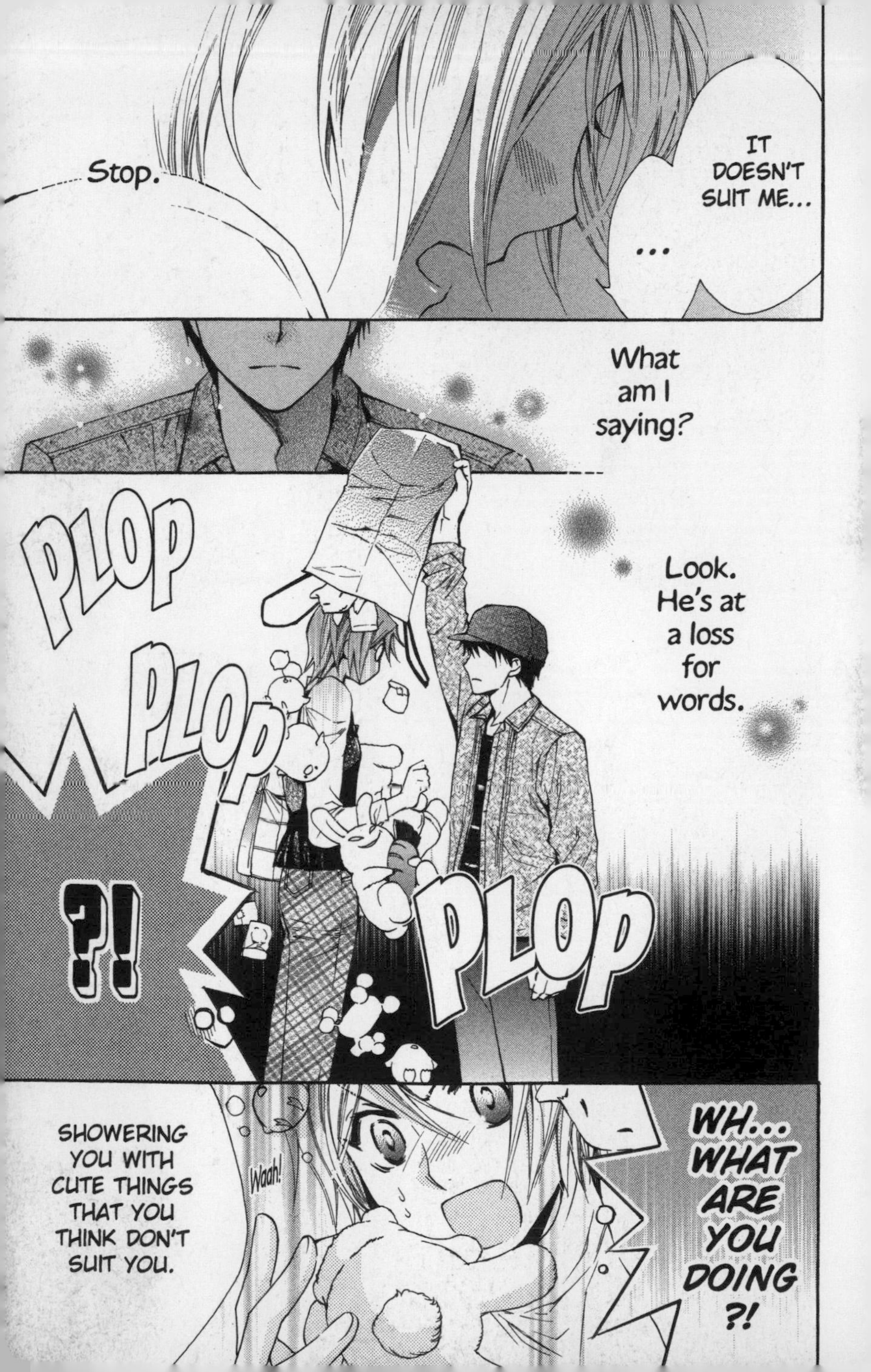
IT DOESN'T SUIT ME...
...
Stop.
What am I saying?
Look. He's at a loss for words.
PLOP
PLOP
PLOP
?!
WH... WHAT ARE YOU DOING?!
Waah!
SHOWERING YOU WITH CUTE THINGS THAT YOU THINK DON'T SUIT YOU.

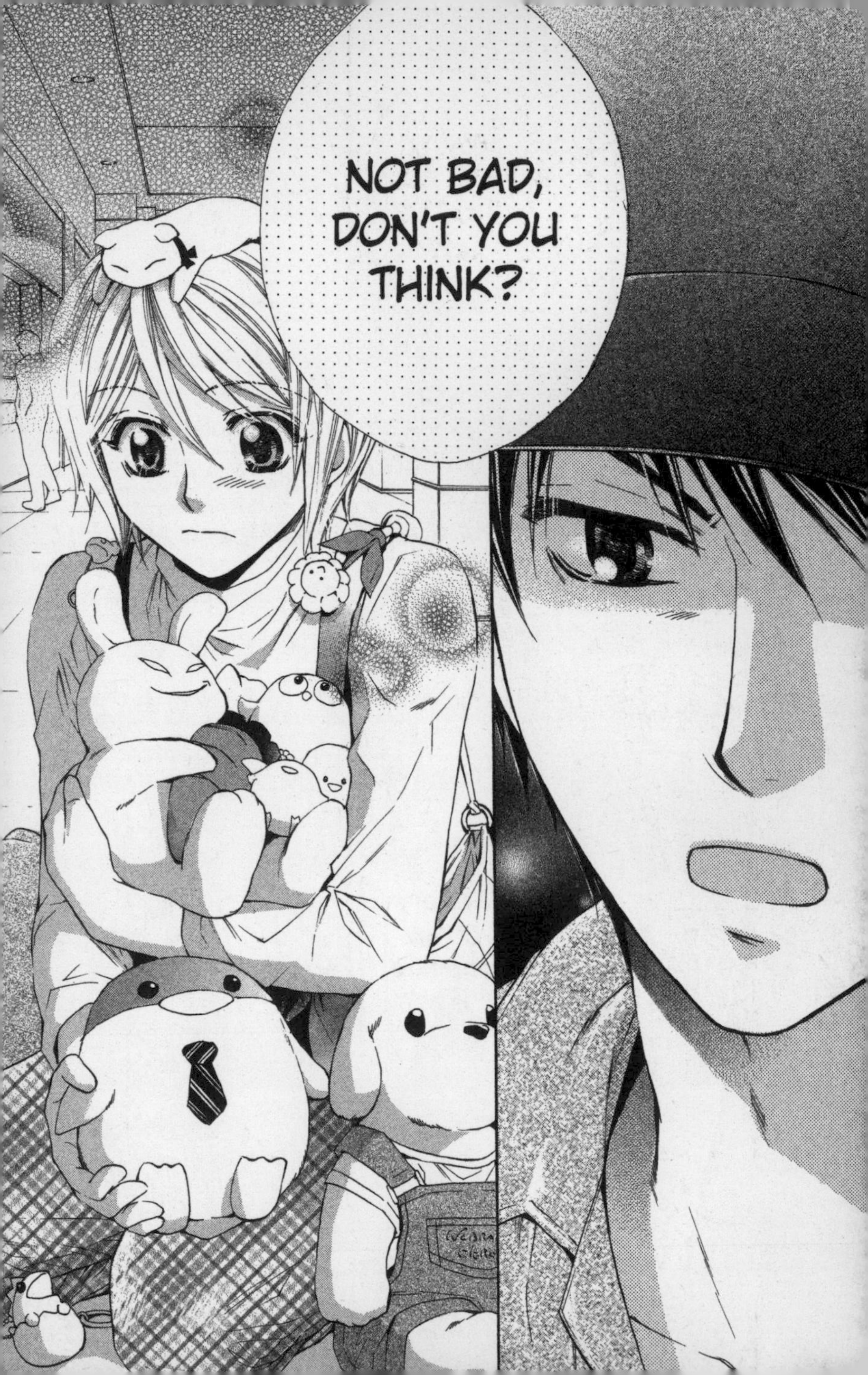
NOT BAD, DON'T YOU THINK?

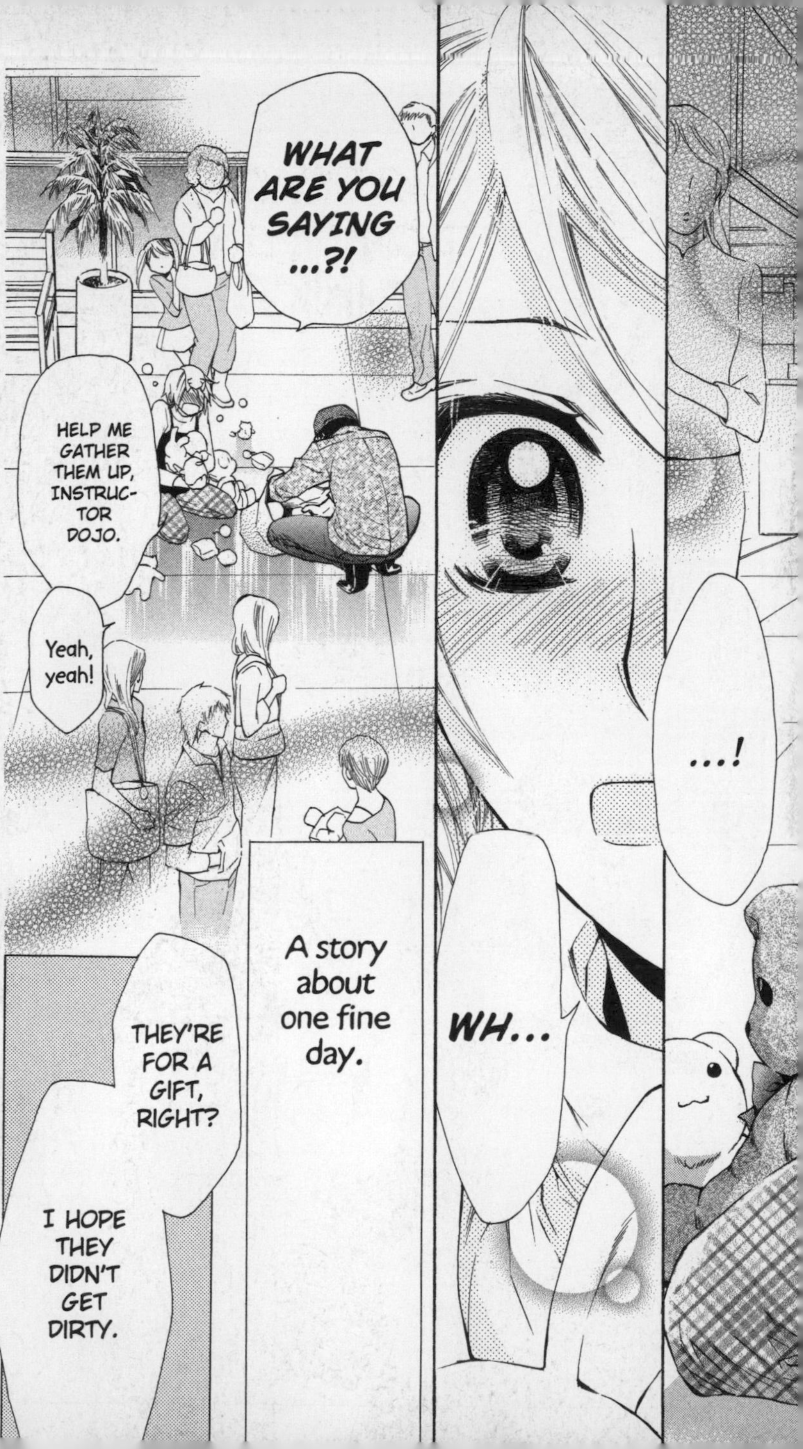
...!
WH...
WHAT ARE YOU SAYING ...?!
HELP ME GATHER THEM UP, INSTRUCTOR DOJO.
Yeah, yeah!
A story about one fine day.
THEY'RE FOR A GIFT, RIGHT?
I HOPE THEY DIDN'T GET DIRTY.

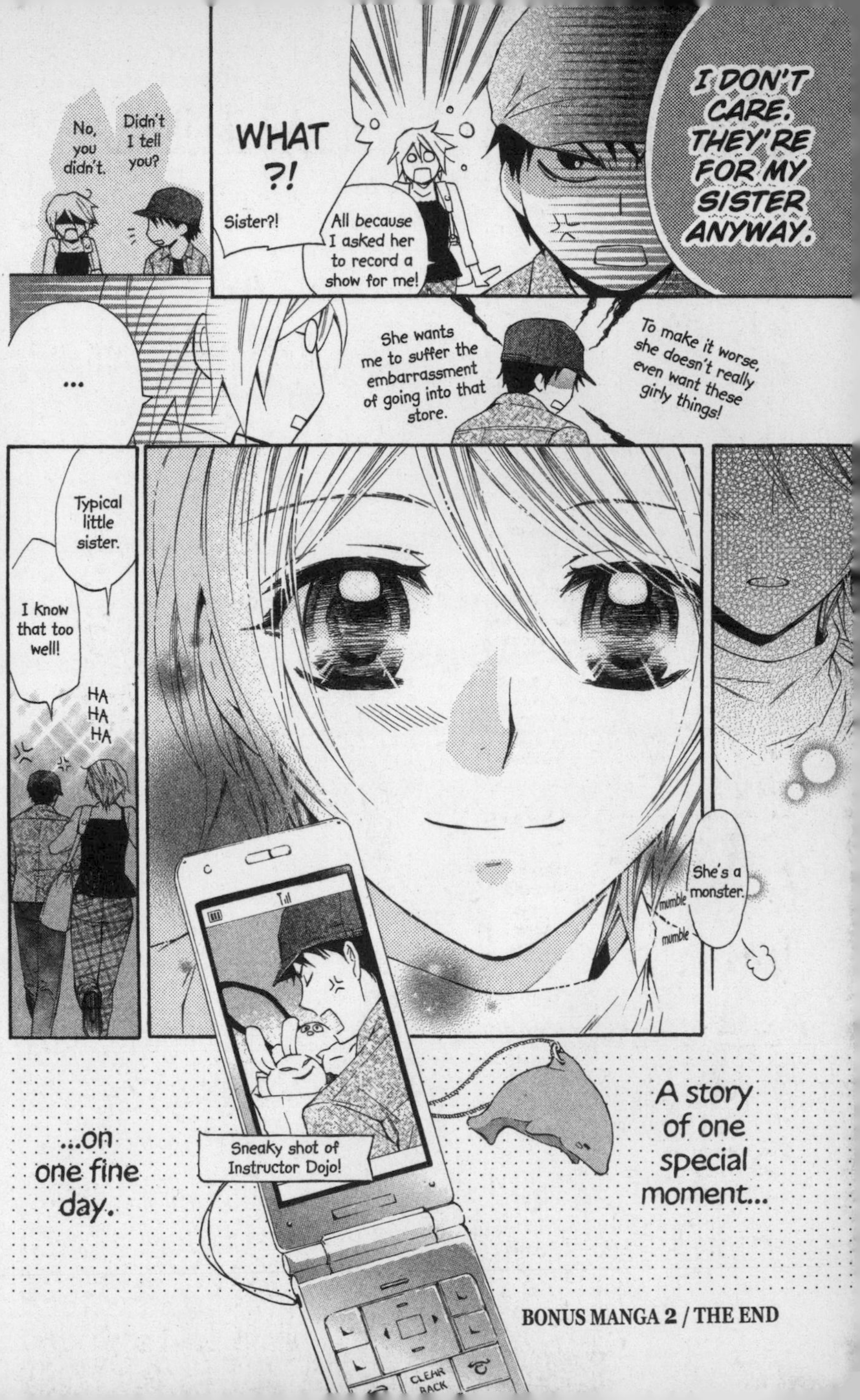
I DON'T CARE. THEY'RE FOR MY SISTER ANYWAY.
WHAT ?!
Sister?!
All because I asked her to record a show for me!
Didn't I tell you?
No, you didn't.
To make it worse, she doesn't really even want these girly things!
She wants me to suffer the embarrassment of going into that store.
...
She's a monster.
mumble
mumble
Typical little sister.
I know that too well!
HA HA HA
Sneaky shot of Instructor Dojo!
CLEAR BACK
A story of one special moment...
...on one fine day.
BONUS MANGA 2 / THE END

Special Thanks !!!

Ms. Arikawa

★

Mamada, Murakami

★

Aoki, Asahina, Otsuka, the entire family

★

Editors

★

Everyone who supports me

★★ Thank you so much!

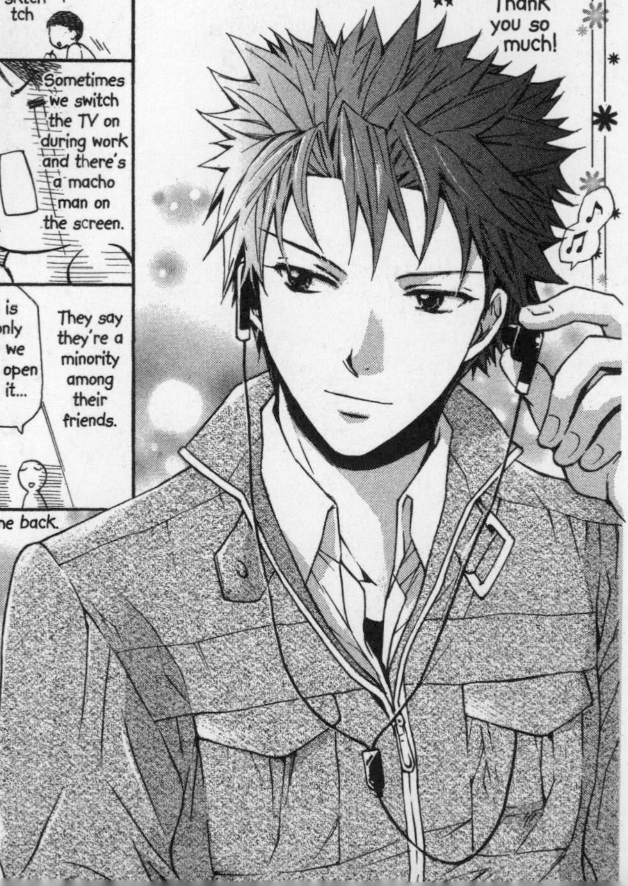

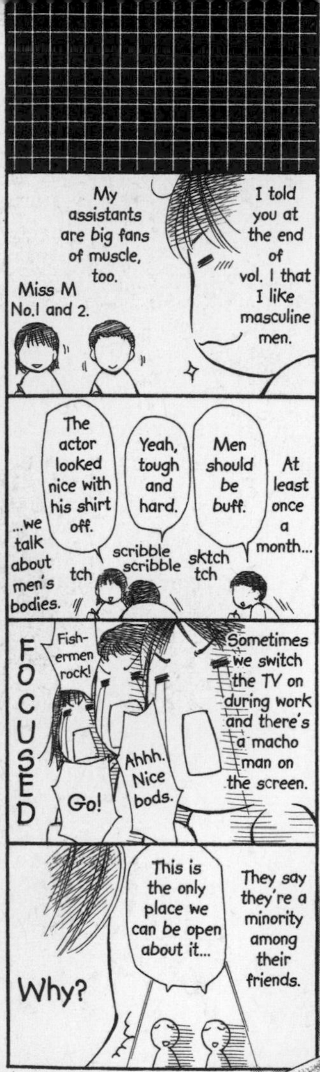
I told you at the end of vol. 1 that I like masculine men.
My assistants are big fans of muscle, too.
Miss M No.1 and 2.
At least once a month...
Men should be buff.
Yeah, tough and hard.
The actor looked nice with his shirt off.
...we talk about men's bodies.
sktch tch
scribble scribble
tch
Sometimes we switch the TV on during work and there's a macho man on the screen.
Fishermen rock!
FOCUSED
Ahhh. Nice bods.
Go!
They say they're a minority among their friends.
This is the only place we can be open about it...
Why?

I've got nothing to hold me back. Lucky me.

I hope to see you again in the next volume!

Kiiro Yumi

End notes

Page 7, author note: Momotaro
Momotaro means "peach boy" and is a popular Japanese folktale about a boy who is born from a giant peach and raised by a childless elderly couple. Later, he leaves his parents to fight the ogres on the island of Onigashima.

Page 21, panel 5: Bogeyman
Namahage in Japanese. In Akita Prefecture, it's traditional for people to dress up as namahage on New Year's and go house to house asking "Any misbehaving kids here?" The parents assure the namahage that there are no bad children in the house and instead give them food or alcohol.

Page 40, author note: Bird, monkey, dog
On his journey to Onigashima, Momotaro befriends a talking pheasant, monkey and dog, who all decide to accompany him.

Page 72, author note: Tiger-striped outfit
Dojo is dressed as an oni (ogre).

Page 73, panel 6: Obon
The Japanese celebration to honor the dead. It is celebrated in the summer, although the exact day differs by region.

Page 115, sidebar: Seibo gift
Or Oseibo. End-of-the-year gifts exchanged between households (rather than individuals).

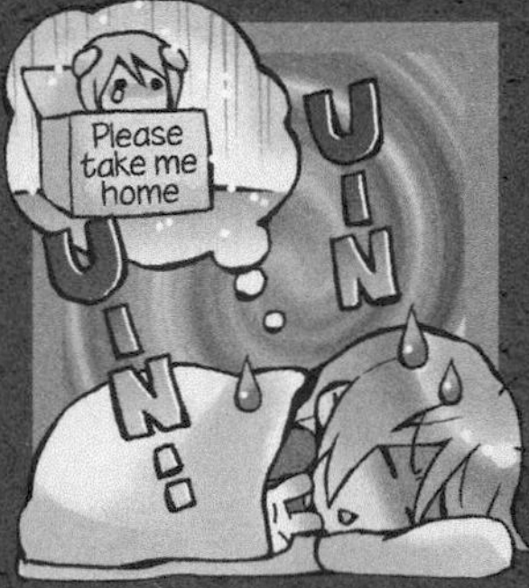
Please take me home
UIN
UIN...

Kiiro Yumi won the 42nd *LaLa* Manga Grand Prix Fresh Debut award for her manga *Billy Bocchan no Yuutsu* (Little Billy's Depression). Her latest series is *Toshokan Senso Love&War (Library Wars: Love & War)*, which runs in *LaLa* magazine in Japan and is published in English by VIZ Media.

Hiro Arikawa won the 10th Dengeki Novel Prize for her work *Shio no Machi: Wish on My Precious* in 2003 and debuted with the same novel in 2004. Of her many works, Arikawa is best known for the *Library Wars* series and her *Jieitai Sanbusaku* trilogy, which consists of *Sora no Naka* (In the Sky), *Umi no Soko* (The Bottom of the Sea) and *Shio no Machi* (City of Salt).

library wars

Volume 3
Shojo Beat Edition

Story & Art by Kiiro Yumi
Original Concept by Hiro Arikawa

ENGLISH TRANSLATION Kinami Watabe
ADAPTATION & LETTERING Sean McCoy
DESIGN Amy Martin
EDITOR Pancha Diaz

Toshokan Sensou LOVE&WAR by Kiiro Yumi and Hiro Arikawa

First published in Japan in 2009 by HAKUSENSHA, Inc., Tokyo.
English language translation rights arranged with HAKUSENSHA, Inc., Tokyo.

Printed in the U.S.A.

Published by VIZ Media, LLC
P.O. Box 77010
San Francisco, CA 94107

10 9 8 7 6 5 4 3 2 1
First printing, December 2010

www.shojobeat.com www.viz.com

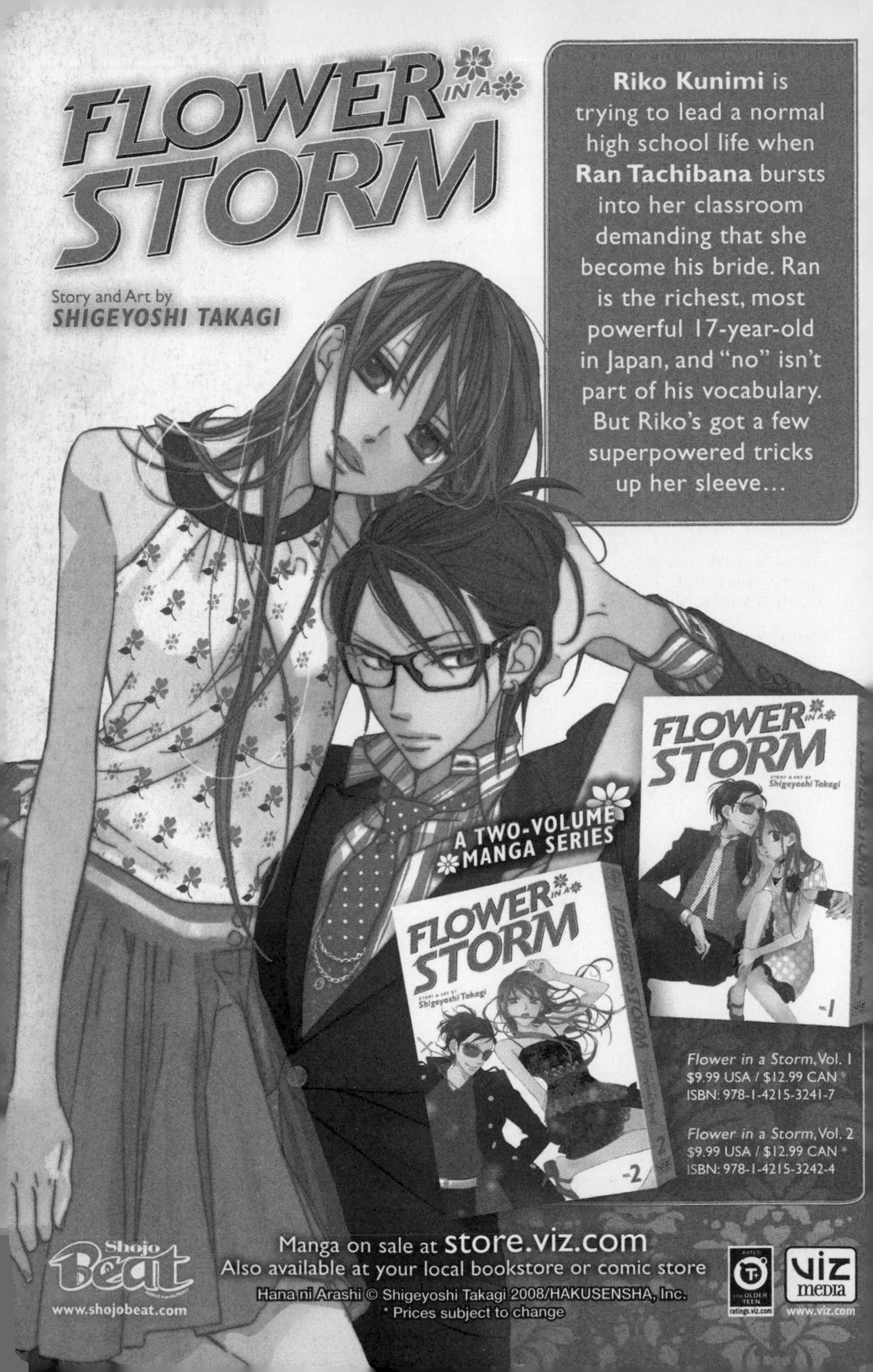
FLOWER IN A STORM
Story and Art by
SHIGEYOSHI TAKAGI
Riko Kunimi is trying to lead a normal high school life when Ran Tachibana bursts into her classroom demanding that she become his bride. Ran is the richest, most powerful 17-year-old in Japan, and "no" isn't part of his vocabulary. But Riko's got a few superpowered tricks up her sleeve...
A TWO-VOLUME MANGA SERIES
FLOWER IN A STORM
Shigeyoshi Takagi
VOL. 1
FLOWER IN A STORM
Shigeyoshi Takagi
VOL. 2
Flower in a Storm, Vol. 1
$9.99 USA / $12.99 CAN *
ISBN: 978-1-4215-3241-7
Flower in a Storm, Vol. 2
$9.99 USA / $12.99 CAN *
ISBN: 978-1-4215-3242-4
Shojo Beat
www.shojobeat.com
Manga on sale at store.viz.com
Also available at your local bookstore or comic store
Hana ni Arashi © Shigeyoshi Takagi 2008/HAKUSENSHA, Inc.
* Prices subject to change
OLDER TEEN
ratings.viz.com
VIZ media
www.viz.com

WELCOME to Imperial Academy: a private school where trying to become SUPERIOR can make you feel INFERIOR!

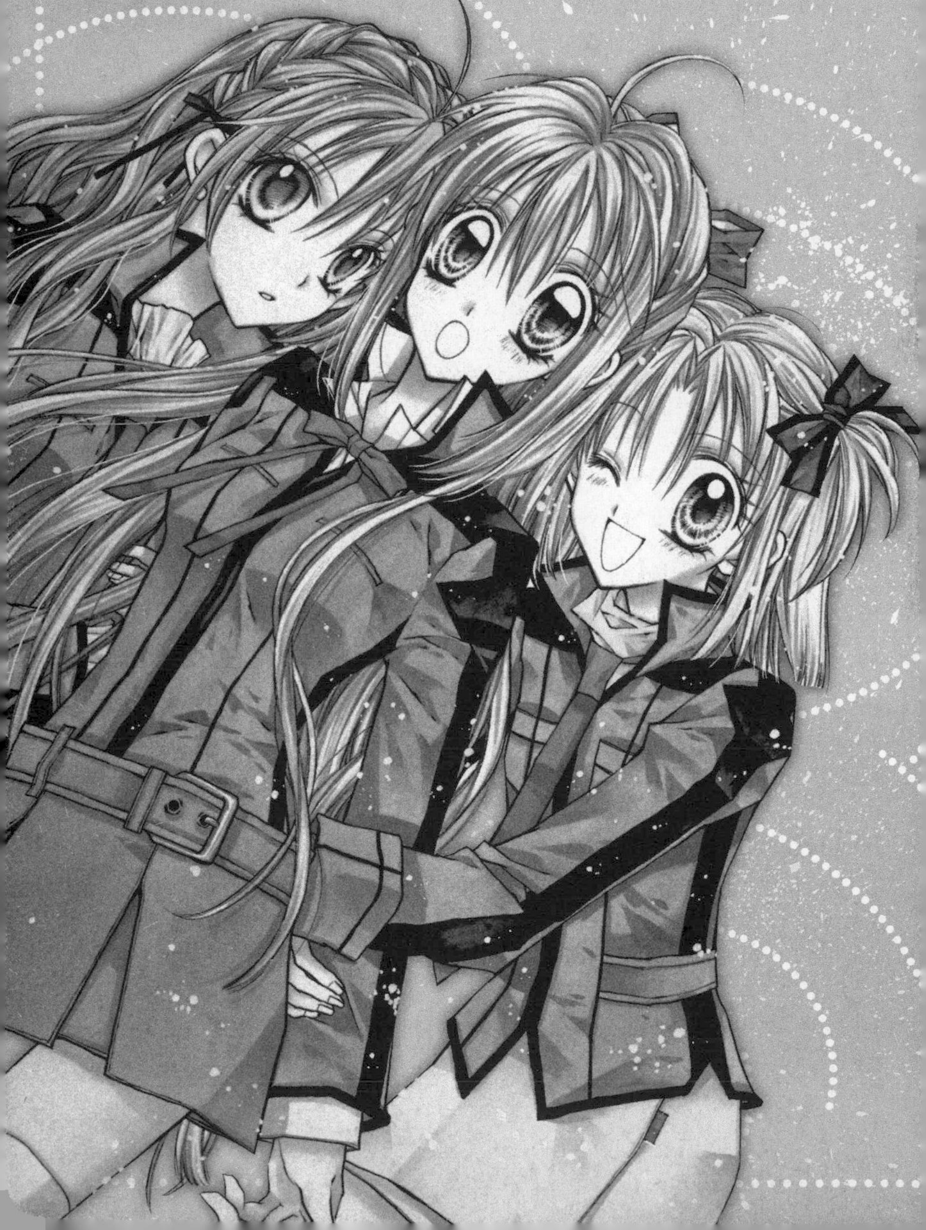

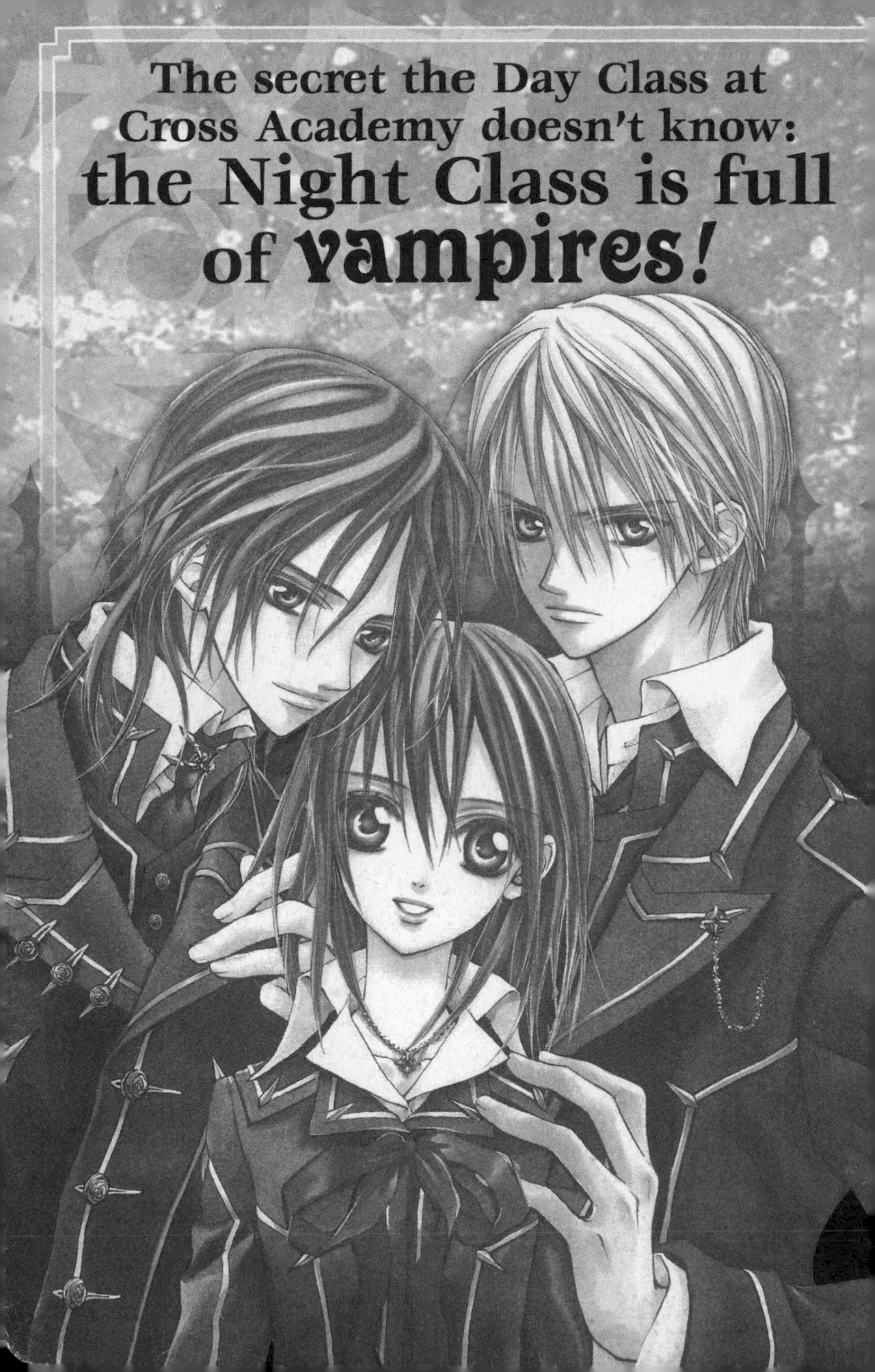
The secret the Day Class at
Cross Academy doesn't know:
the Night Class is full
of vampires!